TO LIVE UPON HOPE

TO LIVE UPON HOPE

Mohicans and Missionaries in the Eighteenth-Century Northeast

Rachel Wheeler

Cornell University Press
Ithaca and London

First published 2008 by Cornell University Press First printing,

Printed in the United States of America

Library of Congress Cataloging-in-Publication Data

Wheeler, Rachel M.
  To live upon hope : Mohicans and missionaries in the eighteenth-century Northeast / Rachel Wheeler.
      p. cm.
  Includes bibliographical references and index.
  ISBN 978-0-8014-4631-3 (cloth : alk. paper)
  1. Stockbridge Indians—Missions—Massachusetts—Stockbridge—History—18th century.   2. Moravian Indians—Missions—New York (State)—Shekomeko Site—History—18th century.
3. Mahican Indians—Missions—History—18th century.
4. Congregational churches—Missions—Massachusetts—Stockbridge—History—18th century.   5. Moravian Church—Missions—New York (State)—Shekomeko Site—History—18th century.   6. Stockbridge (Mass.)—History—18th century.
7. Shekomeko Site (N.Y.)—History—18th century.   8. Stockbridge (Mass.)—Ethnic relations.   9. Shekomeko Site (N.Y.)—Ethnic relations.   I. Title

  E99.S8W54 2008
  974.4'004973449—dc22

2007050005

To my daughter, Sylvia, my parents,
John and Margaret Wheeler,
and the memory of my grandparents,
Leonard and Cornelia Wheeler

Contents

Maps and Illustrations

Acknowledgments

Books do not happen alone. Along the way, I have had the benefit of inspiring mentors, supportive colleagues, and generous institutions. The advice, criticism, and guidance of Jon Butler, John Demos, and Harry Stout were invaluable in the early years of this project, and their unflagging support has helped ensure its progression toward a book. First as a participant in the Young Scholars in American Religion program sponsored by the Center for the Study of Religion and American Culture and later as a member of the Religious Studies department, I have found an especially supportive and stimulating academic environment at IUPUI. Young Scholars mentors, Stephen Prothero and Ann Taves, and my fellow participants, especially early Americanists Doug Winiarski, Martha Finch, and Robert Brown, provided much-needed encouragement and incisive comments. Alison Kalett and the editorial staff at Cornell University Press have been a tremendous help in the last stages of this project, lending just the right amount of encouragement and guidance through the process.

Since joining the faculty at IUPUI, I have benefited from the unfailing support of the department chair, Tom Davis, and the dean of the School of Liberal Arts, Robert White. This book has been substantially improved by careful critiques from colleagues, including Matthew Condon, David Craig, Edward Curtis, Tom Davis, Johnny Flynn, Philip Goff, Kelly Hayes, William Jackson, Ted Mullen, and Peter Theusen. Administrative assistant Debbie

Dale and former student Matthew Williams provided help in preparing the final manuscript. Irakly Chkhenkely, Anna Bellersen, and Anna Huehls all assisted me in working with German texts. Shea Peelples lent her keen editorial eye to the manuscript at various stages. Former colleagues at Lewis and Clark College, including Richard Rohrbaugh, Rob Kugler, Paul Powers, and Jane Hunter, provided support and friendship as I began my academic career. Over the years, I have benefited from conversations with colleagues near and far, including Ava Chamberlain, Kate Carte Engel, David Hall, William Hart, Tracy LaVealle, George Marsden, Michael McNally, Mark Noll, Jon Sensbach, Jan Shipps, David Silverman, Stephen Stein, Doug Sweeney, and Mark Valeri.

This book could not have happened without access to manuscript sources and the ability to read them. Ken Minkema of the Jonathan Edwards Center at Yale has been my guide through all things Edwards, including his crabbed handwriting. Retired archivist Vernon Nelson taught me to decipher the German *Schreibschrift* of the Moravian missionaries and introduced me to the treasures in the Moravian Archives in Bethlehem, Pennsylvania. His successor, Paul Peucker, has graciously provided many of the illustrations for this book. His Herculean efforts are rapidly making the Moravian sources more easily navigable.

A year funded by the National Endowment for the Humanities spent in residence at the McNeil Center for Early American Studies at the University of Pennsylvania provided the time and the stimulating environment to wrestle with the question of how to turn a dissertation into a book. Director Daniel Richter helped steer the project in new directions, while McNeil Center postdoctoral fellow and unflappable realist Brendan McConville became a valued colleague and a trusted friend. A number of institutions have provided generous financial support for this project, including the NEH, the Indiana University President's Arts and Humanities Initiative, the Indiana University School of Liberal Arts, the Woodrow Wilson Foundation, the Pew Program in American Religion, the American Antiquarian Society, and the Massachusetts Historical Society.

In 2001, I was privileged to participate in a conference on the Stockbridge-Munsee Mohican Nation reservation in Bowler, Wisconsin, the result of the inspiration and hard work of tribal historian Dorothy Davids and other members of the tribal Historical Committee. There I made new friends and colleagues, including Lion Miles and John Savagian, and was introduced to Stockbridge Mohican musician Bill Miller, whose music carries on the message of his Mohican forebears.

Portions of chapters 12 and 13 are drawn, in revised form, from my article, "Hendrick Aupaumut: Christian-Mahican Prophet," *Journal of the Early Republic* 25, no. 2 (Summer 2005): 187–220. Reprinted by permission of the

University of Pennsylvania Press. Chapter 7 contains revised portions of my article, "Women and Christian Practice in a Mahican Village," *Religion and American Culture: A Journal of Interpretation* 13 (2003): 27–67. Reprinted by permission of the Center for the Study of Religion and American Culture and the University of California Press.

In my academic wanderings from New Haven to Portland to Indianapolis, I've accumulated many friends who have enriched my life by making sure I didn't spend too much time in the eighteenth century, and for that I am grateful. I also thank my family for listening when I needed to talk and distracting me when I needed to be distracted. And most of all I thank them for providing a center to my life that always tugs me back. My mother and my grandfather, both lawyers, taught me a love of words and a good debate. From my sister, my father, and my grandmother, good Yankees that they are, I learned the value of *doing*.

TO LIVE UPON HOPE

Chapter One

Introduction

Indian *and* Christian

In April 1803, the Stockbridge Mohican[1] chief sachem, Hendrick Aupaumut, delivered a speech to a community of refugee Delaware Indians that had recently settled along the White River in Indiana Territory. Aupaumut recounted for the gathered Delawares how the Mohicans had been introduced to Christianity nearly seventy years earlier. In 1734, the Muhheakunnuk (as they called themselves) received word that Massachusetts officials were eager to send a minister of the gospel. Two hundred tribesmen gathered to debate whether to accept the offer. Although some voiced objections, the result of the council, reported Aupaumut, "was this: not to reject the offer before they should *try it*." It was thus decided that there should be a test village where the gospel would be preached "and let every man and woman go to hear it and embrace it if they think best." Mohicans from various villages began to gather to listen to the minister, but others were suspicious of Christianity, and these, according to Aupaumut, came under the influence of "some wicked Dutch people" and "ardent spirits." Those who did not join the mission community eventually drifted away, some to "live among other nations" and the rest to be "buried under the earth." Consequently, their villages "are, as it were desolated, and possessed by the whites." The test village—a Housatonic Mohican village later incorporated as the town of Stockbridge, Massachusetts—was the only village to survive, "and the descendants of that, who embrace the civilization and Christian religion, are now still remaining as a nation."

Aupaumut believed the Mohican experiment with Christianity and English "civilization" was the key to their survival as a people, so he recommended the same course to the Delaware. If they followed the Mohican example, the Delaware would become "a wise people," happy "indeed in this life and the life to come," and they would be able to "hold your lands to the latest generation, for this is the will of the great and good Spirit." But if the Muhheakunnuk offer to introduce Christianity and civilization were rejected, if the Delaware chose instead to "embrace the cup of the evil minded," then Aupaumut predicted that "you will become poor, in every respect, and you will be scattered; your villages will be desolated or possessed by a people, who will cultivate your lands." And finally, warned Aupaumut, "you will become extinct from the earth."[2]

Aupaumut's address raises a number of difficult questions. Had Christianity and "civilization" really served the Stockbridge Mohicans—or other Indian peoples—so well? Professing Christianity had rarely served to secure Indian lands. By the 1780s, nearly all of the Stockbridge Mohicans' original lands had been deeded into white hands, and the community had relocated to Oneida lands in New York, in a pattern familiar to the many eastern Indians pushed westward ahead of white settlement or pushed to the margins of white society.[3] On the issue of Mohican survival, however, Aupaumut's argument was hard to dispute: the Stockbridges were the only Mohicans to survive as an independent community. They were not, however, the only Mohican community to embrace Christianity.

Interpreting for Aupaumut that day was another Christian Mohican named Joshua. Joshua had been born in a village just thirty miles from Stockbridge and baptized as a boy in the 1740s by Moravian missionaries. He had married the daughter of a Delaware chief, and now he lived among the Delaware on the White River in Indiana.[4] Joshua's parents had been among the first American Indians to be baptized by members of the Renewed Unity of the Brethren, as the Moravians were officially known. The Moravians were one of the many evangelical groups to flourish in the first half of the eighteenth century as part of a transatlantic Protestant awakening.[5] Joshua and his fellow villagers, despite their profession of Christianity and their facility in the skills of European civilization (Joshua, for instance, was a cooper and carpenter as well as a musician and interpreter), had not fared well. Forced from their native village of Shekomeko (in what is now Dutchess County, New York) in 1746, Joshua's community had already moved at least five times by the time the Stockbridge Mohicans left their Massachusetts home in the 1780s. The community professed pacifism, but rather than securing a safe neutrality, their pacifism invited suspicion and violence, especially from anti-British Delaware and Shawnee Indians as well as angry mobs of colonists. At the time of Aupaumut's address to the

Delaware in 1803, Joshua was among the few remaining Moravian Mohicans, all of whom now lived in Delaware settlements.[6]

Viewed historically, it seems that Aupaumut was right—the embrace of Christianity, or at least Anglo-Protestant Christianity helped ensure Mohican community survival. But he was also wrong. Aupaumut's hopes that following the Christian path and adopting English civilization would secure Indian lands were never fulfilled in his lifetime. The Stockbridge Mohicans won some degree of protection through their embrace of Christianity and "civilization"—since 1856 the Stockbridge-Munsee Band of Mohicans has lived on secured reservation land in Shawano County, Wisconsin—but Aupaumut and others had had to confront the realization that, in the end, most whites could not look past skin color and accept Stockbridges as fellow Christians and Americans.[7]

This book explores the histories of the Mohican communities to which Joshua and Aupaumut belonged—Shekomeko and Stockbridge—and their encounters with Christianity from roughly 1730 to 1760, years of tremendous upheaval and change in colonial American society. Major transformations were underway in the realms of demographics, economics, politics, and religion for both European colonists and America's native peoples, though these changes weighed quite differently whether one was white or Indian. If one had to choose one word to summarize the transformations of the early eighteenth century, it would be *diversification*. The populations of the colonies were becoming increasingly diverse, and with the flow of people came an expansion of the economic and religious markets. As colonialists and Indians encountered a greater diversity of people and goods (both physical and spiritual), they were also confronted with the important task of defining their identity.[8] More goods were traded than ever before, and the goods and raw materials traded traveled greater distances. Fish caught off North American coasts found their way to British markets; sugar cane raised by African slaves in the West Indies became rum that made its way to the colonies, often playing a crucial role in diplomatic and land transactions— often of dubious morality and legality—between colonists and Indians; and colonists consumed an ever-increasing variety of British manufactured goods and East Indian tea and spices with great enthusiasm. Indians too were drawn into this complex world market, selling skins and furs in exchange for a wide range of trade goods from rifles to cookware, from cloth to alcohol.[9] The increasing scarcity of land in established English settlements combined with a booming population invariably stoked demand for Indian lands. In the emerging speculative land market, those with the capital to invest reaped fortunes.[10]

Even in New England, the most homogeneous of the colonial regions, there were growing numbers of non-English residents. The middle colonies were far more diverse. Dutch, English, German, Irish, and Scotch-Irish could all be found in New York. In all colonies, in varying percentages, there were Africans who lived as slaves, as freemen, and as indentured servants. Even though entire Indian communities had been ravaged by disease or relocated in response to the pressures of colonial settlement, Indians were still very much a presence in the colonies. Some lived in independent communities, some had intermarried with free black populations, and others lived among their European neighbors, often working in white households or making a living by trading mats, brooms, and baskets. And those Indians who had relocated, whether by choice or by force, often lived in refugee communities with substantial tribal diversity.[11] The Mohicans of the Housatonic Valley and Shekomeko faced similar challenges, in slightly different forms, due to the differing colonial contexts of their locations, Massachusetts and New York, respectively. The founding of the Congregational and Moravian missions (in 1734 and 1740) set the two communities on very different paths. The acceptance of missionaries signaled that Mohicans were struggling to make sense of a world that was rapidly changing around them.

Native choices were constrained by the realities of colonialism, yet Indian agency was not entirely a fiction. Nor was the embrace of Christianity purely instrumentalist—a move calculated to curry favor with their increasingly powerful European neighbors. So the question is not simply what Mohicans hoped to gain by admitting missionaries to their villages, but what Congregational and Moravian Christianity became as practiced by the Mohicans of Stockbridge and Shekomeko. Comparing the experiences of Mohicans at Stockbridge and Shekomeko helps to restore Indian agency to the historical narrative by showing the very different choices two communities made. And comparing the two mission projects makes plain the extent to which political forces shaped the development of distinctive mission practices among Anglo-Protestants and Moravians. Studying Stockbridge and Shekomeko side by side reminds us once again that Christianity is always inculturated; its expression always reflects the historical, social, and cultural context of its practitioners, whether German Moravians, English Congregationalists, or Mohicans.[12]

Understanding the distinctive forms of Congregational and Moravian Christianity and the ways they intersected with broader structures of colonial culture and political power is crucial to understanding the mission experience at Stockbridge and Shekomeko. To an alien observer, Congregationalists and Moravians would likely have been perceived as practicing two entirely distinct religions. Studying the New England mission alongside the Moravian mission serves to make the Puritans strange once again, especially helpful because scholarship on the Congregationalism of New

England Puritans and their descendents has long dominated the field of early American history.

By the 1730s, Congregationalism had been the established religion of Massachusetts for a century, but the close association of religious and civic authority was beginning to crack. The drive of first-generation Puritans for religious freedom had involved no suspicion of merging secular and religious powers; rather, ministers and civic leaders yearned to erect a society in which the state supported and was supported by the *right* form of Christianity, free of the Catholic corruptions they believed still lurked within the Church of England. The Puritans had arrived in what they saw as an "empty" land, free of preexisting European civic authority. Thus, in constructing a "Bible commonwealth," church membership conferred civic status. But in subsequent generations, the Puritan vision of the gathered church of visible saints became increasingly problematic, as fewer and fewer New Englanders took the step of professing their converted state before the congregation to gain full membership. The perceived decline of piety was often interpreted by many New England divines as inviting God's judgment on a sinful nation.

A century after the "Great Migration," New England still bore the heavy stamp of Puritanism, and most New Englanders were Congregationalists. But one could also find Presbyterians, Baptists, Quakers, and even growing numbers of Anglicans. The debates over religion sparked by increasing diversity were in fact debates over the relationship of national, cultural, and religious identities. The transatlantic Protestant evangelical awakening that had begun to brew in the early eighteenth century burst forth in revivals in New Jersey in the 1720s and swept through New England in the 1730s and 1740s. Revivalists from Jonathan Edwards to George Whitfield to James Davenport soon split both Presbyterians and Congregationalists into pro- and anti-revivalist factions. Ironically, just as revivalists were beginning to challenge older theological ideas of social integration—ones that located the individual in concentric covenants between the individual, the church, and the nation with God—the mission efforts spurred in part by those same revivals were insisting that true Christianity was evidenced not only by the state of one's heart but also by one's mastery of the arts of English civilization.[13] Defenders of a more sober religious expression accused revivalists of threatening the social order with their itinerancy and their "enthusiastic" preaching methods. But even evangelicals like Gilbert Tennent sounded a remarkably conservative note when confronted with the Moravians and their successes among the Indians, suggesting that Anglo-Protestantism, whether pro- or anti-revivalist, was heavily invested in religion as a mechanism of preserving social order and, increasingly, racial boundaries.

New England colonists no longer viewed England as the moral wilderness their Puritan ancestors had. Rather, there emerged an increasing sense of a "Protestant interest" that went hand in hand with Britishness. Anglo-Protestant mission efforts like the Stockbridge mission reflected this convergence. There, Indians were to be schooled in the ways of English civilization. But as the history of Stockbridge suggests, New Englanders remained profoundly ambivalent about the prospect of welcoming Christian Indians into the fold. Even as the Stockbridges acquired markers of English civilization such as literacy and English-style houses and served loyally in battle alongside New England colonists, they were consistently denied the same privileges as their white peers. This story is not unique, but it reflects a broader movement, among both whites and Indians, toward increasingly racialized identities.

Moravian Christianity could scarcely have been more different from New England Congregationalism. Whereas Puritanism was very much a religion of the Word—placing tremendous importance on literacy as the means to gain access to God's revealed truths—Moravians emphasized the saving power of Jesus's blood. Through a rich course of rituals, including baptism, communion, songs, and prayer, the power of the blood could be accessed and directed toward the particular needs of the sinner. Moravians themselves were a fairly diverse lot including many different nationalities, social classes, and occupations among the early immigrants to America. And because they had always been a religious minority with considerable internal diversity, Moravians generally shied away from associating particular cultural traits with the Christian life. This tendency was further reinforced in the colonies, where they were a religious and ethnic minority. These disparate expressions of the Christian story translated into dramatically different mission programs.

A comparison of the founding and development of the two missions challenges easy assumptions about the relationships between missionaries and Indians. While Mohican choices were constrained, both communities chose to adopt and adapt Christianity for reasons rooted in native tradition and their current circumstances. Like their European neighbors, Indians too faced an increasing array of religious options. And as in colonial society, greater diversity brought greater divisiveness as individuals, families, and communities sought to construct religious identities that fit the new worlds created by European presence. Some Indians continued quietly to practice the ways of their ancestors. Others, concluding that their acceptance of European ways was the reason for their straitened circumstances, joined nativist revitalization movements, such as that led by the Delaware prophet in the 1740s.[14] Still others, like the Stockbridge and Shekomeko Mohicans, turned to Christianity, often as a means of both preserving community and tapping new spiritual resources.

The power of the European trade, pathogens, and weaponry all worked to constrain Indians options, but adaptation of Christianity did not mean unquestioning capitulation to European colonial aims or embrace of missionary cultural norms. Briefly stated, the Stockbridge Mohicans strove to preserve what they identified as a core value, or at least a core function: Mohicans as cultural intermediaries. In native society, individual identity was defined relationally, and much the same could be said of corporate identity, which was articulated and negotiated in the language of fictive kinship. The Housatonic Mohicans of Stockbridge sought to preserve, or rather re-establish, their position as the "front door" between their fictive kin on either side of their Hudson River homelands—their Delaware Grandfathers, their Shawnee "Younger Brothers," their Iroquois "Cousins," and the increasingly powerful New England "Fathers." The Stockbridge strategy would be to preserve a degree of communal autonomy by becoming fluent in the culture of their powerful New England neighbors. Instruction in English religion, literacy, and husbandry was a means of binding the English to the Mohicans, a relationship they hoped to trade on with their western Indian relations. For the Stockbridge Mohicans, preservation of communal identity did not mean perpetuation of inherited subsistence or unchanged ritual practices but rested instead on the continuation of longstanding diplomatic strategies.

The residents of Shekomeko and the surrounding villages who eventually accepted Moravian missionaries made a different calculation, but one that also attempted to maintain a continuity with the past. Many Shekomeko residents had had considerable experience with other missionaries and wanted no part of the sort of Christianity they had encountered. They only accepted Moravian missionaries once the Brethren had proved that they differed dramatically from other Europeans. These Shekomekoans would seek to enlist the blood of Jesus as a new, powerful *manitou*—the spirits or "other-than-human" beings who animated the world—whose spiritual power could be put to use in traditional (and traditionally gendered) ways. Men sought help on the hunt, for example, while women hoped Christian practice could help to create and sustain self, family, and community. Confronted with the increasing challenges of colonialism, these men and women enlisted the service of an imported European spirit in the project of maintaining and supporting inherited Mohican values. Destructive spirits, like the alcohol and pathogens Europeans brought, would require a European-derived spiritual antidote, in this case the blood of a powerful warrior, Jesus. The Mohicans of Stockbridge and Shekomeko understood their adaptation of Christianity as a means of preserving important elements of what defined them as a people.[15]

Viewed up close, the Shekomeko story could scarcely be more different from the Stockbridge story, but in the end, it serves to confirm many

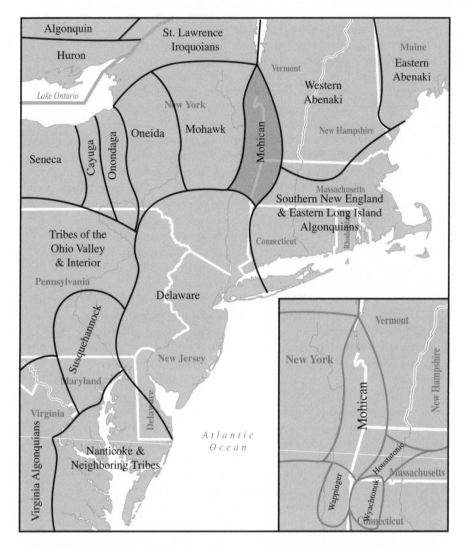

Map 1 Map of Tribal Territories, adapted from *Handbook of North American Indians*, ed. William C. Sturtevant, vol. 15, *Northeast*, ed. Bruce G. Trigger (Washington: Smithsonian Institution, 1978), ix, 198. Created by Ryan Kruse.

Map 2 Indian and White Settlements in the Eighteenth Century. Created by Ryan Kruse.

of the lessons of Stockbridge. Paradoxically, Anglo-Protestants found the Moravian missionaries threatening both because they were generally more successful in winning converts and because they challenged the equation of Christianity with European culture, thereby threatening the line between "Indian" and "white" that British colonial society increasingly depended on as a support for its sense of identity. At the same time, the Moravian disinterest in culture demands attention. In important ways, the Moravians foreshadowed modern sensibilities in defining community as resting on bonds of affection and shared experience.

The emergent mission communities at Stockbridge and Shekomeko were profoundly shaped by forces of politics, economics, religious diversification, and war. The stories of Stockbridge and Shekomeko put a face on these abstract forces, while illuminating the diversity of Indian Christianity and revealing the extent to which debates over the revivals engaged important issues of race and national identity.

This book is part of a growing body of scholarship that builds on the important advances of ethnohistorical scholarship begun in the 1970s while also questioning the tendency of these revisionist accounts to cast the meeting of Indian and white as an inevitable clash of cultures. The driving interest of these revisionist historians and literary scholars was in resistance to Euro-American hegemony.[16] Nativist revitalization movements received considerable scholarly attention, while Indian Christianity received relatively little. When native Christianity was considered, it was usually—with some important exceptions—depicted as a disingenuous mechanism of covert resistance or a course of last resort.[17] Anthropologists and textual critics working in colonial discourse and postcolonial studies have also tended to interpret native Christianity as either a case of colonization of consciousness or masked resistance.[18]

More recently, scholarship on the "Indians' new world" has challenged the earlier "clash of cultures" model of colonial Indian history, providing keen insights into the social and economic lives of northeastern Indian peoples while shying away from studies of religious belief and practice.[19] Uncovering the texture of Indian peoples' religious lives poses significant challenges, but a new generation of scholars has been attempting just such an undertaking, using a variety of methodologies. These scholars have explored the ways various Indian communities have engaged Christianity in a dialogue with native traditions as a means of preserving native identity and securing new spiritual resources with which to confront the challenges of colonialism. Douglas Winiarski, using the tools developed by students of "folk" and "lived" religion in his study of New England's Old Colony, has unearthed a "shadowy world" in which Indians and English settlers exchanged religious beliefs and practices. David Silverman has demonstrated how Christianity was incorporated by the Wampanoags of Martha's Vineyard, facilitating relations with their white neighbors and enabling the preservation of community. And Jane Merritt was among the first to tap into the rich Moravian sources, exploring the ways that Delaware Indians created a religious middle ground through their adaptation of Moravian-Christian practice.[20] Literary scholars have taken a different approach, focusing on the writings of Christian Indians, which had long been neglected because of the presumed taint of the missionaries' imperialist influence. Also in the literary studies vein, Laura Stevens has located missionary writings in a transatlantic context showing the ways that colonial identity rested in part on a particular construction of colonial missions, thus ably demonstrating that cultural encounter was not a one-way street.[21] But while missions have been receiving considerable attention, since James Axtell's monumental *The Invasion Within* there has been relatively little work focused on comparing mission contexts.[22]

This book continues the effort to unearth the diverse paths forged by Indians in early America striving to be both Indian and Christian. It explores the shape of Mohican identity as it adapted two distinctive forms of Christianity as well as the shape of Christianity as it was interpreted through the lens of Mohican tradition and Mohican experiences of colonialism. The proximity—in time and space—of the Congregational and Moravian missions to the Mohicans allows for the benefits of microhistorical studies while also introducing an important comparative element that facilitates examination of the broader historical context. The Moravian sources provide an opportunity to examine the experiences and religious beliefs and practices of Indian individuals in a way that is unthinkable when working from English colonial sources alone. The example of the Moravian missionaries calls our attention to the diversity of European Christianity and its relations with colonial powers. The Stockbridge story provides a window onto the construction of a new body politic that invoked both native tradition and Christianity. It also provides an opportunity to examine how English colonial identity became increasingly dependent on constructions of racial difference.

Before we move on to those stories, the organization of the book needs some explanation, as it does not follow the standard path of a monograph. The form arises from the peculiar challenges of the available sources. What had seemed to me, as a graduate student years ago, a perfect opportunity for a comparative study—two Mohican Indian communities with two very different mission programs founded within five years of each other—proved instead to be immensely frustrating. The two bodies of sources stubbornly refused to answer the same questions, posing thorny organizational as well as interpretive challenges. These challenges forced me to think more deeply about the relationship between historical actors and the types of sources they produced as well as the relationship between the source material and the final form of historical writing. Rather than sweeping these questions under the rug, as I was often tempted to do, I have taken a cue from my sources and attempted to address these questions through style and organization as well as analysis.

In roughest outline, there are four parts to the book. Parts I and IV focus on the Stockbridge story, while parts II and III address the Moravian mission at Shekomeko. Treatment of the Moravian mission is thus sandwiched between the Stockbridge chapters. This organization reflects not only the chronology of the mission—the Stockbridge mission began earlier and continued beyond the existence of the Shekomeko mission—but it also fits with the story that emerges from the two missions. The Stockbridge mission stands as a case study in the larger history of colonization, with emphasis on the reconfiguration of peoples and the formation of racial identity.

The focus here remains on the public and the political, on the body politic. The Shekomeko story, by contrast, provides a rare glimpse into native peoples' subjective experiences of colonialism. The chapters devoted to the Shekomeko community are more like a detailed snapshot showing depth and detail but not change over time, while the Stockbridge chapters might best be compared to an Impressionist painting: from far away the image is of a sweeping landscape, but any effort to focus in on an area of detail leaves one looking at a patch of seemingly unconnected dots. Stylistically, the Stockbridge chapters are narrative and chronological, while the Shekomeko chapters might be said to be phenomenological, focusing on the experience and practice of religion under the circumstances of colonialism.

Within the broader structure, each part consists of a short biographical vignette focusing on two individuals, followed by one or two analytical chapters that take up the central issues raised by the narratives. The aim of the vignettes is to bring alive the historical actors as humans faced with real human dilemmas, rather than simply as data points. Of course, as historian Kenneth Greenberg has written, "those who reconstruct the past are grave robbers. Some treat the corpse with respect, while others mutilate it. Either way, we all rob graves."[23] My project is no different, but I hope that these vignettes help readers to appreciate the humanity of historical peoples whose literal and figurative graves have so often not been treated with respect.

Finally, a few words on methodology and the relationship between the sources and the final product presented here. The most obstinate problem of this project has been how to compare the mission communities at Stockbridge and Shekomeko when the sources available did not answer the same questions. This in turn prompted the question of why the missionaries created the kinds of sources they did. Why do the Stockbridge records contain so little on individual Indian lives, and how has this sparseness constrained the narrative options available to the historian? Similarly, why did the Moravians record the details they did about individual Mohican lives? And if comparison is so difficult, is it even appropriate to lump them together in one book? I have asked myself this question many times, and in the end the answer I settled on is that either story alone would be incomplete and deceptively simple. On its own, the arc of Stockbridge history leaves us with a sense of inevitability: the missionaries enter the scene as agents of colonial power with imperial aims, and before long, the Indians are dispossessed of their lands and seemingly their religion as well. For its part, the Shekomeko story is so short and the sources so different from all other colonial records that it is difficult to gain a broader perspective. Turning to the Moravian-Mohican story after an introduction to the Stockbridge mission allows for a greater appreciation and understanding of Indian experiences, something sorely lacking in the Stockbridge sources. It also provides suggestive possibilities regarding the religious experiences of the mission residents. And returning to the Stockbridge story after the Shekomeko interlude helps us assess the larger meaning of the Moravian missions in the sweep of colonial Indian history.

Missionaries produced the sources at the heart of this project, yet ultimately my subject is neither the missionaries themselves nor the Indians who resided in mission communities but rather the processes of cultural interaction that took place at missions. Missionaries, to be sure, had their hopes and dreams of how native communities would be reborn as communities of Christ (which meant substantially different things to Congregationalists and Moravians), but the Mohicans of Stockbridge and Shekomeko had their own reasons for their alliances with the missionaries, which sometimes clashed and sometimes merged with missionary goals. As we'll see in the chapters that follow, Christianity as practiced by the Mohicans at Stockbridge and Shekomeko was not a monolithic entity. Both communities engaged Christianity in ways that helped them to chart a way forward in a dramatically changed world. What follows is an effort to humanize what has too often appeared in history books as a faceless "clash of cultures." This book attempts to bring to life the experiences of men and women, mothers and daughters, fathers and sons, as they all attempted to negotiate a period of radical and often devastating social transformation.

These human encounters reveal moments of hope tinged by many more moments of disappointment. The title of the book is taken from a piece of paper used by Jonathan Edwards to sketch out his notes for a sermon to the Stockbridge Indians in October 1756, a time when life seemed precarious indeed. Britain and its allies were not faring well in the first years of the French and Indian War. Locally, in Stockbridge, the mission house had been fortified and now served as a garrison for hundreds of soldiers. Rumors swirled of an imminent attack by thousands of French troops, and a company of about thirty Stockbridge Indians had recently departed to the battlefront, including a man named Ebenezer Maunnauseet, who had served often as Edwards's interpreter. Always careful not to waste paper, Edwards wrote his sermon on the back of a piece of paper that had already seen use by Maunnauseet for handwriting practice. Eleven times over—perhaps just before he set out with the militia for an expedition at Lake George—Maunnauseet had written the line, "He who lives upon Hope may dy of Disappointment" and carefully signed his name. The line is apparently a rendering of one of Benjamin Franklin's proverbs from *Poor Richard's Almanac*: "He who lives upon hope will die fasting."[24] Whether the improvisation was Maunnauseet's or someone else's, it seems a fitting commentary on the mission experience.

PART I

HOPE

Chapter Two

The River God and the Lieutenant

On April 25, 1724, in exchange for £460, three barrels of cider and thirty quarts of rum, Umpachenee, Konkapot, and nineteen other Housatonic-Mohican men conveyed a tract of land along the Housatonic River to John Stoddard and other members of the "settling committee" appointed by the Massachusetts government to purchase lands for the creation of two new townships.[1] This deed was not the first to convey Housatonic-Mohican lands into English hands, but it is significant because it records the first known meeting of the principal figures in the founding of the Stockbridge mission a decade later.[2] Beginning our story with this deed and a glimpse into the life circumstances of two signatories, Stoddard and Umpachenee, underscores the extent to which the story of the mission must also be a story of power—of earthly and spiritual power and the intertwining of the two. The deed raises a number of important questions: Why were the Housatonics willing to sell in 1724? And why, just ten years later, did some of the sellers consider the possibility of a Christian missionary on Mohican lands when they had resisted missionary efforts for a century?

Umpachenee and Stoddard lived their lives in vastly different worlds, but their common interest in the lands of the Housatonic Valley and the religious affairs of its inhabitants ensured that their paths crossed with some regularity. The two men must have come to know each other well over the decades as they came together to negotiate issues of primary importance to their native communities. At the time of their first meeting in the 1720s, both men were prominent leaders in their local and regional communities. And both would be centrally involved in the negotiations leading to the founding of the Stockbridge mission. Umpachenee brought the concerns of his community to the attention of Massachusetts leaders; he sought assurances of fair dealing; and he maintained ties with other Indian peoples locally and farther afield. Stoddard served as the primary negotiator for the Massachusetts government; he heard the grievances of the Indian residents when they arose; and he was the one, with his surveyor's chain, who platted the newly incorporated Indian town of Stockbridge. Glimpsing these two men's lives and the state of their communities at the time of the 1724 deed provides the backstory to the official founding of the Massachusetts mission to the Housatonic-Mohicans a decade later.

THE RIVER GOD

Two facts go a long way in explaining the course of John Stoddard's life: He was the son of Solomon Stoddard, one of Massachusetts' most famed ministers, and he was present at the 1704 French and Indian attack on Deerfield, Massachusetts.[3] Given these two facts, it is not at all surprising that Stoddard devoted much of his career to strategizing the defense of New England's frontier and the conversion of Indian souls.

No dearth of sources impedes the reconstruction of John Stoddard's life. Indeed, much of the history of New England could be told through Stoddard's family tree, whose branches linked him to the vast network of "River Gods" that reigned over the Connecticut River Valley with near-feudal power. Ties of kinship coupled with provincial patronage placed Stoddard squarely at the center of judicial, military, and ministerial power in western Massachusetts.[4] A glimpse, then, at Stoddard's life and how it brought him to the signing of the 1724 deed is instructive in setting the scene for the founding of the Stockbridge mission.

Born in 1682, John Stoddard was the tenth child of Esther Warham Mather Stoddard and Solomon Stoddard, who was disparaged by his opponents as the "Pope" of western Massachusetts. In his role as pastor of the Northampton Church, Solomon Stoddard developed a unique version of the New England Way—a sort of Presbyterian revivalism distinct from the increasingly Anglophilic Congregationalism of coastal Massachusetts. Solomon Stoddard presided over numerous "seasons" of revival in his Northampton parish, the fruits of his evangelical preaching and distinctive (among Puritans, anyway) view of communion as a "converting ordinance" rather than the sole privilege of the visibly saved. Through force of personality and kinship ties, the senior Stoddard left his stamp on the religiosity of the region; his sons and sons-in-law propagated the Stoddard way in pulpits up and down the Connecticut River Valley.[5]

But it was not only from pulpits that the Stoddard clan wielded influence. Members of the prominent family ruled—with the nearly unanimous support of the people—virtually every realm of life in western New England, from the religious to the civil to the military.[6] John Stoddard would be active in all three throughout his life, as a militia captain, representative, judge, and promoter of missions. Over the course of his career, he managed to amass substantial wealth, including a thousand-acre grant of land from the government as a reward for his faithful service.[7]

Much of his career still lay ahead of him when John Stoddard served as lieutenant of the local militia posted to protect the garrison at Deerfield early in 1704. The frontier outpost—settled by many of Stoddard's Williams relatives—was still struggling to regain its footing after the devastations of King Philip's War over a quarter of a century earlier. The town was on guard following the announcement of renewed hostilities with New France, the result of the War of Spanish Succession. At the time of the raid, Stoddard was staying in the home of his half-brother-in-law, the Rev. John Williams, pastor of Deerfield since 1686.[8]

When a contingent of French and Indians attacked the town on the morning of February 29, 1704, Stoddard was the lone member to escape from the Williams household; the eleven others were among the fifty killed and the 112 taken captive. Several of Stoddard's captured relatives would eventually be returned from their captivity in Canada, including John Williams and his sons Samuel and Stephen. Stoddard's niece, Eunice, however, would remain throughout her life the unredeemed captive, committing the double betrayal of becoming a Catholic and living as an Indian, married to a Mohawk man at the Catholic-Mohawk community at Caughnawagha. The Treaty of Utrecht signed in 1713 brought an end to the hostilities between New England and New France, enabling Stoddard and John Williams to undertake a journey to Canada in an (unsuccessful) effort to secure the release of Eunice Williams and dozens of other captives.[9]

Stoddard experienced firsthand the vulnerability of the Massachusetts frontier and the power of the Catholic religion over the Indians and even over his Puritan kin. The rest of his career would be largely devoted to protecting the frontier settlements through trade, military might, and missionary efforts. Securing his first government office in 1703 as registrar of probate, Stoddard would accumulate a handful of titles and offices over the coming decades, as justice of the peace, judge of the informal court of common pleas, colonel of the northern regiment of the Hampshire militia, and member of the Massachusetts House of Representatives. With the accumulation of power over the course of his career, Stoddard became, in the words of a contemporary, a "Great Benefactor," offering his loyal support to the legislative agenda of unpopular royal governors in exchange for the considerable largesse that he could distribute among his kith and kin back home, who in turn regularly returned Stoddard and other members of the Williams-Stoddard clan to office.[10]

The signing of the 1724 deed would not have been the first time Stoddard met with Indians from the Housatonic Valley. In 1722, Massachusetts Governor Jonathan Belcher appointed Stoddard to a committee to direct the settlement of Housatonic lands. As early as 1717, residents of the Connecticut River Valley had petitioned the legislature for grant of a township along the Housatonic. A similar petition from Northampton residents was finally approved in June 1722, thus prompting the government to see about securing title to the lands from the Indian owners. The governor turned to his faithful servant, John Stoddard, to head the committee that would oversee the patenting and surveying of the proposed townships. Just a month later, Governor Belcher had another job for Stoddard: together with two others, he would serve on the commission sent by Belcher to a conference being held at Albany with the Iroquois to renew the Covenant Chain, the alliance between the British colonies and the Iroquois Confederacy established in the wake of King Philip's War in the 1670s.[11] Mohican representatives were at this council, and Stoddard likely took the opportunity to seek out an audience for his proposal to purchase Housatonic-Mohican lands. The 1724 deed testifies to his success.[12]

If it was Stoddard's experience at Deerfield that led to the Housatonic deed, then it was likely his father's preaching that fostered Stoddard's commitment to bringing the gospel to the Indians. Solomon Stoddard published a sermon in 1723 asking the *Question Whether God is not Angry with the Country for doing so little toward the Conversion of the Indians?* The first settlers had professed it the principal aim of the colony "to bring the Indians to the knowledge of the true God and Saviour of Mankind," as even the King's charter had it. Yet, concluded the elder Stoddard, "we have done very little to Answer our Profession." Recalling the horrors of the previous sixty years, especially the Indian raids on New England during King Philip's War, King William's War, and Queen Anne's War, Stoddard's providentialism prompted him to ask whether "God has made them a terrible scourge to us" since "we have little care of the Heathen." In short, Stoddard concluded that as "they are instruments to punish us, it may be we have not done our duty to them."[13]

Just one year after the venerable Solomon Stoddard lamented that New Englanders had done more to "make a booty" of the Indians than "gain them to the practice of Religion," his son, John Stoddard, helped to secure more Indian lands that could be turned into New England farms. But it may have been the echo of his father's words that led Stoddard to set relatively generous terms of the deal.[14] And perhaps it was his father's influence that prompted him to broach the idea of a Christian mission so soon after closing the land deal with Umpachenee and the other Housatonic Mohicans. The senior Stoddard had preached that "it is Expected from those that are in Authority, who have Power to send Preachers, and to maintain and Subsist them in doing their Work, to take Effectual Care that the Gospel be Published."[15]

THE LIEUTENANT

Few details of Umpachenee's life can be known with any certainty. John Stoddard, the Englishman best equipped to record details of Umpachenee's life, could have produced rich accounts of their meetings and negotiations over the decades of their acquaintance, but he apparently felt little inclination to do so. And so the outline of Umpachenee's life must be pieced together from a mere handful of scattered references. By one account, he was born around 1696, and by another, as early as 1678, making him either twenty-eight or forty-six when he signed the deed for Housatonic lands.[16] Europeans called him "King," "Governor," "Captain," "Lieutenant," or sometimes simply "Aaron," finding these titles and Anglicized names easier to manage than his Indian names, Umpachenee and Sonkenewenaukheek. Historians and anthropologists have labeled him alternately village chief, chief sachem, or tribal speaker.[17] Although the English tended to grant Konkapot greater status than Umpachenee, that Umpachenee presided over a hundred-foot longhouse in his village of Skatekook suggests that the English were mistaken.[18]

Umpachenee may or may not have been married at the time of the deed. If he was not yet married, he soon would be, to the daughter of the Mohican "King," Etowaukaum, who had traveled to England in 1710 for an audience with Queen Anne. The marriage likely cemented an important alliance between Hudson River Mohicans and Housatonic peoples.[19] Umpachenee's name appears on deeds as early as 1719, confirming that he held an interest in other Housatonic-area lands located near Salisbury, Connecticut. The Salisbury connection suggests that Umpachenee may well have served as speaker for the Mohican sachem, Corlaer, also known as Metoxen.[20]

The range of titles assigned to Umpachenee makes it impossible to determine with any certainty his role in the larger Mohican community. Some help comes from the history of the Mohican peoples written by Stockbridge sachem Hendrick Aupaumut in the late eighteenth century, in which he described leadership structures. Contemporary evidence suggests that this structure was likely in place during Umpachenee's time. Aupaumut described a

Figure 1 *Etow Oh Koam, King of the River Nation,* Jan Verelst (ca. 1648–1734), Library and Archives Canada, Acc. No. 1977–35–1. Acquired with a special grant from the Canadian Government in 1977.

political order that included a Chief Sachem, several Counselors (chiefs), a Hero (war chief), an Owl (speaker), and Runners and Young Men (warriors). Mohicans viewed their Sachem as a "conductor and promoter of their general welfare" who served so long as he "behaved himself agreeably, to the office of a Sachem." The Sachem's office was inherited through the women's lineage, so that when a Sachem died, he was usually succeeded by a nephew, the son of a sister. The Sachem's task, according to Aupaumut, was to contemplate the welfare of the nation and to "take pains to maintain and brighten the belt of friendship with all their allies." When he was called to act for the nation, he was expected to consult first with the Counselors to determine a course of action that would best promote the nation's well-being. The Sachem's Counselors were called chiefs and served by election, not heredity. They were to counsel the Sachem and to promote peace.

A "Hero," according to Aupaumut, was essentially a wartime leader. As was common in many Indian cultures, there was a separate governing body for times of war and peace. When it was no longer possible to maintain peace, the Sachem and his counselors relinquished control to the Heroes, who held their office "by remarkable conduct in the wars, by great courage and prudence." As soon as peace was proposed, governance was returned to the hands of the Sachem and the Counselors. An Owl served as the speaker, and it was his task to "proclaim the orders of his Sachem to the people with loud voice"; as with the Heroes, the office was achieved by merit, not heredity. The requisite skills for an Owl were a good memory, eloquence, and a strong voice.[21]

Based on Aupaumut's descriptions and evidence from the Moravian records, it seems likely that Umpachenee was a local chief, or counselor, to the Mohican sachem. When the Moravians referred to Umpachenee by name, they most commonly used the term *captain* but also occasionally *governor* or sometimes *king*. They also mention the arrival of a runner in 1744 announcing a new "governor" in Stockbridge, likely meaning a new chief sachem. The Moravian records contain references to the captain and governor traveling together, so it is clear it was not the missionaries' general practice to use governor and captain interchangeably.

So who were Umpachenee's people, and why were they willing to sell their lands in 1724? Just as it is impossible to determine with any certainty Umpachenee's life history, so it is difficult to reconstruct the history of Umpachenee's people. But something of the history of the broader community of Indian peoples who lived between the Hudson and Housatonic Rivers can be pieced together from a variety of sources including deeds, official colonial records, and later tribal histories. According to Aupaumut's history, the Mohicans had not always called the Hudson River Valley home but had once lived further west, where they enjoyed an Edenic existence of peace and prosperity. There they lived along the banks of the "waters that are never still" until a famine struck, straining the social fabric and forcing the people to wander in search of better lands. They headed east until they came across the great river, whose waters reminded them of their Muheak-kunnuk homelands, and so there they settled, soon to become important middlemen in an active trade that brought wampum from the coastal Algonquians in exchange for furs from the interior.[22]

The story of the first meeting of Mohicans and Europeans was regularly recounted at later councils between Indians and colonists. Moravian missionary John Heckewelder recorded one account of this early encounter. The Indians at first were astonished "by a phenomenon they had till then never beheld; immense canoes arriving at their shores, filled with people of a different colour, language, dress, and manners from themselves!" The Mohican ancestors, initially believing the new beings to be visiting gods sent by the Great Spirit as messengers of peace, prepared to offer them sacrifices.[23] The Indians were soon disabused of such notions, and a lively and sometimes contentious trade was begun, as recalled in a 1722 address by a Mohican sachem to the New York governor: "When the Christians came to settle this Country they came with a ship & desired to fasten their Cable to the Hills near Housak above Albany, which we readily granted." Since that time, the sachem affirmed, the fat of the beaver served as the grease to prevent the "chain of friendship" between Dutch (and later English) and Mohicans from rusting.[24]

For a time, Mohicans were apparently successful in acquiring furs as tribute from neighboring tribes, thus enabling the Mohicans to remain viable trading partners. Mohicans and Mohawks had likely been at war before the arrival of the Dutch, and hostilities continued into the early trade era. The Mohicans suffered defeat in 1629 or 1630 at the hands of the Mohawks, which forced some Mohicans east from their Hudson River lands, and this movement might well explain the existence of the Housatonic Mohican villages. Some Mohicans eventually returned to their Hudson River homes, but there they were obliged to abide by new rules, including paying tribute to the Mohawks. Peace between the Mohawks and Mohicans was temporarily effected in the late 1660s mediated by English colonial representatives.[25] A failed attempt to regain supremacy over the Mohawks in 1669 with a rebuffed attack on the Mohawk village of Caughnawaga disrupted the uneasy peace. By the late 1670s, Mohicans were considered the "Children" of the Mohawks, living under their protection. Some Mohicans moved west to the Great Lakes region and some north to the St. Lawrence Valley, while others settled at Schaghticoke on the Hoosic River, northeast of Albany.[26]

The Mohican response to these dislocations was similar to that of many other native peoples confronted by the challenges of colonialism: they consolidated populations and sought to secure strategic alliances with European powers.[27] By 1675, the small and loosely affiliated communities along the Hudson formed a confederation with Indians to the east, announcing to the New York governor in 1675, "The English and the Dutch are now one and the Dutch are now English. Thus we Mahikanders, the Highland Indians, and the Western Corner Indians [Housatonics] are now one also."[28] This meeting may have signaled a new alliance that incorporated refugee New England Indians who had fled west to escape King Philip's War.[29] Despite the increase in numbers due to consolidation, the Mohican population suffered a net loss as a result of the repeated waves of epidemic disease that swept through Mohican territory in the second half of the seventeenth century. The colonial wars of the late seventeenth and early eighteenth centuries rendered Mohican existence yet more precarious, not only through the loss of warriors who fought for the English but also in the restriction of Mohican access to western and northern trapping grounds.[30] The declining status of the Mohicans is further evident in the wave of deeds produced beginning in the 1670s exchanging Mohican lands to New York, Massachusetts, and Connecticut colonials for cash, trade goods, and often alcohol. As historian Shirley Dunn suggests, these deeds signified Mohican demand for European goods. No longer able to procure sufficient furs to exchange for the trade goods, they now sold their lands.[31]

By the 1720s, Mohican status as allies and trading partners with both Indian and English had deteriorated significantly; instead of offering shelter to vulnerable European newcomers, Mohicans now sought the protection of the powerful English. The increased dependence of Mohican peoples on colonial powers is clear in Mohican sachem Ampamit's address to New York Governor William Burnet at Albany in 1722, in which he reminded the governor of the kindness Mohican ancestors had shown to the Europeans when they arrived and sought assurances of protection from the colonial government. This exchange between Ampamit and Governor Burnet provides a telling snapshot of the state of Mohican society on the eve of the mission era. "Father," Ampamit started, "We look upon you as a great Tree under whose Branches we desire to shelter, and if there should happen any sudden Tempest or Thunder Shower we hope we shall be admitted to take shelter under that great Tree and be shadowed by the leaves therefore, that no drops may fall on us but that we may live in Peace and safety."

Burnet acknowledged that the "chain of friendship" had been kept "inviolable by your Ancestors from the first time that Christians settled here in this River." Yet now Governor Burnet saw the River Indians as children in need of paternal protection. He praised Ampamit and his people for having "been obedient children and observed the commands of my Predecessors." Finally, Burnet reaffirmed the colony's paternal posture over the Mohicans by warning his "children" against intemperance. While acknowledging the Europeans' greater power, Ampamit placed blame for the abuse of alcohol squarely at the feet of European traders. He conceded that alcohol had ravaged Mohican communities and hindered their ability to provide for the welfare of all. Yet he explained that when his people arrived in white settlements to trade, the traders and townspeople plied them with drink, which made them "crave for more," so that in the end, the proceeds from the trade "goes for drink," leaving the Mohican trappers "destitute either of Clothing or Ammunition." Worse abuses still happened at the hands of "Christians," who, having bought a small plot of land from the Mohicans, "ask us if we have no more." And, according to Ampamit, "when we say yes they enquire the name of the Land & take in a greater Bounds than was intended to be sold them & the Indians not understanding what is writ in the Deed or Bill of Sale sign it and are so deprived of Part of their Lands."[32]

Many of the concerns and critiques registered by Ampamit would be taken up a decade later by Umpachenee when he began to negotiate in earnest with John Stoddard about the possibility of a mission to the Housatonic Mohicans. Stoddard looked to make good on the colony's long-neglected pledge to provide the gospel in exchange for Indian lands. Umpachenee, like Ampamit before him, hoped that his people would acquire the skills of literacy and tools to combat the power of alcohol. And though the founding of the mission brought the Housatonics more fully into the orbit of colonial record-keepers, these men—John Stoddard, missionary John Sergeant, schoolteacher Timothy Woodbridge, and others—committed little about the Indians to paper, tending to record the number of souls baptized, pupils instructed, and acres plowed or sold but providing little detail about the more subjective experiences of life at the new mission community.

Chapter Three

Covenants, Contracts, and the Founding of Stockbridge

It is fitting that the story of the Massachusetts mission to the Housatonic Mohican Indians begins with a deed. New Englanders thought in terms of numbers, contracts, and covenants, whether the commodity was acres or souls. The 1724 deed recorded the exchange of Housatonic lands (lands that had already been patented out to potential settlers) for cash and trade goods: acres, pounds, barrels, and a list of Indian names. The sources created a decade later recording the beginnings of the mission were in many respects not so different from that deed. The body of sources can be read as a ledger: recording expenditures on plows and bibles and salaries and listing the "income" in the form of numbers of souls baptized, numbers of communicants, numbers of students in the classroom.

The first decades of the Massachusetts mission to the Housatonic Mohicans can be understood as a series of negotiated contracts involving different currencies and commodities, both worldly and otherworldly. John Stoddard and the government he represented were buying acres and alliances, and paying off a debt to their God. In proposing a mission to the Housatonics, Stoddard was making payment on a debt he (or at least his father) believed was owed to God while also securing borders and freeing up land for English settlement. And to the Indians, Stoddard was selling a chance at eternal salvation, in payment for which they would have to forfeit their heathen ways and adopt the path of Christian civility.

Umpachenee and his people were active participants in this trade, though they understood the terms quite differently. Despite what Stoddard and other promoters of the mission hoped, the decision by Umpachenee, Konkapot, and other Housatonic Mohicans to accept in their midst a Christian missionary—one determined to teach them the skills of literacy and English husbandry—was far from a rejection of all things Indian. No longer possessed of great military might or access to vast supplies of fur from the interior of the continent, the Mohicans offered their lands in exchange for the trade goods they had come to depend on (or the cash to buy them). With the founding of the mission, Umpachenee and Konkapot hoped to secure a place for themselves in an increasingly Europeanized world; in particular, gaining the skills of literacy not only garnered favor among the English but also (so they hoped) offered protection against fraud. Acquiring competency in other aspects of New England culture and religion similarly would not only secure an alliance, but also provide them with a tradable commodity among their Indian neighbors. And finally, in a world in which the inherited patterns of exchange with the spiritual world no longer functioned to secure a comfortable existence, Umpachenee bargained that an appeal to the Christian God might help, for God seemed to favor the English, even when they fell considerably short of living up to the teachings of their Bible. Ironically, although the conflation of English culture and Christianity meant that Massachusetts civic and religious leaders set out to extinguish the "savage" ways of their proselytes, the acceptance of the mission by the Indians signaled their decision to adapt the tools of English culture and put them to use in preserving community, a bargain many New England Indians had made before them, with varying degrees of success.[1] The different motivations for change inevitably let to clashes.

And for a time during the negotiations and the early years of the mission settlement, it seemed that the parties had agreed on the terms of the bargain; Indian men were eager to learn the ways of English civilization. This honeymoon period was short-lived, however, as tensions present but submerged from the beginning increasingly rose to the surface. The day-to-day and face-to-face encounters that came with the formal start of the mission forced participants to come to the realization that the two parties did not see their agreement the same way at all. By the end of the decade, it seemed to the Indians that the government had defaulted on its promise to grant full protection to the Indian community; to the missionary John Sergeant and other officials, it increasingly seemed the Indians would not so readily abandon their Indian ways.[2]

Ultimately, both parties were disappointed when things did not progress quite as planned. Mohican lands—even when secured under English law to the Stockbridge Indians—proved not to be secure from colonial land hunger. Nor did the Christian God prove effective in preventing further outbreaks of disease or curing the curse of alcohol among the Housatonics. Likewise, Sergeant and the mission backers were disappointed at the slow progress of the gospel and "civilization" among the Indians. English settlers in Stockbridge, brought in as models of Christian living, were quickly on track to displace the town's Indian residents by dint of both higher birth rates and unscrupulous land dealings.

Along the way, despite internal and external tensions, the Housatonic Mohicans of Stockbridge secured a future, no small feat given the pressures faced by native peoples throughout the Americas.[3] In the first decades of Stockbridge's existence, the town served as a haven attracting new residents from native communities along the Hudson and Housatonic Valleys. At Stockbridge, a new Indian identity emerged that was at once Christian and Indian. But if the Housatonic Mohicans were willing to contemplate and construct an identity that merged Indian and English ways, the white residents of Stockbridge—and the Massachusetts officials who sat on the various provincial committees that oversaw town and mission affairs—were generally unwilling to accept Indian Christians as their equals or to apply the same standards of justice the English enjoyed under town and colonial law. The course of events at Stockbridge thus deserves careful examination, as it provides a window onto the creative refashioning of Indian identity and the slide toward a racialized construction of identity among the English colonists.[4]

COVENANTS AND CONTRACTS

By the time John Sergeant was ordained in 1735, the towns of Sheffield and Great Barrington had begun to sprout on the Housatonic lands patented in 1722 and purchased in 1724. Nathaniel Appleton, the Cambridge minister who preached Sergeant's ordination sermon, was worried that the colony had been slow to bring the gospel to the Indians: "It must needs be highly reasonable," Appleton argued, "that we who live among them, and possess their country, should readily expend of our estates, for that which will be of the greatest advantage to them."[5] Appleton was drawing on a long-established trope of colonial literature that envisioned the spread of the gospel as a benevolent act of trade whereby Indians received the invaluable gift of the gospel in exchange for their lands. Following God's mandate to subdue the wilderness, the English would rescue the land from neglect and transform it into a lush garden of plenty: a New Eden.[6]

As early as 1584, England's first booster, Richard Hakluyt, promoted colonization as an act of generosity to the Indians who would be rescued from enslavement to the Spanish and their "popish clergy." An English colony would be "greatly for the enlargement of the gospel of Christ whereunto the Princes of the reformed religion are chiefly bound."[7] This same idea was taken up and elaborated less than a half-century later by the Puritan settlers of Massachusetts Bay. The royal patent for the colony specified the spread of the gospel to heathen nations as the primary purpose of settlement. The same message was proclaimed by the colony's official seal, which depicted an Indian with his hands outstretched, inviting the English to enjoy the natural riches of the New World and pleading, "Come over and help us."[8]

When filtered through the lens of Puritan covenantal theology, the idea of spreading the gospel of Christ became a contract between God and his Puritan agents. The Massachusetts Bay Colony's first governor, John Winthrop, saw God's hand at work in "driv[ing] out the natives before us" and "plant[ing] his Churches here."[9] As early as 1629, Winthrop had justified the English right to Indian land by appealing to the book of Genesis: "The natives in New England, they inclose no land neither have any settled habitation nor any tame cattle to improve the land by, and so have no other but a natural right to those countries." Further, the offer of the gospel was more than generous compensation for the loss of lands: "They have of us," wrote Winthrop, "that [i.e., Christianity] which will yield them more benefit than all the land which we have from them."[10] By imagining that the Indians would gain a chance at eternal salvation and rescue from their heathen ways, the Puritans justified their claims to Indian lands.

Despite the proclaimed importance of spreading the Word, mission efforts trailed far behind expansion. The problem was not simply hypocrisy, as Francis Jennings memorably argued.[11] Rather, in the early decades of settlement, boosters and settlers alike assumed that the Indians would be struck by the superiority of English religion and culture, leading them immediately to abandon their native ways and become Christians.[12] When instantaneous conversions failed to materialize, it took some time for missionary initiatives to emerge, a delay that brought jeremiads from New England's pulpits.[13] The string of Indian wars from the Pequot War to King Philip's War and beyond were interpreted by New England's ministers not as a failure of diplomacy but as God's judgment upon a sinful people.[14]

Such jeremiads rarely prompted New Englanders to open their purses to support missionary endeavors. Most funding for mission work came from across the Atlantic.[15] Memories of the bloody wars with the Indians were fresh in the minds of many colonists living in vulnerable frontier towns. These settlers were likely to view mission efforts as coddling the enemy rather than fulfilling a divinely ordained national duty.[16] One mission promoter observed that many New Englanders would as soon kill the Indians as Christianize them.[17]

There were structural as well as motivational hindrances to mission work. The New England Way of Congregationalism was particularly ill-suited to missionary undertakings, for it made few provisions for church-ing the unchurched.[18] As many Congregational ministers knew all too well, they served at the will of the gathered church. The Puritan commitment to congregational independence was not particularly suited to supporting mission work, as the "heathen" Indians could scarcely be expected to issue a call for a Christian minister of the gospel (and raise the funds to pay his salary) without first being instructed in Christianity. Further hindering mission efforts in New England were the low social and economic compen-sation that came with the job, which made it difficult to recruit capable candidates.[19] And finally, Puritan ministers were family men as well as men of the cloth, a circumstance that generated considerable disincentives to missionary work.

For all of these reasons, Puritan mission efforts were slow to mobilize. When they did emerge, the reigning philosophy was to "reduce" the Indians to civility. As James Axtell memorably described the goal of Puritan mission projects, Christianity was to be constructed over the grave of Indian culture. The very first missions begun by John Eliot in the 1640s embodied this ethic. The "praying towns" instituted regulations that were a hodgepodge of Old Testament precedent and English custom. At their peak on the eve of King Philip's War, the towns counted about 1,100 Indian residents. Regarded with suspicion and often hostility and violence by their English neighbors and allies during the war, many residents of praying towns dis-persed, some fought for or against the English, but many sought asylum on Deer Island in Boston Harbor. Only four praying towns remained at the end of the war, but many residents returned to settle, hoping to maintain a connection to their lands.[20] Indians living on Cape Cod and Martha's Vine-yard faced similar suspicions of their loyalty during the war but were for a time relatively undisturbed in their quiet blending of Christian and Indian traditions.[21] After the war, mission efforts continued but with little popular support from English settlers.

When decades of imperial wars with the French and Indians finally gave way to peace with the Treaty of Utrecht of 1713, new expansionist energies were unleashed. Veterans of the colonial wars sought payment from the land-rich, cash-poor province, and they were often repaid with land grants in the fertile valleys of the western reaches.[22] Meanwhile, a demographic boom meant that many New England fathers found they were unable to set-tle their sons onto lands in the same town. And so young men like Thomas Nash and Joseph Parsons of Northampton (who gained the patents to Hou-satonic lands in 1722) pressured the government to open up more lands for settlement.[23]

Not surprisingly, expansion brought a reinvigoration of the missionary impulse among the colony's religious and civil leaders, as ministers worried that the colony had reneged on its contract with God to supply the Indians with the gospel in exchange for their lands. New mission projects were first proposed in 1733, when the Scottish Society for the Propagation of Christian Knowledge sponsored three fort-based missions.[24] Tellingly, the funding for these missions came from abroad.[25] In the sermon preached at the ordination of the three missionaries, the presiding minister invoked the land-for-gospel rhetoric, encouraging his audience to be generous in their support of missions, "considering GOD hath given us the Possession of this good Land which their Ancestors once inhabited; and that this was the professed Intention of our pious Progenitors."[26] The missions were a pronounced failure, which John Stoddard attributed to their setting, specifically the lack of women and the abundance of alcohol.[27] Trading posts proved to be a poor setting for trade in spiritual goods.

The failure of these fort-based mission efforts reinforced a longstanding fear: although the English were often able to offer a better deal to the Indians in earthly goods, their spiritual wares did not stack up to those offered by the French, as many New England ministers acknowledged. Benjamin Colman, minister of Cambridge's Brattle Street Church, expressed just this fear: "Yet Clouds & darkness do very much encompass this excellent attempt more especially from ye prejudices of Popery sown in ye minds of ye Salvages by ye French jesuits & Friars."[28] Massachusetts missions were of a piece with the larger imperial and spiritual agenda of reducing the French presence in the New World.

The mission to the Housatonic Mohicans emerged from this complex of conditions and motivations. John Stoddard had spearheaded the effort to bring Housatonic lands to English settlers in the early 1720s, and now he hoped to bring Housatonic souls to the Christian faith. Throughout the summer and fall of 1734, the colonial impetus for a mission among the Mohicans of the Housatonic Valley gathered speed. The commissioners of the London-based Company for the Propagation of the Gospel in New England and Parts Adjacent (more commonly known as the New England Company) had been searching for a suitable project in which to invest their funds and energies.[29] Massachusetts Governor Jonathan Belcher shared the clergy's fears that colonists had paid too little attention to Indian souls. "This Government," he lamented, "has done so little from the first Settlement of the Country to this Day for the Conversion of the Indian Natives to the true Christian faith."[30] Stoddard was able to persuade Belcher and the New England Commissioners of the wisdom and chances for success of a mission to the Housatonics, as it would avoid the difficulties of the fort-based missions by introducing settled agriculture and targeting whole communities rather than just the men.[31] Not only would a successful mission open up more lands for settlement by consolidating Indians into praying town type settlements, but the presence of friendly Indians would also provide added protection to the nascent frontier settlements. Finally, converts brought to the Protestant religion would help secure a victory over the French and their Jesuit missionaries. Bringing Christianity to the Housatonic Indians would be a victory for Massachusetts, for England, for Protestantism, and for Christ.

TRADE IN CULTURE

Umpachenee, Konkapot, and the other Housatonic Mohicans who came to endorse the mission project had their own motivations for the new alliance with Massachusetts. Needless to say, they did not view instruction in Christianity as payment for their lands. Nor did they seek to serve as a buffer for English settlers on the frontier. Nonetheless, their choice too reflected a renegotiation of their relationships with earthly nations and with the spirit world. And while they clearly did not desire to be "reduced" to civility, they did seek the tools of English civilization, which they deemed necessary to their survival in a changing world. The experiences of Umpachenee's people during the century of contact prior to the beginning of the mission prompted the renegotiation of economic, political, and social relationships. Villages consolidated as disease took its toll, some moving eastward toward the Housatonic as Dutch and later English settlement encroached. In the midst of these changes, the Mohicans forged new alliances with both Indian and English neighbors.[32]

All of these changes would have entailed a careful look at spiritual relationships, although such changes are difficult to trace through the historical records. In native Northeastern societies, individual and societal well-being depended on the maintenance of proper relationships with *manitou*, the spiritual forces that animated the world. Hunters maintained a relationship with the spirit of the animals they hunted, and healers engaged the spirits that caused illness or learned from spirits who communicated remedies in dreams or visions. Many of these relationships were profoundly altered by the European presence. Encroaching white settlement and pressures from the fur trade meant that game was becoming scarcer. That hunters were no longer as successful as they once had been signaled that the relationship between hunters and their prey was fraying. Traditional healing practices could do little to fend off the epidemic diseases brought by the Europeans. And that whites were not so severely affected by the pathogens that wracked Indians bodies suggested that Europeans were possessed of powerful medicine.[33] The prosperity of neighboring Europeans made a convincing case for Mohican consideration of the Christian God, particularly as many were finding that their religious leaders wielded little power over the English.[34] All of these concerns prompted the Housatonic Mohicans to consider accepting an English missionary in their midst.

What would seem to be a drastic change in course was in fact a variation on a longstanding pattern. In the past, when Mohican fortunes waned, they sought to establish new alliances. Over the course of the seventeenth century alone, some Mohicans moved to the Housatonic region, others joined the St. Francis (Abenaki) Indians of New France, and still others traveled as far as present-day Indiana, where they forged relations with the Miami peoples.[35] Old relationships were failing and Housatonic leaders sought new ways to sustain community by seeking closer alliances with their neighbors, this time the English of Massachusetts. At first, these efforts followed a common practice of cultural exchange, whereby a young member of the tribe was sent to be raised in another community. These children, fluent in their native and adopted cultures, would facilitate relations between the two nations.[36] During the founding negotiations of the mission, Konkapot and Umpachenee both sent their sons to board and study with John Sergeant in New Haven while he finished up his obligations at Yale. The Housatonic leaders' decision was not a concession of English superiority but a continuation of a practice of cultural exchange and an acknowledgment that the next generation of leaders would need a facility in English ways in order to effectively lead their people.[37] Momentum was growing for a closer relationship between the Housatonics and Massachusetts.

By the spring of 1734, the various parties were mobilized to bring the mission into existence: Governor Belcher, area ministers, and the New England Company all endorsed the plan. Umpachenee and Konkapot were willing to hear the proposals, but they still harbored numerous reservations they hoped colonial officials would assuage. The events of the next year leading up to the ordination of missionary John Sergeant in August 1735 highlight the hopes and concerns of both parties as they contemplated this new relationship. In the course of that year, Umpachenee and Konkapot were given commissions by Governor Belcher as lieutenant and captain at the same meeting the official proposal of the mission was made—a bit of multitasking that suggests just how closely tied military and spiritual affairs were. In addition to a number of meetings between Housatonic and Massachusetts officials, Umpachenee and Konkapot met with their townspeople and members of the wider Mohican alliance to discuss the mission proposal—meetings that became debates over the best means of preserving Mohican land and tradition while charting a path for the future in a changed world.

Once both parties had signed off on the proposal, Massachusetts officials enlisted the twenty-four-year-old Sergeant, a recent Yale graduate, to serve as missionary. Sergeant set off in the fall of 1734 for his trial run preaching the Christian gospel to the Housatonics. His sermons attracted sizeable gatherings, while his lessons in reading and writing drew even more people. Sergeant even attended several Mohican religious ceremonies, creating the impression, perhaps, that this experiment would indeed be a continuation of the type of cultural exchange familiar to the Mohicans. This impression was seemingly confirmed the following spring when Sergeant and the recently arrived schoolmaster, Timothy Woodbridge, lodged with their Indian hosts for six weeks.[38] The year culminated in the ordination of Sergeant as missionary to the Housatonics in August 1735 in the midst of a larger council between Massachusetts and several Indian communities.

Throughout the negotiations, Umpachenee and Konkapot's doubts about the mission ran along two basic lines: they were suspicious of English intentions, and they feared that consenting to the mission project could jeopardize their relations with other members of the River Indian confederacy. The two leaders hoped that they could ensure a future for their communities by gaining secured land as well as instruction in reading, writing, and the Christian religion. Head of the village of Wnahktukook, Konkapot was generally esteemed by the English as a more important leader than Umpachenee.[39] Described by one minister as "strictly temperate, a very just and upright Man in his Dealings, a Man of Prudence, and industrious in his Business," Konkapot was apparently the first among the Housatonic Mohicans to express an interest in Christianity. In the words of one English observer, Konkapot feared "that the Religion of his Fore-fathers was not right," perhaps a comment on the declining effectiveness of native traditions. Yet, he explained, "he did not know how to think well of the Christian Religion, because the Christians (many of them) lead immoral lives." He was especially concerned about what he termed the "ill Conversation of Christians."[40]

Umpachenee, then and throughout the rest of his life, harbored even graver reservations about the mission project, skeptical of a religion whose practitioners so often violated its basic precepts. During one meeting with John Stoddard, Umpachenee thanked the colony for the efforts expended to teach Housatonic children to read but explained that there were a few things that "appear'd dark in his Eyes." He wondered first of all why the sudden interest in their souls when the two peoples had long been in contact with one another and no previous efforts had ever been ventured to the Mohicans. Further, he could not help but question whether the Christian Religion was "so true and good" if, as it seemed, there "should be so many Professors of it, that liv'd such vicious Lives, and so contrary to what he was told were the Rules of it." Stoddard attempted to reassure Umpachenee by recounting the long history of Massachusetts mission work dating back to John Eliot's praying towns. Umpachenee's fears were not allayed.[41] They might even have been heightened by the fact that Indians continued to be mistreated despite New England's long tradition of mission work. Christianity had not guaranteed Indians protection from abuses at the hands of Europeans, who often facilitated their abuse of Indians through the twin powers of print and alcohol. Yet relief from these abuses proved to be among the most potent of motivations for the mission.

The suspected purity of Massachusetts' intentions was not Umpachenee and Konkapot's only cause for concern. Equally daunting was the challenge of winning approval for the mission from their own villagers and from the leaders of the wider River Indian Confederacy. In native societies where leaders governed not by fiat but by persuasion, failure to achieve consensus could diminish leaders' authority and cost them important allies. Although the historical record is frustratingly incomplete, it is clear that Konkapot and Umpachenee sought consensus. In the end, the leaders seemed to gain the full support of their villagers but failed to gain the endorsement of the larger confederacy.

From the first talk of a mission, Konkapot expressed his fear that "if he became a Christian, his people would discard him," presumably meaning that those who lived in his village might no longer honor him as their headman.[42] And when Konkapot and Umpachenee first heard the formal proposal of a mission from a group of ministers in May 1734, they expressed some interest, but both made it clear that they had authority to speak for themselves alone. Anticipating that it might be a hard sell, Umpachenee and Konkapot requested that the ministers return again in July when they would debate the mission proposal with the residents of their villages. When the appointed time came, the Reverends Bull and Williams (a former captive taken in the Deerfield raid) traveled to the Housatonic and presented the proposal to the gathered Indians. Williams apparently remained for the full four days of deliberation about the mission proposal, which he frustratingly deemed "too tedious" to record. One remark did capture his attention, however. A man named Ebenezer Poohpoonuc, who would become the first of the Housatonics to be baptized, put the case for the mission this way to the gathered Indians, as rendered by Williams:

> The Indians (says he) continue still in their Heathenism, notwithstanding the Gospel has been bro't so near them, and they are greatly diminished; so that since my remembrance, there were Ten Indians, where there is now

One: But the Christians greatly increase and multiply, and spread over the Land; let us therefore leave our former courses and become Christians.[43]

Apparently, many agreed with Poohpoonuc, and at the end of the deliberations, the Housatonics gave their assent to the mission project.

The bigger hurdle would be gaining approval from the other members of the River Indian Confederacy. The confederacy, first formed in 1675, included the Mohican proper, Highland, and Housatonic Indians. A council was to be held in the late winter of 1735, at which point the Housatonics had hosted Sergeant for several months, listening to his sermons and receiving instruction in reading and writing. Sergeant recorded his trepidation about the meeting, knowing it could "either add Life to our Design, or almost entirely quash it."[44] Word had reached the Housatonics that the Hudson River Indians "highly resented their receiving a Minister and School Master" without the consent of the rest of the tribe. Rumors flew back and forth that there was even a plot afoot to poison the two Housatonic leaders, presumably through the agency of a shaman or "pawwaw."[45]

Two accounts survive of the council, both of them suggestive but problematic. One is the contemporary account written by Stephen Williams. The other is by the Mohican sachem Hendrick Aupaumut, but it dates to nearly seventy years after the meeting. The inconsistencies between the two accounts are nearly as telling as the points of concurrence. According to Williams, the council included 150 to 200 River Indians, including their chief sachem, known as Corlaer, or Metoxen.[46] Williams took the opportunity to deliver a sermon to "one of the gravest, and most attentive Auditories that ever I preached to." Following the sermon, Williams read an encouraging letter from his kinsman John Stoddard, whom many of the River Indian sachems and counselors likely knew personally, and tried to answer objections. Williams happily reported that the Massachusetts delegation had received "encouragement that [the River Indians] would as a Nation submit to Instruction."[47]

Aupaumut recalled the meeting in his 1803 address to the Delaware Indians in an effort to persuade them to receive instruction in Christianity. He told how nearly seventy years earlier, the Christian religion was "offered to my forefathers," prompting a gathering of "the sachems and counselors, who were then living, together with their young men," totaling "about two hundred in number," in order to determine "whether it was best for the nation to accept the offer or not." At the time, according to Aupaumut, many were "prejudiced against [the] Christian religion" because they had fallen under the sway of "the bad white people," most particularly "in drinking the poisonous liquors to excess." The council decided to accept the offer in spite of their doubts, concluding:

not to reject the offer before they should try it, and let it be preached in one
certain village, and let every man and woman go to hear it and embrace it;
if they think best, and Waunahkqtokaher (or Housatonack) was the village
chose, (at this place I was born, and these my companions) then my nation
were collected, such as were disposed to hear the gospel.[48]

The accounts of Aupaumut and Williams are remarkably consistent with
one another—the primary difference is the greater detail provided by Aupaumut. They do, however, cast a different light on the conclusion reached
by the council, and this difference suggests varied ideas of the nature of
civil authority. In Williams's eyes, the meeting produced a decision "as a
Nation to submit to instruction." True religion, for Williams, demanded
obedience to divine authority and submission to God's earthly representatives. Aupaumut's account, by contrast, suggests that the test of religious
truth for the Housatonic Mohicans was efficacy. The mission was to be an
experiment. No leader could simply proclaim the truth of Christianity and
demand obedience of his followers. Rather, its efficacy would be tested: if
Christian profession and practice proved effective in solving the various
challenges faced by the Mohican community, then the religion would be
embraced.

Aupaumut's account, like Williams's, likely casts an overly sunny interpretation on the meeting, a function of his position as leader of the Christian Indian community that grew out of Konkapot and Umpachenee's
actions. That not all of the River Indians were enthusiastic about the decision is clear from a letter dictated by Umpachenee and Konkapot and sent
to Nehemiah Bull, a minister who had attended the meeting of the Housatonics, in early February of 1735, informing him that soon after the general council, two Housatonic men had died and that many from the two
men's villages lay sick. One of the dead was Umpachenee's brother-in-law,
and the other was a young man who had attended Woodbridge's school.
To opponents of the mission, the deaths revealed the dangers of associating too closely with the English. Konkapot and Umpachenee further
reported that they had been taunted at the conference by opponents of
the mission who asked: "What makes you so much like the English?" The
leaders reported that the others "envie and they hate us for what we have
Done but we don't intend to give out."[49] Following the meeting, the Housatonics sent their thanks to the ministers who had participated in the
meeting for the "care and kindness towards us in instructing us in the
Christian Religion," which they acknowledged to be the "best Religion in
the World." In conclusion, they promised their lifelong fidelity, despite
the "great many difficulties in the way."[50] With this split from the River
Indian Confederacy, the Housatonic Mohicans were well on their way to

establishing a distinct identity as the Stockbridge Indians. Their decision to welcome a missionary in their midst can be seen as a constructive re-imagining of Mohican tradition. The leaders who endorsed the mission cast the decision as the continuation of a longstanding tradition of cultural exchange by which Mohicans had ensured good relations with their neighbors and thus ensured their own well-being.

Over the coming decades, other individuals and communities of River Indians joined the mission, but this was by no means the "entire nation," as Stephen Williams had hoped. Considering Aupaumut's account together with other records contemporaneous to the events suggests that in fact the council marked a realignment in the River Indian Confederacy, one that was not entirely amicable. The Housatonic leaders were willing to risk the support of the River Indian Confederacy in the bargain that they would gain greater security in their new alliance with the English and the Christian God. In doing so, Umpachenee and Konkapot were likely drawing on what they saw as the legacy of their forebears. Positioned as they were between the interior Iroquoian and coastal Algonquian peoples, the numerous bands of Indians between the Hudson and Housatonic Rivers had long traded on their facility with neighboring cultures as a means of survival even before the arrival of Europeans. The Mohicans were avid cultural borrowers, adapting those aspects of neighboring technology and ritual that allowed them to maintain community and maintain a presence on their lands. Through shifting trade alliances, wars, epidemics, and relocations, when numbers dwindled or profitable trade was threatened, these Indian peoples turned to native allies and undertook a cultural trade through relocations and population merges. And because of the noncoercive nature of native governance, it was not unprecedented for a group of families—even a whole village—to choose its own path as members reached different conclusions about the best options for their future.

The Housatonics, living in close proximity to the creeping English settlement, gauged it to be in their best interest to immerse themselves in the ways of English culture. In the end, the decision of the Housatonic Mohicans to proceed with the mission plan—and that of the Hudson River Indians not to—likely reflects the desire of both groups to remain on their homelands. Interestingly, as Aupaumut asserted in 1803, it would be only the "descendants of that [Housatonic village], who embrace the civilization and Christian religion, are now still remaining as a nation."[51] In other words, the Housatonic Mohicans came to be the sole surviving definers of Mohican tradition, which in their hands was interpreted to mean not blood lineage alone or the continuation of traditional patterns of subsistence, but rather the continued commitment to cultural exchange, including the embrace of Christianity.

Although it would not be an easy path, from the 1730s on the Housatonic Mohicans would trade almost exclusively in the commodity of cultural knowledge. To the English they could offer their knowledge of the Indian communities to the north and the west, many of which likely counted Mohicans among them. To their Indian neighbors, the Housatonic Mohicans could trade on their knowledge of English ways. Just as for Massachusetts officials the growing demand for land sparked religious concerns, so too did the increased alienation of Mohican lands prompt spiritual questions. These concerns and questions on both sides ultimately paved the road to the Stockbridge mission. And for both communities, the mission was intimately tied to their respective diplomatic agendas. It is not surprising, then, that the ceremonial beginning of the mission was to be part of a larger diplomatic affair.

SUBJECTS AND CITIZENS

The ordination of John Sergeant as missionary was set for the end of August 1735 in Deerfield, Massachusetts. More than the symbolic beginning of the mission, the conference was the occasion to formalize negotiations that by this time had been under way for nearly a year. Both sides expressed their concerns and their hopes for the mission. On the Indians' side, this meant assurances of protection from abuse under English law. For Massachusetts representatives, this meant a commitment from the Indians to live as obedient children under the laws of the gospel, the colony, and the King.

Deerfield would seem to be an odd location for the ceremonial start of the mission: the town was a few days' journey over rugged terrain from the Housatonic mission site. But when we consider the other parties assembled that day, the choice begins to make more sense. For over a week at the end of a hot Berkshire summer, nearly 150 Indians from three different nations— Caughnawaga Mohawks, Schaghticokes, and Housatonics—gathered under a massive tent to meet with Massachusetts Governor Jonathan Belcher and his Council.[52] Governor Belcher and his Council's path from Boston to Deerfield reveals the network of "River Gods" who controlled the civil, military, and religious affairs of western Massachusetts. Along the way, the party was hosted by Colonel Joseph Dwight in Brookfield, Colonel John Stoddard at Northampton, and Captain Israel Williams at Hatfield.[53]

Over the course of the week, Belcher and the tribal leaders exchanged belts of wampum, deer and beaver skins, kegs of rum, and bundles of trade blankets, concluding each exchange with glasses raised to the health of King George, thereby reaffirming the alliance between the British Crown and the various Indian communities. Sergeant's ordination, presided over by a handful of eminent divines, capped off the week's events. The scene symbolizes the extent to which the civil and religious affairs of colonial Massachusetts were of a piece. The Deerfield conference is important in the history of the mission not so much for what was accomplished there—the negotiations had begun long before and would continue afterward—but for what it says about the place of the mission in the larger context of Indian-white relations.

The gathering would have been something of a macabre reunion. Deerfield had not seen such an assembly of Indians since the 1704 French and Indian raid on the garrisoned village. A number of the survivors of that raid were present once again, meeting under very different circumstances. Caughnawagas and Schaghticokes had participated in the 1704 raid, and some of the participants may well have returned to Deerfield, now that peace had prevailed for over two decades.[54] At least two of the English survivors were present, including Joseph Kellogg, who now served as interpreter, and the Reverend Stephen Williams. Both men had sisters who still remained among the Caughnawagas, living as Indians and Catholics.[55]

The records of the Deerfield meeting betray nothing of what must surely have been an emotionally charged encounter; they frustratingly remain focused on the official business of the conference. Governor Belcher's central concern was to reaffirm the peace that had held since 1727 with the Caughnawagha, Schaghticoke, and St. Francis Indians who resided at either end of the Champlain Valley and thus stave off the possibility of renewed hostilities should British relations with France once again turn sour. Friendly relations with the Mohawks would facilitate westward expansion and a profitable trade.[56] The business with the Housatonics was important but secondary. The mission would be one prong in the colony's strategy to make the frontier safe for settlement by British subjects, while also finally and belatedly making good on its promise to bring the light of the gospel to the heathen.

The record of Belcher's dealings with the various Indian delegations is especially revealing, both in the forms of address used and the terms offered. During the opening formalities of the conference, Belcher addressed the Caughnawagas as "my good Friends and Brethren," symbolically wiping away their tears and clearing their throats so that all could speak freely; he also presented a string of wampum with each gesture to confirm his words. In so doing, he placed the Caughnawagas on a plane with the larger Iroquois Confederacy, whose friendship with the British was regularly affirmed through the rites of the Covenant Chain.[57] When the real business began the next day, Belcher reminded the Caughnawagas of the "long Friendship" between King George's subjects and the Five Nations and the "special Covenant" that had been made between Massachusetts and the Caughnawagas eleven years previous. Now, Belcher had come to "renew that Covenant and to brighten the chain, that a good Understanding of Peace and Friendship may be cultivated and continued forever."[58] He sought assurance the Mohawks would remain neutral should hostilities between England and France resume. In return, Belcher guaranteed that Captain Joseph Kellogg, stationed at Fort Dummer (at present-day Brattleboro, Vermont) would ensure that they would "be always honestly dealt with" and that they would receive "such things as you need" and "at a cheaper rate than others can or will let you have them." He acknowledged that the Caughnawagas were "a free people, you are my Brethren" and encouraged them to avail themselves of "the Father" the English had placed at the fort, who would teach the Indians to read and write and "inform them of the Principles of Our Religion."[59] By referring to an English minister as "the Father," Belcher was acknowledging the French success in establishing a spiritual trade with the Mohawks while simultaneously trying to undermine that relationship.

By contrast, in the governor's exchanges with the Housatonic Mohicans, talk of peace and trade was noticeably absent: the Housatonics were not a military threat, nor did they command access to furs from the interior. Their value lay in providing the opportunity to make good on the settlers' collective obligation to God and in serving as a buffer between English settlements and the hostile French-allied Indians to the North. The language and the terms of the relationship with the Housatonics were quite different. With the Housatonics, none of the formal protocols were followed. Rather than "Brethren" and "free people," the Housatonics were "my Children," whom Belcher hoped "were good subjects of King George," deserving of the colony's paternal care. Belcher was especially pleased that the Housatonics had agreed to welcome Sergeant, counseling them that "religion is a serious thing, and it ought to be always born on your Minds."[60] Belcher expected the Housatonics and Schaghticokes, as children and subjects of a Protestant King, to submit to true religion. The Housatonics remained skeptical of Belcher's promise "to always take the same Care of you as of the English." In response, Umpachenee, Konkapot, and the other Housatonic Mohican leaders addressed Belcher as "our Father" but made clear their understandings of such a father's obligations: "and so we think Your Excellency as our Father is willing to do to us upon every account; and we pray that when we are wanting any thing we may be directed to tell Col. Stoddard of it, that he may send to Your Excellency, that what we want may be done for us."[61]

The Housatonic Mohicans at Deerfield sought assurance that if they consented to live in a mission town, not only would they be granted the same privileges as the English but they would also enjoy protection *from* the English. They feared their children would be imprisoned for debt and prayed that they would not be hurt by the severity of the laws. In doing so, they appealed to the paternal care of Belcher: "Our father, we are concerned for our own Children, as we think you, as a Father are for Us, and therefore we pray that it may be given us in Writing (or establish'd by a Law) that our Children after us be not wronged or injured." The Housatonic delegation had reason to be suspicious of Belcher's assurance that he would "take the same Care of you as of the English." Rather than simply showing deference to the powerful English, as Belcher would have interpreted these petitions, the Housatonics were attempting to hold Massachusetts officials to their social mores of reciprocity.[62] This was no idle concern; across New England, Indian children were frequently indentured in order to pay off debts owed by their parents.[63]

Belcher's closing remarks to the Housatonics reveal just how closely tied were ideas of citizenship in the kingdom of heaven and in the kingdom of King George were understood. He let them know he was pleased by "the Expressions of your Duty and Loyalty to our common Father the great King GEORGE." But even more, Belcher was pleased that the Housatonics had showed an interest in "the Gospel of Our LORD JESUS CHRIST, who is GOD as well as Man, and the only SAVIOUR of all Men," for by living in obedience to the gospel, "you will become good Subjects to the King of Kings, and be led in the Way to be happy here, and eternally so in a better world."[64] Living as an obedient, upstanding subject of King George was good training for being an obedient, upstanding subject of the King of Kings. Likewise, living in Christian submission to God prepared the individual for submission to earthly authorities.

The close association of the earthly and spiritual realms meant that failure to meet the qualifications of one often became the basis for denying Indians access to the other. It would become increasingly clear over the early years of the mission that both civil and religious leaders generally came to believe that although allied Indians may have deserved equal treatment in theory, it was because of the Indians' own failings that they rarely benefited from the same protections of the law enjoyed by the English.

Besides being the official inauguration of the Housatonic mission, the Deerfield conference also indicates broader changes and continuities in New England society in the century following the founding of the Massachusetts Bay Colony. The logic of the gospel given in payment for Indian lands was still prevalent, as is clear in Nathaniel Appleton's sermon delivered on the occasion of John Sergeant's ordination. Many New England ministers still believed in the God of Providence who oversaw the well-being of his people, demanding obedience in exchange for his protective care. But, as historian Thomas Kidd has argued, many left behind the narrow, isolationist, sectarianism of early New England Puritanism and began to make common cause in a more encompassing, cosmopolitan Protestantism that had also become more firmly British.[65] "Civilization" had always been understood by Anglo-Protestants as a prerequisite to "Christianization." Now, "civilization" was even more tightly anchored to British culture, and being a subject of King George and of the King of Kings were readily conflated.

FATHERS AND SONS

On the final day of the Deerfield conference, the Rev. Nathaniel Appleton of Cambridge preached a sermon titled "A Consecrated Vessel Fitted for the Master's Use," welcoming John Sergeant into the ministerial fold and giving him the charge for his duties as missionary. The sermon served as a fitting complement to Belcher's addresses to the Housatonics, as it nicely encapsulates the paternalism of Congregational mission projects, while also invoking the logic of the gift of the gospel in exchange for Indian lands. Just as the Housatonics' bodies were to be "Children" to the Governor and subjects of King George, so their spirits were to be under the paternal care of the minister and subject to the King of Kings.

The bulk of Appleton's sermon was devoted to sketching out the nature of the relationship between the missionary and his flock. Appleton relied on the Apostle Paul's metaphor of the household to spell out the relations between God, Christ, the minister, and his congregation. Appleton began his sermon with the observation that "the church of God is as it were a great house, of which Christ is the head and master," in which ministers served as "vessels and instruments for the use and service of this house." Christ rules absolutely over his household and as a good householder, he "makes provision for his church," allowing his dependents to be "fed with the bread of life," and "cloathed with his righteousness." As overseer, Christ sets the rules in his household: "he prescribes rules & orders for his house, which are carefully to be regarded by all the household." Christ was a benevolent patriarch. And as Christ was the patriarch of God's household, so was the missionary the patriarch of his congregation, sent to serve in God's house, "altho' in a dark part of it."[66] The message was clear: Sergeant was God's overseer on earth, and as children under Sergeant's care, the Indian congregants would be subject to the guidance and discipline of their spiritual father.

Before following Sergeant into the field of his mission work, it is worth pausing over Appleton's description of the demands made on missionaries, as it sheds light on the role and status of the missionary in New England society. In keeping with the Congregational emphasis on the centrality of God's word, Appleton listed study and meditation on the scriptures as the first duty of the minister. "In a word," preached Appleton, ministers "must be sober and temperate in all things, suppressing their irregular appetites, and keeping their bodies under."[67] Missionaries were not expected to enjoy their work.

Again and again, Appleton called attention to the sacrifices required of Sergeant, above and beyond the sacrifices required of ministers to English congregations. Sergeant, according to Appleton, had made a great sacrifice in assuming his missionary post, giving up "the agreeable Business he was in as a Tutor of Yale College" in order to take what may "appear mean and contemptible to the men of the world." Further, although some might consider ministry to a band of Indians a mean lot in life, Appleton assured his listeners that Sergeant had "voluntarily devoted himself to the Service of Christ and of the poor Indians," and not out of lack of opportunity elsewhere, for he had "as a fair a prospect as any Candidate for the Ministry whatsoever, to have an agreeable Settlement in any of the Churches."[68] Despite Appleton's protestations, missionary posts were not highly sought after, and Sergeant's choice of career may well have been constrained by several factors, including the accident in his youth that had left him with a lame arm and unfit for life as a yeoman farmer. His choices might have been limited as well by other factors such as social status. In many respects, the twenty-four-year-old, newly minted Yale graduate was an outsider to the circles of River Gods who were ushering the mission into existence. And so, if Sergeant glanced around at his ministerial brethren in attendance at his ordination, he might have wondered whether he wasn't making the wrong choice or lamented that he had not had the family connections to land a more prestigious pulpit.

New England's clerical and civic leaders saw it as their Christian duty to save the heathen who had not had benefit of the divine light of revelation, yet prospective missionaries often found that task difficult at best and repugnant at worst. Ministers who undertook mission work often did so out of a sense of obligation to God, contrary to their natural inclinations. The famously melancholic missionary David Brainerd was similarly warned at his ordination in 1744 that he must be possessed of a spirit of self-denial that would enable him "chearfully to forsake the pleasures of your native Country, with the agreeable society of your friends and acquaintance, to dwell among those who inhabit... uncultivated desarts and the remotest recesses of the wilderness."[69] Brainerd reported just such feelings from his mission post at Kaunaumeek, near Stockbridge: "I have no fellow Christian to whom I might unbosom myself and lay open my spiritual sorrows.... I live poorly with regard to the comforts of life.... I lodge on a bundle of straw, and my labor is hard and extremely difficult; and I have little appearance of success to comfort me."[70] Two decades after the founding of Stockbridge, the missionary Gideon Hawley wrote in his journal a passage that could well have spoken for most English missionaries, as he contemplated whether duty called him to return to his mission among the Oneida in the midst of the French and Indian War:

> Am I willing to sacrifice every Thing to duty & deny myself & at all Events abide by my Mission and not quite [sic] it if God calls me to stand by it?...Do I feel from Day to Day a willingness to deny myself for the Interest of Christ in the World?...But if God calls, if Christ commands, it is my duty....I will pray to God for a Spirit of self denial.[71]

Anglo-Protestant missionaries often set off to their mission posts with heavy hearts buoyed only by the assurance that their work was an act of self-denial and dutiful obedience to God. As they fulfilled their duty to God, they in turn imagined themselves as divinely appointed fathers sent to guide their Indian "children" to salvation through a combination of benevolence and exacting severity. No one expected missionaries to enjoy their job; indeed, the less they enjoyed it the surer they could be that they were acting in obedience to their God. Missionaries like Sergeant, Brainerd, and Hawley generally got what they expected—hardship, frustration, and a lack of social opportunities. As we will see, compared to their Moravian counterparts, English missionaries were miserable.

John Sergeant was a relative late-comer to the mission project. When the Massachusetts Commissioners of the New England Company heard report of the successful meetings with the Housatonics in the spring and summer of 1734, they began their search for an appropriate candidate "to go and reside there as the Minister, to instruct them and their Children in Religion, and in Reading, and to preach the Gospel to them on the Sabbaths" for a salary of £100 (just half of what Jonathan Edwards was paid as minister at Northampton in 1732).[72] Sergeant was not a Stoddard or a Williams by birth or marriage, but his studies under Edwards (kin to both the Stoddard and Williams clans) at Yale were likely at least partially responsible for securing him the job.[73] Stephen Williams and Nehemiah Bull approached Sergeant on behalf of the Company, and in late September, Williams penned a letter to the Commissioners informing them that Sergeant had accepted the assignment. Less than two weeks later, Sergeant arrived at Housatonic for a trial run. In most respects—in his motivations, his theology, and his expectations—Sergeant typified the Anglo-Protestant missionary tradition.

Just as the Housatonics hesitated in casting their lot with the English, so too did Sergeant harbor grave reservations. To his journal, he confided that the sacrifices demanded were daunting: "I must not only lose a great many agreeable Amusements of Life, especially in leaving my Business at College [as a tutor at Yale] ... but also expose myself to many Fatigues and Hardships, and I know not to what Dangers, among a barbarous People." In the end, Sergeant heeded the call to Christian duty, finding that he could not refuse his duty, "for indeed I should be ashamed to own myself a Christian, or even a Man, and yet utterly refuse doing what lay in my Power, to...promote the Salvation of Souls perishing in the Dark, when the Light of Life is so near them." He felt particularly compelled, he wrote, by the advances "in America, and in our Borders" made by the "Romish Church" whose religion "was so corrupted."[74] Having determined that he owed it to God to deny himself a more comfortable existence, Sergeant said his farewells and in October 1734 embarked for his trial period among the Housatonics.[75] His heart was heavy as he and his party made their way "thro' a most doleful Wilderness, and the worst Road, perhaps, that ever was rid."[76]

Sergeant arrived just before nightfall on October 12, and on the following day preached his first sermon to the twenty or so gathered Indians, with Ebenezer Poohpoonuc serving as his interpreter. The sermon was adapted, wrote Sergeant, "to their Capacities and Manner of Thinking." Unfortunately, we cannot know what words Sergeant spoke, what he considered to be his audience's "manner of thinking," how Poohpoonuc interpreted Sergeant's words, or how his audience might have comprehended these words. However, a letter sent by Sergeant later that year to Umpachenee and Konkapot gives us an idea of what he might have preached that first day. He began with an appeal to their native knowledge, expressing his hope that they knew the difference between good and evil and that God would reward the good and punish the wicked. He then argued from Scripture the existence of a wise, just, and powerful God who had a son, Jesus Christ, who was born to save sinners. All are born sinners and thus deserve punishment, and only Christ could save.[77] The theological lessons in his letter could have been drawn straight from the Westminister Shorter Catechism, standard for generations of New Englanders.

Unfortunately, the mission sources provide few insights into the Indian reception of the gospel as preached by Sergeant. In fact, Sergeant's account of the first official Christian rite performed in the mission community obscures more than it reveals. On October 14, 1734, Nathaniel Bull (Sergeant had yet to be ordained) baptized Poohpoonuc, Sergeant's interpreter and the man who had made the case that the Housatonics ought to "leave our former courses" in order to "become Christians." Unfortunately, little is known about Poohpoonuc's life that might help us understand the events of that day. He had apparently lived for a time with an English family and attended school, suggesting perhaps that he had been orphaned or that his family had hired out their son.[78] In response to Bull's questions, according to Sergeant, Poohpoonuc "gave a pretty good Account of the Principles of the Christian Religion, and said, he would rather burn in Fire than forsake the Truth." Poohpoonuc's profession of faith, as recorded by Sergeant, was a concise summary of the core tenets of Congregationalism:

> Through the Goodness of God towards me, in bringing me into the Way of the Knowledge of the Gospel, I am convinc'd of the Truth of the Christian Religion, and that it is the only Way that leads to Salvation and Happiness. I therefore freely, and heartily, forsake Heathenish Darkness, and embrace the light of the Gospel, and the Way of Holiness. And do now, in Presence of Almighty God, the Searcher of Hearts, and before many Witnesses, seriously and solemnly take the Lord Jehovah, to be my God and Portion, Jesus Christ his son to be my Lord Redeemer; and the Holy Ghost to be my Sanctifier and Teacher. And do Covenant and Promise, by the Help of divine Grace, that I will cleave to the Lord with Purpose of Heart, believing his revealed Truths, as far as I can gain the Knowledge of them, obeying his Commands, both those which mark out my Duty, and those that forbid Sin, sincerely and uprightly to the End of my Life.[79]

It is impossible to know whether Poohpoonuc composed this profession himself or whether he read from a standard version provided to him. The latter was common practice, and thus seems likely. Given his plea to his fellow villagers to accept Christianity because he believed it might help preserve Indian lives, it appears that Poohpoonuc had indeed decided to cast his lot with the Christian God.

If Poohpoonuc intended to renounce native religion entirely, he was likely the exception rather than the norm. Native religious traditions generally placed greater emphasis on practice than belief, and religious truth was gauged by efficacy rather than conformity. There were no prohibitions against religious borrowing, and there was no impulse to evangelism; it was generally assumed that different people would have their different religious practices. These assumptions spelled considerable frustration for missionaries who sought to convince Indian peoples of the truth of their particular brand of Christianity. Sergeant discovered this when he encouraged the Housatonics "from Time to Time to let me know, if they had any Doubts with respect to any Thing I had taught them." He found, however, that "tho' they were inquisitive in some Points, yet they never seem'd disposed' to contradict what I said."[80] Sergeant, ready for a rigorous debate, took the Indians' response as acknowledgement of the truth of Christianity. They might well have accepted Sergeant's teachings as true, but not exclusively so, as Sergeant would have wished.

Sergeant continued in the instruction of his congregation, and over the course of the next year, a number of mission residents, including Umpachenee and Konkapot, sought baptism. Konkapot and his wife were baptized on November 2, 1735, the rest of his family (a son and a daughter) the following Sabbath, together with Umpachenee, his wife, and Poohpoonuc's son. Sergeant also performed an English-style marriage ceremony for Poohpoonuc and his wife, complete with the English custom of "publishing the bans," at the request of the couple. By February 1736, Sergeant had baptized about forty residents, whom he found to be "very alive in the business of religion and learning and to hunger and thirst after righteousness." While Sergeant professed to be worried that he might have baptized the proselytes too quickly, he found he "could not persuade them to put it off any longer, they said their hearts were in it."[81] The new Housatonic Christians were likely eager to have access to what they perceived to be the great spiritual powers available through baptism and communion.

The continuation of some native ceremonies further suggests that the Housatonics did not generally expect entirely to relinquish inherited traditions when they admitted Sergeant to their midst. One fall day, Sergeant witnessed a deer sacrifice ritual in which the gathered Housatonics thanked the "great God" for the preservation of the people. On this occasion, Ebenezer Poohpoonuc served as Sergeant's informant and interpreter and answered the missionary's queries about his peoples' religious beliefs. Sergeant took heart from his findings that the Indians believed in one supreme being, knew the difference between good and evil, and had a sense that "God rewards and punishes according to desert."[82] Sergeant observed another ceremony in December 1735, once the mission was well under way, suggesting the continued practice of inherited religious traditions. That winter, several residents approached Sergeant for permission to hold a "Keutikaw," a mourning dance for the dead, to be celebrated together with residents of surrounding villages. The Indians won Sergeant's approval by assuring the missionary that the event was a civil rather than a religious ceremony, suggesting considerable insight into New England society. Sergeant saw an opportunity to evangelize and informed the petitioners that he would be "glad of an opportunity to see some of their people here," insisting only that no rum be available on the occasion, to which the Housatonics readily agreed.[83]

Sergeant, like the backers of the mission, assumed that "civilizing" the Indians was a necessary prerequisite to Christianizing them, yet little mention was made initially of this part of the project. Neither did Sergeant raise any objections when the newly gathered mission residents announced that they would soon be leaving for their sugar huts for the maple-sugaring season. And several months later, when Sergeant returned from completing his duties at New Haven, he took up residence for a time with Konkapot's family. At planting time, the mission residents returned to the villages of Wnahktukook and Skatekook to plant their fields of corn and beans.[84] For his part, Sergeant may not have sought aggressively to purge what he would have seen as pagan practices, at least initially, because he perceived that they were losing favor among the Indians anyway. He remarked at one point that the Indians used to hold "pawwaws" and "conjurers" in high esteem but that they were losing favor because "they confess they have no Power over Christians."[85] One important implication of this comment, though likely unappreciated by Sergeant, was that the acquisition of these new Christian rituals was seen as a means of acquiring power over the Christians. Sergeant heard only an acknowledgment of the superior power of the Christian God.

Far more readily accessible in the mission records are the negotiations of temporal affairs. For both English and Indian, the temporal and the spiritual could not be entirely divorced, but Sergeant and the others who left a documentary trail revealed far more about the practical affairs of the mission. Throughout the fall of 1734, the meetinghouse continued to fill, both for meetings and for school lessons. The reasons certainly varied from individual to individual as to why they chose to cast their lot with the newly arrived missionary. Simple survival cannot be entirely ruled out. The increased dependence on trade for subsistence meant that food was likely more difficult to come by. Beaver had become far scarcer in Housatonic lands, and Mohican hunting sources elsewhere had dried up or been cut off by French-allied Indians. The harvest was now in, and any wages for labor on Dutch farms would have disappeared by this time of the year—some spent on necessaries, some on alcohol. The epidemics that had swept through Mohican territory had decimated the numbers of adults contributing to the food supply of the community. While winter was traditionally the time when villages dispersed to family hunting territories, even these had been encroached upon from all sides by Dutch, German, and English settlement.

Within a fortnight of Sergeant's arrival, construction was under way for housing for several families (the two communities headed by Konkapot and Umpachenee had agreed to settle with Sergeant at a point halfway between the villages for the winter) as well as a public meetinghouse to serve as church and schoolhouse. The Housatonics declared they would stay to hear Sergeant's preaching; in order to learn more quickly, they agreed to spend the winter gathered about the bark church. In the evenings, Sergeant held classes in Christian history, emphasizing especially the "necessity of a supernatural Revelation" and the Christian scriptures as the only repository of revelation, thus imparting the necessity of literacy.[86] Sergeant was pleased to discover that the new settlers displayed a "chearfulness and Engagedness" in hearing the Word preached and in having their children taught to read.[87]

Protestant missionaries held up their commitment to instruction in reading and writing literacy as evidence of their commitment to "raising" the Indians to their level, but in fact, the emphasis on literacy often served to sharpen boundaries between English and Indian. The Puritan stress on "the Word" fueled a tendency toward doctrinal precision that was lacking, for example, in the Moravian missions. Early English missionaries like John Eliot put great effort into translating Christian texts into native languages, while later missionaries tended to place greater emphasis on teaching English to the Indians, believing that native languages were inadequate to the task of capturing the finer points of Congregational theology.[88]

Literacy was indeed a powerful force in drawing new settlers to the mission site, but perhaps not entirely for the reasons that Sergeant imagined. Literacy had clearly come to be seen as a necessary skill for survival of the community. Throughout the winter months, more families came to settle at the new site, apparently drawn by the opportunity to master the power of print and perhaps also to enjoy the company of other villagers. By spring of the following year, Sergeant reported forty scholars in attendance at his classes, including new arrivals from other villages. Young men made up the majority of the pupils in Woodbridge's classes, noted Sergeant: "All the young men from 20 to 30 years, constantly attend school when at home." He further reported that some had even learned to "write as good a Hand as myself."[89] The predominance of young men, future leaders, suggests that literacy had come to be seen as an important qualification for leadership.

Throughout the negotiation process, both Umpachenee and Konkapot continued to press for instruction in reading and writing. A long history of contact with Europeans through trade and land transactions demonstrated the power of print and the ways it could be used against them. At the Deerfield conference, Konkapot insisted that the proceedings be written down by Stephen Williams and then interpreted back to him. Konkapot was wary of verbal agreements with the English and sought written confirmation that the rights of tribal children would be protected in the future.[90] The Housatonic leaders had likely had the same experience that Mohican chief Ampamit had recounted to the New York governor: "Father we have no more Land the Christians when they buy a small spot of Land of us, ask us if we have no more Land and when we say yes they enquire the name of the Land and take in a greater Bounds than was intended to be sold them and the Indians not understanding what is writ in the Deed or Bill of Sale sign it and are so deprived of Part of their Lands."[91]

The proceedings to this point likely convinced the Housatonics that the pace of change would be slow and that they would set the terms. So far, relatively little change had been imposed on the Housatonics, and they were gaining what they had deemed necessary for their continued survival—the tools of literacy and a way to intercede with the powerful Christian deity. Life in the new settlement was a mixture of new and old. The settlers were beginning to acquire skills they recognized as essential to existence in the new world emerging around them, yet they continued to practice many of their old ways.

The Housatonics' strategy of drawing other Mohican settlers to the mission appeared to be working as well. In June 1736, a murder committed by a Mohican Indian prompted Umpachenee and Konkapot to travel to the Hudson River to consult with other Mohican leaders. The men reported back to Sergeant that they had used the occasion to proselytize, spending "almost all their Time in discourse with them [the Hudson River Indians] upon the subject of Religion." They reported further that those they talked with "had favourable Thoughts of the Christian Religion," perhaps a response to the hopeful start of the Housatonic mission and their own continued difficulties.[92]

Soon after Umpachenee and Konkapot's return from the Hudson, eleven mission settlers wrote a letter of thanks (presumably at Sergeant's prompting and with the missionary's assistance) to the mission's benefactors. The letter suggests that the mission settlers viewed the embrace of Christianity as a means of building Mohican strength. The authors expressed their thanks to God for allowing the government to bring them to live in one place and to educate their children in the "Principles of Religion, and other useful knowledge." Being now sensible of the "benefit of the Gospel," the authors wished "that our whole Nation may be brought into the same way." The recipient of the letter was presumably pleased with the Indians' declaration: "We bless God, the Father of Mercies, and Giver of all Good things, that he has pitied us, and put it into your Hearts to use your Endeavours to communicate to us that Knowledge of divine Things, which he has given to you." Yet there was another message that the recipient might not have appreciated: the significance to the Housatonics of having their homeland secured to them, the importance of their children's education, and their hope of a union of Mohican peoples.[93] It seemed the Housatonics' program of cultural exchange was succeeding.

"To civilize will be the readiest Way to Christianize them"

The Housatonics and the English sponsors of the mission had reason to be pleased. The mission community was attracting more settlers, which to Sergeant and his backers was evidence of God's shining light into darkness. To colonial officials, a successful mission promised dividends in various currencies: spiritual, economic, and political. Umpachenee and Konkapot were encouraged that this latest, more drastic form of cultural exchange seemed to be working: more and more of their Housatonic and Mohican neighbors were contemplating resettling at the mission, and they were gaining the skills necessary to secure their future in an increasingly English world. Meanwhile, Massachusetts seemed committed to securing land to the Housatonics according to English custom, which the Indians assumed would provide greater security.

The next stage of negotiations involved the incorporation and surveying of a township granted to the Housatonic Indians. But what would seem to be an unambiguous gain for the mission Indians proved to be the issue that laid bare the very different ideals that the English and Indians held for the mission settlement. Into the planning and execution of the new town's incorporation, Governor Belcher, Sergeant, and John Stoddard all brought with them the expectation that the Indians would form themselves into a town just like other New England towns. In a variation of the land-for-gospel exchange, these men imagined that granting the land to the Housatonics was an act of great charity that effectively obligated the Indian residents to relinquish their culture. To assist in instructing the mission settlers in the "habits of civilization," Sergeant proposed (and Belcher readily agreed) that several model English families should be settled in the new town of Stockbridge for emulation by the Indians. The failure of the Indians to make a full payment on this obligation ultimately became grounds for Massachusetts officials to deny equal protection under English law.

The ideal of "civilization before Christianization" was present in one form or another from the very beginning of English presence in the New World: it was assumed that the Indians needed to be "reduced" to civility before their souls could provide fertile soil for the seed of the gospel. On the one hand, then, it is not at all surprising that the first concerted mission efforts, John Eliot's praying towns, drew inspiration equally from the Bible and English custom. But perhaps it should be surprising. Given their hostility toward what they saw as the depraved culture of Elizabethan England, Puritans might have been expected to develop a missionary program that rejected English cultural norms. Eliot perfectly represents this seeming paradox—his praying towns went further than any New England town in embodying the Puritan ideal of a bible commonwealth. But he also went further than most New England towns in legislating conformity to English custom: many of the civil laws instituted at praying towns originated not in the Bible but in English sensibilities.[94] The paradox can be attributed in part to the fact that English settlers arrived in what they experienced to be an "empty" and often hostile land, which fostered a stronger attachment to the ways of home.[95] Further, ministers and missionaries in New England enjoyed a longstanding, mutually supportive relationship with secular powers that tended to decrease perceived tensions between worldly and otherworldly concerns, with the result that the standard of Christian piety was measured by doctrinal proficiency and display of outward signs of Christian civility.

The same logic of reduction to civility is evident in the origins of the Housatonic mission. Already since 1730, Governor Belcher had been advocating the creation of a township "that should be sufficient to receive a good Number of English and Indian inhabitants, and this Town to be settled at the Charge of the [New England] Company."[96] Like other proponents of mission work before him, Belcher believed the best school for creating new Christians was the "civilized" life. Seeking support for the mission from his Council and the House, in November 1734 Belcher touted the grant of a township as "one good means of civilizing the Indians" and as a way of "better cementing our Friendship with them."[97] And by "civilizing the Indians," the Housatonics would become acquainted with English notions of private property and husbandry and thus be prepared for the reception of the gospel, for, believed Belcher, "to civilize will be the readiest Way to Christianize them."[98] Thus, at the Deerfield conference, Belcher promised the Housatonics that he would recommend to his Council that they give the Indians "Lands to Settle you more conveniently and compact, and what may be enough for your living comfortably upon."[99] Ironically, the land Belcher proposed to grant for the mission was land that had been purchased from those same Indians just over a decade previous and on which the colony had long since recouped its original payment through the selling of shares for the two townships it had already patented. And in this way, the desire for Indian lands fueled religious concerns, which in turn led back to the question of land.

For their part, the Housatonics were eager to have lands secured to them with an English title, which they hoped would be unassailable. Belcher reported to the Massachusetts Assembly of his conference with the Housatonics at Deerfield "what they particularly desired of me, was that they might have a Grant of Land sufficient to support themselves and their families and that it should be so ordered as that they might be settled in a Body together, which would be most comfortable to them, and most commodious for their Instruction in Religion." A committee headed by John Stoddard was promptly appointed to go to Housatonic "to know the minds of the Indians respecting any particularly tract of land they may be inclined to settle." It was rightly suspected that the Indians would desire the intervale lands along the river, but some of this land was now part of the "upper Housatonic" patent from 1722, which subsequently became Great Barrington. The committee was thus charged with trying to negotiate an agreement with both the Indians and the proprietors whereby the English proprietors would relinquish their claims in exchange for the equivalent in unappropriated lands.[100]

The meetings between the committee and Housatonic representatives reveal a pattern that would continue throughout the history of the mission: an act of purported benevolence became a means of acquiring yet more land from the Indians. In this case, the committee, comprised of Ebenezer Pomeroy and Thomas Ingersoll (John Stoddard was unable to attend due to his mother's ill health) arrived at Housatonic on February 5, 1736, and sent for Konkapot and the other Indians, who arrived several days later.[101] The committee presented their agenda to the gathered Housatonics, employing Ebenezer Poohpoonuc as interpreter. Konkapot was clearly wary of the proceedings but eager to have the matter settled because, as he informed the committee, "I and the rest of the Indians should be very glad, because we must plant somewhere." He was clearly eager to have land confirmed to his community and protected by colonial law. The committee attempted to assuage the settlers' fears, assuring them that "we are come in order to promote and cherish your religious disposition and design also to better and benefit you much, with respect to your outward and worldly interest notwithstanding what some people may say and endeavor to persuade you to the contrary." They then inquired of Konkapot whether he and his people were "of a mind to live together in order to receive the Gospel as we before told you," to which Konkapot answered that they were and that they would prefer to settle on the intervale land "above the mountain" and on the west side of the Housatonic River. The committee responded by reminding Konkapot that some of that land belonged to English and Dutch settlers who had bought it from Konkapot, "and if you have that land, we must agree with them people that own it, and give them some other land for it."

The committee proposed that the Housatonics cede the land that they had reserved for themselves in the 1724 deed and asked Konkapot, "have you got no land that way to the east of what you sold to the Committee?" Yes, Konkapot replied, all the land east of what he had sold stretching to the Farmington River and south to the Connecticut line—all of that land was his. The next question was predictable: would Konkapot be willing to cede that land in exchange for the intervale land? They also requested that Konkapot cede some of his land between the road to Westfield and the Farmington River to compensate the proprietors. Konkapot warily agreed, clearly not entirely confident that the committee would indeed come through with the confirmation of the intervale lands.

Next, the committee informed the Indians of its expectation that lots be set aside for Sergeant and Woodbridge for their services as minister and schoolmaster. Konkapot agreed that the plan was reasonable, but he was likely less enthusiastic when the committee informed the Indians "that there should be two or three English Familys there besides the minister and Schoolmaster, to be company for them and their wifes (if any they should have) and also to help and instruct the Indians in their husbandry," the clear implication being that Indian residents could not possibly provide company for the missionary. And so it would go. An act of supposed benevolence came to be quite profitable for the English parties involved, while requiring the Indians to give up more than they had intended—all in the name of bringing "civilization" to the Indians.

Just before the confirmation of the Indian township, a delegation of Housatonic and Mohican leaders including Umpachenee, Corlaer, and Unkamug (Chief Sachem Ampamit's brother) paid a visit to Governor Belcher in Boston. It was clear that the Indians were not coming out ahead in the bargain. In between expressions of thanks for the grant of the township and the support of a minister and schoolteacher, the Indians lodged complaint after complaint with Belcher: there were questions about the boundaries of the land the governor expected the Housatonics to relinquish in exchange for the grant of a township, and there were numerous complaints of unfair trade. In answer to all, Belcher referred the complainants to John Stoddard, who Belcher promised would ensure justice.[102]

It is not surprising, given all of the concessions requested by the committee, that when John Stoddard arrived in April 1736 to survey the new township, Umpachenee had a number of questions for him. Umpachenee was familiar enough with English land practices to be worried about how English law would treat Indian proprietors. Specifically, he wished to know how disputes would be resolved if in the future his children should come into disagreements with the English. He feared that Indian titles would not be considered equal to English ones, and he put the question to Stoddard "how their Titles would be ascertain'd; and what Security they could have, that their Children would be free." Again, Stoddard did his best to alleviate Umpachenee's fears, assuring him that the same protections would be offered Indians as whites, but the Housatonic leader continued to suspect that the interest of the English was purely a pragmatic scheme to secure lands and that the current good will of the English would fade with the subsequent generation.[103]

In May, the township was confirmed: a plot of six miles square was put aside for the formation of the Indian town. The grant by the General Court conveyed to the Housatonic Indians:

the soils, Swamps, meadows, rivers, rivulets, Ponds, Pools, woods, under-woods, Trees, Timber, Herbage, Feeding, Fishing, Fowling and Hunting,

Rights members Hereditaments, Emoluments, profits, privileges and appurtenances thereto belonging or in any ways appertaining TO HAVE AND TO HOLD, the said Tract of land, or Township...unto the said Housatannuck Tribe of Indians...TO their use and behoof forever.[104]

In the end, Umpachenee's fears were well founded: the Indians warily ceded a fifty-two-square-mile tract in exchange for a "gift" of thirty-six square miles laid out for the township, a deal mission chronicler Samuel Hopkins esteemed "no inconsiderable Return for the Favour bestow'd."[105] Interestingly, it was not until two years later, in June 1738, that communion was celebrated at Stockbridge, with eleven Indian participants. This delay is particularly notable if Sergeant adhered to the "Stoddardean" practice of open communion, as an early local historian claimed, suggesting that John Sergeant held the Indians to a higher standard than the English.[106] Land continued to be the first concern, as was clear in the incorporating document, which reserved six lots for Sergeant, Woodbridge, and four model English families.[107]

To missionary supporters, importing English families to the new town of Stockbridge seemed to solve a number of problems. "Interspers'd and settled among the Indians," these families would aid in "civilizing" the Indians. When Sergeant had first proposed the idea to Belcher, the Governor agreed that it was only fair that for their hardships, Sergeant and Woodbridge "might have the comfort of their Neighbourhood, and Society but especially to civilize and anglicize the Indians, and to be a Help to them in their secular Affairs."[108] There was no question but that English civility was a prerequisite to Christianization. The introduction of the four families (by which Sergeant also acquired a wife) set up a new dynamic of exchange by which the Indian residents regularly found themselves indebted, both financially and spiritually, to their English neighbors. The Indians' slow progress in "civility" often became the basis for denying them full protection of the law. A look at John Sergeant's efforts to settle his domestic life reveals much about his attitudes toward his work, as we shall see, which in turn helps to explain why Indians were so often prevented from fully enjoying the benefits of their new township.

Not surprisingly, Governor Belcher turned to John Stoddard to head the committee in charge of selecting suitable candidates. And predictably, Stoddard turned first to his network of kin, inviting the forty-seven-year-old Ephraim Williams of Newton, Massachusetts, to join his many relations already well ensconced in western Massachusetts. In June 1738, Williams arrived with his family, which included a charming and formidable sixteen-year-old daughter named Abigail. It was only a matter of months before Williams began whittling away at Stockbridge Indian lands and perhaps less than that before Sergeant was smitten with the young Abigail.

Sergeant may have been particularly grateful for Abigail's arrival on the scene: his two-year attempt to court Hannah Edwards, sister of famed Northampton minister (and Sergeant's Yale mentor) Jonathan, had failed, and he was likely despairing of ever finding a companion for his life at the mission post.[109] Sergeant's letters to Hannah from 1735 to 1737 reveal much about his attitude toward his work as missionary. They make clear that he expected little in the way of fellowship from his Indian congregation; they also show a glimmer of romanticism about life in the wilderness that suggests that much had changed in New England minds from the early part of the century. By the time of his death, Sergeant would be even more pessimistic about the prospect of "civilizing" the Indians, a failure he had come to attribute to inherent Indian qualities.

In courting Edwards, Sergeant depicted his circumstances as a harsh wilderness far from the comforts of civilization—but also as the perfect place for a romantic idyll. His first letter to Edwards in July 1735—just a month before his ordination—made clear he was looking for a companion to accompany him on his mission. Wrote Sergeant, "I am more than ever I was before convinced of the mighty power of Love. One would have tho't the wildness of this country the Savage manners of the people that inhabit it with the sacred & solemn importance of the business I am ingaged in would have banish'd from my breast the soft & tender passion the tempting pains & pleasing anxiety of love." And in an invocation that would likely have been shocking to Hannah's orthodox Calvinism, Sergeant concluded that Venus, the Greek goddess of love, must have been working against him, "so deep to wound my heart, that I must languish here at so great a distance from the fairest creature in the world."[110]

In the next round of letters, Sergeant described his surroundings for Edwards: "My eyes are saluted with such a horrid prospect of rocks, mountains, and inhospitable woods, that my imagination dare hardly venture over the frightfull impediments that lie between you and me." The stark landscape, he confessed, had led him to be "a Stoic," but now, as the returning sun began "to thaw my frozen passions," he had fallen "out of conceit with the philosophy." Soon he would "try one more experiment more in that philosophy" by living "five or six weeks in the woods with our brown Gentlemen and Ladies," an experience sure to "mortify me to the world in a literal sense." Sergeant closed his letter with a request that he be allowed "to entertain myself with your idea in the woods, for I guess it will be the best company I shall find." That Sergeant believed the chasm between Indian and English to be unbridgeable is clear from another letter written about the same time, this one to the Commissioners of the New England Company, in which he joked about his impending stay among the Indians: "perhaps we [Sergeant and Woodbridge] shall be so taken with them and their way of living that we shall take each of us a wife from amongst, and sadly disappoint all other fair ones that may have any expectations from us." Sergeant clearly found the idea of marrying among his Indian congregants preposterous.[111]

By the following fall, Sergeant had stepped up his fantasies of retreating to the woods with Hannah, imagining "in the closest retreat & retirement from company we should enjoy more pleasure than the world can afford." Part of his fantasy lay in imagining that while the couple could be "the greatest benefactors to the world," they could also be the happiest couple: "innocence & good deeds should finish the day & pleasure crown the night."[112] The mission outpost would be an ideal retreat for a couple in love: "I for my part know of no place," wrote Sergeant, "where you may more securely retreat from the noise & vexation of the world than this: at least I am very willing to think so."[113] Although Edwards's letters to Sergeant do not survive, it is clear that his feelings were not reciprocated, and by April Sergeant had conceded defeat.[114]

Edwards's rejection of Sergeant's overtures likely lent all the more urgency to the missionary's desire to settle four English families at the mission, and he was particularly pleased when Ephraim Williams and his charming daughter arrived in town during the summer of 1738. Just over a year later, John Sergeant and Abigail Williams were married in the presence of ninety Stockbridge Indians. As a political alliance, the match was brilliant: it brought the missionary Sergeant into the powerful River God network, and it linked the Williams family to what was in effect a major public works project that was sure to provide ample opportunity for enrichment. But the political utility of the match did not preclude genuine affection for one another. Apparently fully recovered from his rejection by Edwards, Sergeant counted himself lucky, for it seemed as though God had created Abigail "as if on Purpose for me, and given her to me as if...he tho't it *not good for me to be here alone.*"[115]

Looking back, Sergeant might well have counted that summer of 1739 as the high point of the mission. He was still hopeful about the prospects of the mission, and he had found himself a more than suitable bride and influential in-laws. In May, he had bought four plows for use by the Indians and reported in his diary that they had begun "plowing their Land themselves, which they used to hire done and seemed well pleased with this present."[116] There seemed to be plenty of evidence that the Indians were enthusiastically embracing "Christian civility." Sergeant's optimism was corroborated by a visitor to the mission late that summer. The anonymous author reported that the twenty-five resident Indian families had carefully fenced "fields of Indian Corn, and Beans, and other Sort of Grain." The author was encouraged to find further signs of husbandry, reporting that there were "several Horses among them, and some Cows, Hogs &c." A number of families lived in English-style houses, and many of the women were busy in "sewing Cloth, making Shirts, &c." Many had learned to read, and some could "write a good Hand." The Indian congregation counted sixty baptized souls and fourteen communicants.[117] Construction of a meetinghouse was well under way and would be completed by November of that year, where Sergeant would conduct services in the Mohican language.[118]

The apparent Anglicization of the mission community contained the seeds of many problems. Also that summer, on June 22, 1739, the "principal inhabitants of the Plantation, in the County of Hampshire on Housatannuck River, lately erected into a Township by the Name of Stockbridge," became "fully authorized and impowered to assemble the Freeholders and other qualified Voters there."[119] At the meeting, Ephraim Williams was chosen moderator, Konkapot and Umpachenee selectmen and Josiah Jones constable. Although Sergeant must have counted the event a success, the Indian residents were more apprehensive, as the missionary recorded in his diary that "this affair made some talk and difficulty, as every new thing does among the Indians."[120] Another source of difficulty was introduced that summer, as Konkapot and Ephraim Williams were appointed to divide the common lands and assign individual lots. Again, what might have seemed to the benefit of the town's Indian residents ultimately served to make it easier to alienate Indian lands.[121] Something of the discontent of the Indian proprietors is palpable in Sergeant's diary, which from the fall of 1739 through the following winter is full of references to Umpachenee's "caveling" against Sergeant, Williams, and the English in general. Sergeant attributed the Housatonic leader's dissatisfaction to his drinking and his being "the most turbulent Creature in the world," never considering that the lieutenant might have had ample reason to be upset with the English.[122]

Within a few years, any initial optimism Sergeant had once harbored had evaporated. He was sufficiently discouraged about the progress of his Indian congregation to contemplate a dramatic new approach, one that foreshadows the infamous boarding schools of the nineteenth and early twentieth centuries. Sergeant had virtually given up on teaching the adults and proposed to devote his attention instead to the cultivation of the community's youth, who would be best served, Sergeant thought, by being removed from the influence of their parents and placed in a boarding school. At the same time that Sergeant proposed distancing Indian children from their parents, he had effectively distanced himself from the Indian community. Sergeant and his new bride promptly set about building an elegant house up on the hill near Ephraim Williams, well removed from the Indian settlement in the valley.

Sergeant's plan for the boarding school, as outlined in a letter to Boston minister Benjamin Colman, conceded that simply providing models of

Figure 2 Mission House, Stockbridge, Massachusetts. Photograph by Susan Sheppard. Courtesy of *The Trustees of Reservations*.

"civilization" for emulation by the Indians would not be enough. This plan reflected a change in Sergeant's disposition towards his work. In the early years, he seems not to have believed that a thorough annihilation of Indian identity was necessary for the successful introduction of Christianity. He had even displayed some optimism that the Indians by the light of nature understood something of the fundamental truths of the universe. But his new plan displayed a decided pessimism. The first striking element of the letter is its emphasis on discipline. In this respect, Sergeant's goals for the Indians mirrored in many ways the ideals that had been upheld before him on the occasion of his ordination. In obeying the call of duty to his divine father, Sergeant denied the self and served as a vessel for the communication of God's will. In turn, the Indians were to abase themselves and abandon their heathen ways in order that a new, godly discipline might take its place. They were to show childlike obedience to God's messenger. One means of inculcating this discipline and obedience would be through the introduction of English agricultural pursuits.

The plan included eradication of the Indians' "foolish, barbarous and wicked Customs" in order that civility and Christianity might have a more fertile ground in which to grow. Sergeant aimed to change their "whole Habit of thinking and...raise them as far as possible into the condition of a civil industrious and polish'd People."[123] The best means of cultivating godliness among the Indians was to set them to work in cultivating the earth. And so Sergeant described for Colman his plan to "procure an Accommodation of about 200 acres of Land in this Place." On the land would be built a house in which a number of children would be taught by two masters, "one to take the oversight of them in their Hours of Labour and the other in their hours of Study." In Sergeant's plan, the children were to have their time "so divided between Study and labour as to make one the diversion of the other, that as little time as possible may be lost in Idleness." The plan had the further benefit of rendering the community self-sufficient—the "fruits of Labour" would be put toward the maintenance of the children. As encouragement, some of the profits would be put toward "premiums" to further encourage industry. Sergeant hoped his plan to "root out their vicious habits" would appeal to the benevolently inclined as being well designed to promote the "common good of a very miserable and degenerate part of our Race."[124] In the formula of Christianizing by "civilizing," civilization had become thoroughly equated with English husbandry, and Sergeant's letter is rife with agricultural metaphors: he bemoaned the great difficulty in "cultivating a soil so barren, or rather so overrun with hatefull weeds and pricking thorns."[125] Because English rights to native lands had been based on a belief in the moral superiority of the yeoman life, it would become ever more important to demonstrate the godliness of English husbandry. Thus it was in part the effort to shore up English claims to Indian lands that fed an increasing sanctification of the yeoman life, and this in turn fueled the mandate that Indians must become farmers in order to be saved.

For the most part, Sergeant's experience living among the Indians confirmed his expectations. He had expected to give up much and gain little. He did not expect to find companionship, and he found little. Sergeant found the Indians of Stockbridge "as fickle and irresolute in their Determinations, as any People in the World." Whenever they seemed to be "wholly recovered from their Vice," they were apt to "relapse into their foolish and wicked National Habits," consisting of "idleness and drunkenness and universal suspicion of the English," which he clearly found baseless. Despite such judgments, Sergeant tried to remain optimistic about the prospects for the Indians, at least when appealing to benefactors. Speculating whether Indians might someday reach an equal status to the English, Sergeant concluded that unless the Indians suffered a curse from heaven, he saw nothing "except for their Complection...but that they may be cultivated into as agreeable a People as any other."[126] The bar had been raised again. Once, Sergeant had come close to asserting a fundamental equality between Indian and white, lamenting that the Indians had been "treated with too much neglect by us who in grace alone has made to differ from them."[127] But near the end of his life, Sergeant attributed what he saw as Indian backwardness to the immutable color of their skin.

Sergeant was not the only one whose hopes had waned. It had become increasingly clear to the Stockbridge Indians that securing their lands according to English traditions, attending worship, and receiving instruction in literacy and English husbandry did not raise their status in the eyes of their white neighbors. The roads to English power, secular and religious, remained thoroughly blocked.

It is hard to get beyond the numbers—persons baptized, acres transferred, English houses built—to assess the status of the mission and the thoughts of the resident Housatonic Mohicans. We know that Sergeant had expected to find little comfort and companionship among Indians, and he was not disappointed. He also sought to reform the inner and outer lives of the Mohicans. In some respects, Sergeant had succeeded in this aim but remained skeptical at the time of his death about the possibility of true reform. The "soil" of Mohican souls had proved more difficult to till than he had imagined. Massachusetts government officials had hoped to gain friendly allies and room for expansion on the western frontiers—and they were richly rewarded: mission residents would fight for the English in all the subsequent colonial wars.[128] The province had added substantially to its land reserves, beginning with the Housatonic deed of 1724, and both the province and numerous individuals had profited substantially in the process.

On the Housatonic-Mohican side, the results are mixed as well. The Indians had sought secured land, literacy, access to new spiritual powers, and freedom from the poison of alcohol. Alcohol was a problem not easily resolved. Traders and settlers continued to use alcohol to gain a trading advantage. Umpachenee's fear that English law would not protect Indians' rights against abuses by the English proved all too well founded. While initially intended as a means of securing Indian title to the lands (and, so Belcher and Sergeant hoped, of "civilizing" the Indians), the introduction of English concepts of property and husbandry would ultimately be the means of unseating the Mohicans from their homeland, like the Dawes Act of the nineteenth century. For a time, however, the Mohicans had a land base that served as the center for the consolidation of the remnant populations of nearby Mohican villages. This center would be crucial to the construction of a new identity as the Stockbridge Indians. The new skills acquired in literacy, diplomacy, and subsistence proved essential to Mohican survival for generations to come.

The religious impact of the first decade and a half of the mission on its Indian residents is more difficult to evaluate. Nothing tells us how the several dozen communicants of Sergeant's congregation experienced the Christian sacrament.[129] The Mohicans had hoped that joining the mission would gain them access to a powerful god. They had seen how their Christian neighbors prospered while they faced increasingly straitened circumstances. The power of ritual seemed to have been drained—inherited practices no longer assured the availability of deer or the curing of the sick. Even more troubling, native spiritual power seemed altogether impotent over Christians, a further sign of the Christian god's strength.

The founding of Stockbridge did not resolve the Mohicans' spiritual crisis. But if community is a necessary precondition for religion, then assembling the remnant populations from scattered and often ravaged Housatonic Mohican villages was at least one crucial factor in the creation of a new identity that was both Mohican and Christian. In the final chapters of this book, we will return to Stockbridge to take a closer look at how that new community was forged during the 1740s and 1750s, even as the identity of the English community became all the more entrenched as fundamentally distinct from that of their Indian neighbors. A comparison with a contemporary Mohican community that chose an alternate path sheds further light on the religious life of Stockbridge. We now turn to the experiences of the Indian residents at the short-lived Moravian mission at Shekomeko in New York. The story of the Moravian mission at Shekomeko illuminates the various ways that native peoples responded to the challenge of colonialism. It also calls attention to culturally specific ways that Christianity is lived: Moravian Christianity arguably had more in common with native religions than with Congregational Christianity. But even more, the story of the encounter of missionaries and Mohicans at Shekomeko offers a chance to glimpse, however hazily, something of the inner subjective experiences of native peoples as they constructed new spiritual lives that responded in creative ways to the devastating effects of colonialism. So, in moving from Stockbridge to Shekomeko, we move from the external, the political, and the public to the internal and experiential, a turn facilitated (indeed, necessitated) by the Moravian missionary sources.

PART II

RENEWAL

Chapter Four

The Chief and the Orator

Shabash and Tschoop had good reason to be angry.[1] The two Mohican men had come to New York City in the summer of 1740 hoping to gain satisfaction from the governor for Shabash's ancestral lands, now claimed by a group known as the Little Nine Partners (of which the governor was one) and increasingly overrun by settlers. Since at least the 1680s, Shabash's family had been the recognized owners of a large tract of land in what New Yorkers had begun to call Duchess County. Included in the tract was Shabash and Tschoop's home village of Shekomeko. By this point, Shabash was the respected chief of the village, and Tschoop often served in the role of speaker, carrying on official diplomatic business.[2] The village was nestled into the western side of the Taconic Mountains, midway between the Housatonic and Hudson River Valleys, just one of a number of Indian villages linked to Stockbridge and the larger Mohican network by ties of kinship and diplomacy. Once again (for this was not his first attempt at justice) Shabash was sent away empty-handed. Some years earlier, Shabash had indeed made a bargain with the New York governor by which he ceded much of the disputed lands, reserving for himself and his fellow villagers a one-mile square tract containing Shekomeko. As agreed, Shabash had gone to the appointed place, where he was to receive payment for the land. For four weeks he waited in vain.[3]

Given recent occurrences in Shabash's life, it is not entirely surprising that he had chosen that moment to sign away rights to much of his family's land, for it was around that time that he had become the oldest living member of his family and thus the sole heir to ancestral lands. He was not yet thirty. Shabash's grandmother, Mammanochqua, was likely a sachem and controlled a substantial tract of land that included the village of Shekomeko.[4] Before her death in a smallpox epidemic around 1683, Mammanochqua made provisions that her lands be held in trust for her two young children.[5] Her son was claimed in the same epidemic; only her daughter, Manhat, survived. Years later, Manhat married Argoche, and together the couple had three children, a daughter, and two sons named Shabash and Aminnappau. Scarcely was the last child born when Argoche fell ill and died, presumably also of smallpox. And just a few years later, in 1711, when Shabash was only four years old, his mother was taken prisoner and killed by Mohawks during Queen Anne's War. When he was eight, Shabash lost his sister to disease. The surviving brothers reached adulthood, married, and began families of their own. Another epidemic swept Mohican territory in the early 1720s and claimed Shabash's brother, Aminnappau.[6] It was perhaps the combined toll of these tragedies that prompted Shabash to enter into that first agreement to sell part of his family lands.

We don't know how many additional trips Shabash made to New York to collect on the unpaid debt or what prompted him to try once again in 1738. Perhaps it was that his children were approaching adulthood, making him eager to secure his family's title at least to the village of Shekomeko. This trip elicited fine words from the governor but little else. The governor called the Mohicans his "beloved children," promised payment as soon as the village tract had been properly surveyed, and sent Shabash on his way with ten shillings in his pocket to cover travel expenses.[7]

Sometime that same year, perhaps after the latest futile meeting with the governor, Shabash drank himself into unconsciousness. In this state, he experienced a vision in which a roar of gushing water filled his ears and he saw before him a group of Indians drunk and naked and unable to escape the onrushing water. A voice told him he must give up all wickedness. As the vision continued, a strong light shone all about him, and he heard "a noise like the blowing of a pair of bellows" followed by "a violent blast of wind which dispersed the Indians into the air." Awakening from the vision, Shabash resolved to leave off drinking, and "from that time he entertained serious thought of religion." A year after the vision, Shabash sent a message to missionary John Sergeant at the recently founded Stockbridge mission describing his vision and his desire to find the "way to please God." Two months later, Shabash set out for Stockbridge.[8]

On June 17, 1739, Sergeant noted in his diary that Shabash had arrived in Stockbridge to "inform himself in the affairs of Religion." There, Shabash would have observed about twenty Mohican families engaged in an odd blend of Indian and English agriculture, culture, and religion. Some lived in bark wigwams, others "after the English manner." Perhaps he met with one of the headmen, Konkapot, now a town selectman, in his timber-framed home and surveyed the growing town. Konkapot might have proudly shown Shabash his shingled barn housing cattle and pigs and perhaps even a horse. They might have walked about the edge of the fields, admiring the newly hewn fences "made with their own Hands" and the "good fields of Indian Corn, and Beans." Perhaps Shabash watched with a mix of amusement and shame as Indian men took on women's work, laboring in fields of "other Sort of Grain, as Oats, etc," following behind the unwieldy steel plows recently purchased for the mission by John Sergeant.[9]

Sergeant might have extended Konkapot's tour, showing Shabash Mohican women at work in the schoolhouse, needles in hand, fashioning English-style shirts. And then perhaps on to Timothy Woodbridge's classroom, where Indian children bent over their primers, learning the shapes and sounds of the English language and the fantastic stories of the Bible. By now, five years into his mission, Sergeant's facility with Mohican was sufficient to explain to his visitor some of the basic tenets of Christianity and what he might expect as a new settler in Stockbridge. Sergeant did his best to impress upon his guest "the necessity and importance of religion, and to encourage him with diligence and prayer to inquire after the truth." The young missionary was hopeful, observing Shabash to be "very Desirous of Instruction, and inclined to come and live with us for that purpose."[10] But Sergeant was mistaken. Shabash was not enticed by the missionary's offer to teach the way of the Bible and the plow.

If Sergeant ever found out Shabash's reasons for not settling in Stockbridge, he did not bother to record them. We can imagine, however, what they might have been: a reluctance to leave his home village, the drastic changes required in day-to-day life, and an aversion to the Stockbridge rendering of Christianity. Shabash might well have shared his traveling companion Tschoop's opinion of Christian (presumably Dutch and English) missionaries:

Once a preacher came and began to explain to us that there was a God. We answered, "Dost thou think us so ignorant as not to know that? Go back to the place from whence thou camest." Then again another preacher came and began to teach us, and to say, "You must not steal, nor lie, nor get drunk, etc." We answered "Thou fool, dost thou think that we don't know that? Learn first thyself, and then teach the people to whom thou belongest, to leave off these things. For who steal, or lie, or who are more drunken than thine own people?" And thus we dismissed him.[11]

Neither the gospel preached at Stockbridge nor the economic program seemed to offer a way out of the problems so clearly crystallized in Shabash's vision.

The winter following Shabash's visit to Stockbridge was a difficult one.[12] The next summer, Shabash and Tschoop again went to New York. And again they were turned away empty-handed. Frustrated, the two men turned their steps toward the vibrant trade district of the city and bargained for some rum to lift their spirits or at least to dull their anger before they embarked on the hundred-mile return journey to Shekomeko.[13] While still in the city, Shabash and Tschoop chanced to meet Christian Heinrich Rauch, a Moravian missionary just off the boat from Wetteravia and not two weeks past his twenty-second birthday.[14]

Rauch had been inspired by reports flowing back from the colonies about Moravian mission work among the Indians, accounts that detailed the "miserable circumstances" of the Indians and the great need they had of "teachers who might make known to them the Redeemer of Mankind the Great God."[15] Upon his arrival, Rauch had sought out the Moravian community in the city, seeking fellowship and information about where he might undertake his work of saving Indian souls. He soon met Friedrich Martin, who himself had only just returned from a visit to his mission post among the slave population of St. Thomas.[16] Though Martin knew little of the missionary prospects in the area, he was able to introduce Rauch to some good people in the city who might offer some guidance.[17] But upon hearing Rauch's ambitious plan of converting the local Indians, the people merely scoffed, explaining that many attempts had been made over the years to bring the heathen to Christ, but their efforts were all in vain. The Mohicans remained set "in their old sinful course, and were as much addicted to drunkenness, as ever." To live among them, they warned Rauch, was to risk one's life. Undeterred, Rauch asked where he might find these Indians and was told that two Mohican men were in town to meet the governor.[18]

Rauch sought out and gained an audience with the men. To a recent arrival in the colonies, Shabash and Tschoop must have cut rather imposing figures. Shabash was an honored chief among his people, and bore tattoos in the likeness of a snake on both cheeks.[19] Perhaps they were similar to those of another old warrior from Shekomeko, as described by a missionary:

upon the right cheek and temple, a large snake; from the under lip a pole passed over the nose, and between the eyes to the top of his forehead, ornamented at every quarter of an inch with round marks, representing scalps: upon the left cheek, two lances crossing each other; and upon the lower jaw the head of a wild boar.[20]

The snake figures might have signaled Shabash's status as a *pniesesok*, a man who maintained a special relationship with the spirit being Hobbomok, often represented as a serpent, and who thus had special responsibilities.[21] Tschoop too likely cut an imposing figure to the green missionary—he possessed a "bear-like countenance" and walked with a pronounced limp, having been injured in a fire that left him lame.[22]

Rauch soon discovered he could not converse with the men because they were "frightfully drunk." Finding them sober the next day, Rauch asked whether they would like a teacher to show them the "way out of their blindness and imprisonment to sin." Tschoop, perhaps with a touch of sarcasm, answered that yes, he had in fact had an inclination to "something better than he had hitherto had." Shabash agreed, so the men appointed Rauch their minister and told him to meet them the next day at the house of a German settler, Martinus Hoffmann. Rauch did so, waiting for several days, but the men failed to appear.[23] Still not deterred, Rauch got directions to the men's village and set out.

When he arrived at Shekomeko, Rauch addressed the villagers, explaining that he had come from across the ocean to bring them the news that God loved humans so much that he became a man, lived as all men do, and was nailed to the cross for everyone's sins. God's son had shed his blood and died for all sinners, that they might be saved from sin and granted eternal life. His audience seemed to listen attentively, perhaps out of curiosity, although some seemed quite moved, including Tschoop, who later recalled, "I could not forget his words. They constantly recurred to my mind. Even when I was asleep, I dreamt of that blood which Christ shed for us. I found this to be something different from what I had ever heard, and I interpreted Christian Henry's words to the other Indians."[24]

But Rauch's early success was short-lived. The atmosphere soon changed, and Rauch's overtures were met only with derision, laughter, and threats, a product of warnings from local settlers that the Moravians intended to enslave the villagers' children. On one occasion, a man chased Rauch wielding a hatchet. On another, Tschoop took up his rifle and attempted to scare away the missionary. The message was eminently clear—Rauch was not welcome in Shekomeko. Rauch sought refuge at the nearby farm of Johannes Rauh. Shabash and Tschoop must have thought that that was the last they would see of the strange man.[25]

Farmer Rauh explained to the starry-eyed missionary that it would be easier "to reach up and touch the sky than to rescue the Indians from their baneful condition," for they "could not even understand proper language." But both men saw an opportunity in the situation. Rauh feared his children were in danger of becoming as "wild as the heathen" for lack of instruction, so he offered to lodge Rauch in exchange for tutoring his children.[26] Eager to live near Shekomeko without being burdensome to the villagers, Rauch agreed. He could make himself of use with his medical skills and perhaps eventually regain enough trust among the Shekomekoans to renew his talk of Christ's blood. And so every day, Rauch made the two-mile trip from Johannes Rauh's farmstead to Shekomeko and resumed his talk of Jesus' suffering and the power of his spilled blood. It was certainly rough going for the first months, perhaps even the first year. Yet, despite the challenges, he vowed to "to preach the death of the Lord Jesus, for my soul hungers and thirsts after the salvation of these heathen."[27]

The villagers apparently tired of chasing Rauch away. Eventually, on some unknown day, the guns were laid down, and first one villager, then a few more, including Tschoop, began to change their opinion of the missionary. He didn't seem interested in enslaving their children, as some local whites had insisted. His knowledge of medical arts might well have alleviated some ailments when traditional healing methods failed. He didn't seek land or food from the villagers. He proved himself to be quite different than other Christians they had met. Shabash remained set against Rauch, trying to stir up opposition to the missionary, but sometime before the summer of 1741, he sought Rauch out and professed his desire to know more about the "reconciler of the world."[28] By the end of 1741, Rauch was convinced that the Holy Spirit had indeed showered her grace[29] on the souls of Shabash, Tschoop, Seim, and Kiop, while others in the village remained less enthusiastic about the missionary.[30]

Both support and opposition to Rauch might have been heightened by the difficult circumstances that plagued the village. Rauch reported that the corn supply had frozen, leaving many hungry and susceptible to disease and inclined to "worry more about bread than about the savior." Rauch's assembly dwindled to a few souls, for those who had not fallen sick had taken to the woods in search of food. Nonetheless, Rauch was optimistic enough to promise he would soon travel with several baptismal candidates to see the Moravian leader, the Count Ludwig von Zinzendorf. To Rauch it must have seemed divine providence that Zinzendorf was in the colonies and could thus preside over the baptism of the "Erstlinger," or first fruits, among the Mohicans. In February, Rauch and his recently arrived missionary partner Gottlob Büttner, together with Shabash, Seim, and Kiop, set out for Oley, Pennsylvania, to meet Zinzendorf.[31]

Tschoop's lame leg prevented him from making the arduous 150-mile journey in the winter, and so he sent his regrets in a letter to Zinzendorf.[32]

In it, he described his change of heart, emphasizing the power of Christ's blood:

> My first feeling in my heart was from his blood and when I heard that he
> was also the Saviour of the Heathen and that I did owe him my heart I felt
> a drawing towards him in my heart.... Untill our teacher came and told us
> of the Lamb of God, who shed his blood and died for us blind and cursed
> men. I wondered at it and as often as I heard a preaching of it, I thought,
> there must be something in it, for my heart got every time warmed by it.
> I did often dream as if our teacher did stand before me and did preach to
> me of the blood of our Saviour and I longed in the morning for his coming
> to me, that I could tell him my dream.

Tschoop continued to struggle because "there were so many things I was attached to." Evoking the uncertainty of Mohican life, he confessed, "my belly was my God. My wife and Children my Joy and I was afraid of men." He himself had been "the greatest Drunkard and the most willing slave of the Devil." He wavered for a time, before coming to feel that only the Savior could help him, "but now I feel that I believe that only he can help me with his blood." He felt a "power in my heart" that led him to desire baptism: "Blood, I finally heard. I should give my wicked heart to the Savior and let him wash it with blood."[33]

The blood of Christ promised new spiritual powers that could be used to improve lives, sometimes by challenging the status quo. In his letter to Zinzendorf, Tschoop wrote of being freed from the tyranny of his mother-in-law. Once he began to believe in the blood, he wrote, "my nearest friends [grew] enemies—my Wife, my Children and the greatest enemy was the mother of my wife, who said I was not so good as a dog if I would no more believe in her God." Now, it seemed "it was foolishness to me, what she said." His mother-in-law had inherited her claim to religious leadership from her grandmother in the form of a medicine bundle, made of leather and "in the Shape of a man and adorned with wampum and as she was the oldest she gave him to us to pray before him and we did so."[34]

Leaving Tschoop behind, a small party readied for the journey to Pennsylvania. What may at first seem an odd location for the baptism of the three "firstlings" into the Moravian faith makes more sense when considered in the context of Zinzendorf's ambitious ecumenical project. The February meeting in Oley was the third synod of seven held over the span of as many months; the meetings brought together many varieties of colonial German Protestants. The synods were Zinzendorf's effort to create a "Church of God in the Spirit," a nondenominational union committed to universal Christian ideals. But by this third synod, many of the participants, including the Mennonites, the Schwenkfelders, and the Dunkers, had realized that ecumenism to Zinzendorf effectively meant the freedom to agree with the Moravian way and so had withdrawn from the project.[35]

With ecumenical ideals rapidly crumbling, the inauguration of the Mohican church gained in significance. Zinzendorf by this time was thoroughly frustrated with what he believed to be the pettiness and divisiveness of Pennsylvania's many religious sects, prompting him to pine nostalgically for Europe, whose religious politics now seemed harmonious by comparison. In the colonies, lamented Zinzendorf, he found "nothing but enthusiasts, or proud saints, or rude, scornful people, which made the preaching of the gospel very hard for him."[36] Zinzendorf might well have hoped that baptizing the first Mohican converts in the presence of the assembled denominations would stand as testimony to Christian universalism: surely, if heathen Indians could join hands with Moravians, those who differed so much less should be able to join the cause.

The party from Shekomeko arrived in Oley on the evening of February 9. Already present were members of the General Synod as well as a group of Delaware Indians, there to observe the goings-on. (Just three years later, Rauch would preside over the baptism of the first Delaware converts.) Although no lengthy description of this first baptismal ceremony survives, the ritual is described at length elsewhere in the Moravian records.[37] The candidates would have been led into the center of the room, robed in white and accompanied by their sponsors. Next followed a short discourse on the qualifications for and meaning of baptism, likely intermingled with spontaneous hymn singing.[38] Moravians understood baptism as "a gift of grace" that depended not on any demonstration of a "knowledge and understanding of the truths" but only upon the candidate being "sensibly touched with and convinced of ones miserable Condition" and desirous of deliverance with "a hunger and thirst after our Saviour."[39]

In preparation for baptism, the candidates would have been asked several questions, including whether it was the "whole desire of your Hearts to be baptised in the blood and death of Jesus," and whether they believed that "by the Blood and Water from our Saviour's side which is now about to be poured out upon you in Baptism, all your sins will be washed away and you eternally released from all Condemnation, Curse and Misery." The Brethren responded to the candidates' affirmative answers by promising "in the name of our Husband, his Father and our Mother, the Holy Ghost" that they would become "children of God" ensuring that the Saviour "will give you the Priviledge, to become happy in his pierced side, to find your Habitation therein and for the time to come to be free from every power of sin and darkness." Further, the Brethren "promise[d] and assure[d]" the candidates that "our dear Mother [the Holy Spirit] will take you into her nursing Care." Finally, the missionary assured the candidates that "ye shall

A. *Der Priester welcher tauft.*   TAUFE   C. C. *Die Arbeiter von ihrer Nation.*
BBB *Die Täuflinge.*   der Indianer   D. D. *Die Indianer-Gemeine.*
   in America

Figure 3 "Baptism of Indians in America," [Moravian Church], *Kurze zuverläßige Nachricht* (1757). Courtesy of Moravian Archives, Bethlehem, Pennsylvania.

participate in all the Blessings of the Church." At that point, the Brethren laid hands on the kneeling candidates and offered a prayer to cast out evil spirits: "We command hereby every Power of Darkness, sin and Satan... totally to depart from every one of you this Instant, and for the Future not dare attempt to approach hurt or disturb you in the Grace and Peace which shall be imparted to you through the Blood of Jesus."[40] This casting out of evil spirits may well have had special resonance with the Mohican candidates, who would have shared with other northeastern Indians a belief that sickness and ill-fortune could be the result of powerful people who invoked evil spirits to do their bidding.[41]

After the casting out of spirits, the Saviour was entreated to take the neophytes into his care:

> Take Thou possession of them and baptise them in thy divine Blood, bedew them in Baptism, with thy sweat in Pennance-Agony, Body and Soul!

Make them thy Children and fellow inheritors with us of eternal life! And release them this moment, from all their misery and corruptions from their unbelief and enmity against thee, thou Lamb of God! Keep them eternally as thy Inheritance that none may be able to tear them out of thy hand, but that they may be preserved happy till thou callest them Home, to kiss the prints in hands and feet, and to reside eternally in thy wounded side.[42]

The ceremony at Oley concluded with the candidates being "overstreamed" with water, to the words: "Abraham, Isaac and Jacob, I baptize you in the name of the Father, and of the Son and of the Holy Spirit, with Jesus' death." Then came the laying on of hands and a hymn to conclude: his Blood "washes us clean, makes snow-white that which is red, in him one can rejoice with a hero's courage, no judgment to shrink from, as a sinner usually does."[43] From that day on, Shabash, Seim, and Kiop would be known as Abraham, Isaac, and Jacob, patriarchs of a new nation of believers. Tschoop was baptized two months later in Shekomeko, receiving the name Johannes, perhaps in honor of John the Baptist. Within the year, all three men's wives were baptized: Sarah, Rebecca, and Rachel.[44] But that is not the end of the story.

Tschoop and Shabash had gone to New York seeking justice and returned with a missionary instead. In the absence of justice, Tschoop and Shabash, now known as Johannes and Abraham, found new sources of spiritual power that helped them to function in a world that was increasingly hostile to Indian existence. Both found a means of overcoming the destructive power of alcohol and a means of reinforcing their leadership roles within their community. Baptism into the Moravian faith, however, was no panacea—it could not protect their land, stave off disease, or ensure Christian fellowship with European Christians outside of the Moravian fold. The lives of the two men are instructive in what they tell us about the possibilities and the limitations of affiliation with the Moravian mission project.

Johannes became a renowned preacher in Shekomeko and the surrounding Indian towns. The skills he had developed in the office of speaker for the chief—once used in the conduct of diplomacy—were now redirected toward proclaiming the power of Jesus' blood. The larger Mohican confederacy no longer played the role it once had in colonial-Indian relations. Johannes's message preached to his fellow Mohicans related his acquaintance with a great spiritual warrior and the protective and sustaining power offered by the Moravian Savior. Like later prophets such as the Delaware prophet, Neolin, or the Shawnee prophet, Tenskwatawa, Johannes left behind a life that had been plagued by alcohol and preached a message of cultural renewal through ritual practice.

The eruption of the King George's War between England and France in 1744 brought an end to a few relatively peaceful years at Shekomeko.

Suspected of being "papists," Moravian missionaries were prohibited by New York authorities from preaching to the Indians.[45] On the one hand, the prohibition on Moravian preaching put leadership of the nascent Indian Christian community squarely in Indian hands—Johannes and Abraham led most services. On the other hand, the Shekomeko Indians' affiliation with the Moravians rendered their status in British colonies yet more tenuous, as local English settlers began toting guns to church for fear of the Shekomeko Indians.[46]

Johannes's role as preacher was not unlike that of tribal speaker, but as preacher, he found a means of challenging the authority of white settlers, who were often suspicious at best and hostile at worst toward their Indian neighbors. He also found a means of leaving behind aspects of his native culture—such as the religious authority of his mother-in-law—that he found problematic. But Johannes's Christian practice could not ward off the powerful diseases brought by European settlers. In August 1746, just four months after a party of Shekomeko residents had left their village, hoping that they might find a better life settled with the Moravian congregation at Bethlehem, Pennsylvania, Johannes contracted smallpox and died within a week. Johannes was buried in "Gottes Acker," or "God's field," where the "Hütten" or "tabernacles" of departed Brothers and Sisters were planted, from which their souls arose to return to their Creator.[47]

Abraham followed a more varied path. In the years following his baptism, Abraham, like Johannes, was an active preacher. He regularly sponsored village feasts at which he often preached late into the night about the power of Jesus' blood. And like Johannes, he regularly led services in Shekomeko following the ban on Moravian preaching in New York. But when the choice came in the midst of King George's War whether to remain in Shekomeko, remove to Bethlehem, or move to the Susquehanna Valley with other Indian peoples seeking refuge from the pressures of white settlement, Abraham stayed behind, still hoping he might retain title to his home village and receive a long-delayed payment for his other lands.[48] He had recently been named as an important counselor to the Mohican chief sachem at Stockbridge. Even though he had not wanted to settle in Stockbridge, he might have hoped that the Stockbridge Indians' close ties to the Massachusetts government could be of help in negotiating with colonial officials.[49]

But life in Shekomeko quickly became untenable: the creditors came knocking, and with war raging between the British and the French, the allegiance of all Indians became suspect. In addition, by the spring of 1747, Abraham and Sarah were expecting another child, and there seemed to be no future in Shekomeko. And so the couple decided to relocate to the new mission settlement, named Gnadenhütten, or "Huts of Grace," near Bethlehem. They arrived just weeks before Sarah, at around forty years of

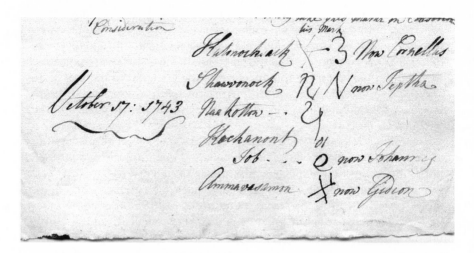

Figure 4 Signatures of Indian leaders, witnesses to Abraham's petition, including Cornelius of Shekomeko; Jeptha, Esopus Indian of Shekomeko; unknown; Benjamin Kokhkewenaunaut "King Ben" of Stockbridge (sachem of Mohicans by 1750); Johannes of Shekomeko; and Gideon, Wampanosch of Pachgatgoch. October 17, 1743, 113/5/9 RMM, Courtesy of Moravian Archives, Bethlehem, Pennsylvania.

age, gave birth to a son, whom they named Isaac.[50] Abraham received several acres at Gnadenhütten to plant, deciding that it was more profitable than trying to support his family by hunting.[51] But after about seven years in Gnadenhütten, Abraham somewhat reluctantly left the Moravian community. Having accepted the position of war captain from the Mohican chief sachem at Stockbridge in 1753, he was called upon to accept the invitation (or command, rather) from the Iroquois to remove to Wyoming on the Susquehanna.[52] Abraham clearly resented being forced to choose between his allegiance to the Moravian community and his obligations as a captain among the Mohicans. Abraham died in December 1762, just months before the Treaty of Paris put an end to the French and Indian War.[53] On his deathbed, he exhorted his wife Sarah to return to the Brethren, which she did.[54]

After his death, Abraham's family carried on his legacy. Two of Abraham's sons took up their father's quest for justice. In September 1763, nine months after their father's death, even as Pontiac's War raged around them, "two Sons of Old Abraham a Mohicander" appeared before the British superintendent of Indian affairs, William Johnson. They complained that the patentees of the Little Nine Partners had never paid their father for his land but instead had "always trifled" with him. Understanding the importance of symbolic gestures of reciprocity, Johnson inquired as to "what consideration would satisfy them." They replied that they would be content with £100, although they knew that farms on the land had sold for five times that amount. Johnson promised to look into the matter and then sent them away with "2 Black Strowds" to cover "the Grave of Old Abraham, their late Father."[55] That was likely all the satisfaction Abraham's family ever received.

Chapter Five

Moravian Missionaries of the Blood

When Tschoop—baptized as Johannes—looked back on Rauch's arrival, he registered his surprise that a white man would calmly lie down and sleep: "When he had finished his discourse, he lay down upon a board, fatigued by the journey, and fell into a sound sleep. I then thought, what kind of man is this? There he lies and sleeps. I might kill him and throw him out into the wood, and who would regard it? But this gives him no concern."[1] In another version of this encounter, Tschoop threatened to kill Rauch, to which Rauch responded, "I trust in Jesus." Rauch's claim to be protected by a man named Jesus left Tschoop to wonder "what kind of man is this little fellow? . . . Who is this Jesus? I, too, will find the man."[2] Clearly, Rauch was not like most other Europeans. He did not recoil, as many Englishmen did, at the prospect of sharing an Indian dwelling. Neither did he regard Tschoop as "savage." But what most distinguished Rauch was his talk of blood and the assurance Rauch exhibited that he was protected from harm by Jesus's blood, which Johannes remembered as "something different from what I had ever heard." Even though it would be months before Rauch was allowed to stay and preach on a regular basis, his words haunted Tschoop: "I could not forget his words. They constantly recurred to my mind. Even when I was asleep, I dreamt of that blood which Christ shed for us."[3] It was Rauch's manner and his message about a powerful protector spirit that Johannes emphasized in recalling Rauch's visit. That

Rauch seemed as comfortable among the Shekomeko settlers as among the neighboring German farmers sent a powerful message that perhaps Rauch was capable of appreciating Indian humanity.

This one encounter prompts a series of questions about the Shekomeko experiment. Why did Rauch act the way he did? Why was Tschoop so surprised by this behavior? Why did Rauch begin his proselytizing efforts with talk of the blood and wounds of Christ rather than with the existence of God and the story of the Creation and the Fall, as other missionaries had? And just why did Tschoop find this talk of the blood of a persecuted and tortured god-man so compelling?

The lives of Tschoop and Shabash suggest some of the answers to these questions. Except for the level of detail recorded about their lives, little marks their experiences as unique among native peoples in colonial America. Shabash's troubles retaining title to his ancestral lands highlight the very real and threatening presence of colonists, who were rapidly multiplying (both by immigration and procreation) and increasingly emboldened by the long peace that had prevailed since the end of Queen Anne's War in 1713. His loss of nearly all of his family to disease and war puts a human face on the demographic catastrophe that all Native Americans faced. Directly or indirectly, illness often became the impetus for interest in Christian practice. Shabash and Tschoop's troubles with alcohol testify to a further cost of the extreme social dislocation that came with the ever-increasing European presence.[4]

Neither was Rauch's story entirely unique. He was one of many individuals on both sides of the Atlantic to have been caught up in the rising spirit of religious awakening (or "enthusiasm," in the view of its detractors). The rapid growth of the Moravian community beginning in the 1720s in Herrnhut had fueled tensions with local religious and civic leaders in Saxony, and Moravian missionaries in the New World did not escape their share of controversy—they arrived just as tensions over religious revivals were heating up across the northern British colonies. And when war resumed between Britain and France in 1744, the Moravians almost immediately came under suspicion as "papists" whose allegiance lay with Catholic France. The irony of the Moravian-Mohican encounter was that it was precisely the Moravians' outsider status in the colonies that facilitated a different sort of religious exchange, one that did not seek complete transformation or eradication of Mohican culture. And just as Shekomekoans were in the midst of revitalizing their community by indigenizing Moravian Christianity, imperial wars intruded, and the Mohican affiliation with the now-suspect Moravians rendered the Shekomekoans' status yet more tenuous.

Moravians were like no other Europeans the Shekomekoans had encountered. The contrast with the Stockbridge program of "civilization before

Christianization" could scarcely have been greater. The unique communal organization of the Moravian community placed relatively few demands on Mohican resources while also providing a highly structured support system that could provide economic, social, and spiritual sustenance where indigenous systems had been seriously compromised. Further, in their understandings of spiritual efficacy—the means of accessing spiritual power—Moravians and Mohicans were not so different from each other. Whereas Congregational missionaries like Sergeant emphasized literacy and doctrinal competency, Moravians scorned theological disputation, focusing instead on the blood and wounds of Christ as the locus of human redemption and insisting only that sinners feel the blood of the Savior in their hearts in order to experience Christ's saving power. This power not only gained believers a place with Christ in the next world but could also be directed to very real and immediate needs. Viewed through Mohican eyes, Moravian Christianity offered the protection of a powerful warrior spirit who willingly sacrificed his life to free humans from suffering. And the Shekomekoans were clearly suffering.

The stories that emerge here challenge the conventional wisdom about the role of missions in colonial American society. Moravian missionaries did not serve as agents of colonial power. The Mohicans of Shekomeko did not feel compelled to adopt Christianity: they had turned away missionaries before. The adoption of Christian practices by Tschoop, Shabash, and others signaled neither a wholesale rejection of traditional ways nor a full embrace of Moravian piety or cultural norms. Recent studies have begun to emphasize the ways native communities adapted Christianity to preserve and construct community. The Moravian mission records, rich in details of individual Indian lives, provide a unique opportunity to observe a "culture in motion."[5] The Moravian records are of such interest not only because they offer a glimpse into the emergence of an indigenized, Mohicanized, Christianity but also because that newly emerging Christian practice stands as a powerful witness to the devastations of colonialism on Indian individuals and communities and to the reserves of the human spirit.

INDIAN VIEWS OF CHRISTIANITY

Shabash and Tschoop had been ready to turn away the eager Moravian missionary, Christian Rauch, just as they had other missionaries before him. They feared that the missionary would preach simple truths they already understood—truths that Christians, in Mohican experience, often failed to live by. They had yet to encounter a missionary whose God worked in the familiar ways of *manitou*, the spirits that enlivened the Mohican world. In fact, by the time of the Moravians' arrival, there had emerged among northeastern Indian peoples a fairly standard critique of European

missionary efforts that rested on three interrelated claims: the separate creation of Indians and whites, the bad behavior of professed Christians, and
the superiority of Indian ways.

All three of these critiques were presented by an elderly Shawnee
chief in his response to Moravian leader Ludwig von Zinzendorf's proposal to start a mission at Shamokin, an important intertribal settlement
on the Susquehanna River in Pennsylvania. The chief politely declined
Zinzendorf's offer to send missionaries, in an explanation (as recounted by
interpreter Conrad Weiser) that bears quoting at length:

> He believed in God, who created the Indians as well as the Europeans, only
> there was this Difference, that the former were created Brown, the latter White,
> the latter prayed with words, the former in their Hearts, which God saw and
> was very kind to the Indians. He himself was an Indian of God's creation and
> he was satisfied with his condition had no wish to be a European, above all he
> was a subject of the Iroquois, it did not behoove him to take up new Things
> without their Advice or Example. If the Iroquois chose to become Europeans,
> and learned to pray like them: he would have nothing to say against it, but as
> a matter of fact there was not much behind the Prayers of Europeans. They
> were mostly bad People. He liked the Indian way of Life. God had been very
> kind to him even in his old Age and would continue to look well after him.
> God was better pleased with the Indians, than with the Europeans.[6]

Other ministers and missionaries active in the northeast around the same
time encountered nearly identical sentiments.[7]

David Brainerd, the Presbyterian missionary who inspired far more future missionaries than he did Indians, found similar sentiments among the
Delaware. The Indians, noted Brainerd, were "obstinately set against Christianity" and blamed Europeans for introducing many vices among them,
especially alcohol, which "made them quarrel and kill one another." When
he attempted to counter this argument by distinguishing between "real"
and "nominal" Christians, Brainerd was met with still greater opposition:
"If all those who will cheat the Indians," retorted the Delaware, "are Christians only in Name, there are but few left in the Country to be Christians in
Heart." Worse, Brainerd found that missionaries were suspected of having
been sent "to draw them together under a pretence of Kindness to them,
that they may have an Opportunity to make Slaves of them as they do of the
poor Negroes." But what most galled Brainerd was the Indians' presump-
tion of the superiority of their way of life:

> 'Tis certain they look upon themselves and their Methods of living (which,
> they say, their God expressly prescrib'd for them) vastly preferable to the

white People and their Methods. And hence will frequently sit and laugh at
them, as being good for Nothing else but to plow and fatigue themselves
with hard Labour; while *they* enjoy the satisfaction of stretching themselves
on the Ground, and sleeping as much as they please, and have no other
Trouble but now and then to chase the Deer, which is often attended with
Pleasure rather than Pain.[8]

Given the Indians' general antipathy toward colonists, with their toilsome
way of life and their Bible that seemed so difficult for whites themselves
to follow, it is not surprising that Christian Rauch was met with jeers and
threats when he attempted to preach to the Shekomekoans of the Christian
God. So when and why did the villagers eventually put down their rifles and
hatchets and begin to warm to this strange visitor?

Part of the answer is to be found in the Moravian approach to mission
work, and their differences from other Europeans. It was certainly rough
going for Rauch in the first year. Eventually, Rauch's presence became tol-
erable and even welcome.[9] Rauch and other Moravian missionaries attributed their success in gaining an audience to the power of the gospel and
the labors of the Holy Spirit, but other more prosaic forces were at work as
well: the Moravians confounded the Shekomekoans' expectations of European behavior. Rauch proved himself to be quite different from the Dutch
and English Christians Shekomekoans had encountered, and the Savior
that he spoke of was quite unlike the God described by other missionaries.
By and large, the Moravians agreed with Indian critiques of white society,
and they quickly came to understand that the more they were able to set
themselves apart from other Europeans, the greater were their chances
of being heard. Zinzendorf himself claimed he was "ashamed to pass for
a European Christian."[10] Mohicans and Moravians agreed that the better
part of professing Christians fell short of practicing what they preached.
The distinctive Moravian interpretation of Christianity can be traced to the
circumstances of the emergence of the Renewed Unity of the Brethren in
Saxony in the 1720s and 1730s.

MORAVIAN HISTORY AND MISSION POLICY

The Moravians' mission program was quite distinct from other mission
programs active in the colonies.[11] Two factors were particularly important
to the development of the Moravians' unique missionary program: an identity anchored by a long history as political outsiders and the colorful personality of Count Nicholas Ludwig von Zinzendorf, the dominant force
behind the renewal and transformation of the ancient Hussite faith into

a modern, global, and pietistic Church, part of a transatlantic Protestant religious awakening.[12]

Zinzendorf's own religious experience bore the marks of his upbringing; he was born in 1700 and was raised as a member of the nobility by his maternal grandmother, a highly educated woman who took deep personal and financial interest in the emerging Lutheran Pietist movement. Although deeply influenced by the Pietism he encountered during his studies at the University of Halle in Saxony, Zinzendorf ultimately became disenchanted with the Hallensian view of conversion as a spiritual struggle, which did not match his own experience of the joy of Christianity. Zinzendorf's primary interest remained theology even as his family steered him toward legal studies and a career more befitting his social status. By his early twenties, Zinzendorf had accepted a judicial position with the Saxon government in Dresden and was beginning construction on a manor house when he received word through the local Lutheran pastor that some Protestant dissenters were seeking refuge from increased persecution in the neighboring, Catholic-controlled Austrian territory.

When the young Zinzendorf granted asylum to the small band of religious refugees in 1722, he little expected to become the motivating force behind a worldwide evangelizing project. These refugees from Moravia traced their roots to the ancient Bohemian Unitas Fratrum (Unity of the Brethren) that had emerged in the fifteenth century in the wake of the reformer Jan Hus's martyrdom.[13] Zinzendorf was drawn to the simple piety of the refugees. And when he began reading the work of the seventeenth-century Moravian bishop Comenius, Zinzendorf found a kindred spirit.[14] The basic tenets of Moravian faith were that the Bible is the source of all religious truths; that Christ, not the Pope, is the head of God's church; and that piety and ethical conduct must be emphasized over doctrine. To these, Zinzendorf, as the emerging spiritual leader and spokesperson for the Brethren, brought his own experiences with the Pietists at Halle lending to the traditional faith of the Unitas Fratrum an affirmation of the primacy of the heart over the head as the wellspring of true religion. Zinzendorf resisted sectarian labels, fostering instead a philadelphian vision of Christian fraternity. The growth of the community at Herrnhut worried local authorities, and in 1736, Zinzendorf was forced into exile for harboring dissenters.[15] Pennsylvania soon became the focus of Zinzendorf's ecumenical and missionary hopes.

During these same years, the Moravian missionary program took shape. Already in 1727, several of the Brethren at Herrnhut had organized a mission prayer group, devoting themselves not only to prayer but also to acquiring the skills they believed would be necessary for mission work, including study of languages, medicine, and geography. Zinzendorf's encounter in Denmark with a freed slave from St. Thomas fueled his interest in mission work. The first Moravian missionaries set out in 1732 for St. Thomas, and the following year a mission was founded in Greenland, where a Pietist Lutheran missionary had been laboring unsuccessfully for a decade.[16] The Moravians learned a number of important lessons from these early missions, which initially followed much the same program as their Anglo-Protestant counterparts, beginning with the doctrines of God's existence, human sinfulness, and the righteousness of punishment for sin. After six fruitless years, the Herrnhut congregation prayed on the issue and came to the conclusion that their missionaries in Greenland ought to focus their message on the crucifixion if they expected any blessing among the heathen. The Greenland missionaries did as instructed, emphasizing the suffering and death of Jesus, and they were rewarded with an awakening among the native Greenlanders.[17] This would be the central focus of Moravian preaching to the Indians of North America.

Moravian mission efforts in North America began inauspiciously. The first Moravian missionaries to serve in North America arrived in 1736 with the aim of converting local Creek and Cherokee Indians as well as black slaves in Georgia. The mission quickly folded due to a combination of internal conflicts within the community and tensions with the surrounding settlers, who were suspicious of the Brethren's pacificism.[18] The Moravian bishop, August Spangenberg, who had overseen the failed Georgia experiment, now turned his energies to missionizing among the Indians of Pennsylvania. Spangenberg's report to Herrnhut on what he saw as the desperate spiritual plight of America's Indians heightened interest among European Moravians in mission work. One young man who caught the missionary fire from Spangenberg was Christian Rauch.

In the spring of 1740, Rauch set sail for America, instructed to seek out opportunities to bring word of the Savior to the heathen.[19] Within two years of Rauch's arrival, the Moravian headquarters at Bethlehem, Pennsylvania, was founded, populated by members of the original Georgia contingent as well as the missionaries of the "Sea Congregation" recently arrived from Europe.[20] Bethlehem was unique among Moravian settlements. The community was a *pilgergemeine*, or pilgrim congregation, whose primary purpose was to support mission work among the Indians. The communal economy instituted in 1744 grew not out of a Christian-socialist utopianism but out of pragmatism as the best means of facilitating a rapidly expanding mission program.[21] This arrangement had important implications for the Moravian missionaries' interactions with the Indians of Shekomeko.

When Rauch approached Tschoop and Shabash in the summer of 1740, he represented a religious community with a dramatically different missionary style, a style that can be linked not only to Moravian theology but also to the social location of the *Brüdergemeine* in both Europe and the colonies.

Rauch did not represent any colonial power, he was not attached to a community of settlers eagerly eyeing Mohican lands, he had no large family to support, and he did not presume that the Mohicans must first be "civilized" before they could be "Christianized," as most of his Anglo-Protestant counterparts believed. Instead, Rauch at first boarded with a nearby farmer, Johannes Rauh, offering his services as a tutor to Rauh's children in exchange for room and board. He tried to make himself useful among the Shekomekoans by offering what medical services he could. In the meantime, Rauch worked at learning the local language, likely tutored by Rauh's daughter, Jannetje, who was fluent in Mohican. When he finally gained permission to settle in Shekemeko, Rauch and the other missionaries who joined him continued to work for their own maintenance, supported when necessary with aid from the newly established headquarters at Bethlehem.

What is perhaps most striking about the Moravian mission efforts is what they did *not* do. Compared to their counterparts of other denominations active in the colonies, Moravian missionaries were culturally non-aggressive, a result both of pragmatism and idealism.[22] Practically speaking, the Moravians were colonial outsiders. Moravian missionaries were not concerned with furthering imperial projects, although their work often did in fact facilitate the spread of European settlement. The kind of secular power that would have made demands of cultural transformation more tenable, Moravians construed as corrupt.[23] As Zinzendorf wrote, sounding remarkably like the seventeenth-century sectarian, Roger Williams, "If the Christian Princes and Divines should go so far as to convert the Heathen Nations to their Customs and Ways in our Days, they would thereby do the greatest Piece of Service to the Devil."[24] The Moravians' status as outsiders—both in Europe and the New World—militated against the equation of European culture with the true Christian life.

Moravian mission efforts remained fairly modest; they did not aim to attach native peoples to government interests, nor did they expect to convert whole nations. While this approach was certainly pragmatic, it was also rooted in theology. Zinzendorf believed that God, through the Holy Spirit, "must first have spoken to their Hearts" before there was any hope of successful mission work.[25] Thus, in assessing a potential mission site, the missionaries were to discern whether "there be here or there a person, whom God himself is preparing, by his grace, to hear and receive a word concerning Christ Jesus, and of our salvation in him."[26] If not, then a mission was not to be attempted. This policy prevented the missionaries from establishing missions where they were unlikely to gain an audience. For example, after a chilly reception during a 1742 tour of Iroquois territory, Zinzendorf announced that he was "unable to discern any promising indications or signs of grace among them, excepting in the case of a few individuals" and so concluded that "the time of the Heathen is not yet come."[27] In practice, this policy served to keep Moravian expectations of conversion low while also providing the missionaries with a reason to withdraw from any unpromising endeavor without admitting defeat.

If Moravian missionaries were not flat out turned away, they were still instructed to be cautious. They were not to begin with labored proofs of God's existence or "the absurd doctrine of the cross," neither of which could be proven to the intellect. Zinzendorf believed that God's existence had been revealed to all peoples, and so attempts to prove his existence would simply betray the missionaries' ignorance. Instead, missionaries should make known the saving truth of the gospel in their actions before beginning to preach.[28] An entry in the Bethlehem diary written soon after the arrival of a number of Shekomeko residents suggests just how seriously this tenet was taken. The congregation was reminded not to "ask curious questions of the Indians who came to visit us, and also not to get in religious discourse with them. We do not want to begin with them from doctrine. First they must get a different concept of Christ and His people from our behavior."[29] Other missions had failed, Moravian leaders believed, because they started with efforts to teach doctrine rather than with the testimony of their example.

Before they began to preach, Moravian missionaries were to make themselves useful by laboring to support themselves, while also studying the language of their hosts. The Moravian dedication to learning native languages further eased the missionaries' entrance into Indian communities. This was not only for the obvious reason that communication was facilitated when the need for an interpreter was eliminated, but as Spangenberg observed, as long as the missionaries could not speak, they were obliged to teach by example. The Indians would then have opportunity to "look at them while at work, and get an impression of them, as of a good and outwardly useful people." Once the native hosts observed that the missionaries could be productive members of a community, the apprehension "which easily arises in them, when they have to do with the Europeans" would be removed.[30]

Missionary Martin Mack's experience bears out this observation. Mack joined Rauch at Shekomeko in the winter of 1742–43. From his base in Shekomeko, Mack ventured to nearby villages, including Pachgatgoch and Potatik, where he hoped to establish new missions.[31] When Mack and his wife Jannetje (Rauh's daughter) arrived in Pachgatgoch in the middle of a February snowstorm, the villagers were amazed "that we should come there in such bad whether [*sic*], saying, we must certainly love them very much."[32] From Pachgatgoch, Mack lit out for Potatik, seeking a meeting with the captain of the village, a man known for his violent opposition to Christianity. By assuring him that he intended only to visit and not to preach,

Mack managed to persuade the captain to meet with him. The two men met briefly, but the captain told him he wanted nothing to do with Mack's religion, for "he had been so often deceived by the White People." Mack finally obtained permission to visit at greater length and dined with the captain. After the meal, Mack took up an axe and chopped wood for his host, to the amazement of those who had gathered to see this curious sight.[33] On a later trip to the Susquehanna in Pennsylvania, Mack observed, "Our walk and behavior preached amongst them and showed that we loved them."[34] Mack and other missionaries often worked side by side with their Indian hosts: chopping wood, building houses, planting fields, and working the harvest, occasionally even receiving wages from the Indians. The missionaries sometimes hunted and fished as well, but they generally left these tasks to the Indians.[35] Whites and Indians reacted very differently to this commitment. It did much to increase the suspicions of surrounding whites even as it allayed the fears of prospective Indian neophytes who generally experienced missionaries as a drain on local resources.

The missionaries were never able to be entirely self-sufficient and regularly relied on Bethlehem to supply the needs of the mission.[36] Bethlehem was well organized to meet the needs of its missionaries in the field. Indeed, the primary purpose of Bethlehem was to support the Brethren's ambitious missionary plans. The distinctive communal economy instituted by Spangenberg in 1744 was not an expression of utopian Christian communalism but simply an efficient means to an end. From a purely practical standpoint, the arrangement was well suited to supporting missionary work. Communal housing, in which peer groups lived together, cut down on initial construction costs and eased the burdens of providing for a growing community through an efficient division of labor. The specialization of labor (including child-rearing) made it possible for residents to go out on missionary tours with relatively little impact on the functioning of the community. For example, in 1747, fifty out of a total population of four hundred residents were abroad in the mission field.[37] And finally, the economy made it possible for missionaries to serve as couples, providing not only companionship but also an important connection with the Indian women.

The benefits of this system can be seen in the operation of the Shekomeko mission. The Bethlehem *Gemeine* (congregation) took a keen interest in its role as supporter of mission work, as the frequent references in the Bethlehem Diary make clear. Bethlehem served as an important spiritual resource to which missionaries could return for rest, renewal, and support. Christian Rauch did not remain a lone missionary but was soon joined by a minor fleet of coworkers, including Gottlob Büttner and Johann Martin Mack in 1742, and Joseph Shaw, Joachim Sensemann, Christian Friedrich Post, and Christoph Pyrlaeus the following year. In those two years, all five missionaries married and were joined in their labors by their wives.[38] Two of these marriages were particularly important to the mission: Mack married Jannetje Rauh, daughter of the farmer who had lodged Rauch and fluent speaker of Mohican. Post, a joiner from Prussia, was determined to marry an Indian woman, and in August 1743 he married the twenty-one-year-old Amanariochque, recently baptized and given the name Rachel.[39] At times, there were a dozen missionaries at Shekomeko.

This cadre of missionaries functioned effectively as a guild, with all the benefits of efficiency and camaraderie a guild provided. Most of the missionaries were in fact tradesmen, rather than university-educated ministers.[40] At Shekomeko, the physical and spiritual labor was divided among the missionaries, men working primarily with the Indian men and their wives working among the Indian women. In addition, the men built the mission house and other structures, fenced fields, worked in the fields, cut timber, butchered pigs, and even knit stockings. The women cooked for the mission, spun wool for Johannes Rauh, and taught school among the children and the Indian Sisters.[41] In part because missionary work was so highly regarded missionaries generally experienced a very high degree of job satisfaction, a sharp contrast to Anglo-Protestant missionaries, who often felt overworked, isolated, underappreciated, and undercompensated. Moravian missionaries often expressed in letters their feelings of love for their Indian hosts. This love was part of the job description, for the missionary was called on to be "a servant of Jesus" and "a lover of all men." However, their expressions of affection went far beyond duty.[42] For example, Gottlob Büttner recalled his first meeting with the residents of Shekomeko by exclaiming that he had experienced such an "Extraordinary Love the first moment I saw them that my heart continues set to them."[43] Martin Mack remarked in his journal during a trip from Bethlehem to Shekomeko that "my heart longed very much after Checomeco so that I could not sleep in the night being so near to it."[44] Johannes Hagen closed a letter to the Indian congregation with greetings to the leaders of the various villages: "Abraham I kiss you with a mouth smeared with Jesus' blood. Brother Jonathan, and Gideon, Lucas, Cornelius, O Cornelius, you know how Jesus sweat blood for us. . . . I love you and your people with all my heart."[45]

This love expressed by the Moravian missionaries for their Indian hosts was rooted partly in the conviction that the Holy Spirit must first have acted before they could be successful. Ironically, this belief meant that these remarkably active missionaries claimed little agency for themselves. They understood themselves to be witnesses of the Savior's work, watching the unfolding of sacred history. In the seeming simplicity of native society, the Brethren found echoes of the ancient Hebrew patriarchs and the primitive Christian church. It was thus no accident that the first three men to be baptized took the names Abraham, Isaac, and Jacob, and their wives were baptized as Sarah, Rebecca, and Rachel. Tschoop, baptized as Johannes, was a Mohican John the Baptist paving the way for the emergence of a new Christian community. Not only did the Moravians find ancient Hebrew patriarchs among the Mohicans, but they also found Protestant heroes, such as when the bishop August Spangenberg, upon first meeting Johannes, exclaimed that the heavily tattooed man with a lame leg "appeared with a very particular Look, just so as Luther is painted."[46] One can scarcely imagine John Sergeant finding the likeness of Calvin in an Indian visage!

The Moravian missionaries' affection for their Indian hosts did not go unnoticed. In fact, it was arguably the central factor in gaining an audience for the Moravian message among Indian communities. As the story of Tschoop and Shabash makes clear, the Mohicans of Shekomeko were savvy students of Christianity. They were quite capable of discerning differences between missionary programs. And when they agreed to accept the Moravian missionaries, it was because they believed the Moravians recognized their humanity. Again and again, the Mohicans of Shekomeko commented on the affective bonds between missionary and villager, something they had rarely experienced with whites. For example, Abraham expressed his affection for Christian Rauch, remarking, "There is not another such person in the world."[47] On his deathbed and suffering from smallpox, a convert named Jonas spoke to those gathered about him, recalling his first encounter with the Moravians, whom he found to be a "people who from the bottom of their Hearts acted faithfully towards the poor Indians."[48] When the sickly missionary Gottlob Büttner was ordered to appear before New York officials, Johannes's wife, Martha, wondered, "What are they doing with my brother. . . . Why are they bothering him so and keeping him from home when he is so sick?"[49] And when two other missionaries, Friedrich Post and David Zeisberger, were detained in 1745, Johannes and Abraham decided to prepare a wampum belt in appeal to the New York governor.[50]

Indians from other communities remarked as well on the distinctive Moravian manner. One Indian woman dictated a letter to be carried to the Moravians. Having encountered members of the Brethren in Philadelphia, the woman wrote how much she liked them. According to Mack, she "could not express with what great love she had been received by our People in Philadelphia but particularly that the women had kissed her. She said, it had made a great Impression on her Heart, for she had never before been treated in that manner by white People."[51] And when the leaders of the Stockbridge Indian community traveled with Abraham to see the Governor of New York about Mohican lands, they lodged with white members of the *Brüdergemeine*. When they returned, the Stockbridge leaders reported their astonishment "that they were so well accepted by white people and said they would never in their lifetimes forget it."[52]

Not surprisingly, it is more difficult to track resistance to the Moravians in the mission records. There were surely many who did not find the Moravian gospel appealing or who actively opposed the presence of the missionaries, but the references to such resistance in the mission records are fleeting—those who strongly opposed the missionary presence quickly moved out of the Moravian orbit. For example, Johannes's wife Martha remarked that her brother often warned her son (Johannes's stepson) not to follow the Moravians, "for if he did the Brethren would put him in a great ship and carry him over the great water." Missionary Büttner reported of Martha's son that he had "determined that as often as we went into the Church to sing, he would go outside and pipe and dance."[53]

Far more common than vehement opposition is evidence of dissatisfaction with mission leadership, which appears most often in the minutes of the weekly conferences held among native and white leaders to discuss mission affairs, though sometimes they made it into the official diaries as well. For instance, Cornelius, who was likely the village chief before Abraham, occasionally registered his objections to the decisions of the conferences.[54] During the weekly meeting, one woman from Potatik expressed her frustration, saying she was unhappy with the missionaries "because we had dealt harshly with her and she would say nothing more from her heart in her life."[55] There were surely far more who were critical of the Moravians—either actively or passively—whose views were not recorded by the missionaries. However, that the Moravians recorded as much criticism as they did suggests that there was not a systematic attempt to keep dissent out of the records.

Although Moravian missionaries generally found their work spiritually rewarding rather than trying and although they did not focus in the early years of the mission on the cultural transformation of Mohican society, they were not entirely free of prejudice. This tension, or ambivalence, is perhaps best exemplified by Zinzendorf's breathless delight in being welcomed into Shekomeko on his first visit and lodged in a "perfect palace of bark" even while deeming the Mohicans to be "a confessedly worthless tribe of Indians."[56] Zinzendorf, whom the historian Paul Wallace colorfully and aptly described as "a kind of Christian mastodon, trampling ruthlessly over all obstacles that stood between him and the Lamb of God," was a member of the nobility and his sentiments arguably reflect those of his class.[57] Most of the missionaries laboring in Shekomeko, by contrast, were of far humbler origin and generally paid very little attention—positive or negative—to native culture, focusing far more intently on Indian individuals. Over the years, Moravian missionaries became more interested in native culture, arguably signaling the emergence of starker cultural barriers and a growing identification with their Anglo-American neighbors.

These were the people who approached the Mohicans of Shekomeko with a proposal to teach them about the blood and wounds of a Savior who died to save Indian and white alike. They were compelled by an ethic of brotherly love and a desire to witness the outpouring of the grace of the Holy Spirit. Their mission to the Indians was to be a recapitulation of Christ's love for humanity. The mutual hostility between the Moravians and secular powers meant that there was a high degree of differentiation between believers and the broader culture. Those who became missionaries tended to be prepared for exclusive demands on their inner and outer lives, and they prided themselves on differentiating themselves from other Europeans in their relations with Indians. Rather than seeing their work as a sacrifice, they understood it as an occasion to experience the Savior's work in the world.

On the whole, compared to other colonial models of mission work, the Moravians were low-impact missionaries, more out of indifference toward rather than respect for native cultures. Initially, Moravians were quite successful in generating interest among the Mohicans precisely because the Moravian way contrasted so sharply with that of other Europeans. And because Moravian missionaries saw themselves as witnesses to the great work of the Holy Spirit and because they believed the Holy Spirit was as likely to shower grace on native individuals as European, they expressed a level of interest in individual Mohican lives. It is this interest, this sense of witnessing the unfolding of sacred history, that accounts for the incomparably rich body of mission records created by the Moravian missionaries. These records make possible an attempt at reconstructing the meanings behind the Christian practices of many Shekomekoans during the period of intense spiritual awakening from the baptism of Abraham, Isaac, and Jacob in February 1742 to the disbanding of the mission at Shekomeko in April 1746.

REVIVAL

Geographically speaking, Shekomeko was at the center of the Great Awakening—the revivals that swept the northern colonies in the early 1740s—and so the villagers were likely quite familiar with the range of evangelical wares being proffered by itinerants of all stripes.[58] The English revivalist George Whitefield had recently crisscrossed the American colonies on several preaching tours in 1739 and 1740.[59] In August 1742, David Brainerd preached for the first time to the Indians at the village of Pachgatgoch, near Kent, Connecticut, having resolved to devote his life to bringing the gospel to the heathen after being inspired by Whitefield and the revival he helped fuel at Yale. Just a few months later, Pachgatgoch Indians arrived in Shekomeko to hear Moravian preaching for the first time.[60] But the only spark of revival that caught among the Indians of Shekomeko and Pachgatgoch was that generated by the Moravians. By 1743, there were upwards of a hundred Indians from Shekomeko and neighboring communities gathered to listen to the Moravians' story of the son of God and brother of man who came to this world in love to save the halt and the lame. Ritually tortured and killed, this god-man offered up his body and blood to all who were hungry and thirsty and who had lost all hope.[61] The story resonated and soon, Shekomekoans offered testimonials to the power of Jesus' blood. It had washed their hearts clean, helped them recover from illness, conquered the powerful evil spirit of alcohol, and even guided them to the deer as they hunted. By the end of 1743, sixty-three of the roughly one hundred residents of Shekomeko had been baptized, and many of the unbaptized attended services as well.[62]

It should not be assumed that those Shekomekoans who chose baptism were choosing also to relinquish their native identity. In fact, the flourishing of Christian practice at Shekomeko seems to have been a revival movement by which members sought to counter many of the worst effects of colonialism and express traditional values in ways that made sense of a rapidly changing world. Many Shekomeko men turned to the blood of Jesus seeking a renewed connection with the spirit world. Having renewed this connection, they put that power to work in familiar ways: seeking protection from harm, including alcohol and ill health, and attainment of good, including success in hunting and reinforcement of a frayed social fabric.

The ever-increasing presence of Europeans posed many challenges to the Indians of the northeast, not least of them spiritual. The link to European markets altered the dynamics of trade. Overhunting and continued encroachment by European settlers left game in short supply, disrupting the relationship of the hunter with the spirits of the animals. New diseases wracked Indian bodies and refused to respond to traditional cures. The introduction of alcohol posed a host of physical, cultural, and spiritual questions. And while native populations declined precipitously, European numbers increased exponentially. Abraham's vision—in which he lay surrounded by naked and immobilized Indians in the path of onrushing water—is eloquent testimony to the psychic costs of colonialism and the profound sense of helplessness that pervaded the community at Shekomeko. It was in response to this feeling that Abraham first considered Christianity as a new source of spiritual power. Abraham was certainly not alone. David Brainerd recorded a similar vision experienced by Moses Tatemy, a Delaware man. In the vision, there seem'd to be an impassable Mountain before him. He was pressing towards Heaven as he thought, but his Way was hedg'd up with Thorns that he could not stir an Inch further. He thought if he could but make his Way thro' these Thorns and Briers, and clime up the first steep Pitch of the Mountain, that then there might be Hope for him, but no Way or Means could he find to accomplish this.[63]

In Tatemy's vision, like Abraham's, the once familiar natural environment had become forbidding, rendering the seer helpless. Many Shekomekoans expressed similar states of being spiritually mute or immobilized, though rarely were their experiences recorded in as much detail as those of Moses and Abraham. The records of the Moravian mission at Shekomeko reveal a community faced with a loss of spiritual mastery struggling to regain control.

While no Indian community could escape these challenges, they met them with a wide range of responses throughout the eighteenth and early nineteenth centuries. Delaware, Shawnee, and Seneca prophets inspired new religious movements that often blended rejection of European goods and the creation of a pan-Indian identity.[64] Adaptation of European-style agriculture and Christianity was another option, as exemplified by the Mohicans of Stockbridge. Somewhere in between was the path chosen by Abraham and Johannes and other Mohicans of Shekomeko, who found in the blood of Jesus a new source of spiritual power, or *manitou*, which could be deployed to address the problems brought with colonialism.

So what did Christianity become in the hands of the Mohicans? To answer this question, it is necessary to try to view Moravian Christianity through Mohican eyes. And in many respects, Christianity as practiced by the Moravians was not entirely unlike traditional Mohican religion. In their understanding of the source of spiritual power and the ritual means of accessing that power, Moravians and Mohicans were not so different. Moravian Christianity was arguably closer to Mohican religion than it was to New England Congregationalism.

Christian ritual as practiced by the Moravians provided enough points of similarity with the modes of Mohican practice that it did not seem wholly foreign to the Shekomekoans. At the same time, it was different enough that there was reason for Mohicans to enlist Christian ritual practice in the effort to cope with the new world emerging around them.[65] When familiar spirits no longer spoke as clearly as they once had, the Moravian Savior offered a powerful alternative. The forms of Moravian ritual practice opened the way for Mohicans to add Jesus to a pantheon of powerful native *manitou*. The new course of rituals introduced by the missionaries offered hope that some of the worst ravages of colonialism could be countered with spiritual means. Mohicans enlisted the power of Christ's blood to purposes that both were rooted in native culture and reflected the severe strains placed on Mohican individuals, families, and communities by more than a century of European colonial presence.

The Moravians practiced a course of ritual that sacralized every moment of a member's life, and in this way, the *Brüdergemeine*'s religion was akin to native traditions in which religion was not a set of doctrines to be affirmed but rather a way of life. It was how one lived. Moravians sought to erase the lines between sacred and secular, much as the early Protestant reformers had envisioned but which had been difficult to sustain.[66] *All* of life was to be lived for the Savior, not only worship in the church or appointed ceremonial days.

Moravian worship was Christocentric in the extreme. Members of the *Brüdergemeine*, of course, believed in the Christian God, yet they rarely spoke of God the Father. Rather, worship focused almost exclusively on Jesus, the Son of God. They attributed great powers to Jesus, yet it was his humanity that formed the focal point of Moravian spirituality. For Zinzendorf, the Incarnation was Christianity's most important idea, for it rendered Christ accessible to all humans. Christ on the cross was the perfect embodiment of the human condition—absolute human misery and redemption.[67] Jesus' life provided a precedent and thus guidance for the full range of human experience. Out of love for humanity, Jesus had become fully human, lived and suffered as humans do, and willingly sacrificed his life, and in so doing offered up his spiritual powers to those who would call on him. The Moravian *Heiland*, or Savior, was understood as very much an active agent in human lives, as evidenced in the 1741 decision to appoint Christ as the Chief Elder of the *Brüdergemeine*. By means of the lot, the Savior was thought to make his will known on issues large and small: he offered his consent or objection to baptisms, marriages, first communions, and innumerable other issues.[68] The Moravians' belief in the constant intervention of the Savior was derided by outsiders, as when Lutheran leader Henry Melchior Muhlenberg made it safely across the Susquehanna River in stormy weather and remarked that he "prayed the dear God to be pleased to punish us at some other time in accord with His will in order that the Moravians, who take a malicious joy in others' misfortune, might not put a perverted construction on it."[69]

Evil, embodied by Satan, also played an important role in Moravian theology. Zinzendorf believed that God's power had ultimately triumphed over Satan—the sacrifice of his son bought victory over Satan and thus human salvation. But God, or rather the Savior, suffered Satan to continue to tempt people in order to accomplish his higher ends.[70] In practice, Moravian missionaries often interpreted any mishaps or opposition as the workings of "the enemy." For example, while on a mission tour in Pennsylvania, Martin Mack described the opposition he faced: "We had been a good while before afraid that the Enemy would endeavour to do something from that Quarter, since he is so much against our living here among the Indians, and therefore he tries all Ways and means to get us away again, for we are a Thorn in his Eyes, this we can often see."[71] For Moravians, life was a battle between the spirits of good and evil, yet they were consoled by their confidence that the Savior stood ready to assist the faithful.

For Mohicans as for Moravians, the world was animated with vital forces that the Mohicans called *manitou*.[72] Every aspect of an individual's life was guided by the effort to maintain good relationships with *manitou*, who held the power to show or withhold their favor to individuals and communities. As described by Stockbridge sachem Hendrick Aupaumut, writing in the late eighteenth century, the Mohicans believed in "one Supreme Being" who dwells above, called "Waun-theet Mon-nit-toow" or "the Great, Good Spirit, the author of all things in heaven and on earth." They also believed in an evil spirit called "Mton-toow" who was the source of all mischief and evil in the world.[73] The affinity between Moravian and Mohican conceptions of the spiritual forces of good and evil can be seen in a report of preaching by Jonathan (Abraham's son), who warned his listeners against being led astray by the devil.[74]

Just as the Moravians focused their worship more on the Son of God rather than God himself, so Mohicans rarely entreated the Great Spirit directly, instead petitioning those *manitou* who were more readily accessible to humans. These lesser *manitou* were often understood as sacrificing themselves to ensure the well-being of humans in exchange for proper ritual devotion. Such relationships can be glimpsed in the myth recounted to Stockbridge missionary John Sergeant by a Housatonic Mohican. The man told Sergeant that his people understood the stars to be Indians dancing in heaven and that the seven stars of the Big Dipper were seven hunters who began their hunt for bear in the spring, continued it through the summer, and "by the Fall they have wounded it, and that the Blood turns the Leaves red; by the Winter they have kill'd it, and the Snow is made of its Fat; which, being melted by the Heat of the Summer, makes the Sap of Trees."[75] Such myths exercised great explanatory power, accounting for the world around them and, presumably, prescribing the proper terms of relations between humans and other spirits. Sergeant's interlocutor might well have gone on to explain that the celestial bear allowed himself to be killed by the hunters, and that the spirit bear's earthly relations would continue to sacrifice themselves so long as hunters paid the bear spirit proper respect in the form of offerings.[76]

Guidance also came from dreams and visions. An animal spirit might appear to an individual in a dream or vision, offering its powers in exchange for the individual's devotion.[77] These *manitou,* according to Moravian missionary Heckewelder, "look down particularly upon the Indians, to see whether they are in need of assistance, and are ready at their call to assist and protect them against danger." In order to solicit the help of these *manitou,* humans must acknowledge their help and offer sacrifices.[78] David Brainerd catalogued the devotion of the Delawares to "Beasts, Birds, Fishes, and even Reptiles," and especially to the powers that presided over the four corners of the earth. The spiritual power did not inhere in creatures, according to Brainerd's understanding, but was infused by the spirit, which communicated to the particular animal a great power to do good for certain people. When a spirit helped a human, it became sacred to that person, and the human was then obligated to the animal-spirit.[79]

Moravians and Mohicans believed in an all-powerful God who kept himself at some distance from his human subjects. They believed, too, that there were other spiritual powers more intimately involved in the lives of humans. Moravians attributed a range of powers to a single being, while Mohicans experienced the world as animated by a pantheon of spirits that could be enlisted to the aid of humans. For both Moravians and Mohicans, however, ritual was the means by which the power of the spirits could be tapped in support of human thriving.

Moravian liturgical life in the mid–eighteenth century was particularly rich, displaying none of the iconoclasm of other Protestant sects. This quality of their worship rendered Moravians suspect to their colonial neighbors, who accused them of being "papists," but it also constituted part of the appeal to their Indian hosts.[80] Their worship services engaged all of the senses and were especially rich in the application of music and imagery as key elements of devotional practice. The Moravian liturgical calendar marked the cycles of the day, week, and year with "singing hours," weekly Sabbath, and the annual cycle of events commemorating the birth, life, death, and resurrection of Christ.

The central distinguishing feature of Moravian worship—and what so animated their many detractors—was their emphasis on the blood and wounds of Christ rather than the more traditional Protestant symbolism of the cross. The cross, believed Zinzendorf, too easily became abstracted into symbol, allowing the meaning of Christ's death and resurrection to dissipate into theological speculation. The wounds and the blood that was shed from them, however, functioned to keep the humanity of Jesus fully before the believer. This distinctive theology is encapsulated in the Litany of the Wounds, first introduced in 1744 at the height of the period of spiritual devotion that came to be known as the "Sifting Time."[81] But even before this time, devotion to the blood and wounds of Christ formed the central component of Moravian worship. Missionary Büttner, for example, referred to the first communion service at Shekomeko in March 1743 as "the meal of the wounds."[82]

Litanies, standardized prayers used in church services, were a common feature of Moravian worship, and the Litany of the Wounds was among the most important. The Litany of the Wounds was introduced by Spangenberg in 1744 and was soon in use at Bethlehem and at mission sites.[83] The Litany of the Wounds is worth pausing over, as it was so central to Moravian worship during this time. The Litany began with a series of supplications, beginning "Hail! Lamb of God. Christ, Have mercy! Glory to the side wound!" After acknowledging the distinctive work of the members of the Trinity, believers called on the wounds to save them from a variety of ills. Next, participants appealed to particular aspects of Jesus' life to supply assistance: "May your painful first birth," for example, was answered: "*Make us love our humanness!*" "May your willing passion" was answered: "*Teach us tolerance.*" The particular wounds and sufferings of Christ on the cross were then recalled: "Pale lips, *Kiss us on the heart!*" and "Bloody foam from your back, *Wash our feet!*" And finally, the wounds were exalted and described in all their powers: "Wondrous wounds of Jesus, *Holy fissures, you make sinners holy!*" and "Powerful wounds of Jesus, *So moist and gory, bleed on my heart so that I may remain brave and like the wounds.*"[84]

The Litany of the Wounds was just one ritual by which worshippers were brought close to the Savior. Members of the *Brüdergemeine* experienced the blood and body of Christ vividly and viscerally as active forces in their lives flowing directly from ritual practice. They were baptized in the blood of Christ, they sang of swimming in the wounds of Christ, they desired to crawl into the side hole of Christ, they were revived and sustained by drinking Christ's blood, which "tasted very sweet and juicy."[85] The wounds offered sustenance, respite, and often, spiritual ecstasy, expressions of which can readily be found in hymns, litanies, letters and diaries. Nearly every aspect of life in Bethlehem was oriented by the blood and wounds theology.[86]

Human striving was useless, Moravians believed, without divine assistance accessed through ritual. Ritual action brought spiritual power. In Zinzendorf's words, "One needed not to contrive so much, how to avoid Sin and lead a godly Life, but also how to learn to know Jesus as one's Saviour," and the rest would follow.[87] It was this last point—the assertion of direct, almost magical power—that so disturbed other colonial Protestants. Recounting a meeting with Martin Mack, the Congregational minister (and disciple of Jonathan Edwards) Joseph Bellamy expressed his fears about Mack's theology. Bellamy was particularly disturbed that Mack "seemed to be more taken with the blood and wounds of Christ than with Christ himself" and that he "seemed to talk as if a law work was not so very needful, but all sinners have to do, is to believe."[88] Moravians eschewed doctrinal precision, much to the annoyance of those who tried to engage them in theological debates.[89] But what other colonial Protestants found so disturbing about the Moravians was precisely what appealed to the Shekomekoans and other Indians.

Mohicans found Moravian rituals of supplication to powerful spirits familiar, and they readily infused these new rituals with meanings drawn from their own experiences. And if Mohicans understood Moravian ritual within a native frame of reference, they also sought to deploy the powers of the ritual to purposes specific to their circumstances. Thus, while European-Moravian expressions of piety are best understood as partaking of a mystical Christian tradition whose goal was union with the divine, Mohicans invoked the blood and wounds of Christ as a means of securing spiritual intercession toward the sustenance—spiritual and physical—of self, family, and community.[90] Mohican devotions were far more concrete than those of European Moravians, reflecting a continuity with traditional ways of life, where food, health, and other necessities of human life were understood to be directly contingent on proper ritual practice.

A full account of Mohican ritual life on the eve of the mission era is impossible, but what can be gleaned from various sources suggests that Mohicans would have perceived Moravian religiosity as far less foreign than the other sorts of European Christian practice they had encountered. Mohicans, like other northeastern Indians, believed that in order to live a good life, humans had to align themselves with the spiritual powers of the universe. Proper remembrance and observance of ritual ensured a people's well-being by maintaining the balance between humans and the *manitou* that animated the world and made human existence possible. Individuals made offerings to the guardian or tutelary spirit who was responsive to his or her particular needs. A traveler might offer a bundle of tobacco to the river to bring swift passage. Communities gathered to offer a sacrifice in thanks for the harvest or a fruitful hunt. Relationships between humans and *manitou* were often conceived in kinship terms, and ritual practice served to reaffirm the terms of the relationship. *Manitou* offered their power in exchange for the gratitude and devotion of humans.[91] Ritual practice might be individual or communal and corresponded to one's life-stage, gender, and status.

With its emphasis on practice and efficacy, Indian religious practices were readily adaptable to innovation. Intermarriage, warfare, and village consolidation could introduce new spirits and new ceremonial practices. Mohican religion, like most native religions, was not dogmatic and contained no prohibitions against borrowing from other traditions. The test of religious "truth" was efficacy. The challenges posed by colonialism prompted an interest in new ritual practice. The slaughtered lamb of the Moravians operated on familiar terms. Recognizing as familiar the god of a different culture is one thing, but calling on that god for help suggests confidence that that god will respond to a supplicant's entreaties. This could not have happened simply by dint of Moravian affirmations of the truth of the Bible—Mohicans by this point had good reason to be deeply suspicious of the printed word. That Moravian missionaries emphasized the power of blood where other missionaries emphasized "the Word of God," which was naturally something external to the self, may well have influenced the decision to admit the Moravian missionaries where they had turned others away.

Moravians, compared to their Anglo-Protestant neighbors, placed relatively little emphasis on the authority of the Word, stressing instead the authority of direct experience. They expected that the Holy Spirit would work on the heart of the sinner, causing the generation of a "new heart," thereby empowering the individual to live well in this world. Most importantly, Moravians emphasized that confirmation of the truth of their message would be found internally, in the promptings of the heart. As Christian Rauch explained the Moravian message to an unnamed Presbyterian missionary: "One must first begin with telling them of the slaughtered Lamb and his wounds" and continue to focus on Christ's sacrifice "until they find their hearts, and then their own hearts will tell them, 'yes, that is true what I have heard.' "[92] Examples abound of the application of this principle at mission sites, as when Jonathan sought out Rauch for advice, the missionary counseled Jonathan to "search his own heart which would soon tell him."[93] The Moravians told the Indians that they could find all they needed to know in their own hearts. In this way, Moravian mission strategies affirmed rather than undermined the authority of Indian experience.[94]

The Moravian message to Indians was consistent. In essence, they said, "Here is a powerful spirit, see if it works for you." Although it is impossible to prove definitively, the first stage on the way to enlisting Jesus's blood must have been an experience that convinced Shekomekoans that Jesus could hear and would respond to Mohican pleas. In other words, Mohicans had to come to *know* that missionary descriptions of Jesus's powers were true. And in fact, those Indians who joined the mission community often spoke of coming to believe the Moravians' message because they felt it in their hearts to be true. For example, after hearing Mack preach, one Pachgatgoch resident remarked to another, "God has surely sent the Germans to us, that they should shew us the strait way to Him, and that is the Strait Way, *for the words which they speak, we feel.*"[95] Similarly, Johannes expressed the familiarity of the Moravian message in a letter to the Bethlehem congregation in which he proclaimed that he believed what the Brethren told him "because I find it also in my heart that it is so, that my heart is like a book, for when I hear something and I look into my heart, I always find it written there what my friends preach and say."[96] When Joshua explained the nature of faith in the Savior to a visiting Delaware man, he assured him that "even if I cannot read the bible, I can read it in my heart."[97] Moravian missionaries likely heard these sentiments as evidence of the work of the Holy Spirit on Indian hearts, but they might be read instead as evidence that Mohicans found affirmation of traditional ways of experiencing the spirit world within the Moravian message.

The Moravian missionaries encouraged their Indian hosts to test their message and that of other ministers against their own experience. And indeed, the Mohicans of Shekomeko embraced the invitation to judge ministers against the promptings of their heart. Not surprisingly, many of the instances of Indians evaluating and comparing Moravian and other missionaries reflect positively on the Moravians. But though these quotes must be read as participating in a larger interdenominational dialogue about the nature of true Christianity, this should not prevent us from seeing the strong thread of Indian agency that runs through these often comical exchanges.

On one occasion, a visiting New Light (revivalist) minister sought permission to preach at Pachgatgoch. Missionary Martin Mack and his Indian host (presumably the head man, Gideon) consented. The unnamed minister proceeded to preach, in Mack's words, "how angry God was with them, and how he would cast them in Hell, and that continued about 2 hours." When he finished, Mack reported, "One of the Indians asked me if that could be right? and another came and said, I don't like that!"[98] The following week another villager, newly empowered by the Moravian message, took the opportunity to upbraid an English neighbor who had come to witness the spectacle of the Moravian preacher. The villager railed at the Englishman for having lived so long near the Indians and never telling them about Jesus's blood. Mack was different, the man continued his assault, for he "don't babble and pray so much as ye, but he says what He has Experienced in his Heart," whereas the English "pra'd Babbled and read Books only and said always the Indians must also do so, but did not themselves what they said."[99] Abraham's son, Jonathan, drew similar conclusions from an encounter with neighboring whites: "These people do not have the Savior. . . . One says 'this is so' and another, 'this is so' and none knows what is right, they clearly know nothing of the Savior's business."[100] On another occasion, Gideon made a passionate appeal for religious freedom in responding to a local minister's suggestion that the village secure orthodox ministers and schoolteachers from New England:

> You never disturb your people in their way of living, let it be ever so sinful, and therefore do not disturb us, but suffer us to live as we are taught. There

are many churches in your towns, and various sects, each of whom calls the doctrine it professes, the only right way to heaven, and yet you grant them full liberty; therefore permit us likewise to believe what we please, though you should not think it right.[101]

The Moravian message of the power of the blood of Christ appealed in no small part because it enabled many Mohicans to articulate their complaints against colonists in the colonists' own terms. Their criticisms reveal the Mohicans to be far savvier in their understanding of New England sectarian divisions than their English neighbors suspected.

The Moravian missionaries interpreted Mohican statements about the promptings of their heart as evidence of the prior work of the Holy Spirit. But in fact, the Indians were effectively saying that they recognized in Jesus a powerful *manitou*. For example, an older man named Jephta was known to walk in the woods singing hymn verses to the wounds, a practice not unlike native traditions of offering thanks and praise to the spirits who assisted human life.[102] Another older man, Nicodemus, frequently shared his thoughts and dreams with the missionaries. Two images provided by Nicodemus suggest that Christ might have appeared to Shekomekoans as a spirit helper who offered protection to humans. Nicodemus compared his body to a canoe; his heart was the rudder and the "spirit of the little lamb" was the "man who sat in the canoe and held the rudder, steering the heart toward the wounds of Christ."[103] In a similar vein, he compared his heart to a wheel connected with other wheels, like a sawmill. "And when the stream from the bloody fountain doesn't flow, so the wheel is dead and stands still. But when the bloodstream flows, so everything comes into life."[104]

In native societies, dreams and visions were often a source of spiritual guidance, and they continued to be important to Mohicans, with Jesus appearing regularly in dreams and visions.[105] When Shekomeko resident Jonas lay dying he experienced a number of visions. In one of his final visions, the dying man "saw many strange Indians before him." In this state, he asked missionary Rauch "what those Strange Indians on Yonder Hill wanted?" He was concerned for them "and believed they would perhaps hear something of our Savior."[106] Nicodemus had a number of visions and dreams that he reported to the missionaries. One Christmas morning, Nicodemus experienced an elaborate vision in which a brilliant ray of light came down from the sky and illuminated a manger with the Christ-child, surrounded by all of the Brethren and Sisters from Bethlehem. He saw Joshua as well and queried the Savior, "Do you also have Joshua? Hold him tight." Two weeks later, Nicodemus described how in a dream he had seen Jesus sitting in a tree and that he had gone to kiss the Savior's side wound.[107] A comment by Büttner in his diary suggests that Jesus had indeed come to serve as a *manitou*. As Büttner reported, "Boas came to me and told me how it was in his Heart and that it was quite otherwise than before his Baptism and his Heart was in the Night time with our Saviour."[108] The Gnadenhütten diarist recounted a dream experienced by Joshua in which many Indians from a nearby town came to his house and listened as Joshua preached to them about Jesus' wounds. Several days later, a party of Indians indeed arrived.[109] Visions and dreams continued to be an important means of communication between the visible and the spiritual worlds.

Moravian missionaries appealed to the Mohicans of Shekomeko where Anglo-Protestant missionaries like John Sergeant of Stockbridge had failed. They gained an audience because they distinguished themselves from other Europeans, most particularly by showing respect for the Indians' humanity. Moravian forms of religiosity were familiar enough for some Mohicans to imagine that the Moravian Savior could be enlisted as a powerful *manitou* to help solve a host of problems that plagued Mohican society, most of them a result of European colonization. The next chapter explores in greater detail the ways that Mohican men practiced Christianity, and through that practice gave voice to their experiences as Mohicans living in conditions of considerable stress.

Chapter Six

Mohican Men and Jesus as *Manitou*

In recalling his first perception of Jesus' blood, Johannes recalled that before, he had been "as cold as ice and dead as a stone, but the blood of our blessed maker has melted me and made me burn." Now, he wrote, "I find it so that one can do everything, if only the savior is merciful."[1] Throughout the rest of his life, Johannes attempted to persuade others of the power of Jesus' blood, as when one woman visited and promised that she would turn to Jesus as soon as she had a good heart. Johannes retorted, "You want to walk on your head! How can you get a good heart, unless you come first to Jesus?"[2] While Johannes's words sound like standard evangelical fare, they contain hints of the distinctive forms of Indian Christianity that emerged at Shekomeko.

Johannes and other Mohicans found in Moravian Christianity a conception of spiritual efficacy that accorded with inherited forms of native religious practice. For both Mohicans and Moravians, ritual brought transformative power. Once Shekomekoans recognized Jesus as a spirit being with whom they could communicate, they began to harness the perceived power of the Savior to particular ends. The Mohicans of Shekomeko sought aid from the blood of Jesus as a form of *manitou,* and they used this power in the service of maintaining inherited ideals and values in the face of the dramatic disruptions of colonialism. Mohicans sought access to new sources of power, both physical and spiritual, that might be used to excise some of the most insidious effects of European invasion, such as disease, threats to traditional modes of subsistence, and alcohol-induced social disturbance. The Indian men who joined the emerging Christian community practiced Christianity in gendered ways. They sought help as individuals in their lives as hunters, warriors, and victims of disease. They also sought help in supporting and maintaining their public roles as leaders, as orators, and as diplomats.

A closer look at the emerging forms of Mohican-Christian practice suggests that appropriation of Christianity did not signal a rejection of native identity but instead was often an affirmation of traditional Mohican values. The embrace of Christianity often functioned as a means of restoring power and recapturing a past state free of the alcohol, disease, and decimated game supplies that increasingly plagued native societies. And where that failed, Mohicans often found comfort in Moravian theology, which lent redemptive meaning to suffering. As the stories of Abraham and Johannes suggest, affiliation with the Moravians could serve as a means of enhancing men's power at a time when the traditional indicators of status were increasingly difficult to maintain. In an earlier age, the men of Shekomeko might have expected to command the respect of their fellow villagers as warriors, diplomats, or skillful hunters. But the increasing presence of Europeans made all of these activities more problematic, arguably disrupting men's activities more drastically than those of women. But as Johannes's story of challenging his mother-in-law's religious authority demonstrates, the adoption of Christianity cannot simply be understood as a veneer that served as cover for the perpetuation of native traditions. Johannes's role as preacher in the emerging Christian community arguably confirmed his prior role as tribal speaker while also enabling him to cast off aspects of inherited tradition that he found problematic. As a preacher of the gospel, Johannes gained greater religious authority than might have been available to him otherwise. Although Mohicans were clearly empowered in profound ways by the Christian rituals introduced by the Moravians, the uses for which they harnessed that power testify to the social, physiological, and spiritual costs of colonialism.

In Christ's blood, many men of Shekomeko experienced the power to effect personal transformation when they themselves felt particularly powerless. These men also engaged Moravian communal forms and rituals in the effort to reinforce a social fabric under severe strain. Abraham, Johannes, and other men of Shekomeko practiced Christianity in ways that enabled them to fulfill, transform, and sometimes challenge the traditional male roles as hunter, warrior, and chief.

Moravian theology and ritual practice, with its focus on the blood and wounds of Christ, played a key role in facilitating the adaptation of

Christianity by Mohicans. By viewing Mohican expressions about the blood and wounds of Christ in the light of native traditions of warfare and, in particular, rituals of torture enacted against enemy captives, it is possible to see how Christianity both facilitated a continuity of tradition while also offering revised spiritual practices that spoke to the current circumstances of many Mohican men. Warfare had traditionally been a defining activity in the formation of male identity. As Daniel Richter has suggested in his monumental study of the Iroquois, the traditional calculus of warfare was fundamentally transformed by the arrival of the Europeans. Warfare became far deadlier, and the tradition of the mourning war by which tribal losses were avenged meant the constant escalation of intertribal warfare.[3] Since the seventeenth century, Mohican fortunes had declined significantly, and the costs of warfare were great. While many Mohicans, including those at Stockbridge, continued to fight in the wars of the eighteenth century, maintaining peace remained an ideal to be pursued. And Abraham, who at the request of the Stockbridge sachem in 1753 assumed the role of war captain, seems to have endeavored throughout his career to preserve peace and keep his people out of war.[4] Moravian pacifism, coupled with the Moravian understanding of communion, offered a way out of warfare while presenting a spiritually compelling substitute for some of the traditional benefits of war.

Abraham and possibly others had close personal experience with the rituals of war: when he was just four years old, Abraham's mother was captured and killed by Mohawks during Queen Anne's War. Although ritual torture of captives is most commonly associated with the Iroquois, there is considerable evidence that it was practiced by Mohican and Delaware peoples as well. In these wars, captives were seized from enemy tribes to appease the deaths of family members. The power, and the obligation, to quench the crying blood of lost relatives belonged to women, who could appease the death either by adopting the captive or by mandating torture and death, which was also understood as a sort of adoption. If the captive was to be killed— a more likely fate for men than women and children—the whole village gathered to participate in the ritualized torture of the victim, with women playing a central role.[5] As captives endured the villagers' torments, which often included applying burning brands, removing fingernails, or pouring hot liquids or sand over the victims, they strove to conceal their suffering, thereby displaying spiritual fortitude and power.[6]

Adriaen van der Donck, a Dutch observer, described similar practices among the Mohicans. Captives taken during war were uncertain of their lives, as their captors accepted no ransom. Their only hope of survival was if "they are given over to persons who have previously lost connections by blood in war." Those not so fortunate would be subjected to torture over the course of several days, during which the victim "continues to sing and dance until life is extinct, reproaching his tormentors, deriding their conduct, and extolling the bravery of his own nation."[7] Captors admired the stoic suffering of their captives, for it testified to their great spiritual power—a power that the captors could appropriate through ritual consumption after the victim expired. As Daniel Richter has suggested, discerning the spiritual meaning of these rituals with any certainty at such a great historical and cultural distance is impossible, yet the evidence suggests that the ritual torture and consumption of the victim involved a negotiation and transfer of spiritual power.[8]

The Moravian symbolism surrounding communion intersected in powerful ways with native rituals of warfare. Moravians placed especial emphasis on Christ's gruesome death, describing in great detail the spear wounds, the blood that ran like sweat, and his stoic death upon the cross. Further, the *Abendmahl*, or communion, was often referred to by the Moravians as "Streiter-Mahl" (fighters' meal). Consumption of Christ's flesh, as represented by the bread, brought transformative powers to the participant.[9] Communion, as practiced by Mohican Christians, did not require the risks of warfare but conveyed many of its benefits. Through the ministration of the missionaries, who functioned much like native shamans, the bread and wine became the body and blood of Christ. Here was a powerful warrior who willingly sacrificed his life for the benefit of those in need—and with none of the dangers of spiraling warfare.

Shekomekoans frequently spoke of hungering and thirsting after the body and blood of the Savior and its sustaining power. For example, Abraham told his fellow Christians just before a communion service that he had "long felt a hunger and thirst again after the Flesh and Blood of our Saviour." He often felt himself poor and weak and found that it was "this Meat and this Drink...gives me Life and Supports me." On the same occasion, Johannes declared his faith that the blood and the wine were truly Jesus's blood and flesh, perhaps attempting to allay fears that the absence of true flesh would hinder the efficacy of the sacrifice.[10] Philip reported that he "felt the savior's blood that made my heart warm.... I am hungry and thirsty. I would like to eat and drink."[11] On one occasion, Nicodemus entreated the missionaries to celebrate communion soon, because he "hungered for it so greatly and his heart was thirsty for the hot blood."[12] Mohicans' desire for this type of empowerment suggests that inherited rituals were no longer functioning.

Mohican men frequently turned to Christian ritual practice for assistance in the hunt, suggesting that the pathways of communication with the spirit world had been disrupted. Already in the seventeenth century, Mohicans informed one Dutch observer "before the arrival of the Christians, many more deer were killed than there now are, without any perceptible decrease of their numbers."[13] According to van der Donck, Mohicans hunted for bears, wolves, beavers, and deer, often traveling in large groups and remaining away from their home villages for one to two months. Van der Donck provided a rare glimpse into the religious practices associated with hunting when he remarked that on the hunt, hunters "usually cast a part of what is first taken into the fire, without using any ceremony on the occasion, then saying, 'stay thou devil, eat thou that.'"[14] This report suggests that the Mohicans likely shared in the worldview common among northeastern Indian peoples, in which successful hunting depended on maintaining proper relationships with the spirit world. Any number of different spiritual negotiations might go into producing a successful hunt: proper sacrifices to the "keeper of the game," observance of a fast before the hunt in order to induce dreams by which the hunter might be "informed of the haunts of the game, and of the best method of appeasing the wrath of the bad spirits," the use of *beson* (medicine), and, finally, the observance of certain taboos in killing and processing the game in order not to offend the animal's spirit master.[15] Presumably, the men of Shekomeko continued to draw on similar hunting practices during the mission era, although the mission records provide very little evidence on ethnographic matters. A single reference dating to 1750 suggests that the sweat lodge was still being used as a place to prepare for the hunt.[16] Whatever the extent of continuity with inherited hunting traditions, they were often practiced together with new Christian adaptations.

Jesus was invoked as a helper spirit who could assist hunters in their pursuit or could find other means of providing if he saw fit. Isaac, one of the first Shekomekoans to be baptized, recounted his experience hunting to the missionaries. He reported that he had been out to visit a friend and looked down at his feet, then entreated Jesus, "You, beloved savior! I have no shoes and no coat. You can surely see that I need a pair of shoes." Then, according to the missionary, Isaac turned and continued on his way. When he had nearly reached his destination, a deer jumped across his path. Isaac took aim and killed the animal. And so Isaac had food for his family and a deerskin for new footwear.[17] Jonathan recounted to the missionaries that now that his heart was with the Savior and his wounds, the Savior guided him to the deer. "O Lamb, give me your blood in my heart," entreated Jonathan. In speaking of Jesus's aid in the hunt, Jonathan explained that Jesus not only guided him to the deer, he also enabled him to be satisfied even when he was unsuccessful, perhaps with the reassurance that the Savior could provide through other means. Jonathan envisioned the Savior as the "keeper of the game," believing that "the woods and all the animals therein were His." When asked by a white neighbor whether it was Satan who guided the non-Christians to the deer, Jonathan answered no, that the

Creator looked out for all, suggesting that Mohican Christians refused to make the distinctions between converted and unconverted that Europeans encouraged.[18] Others found that the Savior not only led them to the game but also helped them to avoid dangers along the way. When Nathanael was out bear hunting and escaped some sort of danger, he attributed his safety to the Savior's intervention.[19]

Certainly not all Indians believed that the Christian God assisted in the hunt, and some even attributed failure in the hunt to the presence of missionaries.[20] But those who did adapt Christian ritual to hunting practices accomplished a dual purpose; they maintained a continuity of practice by entreating a powerful spirit for assistance in the hunt, but they also broke from tradition by reinterpreting failure in the hunt. Traditionally, a failed hunt might be attributed to a ritual lapse, and thus the hunter would have been to blame. In the newly Christianized hunting rituals, a hunter could console himself that the powerful spirit Jesus intended to provide for his followers in other ways. Changes in environment necessitated spiritual changes, and some found consolation in a Savior that could guide hunters to the deer or provide through other means.

Some Shekomeko men had come to call on the Savior's blood either to supplement or supplant hunting *beson*. Many also turned to the Savior to carry out another important function of *beson:* preservation and protection. Although little is known specifically about Mohican rituals, common among many Northeastern Indian peoples were ritual supplications to the spirit world, in Gregory Dowd's words, "to give them spiritual armor, foretell their success or failure, disclose the location of the enemy and his numbers, and subdue this enemy, body and soul."[21] Individual warriors often carried with them *beson* to ensure protection on their expedition. The early Moravian sources reveal little about the practices of those Indians who continued to enlist for service in colonial wars (contrary to the pacifist commitment of the Moravians), but the persistent language of preservation and protection would suggest that men in particular felt under siege and in need of spiritual protection from possible dangers. Writing of his experience among the Delaware, Moravian missionary John Heckewelder described the practice of war songs by which men entreated the spirits for protection for the sake of their families.[22] While war never encroached physically into Shekomeko, the threats to the village's existence were no less real, and many Mohican men turned to the blood of Christ seeking preservation and protection.

The desire for preservation appears particularly clearly in the writings of Shekomeko residents. One hymn attributed to the missionary Pyrlaeus and Joshua reads, "Hide us in your side, / which is open to our souls. / Take away what makes harm, / and bring us to safety, O Jesus! / Let us see that / you are crucified / and how you have spilled / your dear blood."[23]

These same themes emerge in the letters sent by Mohicans to their friends and family who lived in other villages.[24] Joshua wrote to the missionaries, informing them that "I thirst every Day after the spilled Blood, because I feel that I am poor in my Heart.... I have found a Place where I can rest with my heart, and where Satan can't touch me, that is in Jesu's Blood." Jonas wrote from Bethlehem to his friends in Shekomeko, sending a special greeting to Jonathan: "I will also tell you something: when one abides by the Wounds, one can then allways see well and is afraid of nothing, but remaineth happy." He also assured his mother she should not worry about him, for "I am in the wounds, where I am kept safe." Zacheus reported that in Bethlehem "I am as if I was in a Fort to which the ennemy can't come." Joseph echoed Zachaeus's sentiments, "I feel myself so secured as if I was in a Castle with Walls & Towers... the Ennemy can't come at me." Michael greeted Isaac and Rebecca, informing them he was "right contented and it is as if I was so inclosed that no wind which could do me any hurt could come at me."[25]

The men of Shekomeko sometimes found courage in addition to protection in the wounds, as Nicodemus wrote in a note to his wife, letting her know he was happy in Gnadenhütten: "The dear Saviour hath taken him as a miserable man out of Satans Hands and brought him to his Wounds and therefore he felt boldness."[26] With their lands, their livelihood and even their lives under attack, the blood of Christ and the community of the Brethren offered to some security and protection. The pervasiveness of the language of protection and shelter is a stark indicator of the extent to which the Mohicans were a people under siege. One of the most potent threats to native peoples everywhere was disease brought by Europeans.

Mohican villages had been decimated in successive waves of epidemics since the first arrival of the Europeans. At the turn of the eighteenth century, no medical practitioners, European or Indian, had an effective treatment for smallpox. There was no cure—only acquired immunity could prevent infection. Lack of immunity combined with the conditions of relative poverty inherent to colonization were devastating to Indian communities. Smallpox presented an unwinnable challenge to native healers. Traditional healing practices relied heavily on purgative measures that tended only to worsen the patient's condition and speed up the transmission of the deadly virus.[27]

According to van der Donck, Mohicans believed that all that happened on earth was determined by the devil, which presumably was van der Donck's rendering of the concept of *manitou*. They believed in a chief god who dwelled in the sky but who did not concern himself with the everyday affairs of humans. All accidents, illnesses, or diseases, however, they believed were sent by "the devil." If they suffered some sort of internal malady, they would say "the devil is in me" and attempt to palliate the spirit by casting something in the fire as a sacrificial offering.[28] In northeastern Indian societies, disease was typically understood as the result of either a failure of ritual or the active malevolent intervention of spirits called to action by another human, often through the interference of a "juggler" or "paw-waw," as colonists frequently called them.[29]

In a belief system that attributed illness to the neglect of proper ritual observance or the working of *beson*, the outbreak of an epidemic created spiritual and psychological stress. In some instances, Mohican men turned to the blood of Christ seeking a cure, as suggested in a hymn: "strong wounds. / Whoever drinks the sap / that flowed out of your body is / the one who becomes healthy."[30] Some attributed their recovery of health to ritual contact with the blood and wounds. For example, Joseph explained to his parents that before his baptism, he had "been sick a great while" but was now "quite well in Body and Soul." He counted his illness a blessing, for it was then that he felt "the need I had of our Savior and his Blood." Joseph resolved to "give my self wholly up to him" and was rewarded by the Savior who had had "mercy on me ... and given me rest and ease in my Heart."[31] An unbaptized Pachgatgoch Indian had told Gideon, chief of the village, that he had "been lately sick, and had saw himself in a very lost Condition, and determined within himself to turn to God, who had died for Mankind and Now he was well."[32] In an especially revealing account, Nathanael from Shekomeko reported on a conversation he had had with a visiting Delaware man who had been set against the Moravians until his child became sick. The man became very anxious that the child would die without being baptized and thus would not have life after death. As he was wandering in the woods and trying to decide what to do, the man cried out to God to protect his child. He promised God that if he healed his child, he would give his heart to the Savior and would immediately go to the Brethren at Gnadenhütten. When he returned to his house, he found his child restored to health, and so the man set off for Gnadenhütten.[33] In the eyes of some Mohicans, the Moravian Savior had been tested as a healer and proved his power.

When illness proved incurable, some Shekomekoans found comfort in aspects of Moravian theology that redefined the meaning of illness. Moravians spoke of death as "going home to the Savior," where the believer was united in eternal union with Christ the bridegroom. Zinzendorf even went so far as to suggest that illness was a gift from the Savior that made it easier for the believer to depart this life and return to the Savior.[34] As in hunting, Moravian theology offered a different explanation for failure: illness was no longer the result of a failure of ritual but rather a mark of special love conveyed upon the believer by the Savior. For example, when Daniel was sick, he found comfort that the Savior had a larger purpose in allowing him to be sick.[35] And when illness proved fatal, Shekomeko Christians were comforted that the Savior had a comfortable place prepared for the dead. When an infant died in Shekomeko, Abraham oversaw the burial, praying "that the Savior might graciously receive this child to himself" and exhorting those present "to receive the Saviour who was come into the world to save them by his Blood."[36]

New illnesses and alcohol posed new challenges to Mohican spiritual resources. Traditional practice could do little against smallpox, and there was little precedent for dealing with alcohol, so some Shekomekoans turned to the powerful spirit introduced by the Moravian missionaries. Moravian missionaries were not able to cure smallpox or the other devastating new diseases Europeans introduced, but they did offer a theology that affirmed the redemptive power of suffering. Because Christ himself experienced sickness and death, he sanctified these universal human experiences. The believer could take comfort by meditating on Christ's sufferings. The Litany of the Wounds, and the blood and wounds theology more generally, offered up a means of making sense of the great suffering that many Mohicans were enduring.[37]

Beyond a cure for illness or at least solace in suffering, Mohicans often found in Moravian ritual the power to counteract the *beson*, or medicine, of alcohol. Like other forms of *beson*, alcohol could be deployed for good or ill. Alcohol was valued for its ability to induce visionary states, and because of its power, it was often employed in ceremonies.[38] Alcohol was commonly used as an offering or sacrifice, made sometimes to appease the spirits of the dead or the spirits that caused harm in the form of a headache or toothache. In the former case, a group would gather around the grave of the deceased and rum would be poured on the grave while the leader of the ceremony, commonly an old man, addressed the soul of the deceased. The rest of the rum was then consumed by the guests.[39]

Despite its occasional ceremonial use, the social costs of alcohol were clear, and some villagers believed that in order to restore Mohican society to its proper order, the use of alcohol would have to be more strictly controlled. Alcohol literally upset the balance between self and surroundings and continued to disrupt village life, claiming the lives of at least two Shekomekoans and causing innumerable social conflicts and physical injuries.[40] Abraham's first impetus to visit the Stockbridge mission had come after a bout of drinking. In his vision, Abraham saw drunken Indians helplessly immobilized by alcohol and unable to escape the onrushing water. Alcohol induced a feeling of helplessness and a fear of natural forces, once familiar but now grown ominous. Alone, Abraham had not been able to fight the power of rum, and his visits to Stockbridge had suggested that that community had yet to find a satisfactory solution either.[41]

Although Abraham did not elaborate on his understanding of alcohol's power, later Moravian sources suggest that alcohol was seen as a powerful *beson* bewitched by whites. One Delaware man even speculated that alcohol was the devil's blood. A conversation between missionary Heckewelder and another Delaware man elaborated this belief. As they walked together, the man, having consumed a small amount of alcohol, mistook a sapling for a snake. He feared what he might do if he drank more: what if he were to confuse a friend for a bear and try to kill him? The man reasoned that either the alcohol itself was *beson* or white sorcerers bewitched it as a means of deceiving those who drank it. Because whites seemed not to be affected so adversely by the drink, the man concluded that white conjurers had bewitched the alcohol in order to destroy Indians.[42] If indeed alcohol was understood as exercising its power because it was the devil's blood, perhaps the blood of the Savior could be the antidote. And this would appear to be just how Abraham understood matters.

On one occasion, Abraham was confronted by the wife of Philip Livingston, one-time New York commissioner of Indian affairs, who told him the Moravians were not true ministers because they had not been appointed by the government. Abraham responded passionately:

> Don't you see there my drunken friends there lying before your doors? Why don't you send ministers to them? If you have any true ones that can do any thing for them, so send them to them and let them make them otherwise. Look, 4 years ago I myself lay in that very place in the same condition as they, and no one ever told me, nor how I could be delivered from that unhappy condition; 'till the Brethren came and told us of the Savior and his Blood. He has delivered me, and made me another man. If now your ministers can do any thing, O see that my poor friends be made otherwise, that they may not perish in their misery. If our ministers are right ministers or not I can give you no other proof, than this, They have told us that the Blood of Jesus would help us, when we believed on it, out of all our Sins, and that we have experienced to be true: It has delivered me and many of my Friends.[43]

The blood of the Savior proved to be a powerful antidote to the *beson* of alcohol. New problems necessitated new sources of spiritual power to combat them.

For Abraham and others, it was the blood and wounds of the suffering Jesus that provided a measure of defense against alcohol's evils. Like Abraham, Johannes believed that it was the blood and wounds of Christ that enabled him to give up alcohol. Rauch assured Johannes that if he had blood in his heart, his drunkenness would fall away.[44] Johannes apparently took the message to heart, and wrote in a letter to Zinzendorf, "Now

I believe that he can help me with his blood."[45] For these two men at least, the blood of the Savior proved an effective remedy: so long as they continued their Christian practice, they were able to abstain. Abraham attributed one relapse to the departure of the missionaries from Shekomeko.[46] The abstinence of Moravian Indians was enough to impress colonists: when Abraham, Isaac, and Jacob visited Philadelphia, they met with William Penn's agent, James Logan, who deliberately tested the Indian men's ability to abstain by offering them all a drink. While missionaries Büttner and Rauch joined the trader in a glass of wine, "the others would taste nothing but water."[47] Again and again, Mohican neophytes emphasized the power of Christ's blood to enable the believer to accomplish seemingly impossible feats.

Delaware Indians who later joined the mission community at Gnadenhütten found a similar liberation from alcohol through their alliance with the Moravians. When non-Christian Delawares suggested that the Moravians intended to enslave their Christian converts, the Moravian Delawares responded that alcohol was the real instrument of slavery:

> when the traders come and offer their rum to you, you suffer yourselves to be immediately deceived; you get drunk, and then they can do with you what they please, therefore your bad hearts cannot defend you against them, but make you an easy prey to their cunning. But when they come to us, we refuse their rum and thus they cannot treat us as they please; our hearts, which believe in Jesus, resist their temptations and defend us against them.[48]

Ironically, then, Mohicans and Delawares came to believe that the Moravian missionaries offered a mode of defense against some of the worst ravages introduced by white society.

In addition to spiritual responses to the problem of alcohol, the community at Shekomeko instituted civic measures as well. Through the establishment of new social structures, the missionaries and villagers together provided moral support to those suffering while putting into place a policing mechanism that effectively established taboos against drinking. Johannes Hagen recorded in his diary the actions taken against alcohol consumption: "If any one resident here dared to get Drunk, in order to perplex & trouble them thereby, then the 4 Brn whom they had appointed for it, viz. David, Jonas, Boas & Josua, sho'd imediatly Bind them, & if they then wo'd not be quiet but endeavour to do Mischief, they sho'd Whip them, that no one may for the future dare to do so." The committee had been established soon after Isaac and Rebecca's house had burned down. Rebecca attributed the loss of all of her possessions in the fire to punishment for her continued trade in rum.[49] Even before the institution of the committee, a similar practice was in place. Gottlob Büttner recorded one instance in which a young man in Jacob's house was drunk and making an "astonishing racket." Boaz and Joachim (Abraham's son) managed to bind the man in order to prevent harm to himself or others. Apparently this was not the first time the young man had been restrained. As he begged to be released, Joachim addressed the man: "I have warned you not to drink and then I let you go. But now you have bound yourself, so it will be." He continued all night, threatening to kill anyone who came near him, but by the next morning, Büttner reported that the man had quieted down and that he had hopes "he could be won to the Lamb."[50] The measures were certainly harsh, but the fact that the policing remained in the hands of the villagers strongly suggests that it was not only the missionaries who desired such policies. Men like Abraham and Johannes sought personal empowerment and preservation through Moravian ritual. And as leaders in the Shekomeko community, they also sought new resources to mend a frayed social fabric. The Moravians' unique social arrangements served to support rather than undermine native patterns of leadership and community.

COMMUNITY LIFE

The events of Moravian leader Ludwig von Zinzendorf's visit to Shekomeko in August 1742 go a long way in explaining how and why the Moravian missionaries sanctioned native leadership and encouraged the newly baptized to begin preaching. It was a busy few days. Zinzendorf and Rauch conferred and drew up a list of objectives for the mission, which included, among other things: gathering the Mohicans into a congregation, baptizing twelve Indians (presumably to serve as disciples to their people), and appointing native assistants for the "infant congregation." Another was "to confer with Abraham, Isaac, Jacob and John [Johannes] on our method of laboring among the heathen, and on its object, which is not the indiscriminate acquisition of large numbers but the admission into the congregation of souls that have been renewed to life in Christ." After having met in conference with the "firstlings," Zinzendorf reported with some surprise that he found the four men "in all respects incomparable Indians, and men of God. When met in conference on affairs of the mission, they deliberated in a manner which astonished us."[51] Following the conference, the four Shekomeko men were ordained into service: Abraham as elder, Johannes as teacher, Isaac as sacristan, and Jacob as exhorter.[52]

In appointing Abraham as elder, the Moravians were effectively ordaining him as the primary spiritual leader of the community. This office of elder was important for several reasons. It lent additional sanction to Abraham's role as leader of the village, a role he had likely inherited together with the land from his grandmother, Mammanochqua; further, it symbolized the Moravian commitment to building on preexisting structures; and finally, it offered new categories and duties of leadership that could provide a means of redefining community and relationships within that community to meet changing circumstances. With his family and his community decimated by the ravages of disease and war and his land in jeopardy, Abraham would have found it difficult to perform the functions needed to secure the continued support of villagers.[53]

When Mohican men called on the blood of Jesus in the hunt or entreated the Christian Savior for renewed health, they sought individual empowerment. But with the arrival of the Moravian missionaries also came new modes of communal worship and community regulation. The men of Shekomeko adapted Moravian forms of Christian practice—lovefeasts; annual festivals commemorating Jesus' life, death, and resurrection; and preaching—blending them with native traditions in hopes of reinforcing a frayed social fabric and enhancing their position within the community.

During the heady years of 1742–46, Shekomekoans adapted many Moravian forms and infused them with new meanings rooted in Mohican tradition and the circumstances of the Shekomeko community. Through various public functions, including feasts, preaching, and diplomacy, Mohican men blended Moravian and Indian elements in the effort to revive and create community. Christian ritual in some respects carried on indigenous traditions, yet they were not simply a cover for the continuation of native ways. Rather, Christian public rituals, as presented by the Moravians, were perceived by the people of Shekomeko as an apt expression of Mohican civic values. In holding lovefeasts and Easter services and preaching to visitors, Shekomekoans participated in the work of indigenizing and inculturating Christianity.

The lovefeast, for example, became an important ritual feast in Shekomeko whereby leading men of the village confirmed their credentials for leadership by demonstrating their ability to provide for the community. Easter services were an opportunity to channel the grief of mourners and to imagine a better world beyond the present. On these occasions, Shekomeko men, especially Johannes and Abraham, regularly preached to the gathered community, testifying to the powers of Jesus' blood. Mohican preaching was at once new in that it promoted a new source of spiritual power but also old in that it carried on native traditions of public oratory.

Indian and white Moravians shared in a rich course of communal rituals at Shekomeko. In addition to the elaborate baptismal celebration such as that described in the opening narrative of Tschoop and Shabash, the Moravians practiced a host of communal rituals that sacralized the passing of time and the practice of community. It is impossible to know for sure to what extent these new ceremonies took place alongside traditional ceremonies and to what extent Christian and traditional practices were considered mutually exclusive, either by the missionaries or the Indians.[54] The Mohicans of Shekomeko seem to have found in Moravian ritual an apt vehicle for the perpetuation of Mohican culture. Lovefeasts, Easter celebrations, and public preaching all became expressions of Moravian piety and Mohican ideals of community.

On Christmas Day 1742, less than a year after the first baptisms of Shekomekoans, Abraham and Moses, the leader of nearby village of Wechquadnach decided to host a lovefeast. Nearly one hundred Indians—both baptized and unbaptized—had gathered to join in the feast, which likely consisted of a number of deer recently brought by a hunting party. Missionary Büttner preached a sermon from Luke 1, recounting the story of John the Baptist. After the meal, Johannes, as the Mohican John the Baptist, testified to the power of Jesus' blood that he had experienced in the previous year.[55] Among those at the meal were a number of Indians who had been baptized just two weeks earlier. Gadrasachseth, "the Old Captain," had taken the name Cornelius, evoking the biblical Cornelius, the proto-Christian and beneficent Caesarean leader.[56] Callabash, an older Wampano man, became Nicodemus, his baptismal name perhaps recognizing his status as a village elder.[57] As an elder in the Christian community, Nicodemus served as an important spiritual counselor, mediator, and exhorter. Aguttamack became Moses, symbolic of missionary hopes that he would lead his people to the freedom of the Christian gospel.[58] From early on, mission residents directed communal ritual life, as when Johannes announced his intention to hold a lovefeast for his clan, perhaps to celebrate the recent baptisms. About thirty villagers gathered for the meal, at which Johannes offered a prayer before distributing the food.[59]

From the missionaries' perspective, these lovefeasts were celebrations of God's love, and native preachers were testifying under the inspiration of the Holy Spirit. From the Indians' viewpoint, the lovefeast likely did not look very different from traditional feasts held on the occasion of a hunter's successful return. They presented a chance for community leaders to demonstrate their leadership qualifications by directing the redistribution of food within the community. In his preaching, Johannes offered public recognition for the favor the *manitou* Jesus had shown him, perhaps elaborating on how it had helped him conquer the spirit of alcohol.

For the Moravians, the lovefeast was one of many "rituals of *Gemeinschaft*," or community, as historian Craig Atwood has called them. Like many sectarian Protestants, the Moravians sought to create a community fully in accord with gospel precepts. As restorationists longing for the purity of the primitive church, Moravians grounded their ritual life on New Testament precedent. In addition to baptism and communion, the Moravians cele-brated *agape* (lovefeasts), *pacem* (the kiss of peace), and *pedilavium* (foot-washing).[60] Lovefeasts were a simple meal, consisting most commonly of coffee and bread, given liturgical form and significance as the ritual com-memoration of divine love. The food was no different from other meals, but conversation was focused on spiritual matters. In Bethlehem, lovefeasts were regularly held on Saturdays, commemorating Christ's rest in the grave and the Sabbath. Lovefeasts might also be held to commemorate im-portant church or choir festivals or to celebrate the completion of a com-munal work project—after a Sisters' choir had finished their spinning or the Single Brothers' choir finished reaping the harvest.[61] Private lovefeasts could be sponsored by an individual brother or sister in commemoration of an important anniversary or event. The meaning of lovefeasts was often heightened by the use of hymns and visual art, such as representations of Christ on the cross. Generally speaking, then, lovefeasts functioned to consecrate the work of everyday life to the Savior. This sacralizing of work is vividly conveyed in a 1746 letter from Bishop Spangenberg to Zinzen-dorf in which he reported, "They [the Brethren] mix the Savior and His blood into their harrowing, mowing, washing, spinning, in short into everything."[62]

The embrace of a rich liturgical practice that ordered time and sanctified life and labor distinguished the Moravians from their Reformed Protestant brethren. It also rendered the Moravians less foreign to their native hosts, who also believed that all aspects of life involved communication with the spirit world. At root, the Moravian lovefeast was not unlike traditional com-munal feasts common among Mohicans. Writing in the mid–seventeenth century, van der Donck noted that feasts were held among the Mohicans for any number of reasons, including "peace, war, alliances, treaties, and devo-tions, or to counsel the devil on some approaching event, or in relation to the fruitfulness of the seasons, or to celebrate some successful occurrence by frolicking and dancing, as at the conclusion of a peace, or to make war with some neighbouring people."[63] Evidence for Mohican ceremonial life on the eve of the missionary era is scant, but a deer sacrifice ritual observed by Stockbridge missionary John Sergeant in 1734 at Konkapot's village sug-gests that native traditions might have blended easily with the forms of the Moravian lovefeast. The feast witnessed by Sergeant was presided over by an old man who bent over the skin of a deer and called out thanks to the provider, "O great God pity us, grant us Food to eat, afford us good and comfortable Sleep, preserve us from being devoured by the Fowls that fly in the Air. This Deer is given in Token that we acknowledge thee the Giver of all Things." After the invocation, the officiant "halloo'd pretty loud, that God might hear and take Notice of what they were doing," and then the meat was boiled and distributed to all present, reserving an extra portion for a widow.[64]

Timothy Woodbridge witnessed a divining ceremony in 1735 resembling what van der Donck described as "driving the devil." At such ceremonies, wrote van der Donck, "they assemble in the afternoon towards evening, and then some of them do, most singularly indeed, endeavour to enchant and charm the devil and carry on witchcraft." After a time, "the devil, as they say, appears to them in the form of a beast," and, depending on the spirit's form, the participants may have the answer to their query.[65] The purpose of the ceremony observed by Woodbridge in 1735 was to determine the identity of those who had "poisoned" two members of the community, presumably by interceding with powerful spirits. An older man presided over the ceremony, leading the invocation, chanting, and dancing, which lasted through much of the night.[66] Communal rituals were means of communicating with the spirit world in order to offer thanks, to divine important knowledge, or to stave off harm.[67]

Moravian and Mohican ceremonies were an occasion to gather the whole community to offer thanks to the spirit forces for their care or entreat them for continued assistance. In both, an elder, esteemed member of the community presided over the services, likely procuring food, directing its preparation and distribution to the gathered members. In the Mohican deer sacrifice ritual as in the lovefeast, the participants expressed their thanks to the spirits for providing for the needs of the community. In the ceremony that van der Donck identified as "driving the devil," the goal was not to give thanks for the protection of *manitou* but to persuade *manitou* to reveal information that would contribute to the health of the community.[68] Since 1741, the Moravian community looked to Jesus as chief elder of the Church and often sought his advice through use of the lot, a practice that must have appeared to their Indian hosts as a form of divination.

Lovefeasts were regular events at Shekomeko, held by the Indian residents for any number of reasons, public and private. The smaller, private lovefeasts generally celebrated a special occasion such as the birth of a child, the anniversary of a baptism, the return of a family member, or a successful hunt.[69] Indian converts often sponsored lovefeasts for the white Moravians, as when Thomas gave a lovefeast in February 1745 "to ye Elders of the Bethlehem Congregation and the Heathen Messenger [missionary] which had been in Chekomecko." The feast consisted of "Mush and Indian Cakes."[70] Later that year, Nathanael hosted a lovefeast for the missionary Christian Rauch upon his departure from Shekomeko.[71]

Larger lovefeasts served as occasions to confirm the status of the leading men, such as Abraham, Johannes, and Moses. According to anthropologist Kathleen Bragdon, men of high standing in Algonquian communities were to "act with dignity on all occasions, to show generosity and fairness, to seek consensus, and to act with wisdom and knowledge."[72] Their rank was demonstrated by their ability to provide for the community. Native leaders of Shekomeko and other surrounding communities sponsored lovefeasts, sending out a hunting party for provisions.[73] The Christmas lovefeast seems to have quickly become an important ritual and social occasion, drawing hunters back from their winter hunting lodges.[74] For the Christmas celebration of 1743, several Shekomeko men announced that they wanted to hold a lovefeast for Shekomeko residents and the many visitors they were expecting "if the Savior would give them some deer."[75] Shekomeko residents took pride in being able to contribute to the feasts, as when Joshua and his wife, Bathsheba, announced that they had contributed to the community a pair of baskets specifically intended for use at lovefeasts.[76] Lovefeasts, like traditional feasts, were an opportunity for leaders to show their good standing with the spiritual world in procuring food for the feast and an important mechanism of social welfare by providing for the needy in the community.

In function, then, Moravian lovefeasts were similar to Mohican ceremonial feasts. Both functioned on several levels. As practiced at Shekomeko, lovefeasts were occasions of sacrifice and thanksgiving to the spiritual forces, they ensured communal welfare by redistributing food, and they could enhance the status of the host by demonstrating the ability to provide. Baptismal lovefeasts may well have had much in common with traditional naming ceremonies, in which it was common for someone outside of the clan to provide a person with a name that the namer had dreamed. The name in turn would convey something of the power of the namesake. And so when Shekomeko residents were baptized with biblical names and became Abraham, Moses, Cornelius, and so on, they were gaining access to a wealth of powerful spiritual ancestors.[77]

Lovefeasts, as celebrated in the mission community, melded Moravian and Mohican traditions of thanksgiving and community. Similarly, the observance of Easter and funeral practices merged native and European customs. The most important event in the Moravians' liturgical year was the annual Easter cycle. Throughout the week, accounts of Jesus' suffering were read and commemorated in hymns. Rather than being a somber occasion, Good Friday celebrated the side wound inflicted on Jesus by the centurion's spear, marking the beginning of the church, which Moravians understood as having been birthed through Jesus's side wound. Easter Sunday began just before dawn with a procession to God's Acre (the burial ground), where the graves of the deceased were visited. There, the Easter litany was performed, which included a prayer for union with those who had "gone home" to the Savior in the previous year: "I believe that our Brethren {name} and our

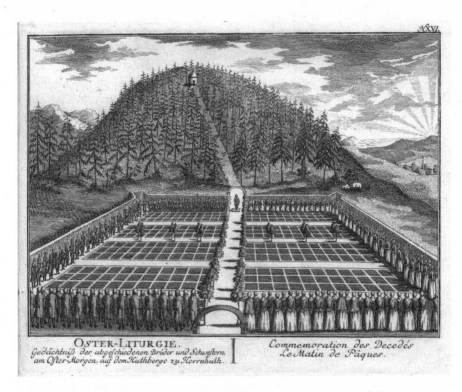

OSTER=LITURGIE.
Gedächtniß der abgeschiedenen Brüder und Schwestern,
am Oster-Morgen, auf dem Huthberge zu Herrnhuth.

Commemoration des Decedes
Le Matin de Pâques.

Figure 5 "Easter Liturgy," [Moravian Church], *Kurze zuverläßige Nachricht* (1757). Courtesy of Moravian Archives, Bethlehem, Pennsylvania.

Sisters {name} are gone to the church above and entered into the joy of the Lord; the Body was buried here." The service was a celebration of the community of the living and the dead.[78]

Shekomekoans who came to participate in Easter services with the Moravians may well have understood the rituals as carrying on the traditions of the "Keutikaw" ceremony, which marked the end of a year of mourning for the deceased. As described by John Sergeant, the Keutikaw was sponsored by the principal mourner, who invited guests to attend the ceremony. Guests were expected to bring presents for the relatives of the deceased in order to "make up their Loss, and to end their Mourning." A special speaker appointed for the occasion received the gifts, and then distributed them to the elderly in attendance, explaining the significance of the gifts. Once the gifts were distributed, the mourners were entreated to forget their sorrow and accept the condolences, after which the community feasted on a celebratory meal.[79]

The descriptions of burial practices left by van der Donck in the seventeenth century and Heckewelder in the eighteenth suggest common and enduring features of burial practices. According to van der Donck, the deceased was buried in a seated position accompanied by wampum, utensils, food, and other goods needed for the journey to the spirit world. Mourners wailed at the burial site for several hours, and in the months and years to follow, relatives of the deceased tended to the grave with great care.[80] Heckewelder described very similar burial rituals, including a feast held after the burial in which the presents were redistributed to the community, the most valuable going to the chief mourners.[81]

The Moravians brought with them new rituals of death and burial. But particularly in the early years of the mission, these customs seem to have blended easily with Mohican tradition. When a young girl died in December 1742, a delegation of missionaries and Mohican men including Abraham, Johannes, and Jacob set out to identify a burial site, which the Moravians called "God's Acre."[82] Friends of the young girl prepared the grave, and then the gathered community assembled to sing a few hymns before setting the body into the earth. Büttner remarked favorably that the ceremony had taken place without the "customary wailing," but it is impossible to know whether the shift in mourning practices was brought about under pressure from the missionaries or whether the Shekomeko mourners found in hymn singing a suitable expression of their grief.[83] When a baptized Indian, Daniel, died in March 1744, Rauch held a conference with several Indian leaders in order to decide on the arrangements for his burial. Because there was too much snow on the ground for an outdoor service, the body was brought into the *Saal* (main worship hall), where Rauch delivered a "corpse sermon" and then sang several hymns together with the congregation, after which a procession of Indian and white Brothers and Sisters bore the body to the burial site, where several more verses and prayers were offered about the Day of Judgment. After Rauch finished his prayer, Johannes offered his thoughts on the meaning of the verses, though unfortunately the diarist did not record the content of Johannes's remarks.[84]

Some clues about how Moravian and Mohican views of death might have converged surface from comments made by Nicodemus. Not long after the death of his friend Jonas, when he himself was not far from death, Nicodemus offered his thoughts on the Resurrection. He remarked, "I am now old and will soon go home [die] and my body will be planted in God's Acre from which something wonderful will come. And when the Savior says the word, the brothers who have long been sleeping, and even my brother Jonas, will come forth beautiful and new."[85]

These statements are remarkably similar to a Narragansett tradition recorded in the seventeenth century, according to which

> the body was planted in the ground from whence corn and other plants sprang, and the soul traveled to the southwest from whence corn originated. The body entered the womb of earth-mother via the grave and enriched her, bringing forth more corn, while the soul returned to the southwest and joined Cautanowwit and the ancestors, thus enriching the group's tradition. Thus the relationship between birth and death was a cycle of continuous renewal for both the community of the living and the community of the ancestors in Cautantowwit's house.[86]

Van der Donck reported similarly that Mohicans in the seventeenth century believed that upon death the soul separates from the body and "removes to a place toward the south, where the climate is so fine that no covering against the cold will be necessary." Those who were good would go to that place to the south, while the wicked would be forced to roam the woods at night.[87] Perhaps surprisingly, the missionary Christian Rauch enthusiastically embraced Nicodemus's rendering of Christian doctrine. In fact, Rauch continued the discourse, comparing the grace that came from Jesus' death and burial to the potential of a seed planted in the ground in hopes of a fruitful harvest.[88] This scene, in which Nicodemus evoked inherited understandings of the afterworld using Moravian-Christian terms, suggests the importance of metaphor in facilitating cross-cultural interaction. Rauch and Nicodemus may well have had quite different images before them, but they both experienced a sense of deep affinity.

As these lovefeast and death scenes make clear, the men of Shekomeko became preachers as well as practitioners of Christianity, and this with the full support of the missionaries. Johannes, Abraham, Jonathan, Isaac, and Joshua also became regular exhorters, preaching at lovefeasts, gravesides, and inter-village and inter-tribal gatherings. Although the sources must be read with care, the Moravian records are quite revealing about both the theology and the function of Mohican preaching, in part because the missionaries fully expected that the Holy Spirit, when it fell upon members of any nation, would inspire those individuals to convey the message in terms most readily understood by their compatriots. Indian preachers were encouraged by the missionaries, who believed that the sole qualification for preaching was experience of the power of Christ's blood, not rigorous study and training. But the Moravians were also mindful of worldly status: all of the regular Indian preachers came from prominent families, due in part to the Moravians' tendency to target the elite in their mission work, believing that their influence would be important to spreading the gospel. For their part, native leaders found the alliance with the Moravians useful because it reinforced their status. But Mohican preaching was not simply pragmatic: it also expressed the hopes and anxieties of a people struggling to find their way in a rapidly changing world.

In many respects, Mohican preaching continued the same themes that emerged in the development of Mohican-Christian ritual practice: Shekomeko men testified to the protection, power, and health that they had found and that was available to others through supplication to the Savior. In doing so, they developed distinctive styles and methods of preaching. Theologically, Mohican preachers picked up on and expanded on Moravian leanings toward universalism by emphasizing again and again the desire of the Savior to empower all who sought help. And finally, functionally, Mohican preaching carried on native traditions of public oratory that served to build consensus, confirm the authority of leaders, and conduct the business of diplomacy.

Not surprisingly, native preaching reflected Mohican experiences. Moravian missionaries noted the distinctiveness of Mohican preaching, remarking on its forceful imagery. Mohican men often began preaching very soon after their baptism, sometimes even before. Johannes was one of the most active native preachers at Shekomeko. Just six months after his baptism, Johannes was ordained as a teacher by Zinzendorf himself. As a teacher, his task was to translate and interpret the words of the missionaries, but it was also far more than that. He was encouraged by the Moravians to present the Christian message in a way that resonated with native experiences. Perhaps it was pure luck on the missionaries' part, but their expectations of Johannes as teacher coincided with what was likely the role he already filled as tribal speaker.[89] A speaker represented the village or tribal leaders and was expected to be able to present the key points of business before the audience in a fluid and persuasive address. Speakers were responsible for observing proper protocol and were thus central to diplomacy. If a boy showed particular aptitude in memory or eloquence, he would be specially trained for the job.[90] Johannes may well have been one such child. With the advent of the Moravian mission, Johannes came to apply his skills as a speaker to the new task of spreading the Christian gospel, which the Shekomeko Christians arguably attempted to make the new currency of diplomacy.

When the missionaries decided in the late winter of 1743 to scout missionary prospects at the village of Potatik, they made sure that Johannes accompanied them, not only because of his preaching skills but also because many of his relatives or clan members lived in the village.[91] Mack had first preached in Potatik early in February 1743 and returned at the end of the month with a party of twenty Pachgatgoch residents as well as Johannes. When Mack preached, an old man ran out of the house in protest. But when Johannes preached afterwards, Mack reported that the gathered

Indians were "all full of wonder at him," exclaiming that they "never had heard the like in all their lives." Mack seems not to have minded being upstaged and readily acknowledged Johannes's skill: "It is true, he is a wonderful preacher, and every one has not his Method." Mack believed that Johannes's sermon made "a far greater Impression, than all the Studied and contrived speeches of the Learn'd could have done."[92]

Mack then went on to describe Johannes's style of preaching: "He paints the Bad Heart out, and to that end he takes a little board, and draws a heart thereon with a Coal, and all round about it spikes, pricks, and thorns, and then says Schineao (behold) so is a Heart when Satan Dwells in it, and from within comes all Wickedness."[93] Mack interpreted Johannes's drawing as depicting the evil that emanates from the sinner's heart, but one wonders whether Johannes might have intended to show instead that without the protection of Christ's blood, one's heart stood vulnerable to stings and arrows. This would seem to be more in keeping with Johannes's own description of his preaching method, in which he said he looked into his heart "and there I find likewise all what to say to my people, for the blood of my happy maker becomes clearer in my heart and that it is which helps me in all that I speak at any time."[94] Interestingly, Mohican preachers seem not to have used the Moravian rhetoric of being washed and purified by the blood of the Savior but emphasized instead the power of the Savior to protect individuals from harm and exorcise bad spirits. Mack's colleague Gottlob Büttner confirmed Johannes's skill in a letter, remarking that he "interprets very well what we preach or say" and that he was himself a "great preacher among his people."[95] Native preachers couldn't win over all opponents however, as the chief of Pachgatgoch discovered. When Gideon began to preach, one man held a gun to his head and threatened, "Now I'll shoot thee for thou speakest continually from the Savior. If thou hast anything so keep it for thyself." Gideon responded by assuring the man, "when [if] my Savior does not permit thee, thou canst not shoot me."[96]

But often, Shekomeko preachers found an audience where Europeans had not, as when Joshua preached along the Connecticut coast. Joshua testified about the power he had received from the Savior with his baptism, saying that "he felt our Saviour Hourly on his Heart." His message was to dwell on the wounds of Christ in order to be able to abandon sin. Upon hearing him preach, one native listener remarked, "But the English don't preach that." Responded Joshua, "Verily...if they don't preach that they have it not."[97] Interestingly, Joshua's answer echoed revivalist rhetoric about the "dangers of an unconverted ministry," but here it was infused with distinct meanings. Joshua and other native preachers emphasized the power conveyed with the blood of Christ and came to see belief in the blood as the test of European Christians. One man, likely Gideon of Pachgatgoch, informed Mack that he did not want to be "baptiz'd by one who did not know the Savior himself."[98] Native preachers found an audience among other Indians, and they used these occasions not only to assert the power of Jesus' blood but also to claim their own authority by announcing the danger of an unconverted ministry.

A common feature of Mohican Moravian preaching was an emphasis on the universality of Christ's atonement. In part, this reflects the Christian message as delivered by the Moravian missionaries. When debating in theological circles, Zinzendorf denied a belief in universal salvation, but the missionaries in the field stressed that Christ's blood was shed for all—Indian and white alike.[99] Martin Mack preached a similar message in his travels, telling the story of the humanity of Jesus and the possibility of universal grace. Even the worst sinner, Mack asserted, could be saved if he felt the blood of Christ in his heart.[100]

When Mohican preachers took up this theme, they tended to focus less on the universality of salvation, stressing instead the universal availability of power through the blood of Christ. In January 1746, when Johannes led services, he chose his text from 1 John 2:1: "And if any man sin, we have an advocate with the Father, Jesus Christ the righteous."[101] Similarly, Gideon of Pachgatgoch assured a fellow villager, "if you come to our Saviour, and you are in earnest, to become acquainted with him, he has spoke this everlasting Truth, for you, 'He that commeth unto me will in no wise be cast out.' "[102] One Mohican man was recorded as preaching: "I have nothing to say to you but a few words concerning Jesus." Jesus had labored hard "to gain salvation for us, even so that his sweat was as great drops of blood falling to the ground." Now the man spoke directly for Jesus, offering salvation to all: "I have redeemed you all, I have given my life and blood for you." The offer is universal, "whosoever believeth in him, shall live eternally." All may have eternal life "if they come to Jesus, for he will receive them gladly."[103] Joshua preached a similar message at the sickbed of a Gnadenhütten resident, asserting that one didn't have to be perfect before approaching the Savior, but anyone who came to him with a "poor heart," the Savior "helps . . . right away."[104] For Mohican preachers, the central message was the power available through Jesus' blood, a power available to all who sought help.

Mohican preaching was not limited to formal addresses before large gatherings. The mission records mention Shekomeko men preaching on the hunt and in the sweat lodge. Joshua reported to the missionaries that while he had been in the sweat lodge with a Delaware visitor, the thick steam had "given him the occasion to talk to Armstrong about the blindness of men on whom the light of the wounds doesn't shine."[105] The Moravian records also suggest that winter hunting lodges provided a venue for talking about the power of Jesus' blood.[106]   '

The message of Mohican preaching was clearly important, but equally important was the context of these exhortations. Most mentions of Mohican preaching in the Moravian records refer to occasions on which Mohican leaders addressed inter-village and often inter-tribal gatherings. Shekomeko leaders like Abraham seem to have drawn on Christianity as a means of both fulfilling and sometimes renegotiating diplomatic relationships. By the mid–eighteenth century, Mohican peoples had lost considerable standing—they were no longer the power in trade and war they had once been. Where once English and Dutch authorities competed for the advantage in trade with Mohicans, colonial authorities now lost little sleep in pondering the best strategy for maintaining Mohican allegiance.

At a time when the world was changing dramatically around them and their status seemed to be spiraling downward, Christian affiliation promised a new means of forging and maintaining relationships with colonists and other native peoples. The Moravian way offered hopes of a peaceful existence with whites and other tribes articulated through the use of kinship terminology. A look at the Moravian and Mohican use of fictive kinship terminology as a means of ordering social relations sets the stage for a consideration of the diplomatic program followed by the Mohicans of Shekomeko.

Zinzendorf, like many Christian theologians before him, articulated a philosophy of Christian social relations—between humans, between humans and the divine, and among the members of the Trinity—by drawing on kinship metaphors. Zinzendorf, however, was anything but traditional in his understanding of the Trinity. His emphasis on Jesus' humanity (as opposed to Christ's divinity) meant that the central relational principle of Moravian spiritual life was the fraternal bond. By becoming human, Jesus chose to relate to humans as one of their own. The Incarnation was the perfect expression of fraternal and divine love. The Church was the spiritual offspring of God the Father and the Holy Spirit, the Mother, born from Jesus' side wound. From this principle flowed a view of the Church as the *Brüdergemeine*—siblings to one another in the Church family, all children of the Holy Spirit and spiritual siblings to Jesus. Christians were thus bound to one another by ties of fraternal love. Manifestations of this central idea are found on nearly every page of the Moravian records: Moravians called each other Brother and Sister, and corporately they were the *Geschwister* (siblings) or the *Brüdergemeine*. Moravian missionaries employed the same fraternal language with the Indians of Shekomeko: all Christians, Indian or white, were brothers and sisters in Christ. The centrality of the fraternal relation meant that the Moravian missionaries viewed their work as an act of brotherly love rather than an exercise of paternal benevolence toward childlike Indians undertaken in obedience to a heavenly Father, as Anglo-Protestant missionaries tended to understand their work.[107]

Fictive kinship had always been central to inter-tribal relations, and the language of Christian fraternity became an important means of re-establishing these relationships in a changing and increasingly European-dominated world. In traditional intertribal diplomacy, ceremonial practice was particularly important in maintaining good relations between peoples. When Moravians called the Shekomekoans "Brother" and "Sister," it did not go unremarked. For the Mohicans, it was particularly astonishing to be called "brother" by Europeans. While British colonial officials had adapted the Indian custom of fictive kinship terminology for diplomatic purposes (though Mohicans were generally addressed as "Children" rather than "Brethren"), they rarely invested it with a meaning that transcended political calculus.[108]

The language of fraternity was readily understandable by the Indian communities approached by the Moravians. Mohicans, like most inland, riverine Algonquin peoples (and in contrast to some coastal Algonquians) were matrilineal, meaning that fraternal relations were of greater significance than paternal ones. Children inherited clan membership from their mothers. In the case of a mother's death, children were often raised by a maternal uncle rather than the father. Where leadership remained within a family line, it generally passed through the maternal line.[109]

Kinship for Mohicans was not limited to biological relations but shaped the political and the spiritual realms as well. Fictive kinship was the language of diplomacy. Relationships with other tribes were defined by their kinship designations. For example, the Mohicans addressed the Delaware as "Grandfather," the Iroquois as "Uncle," and the Shawnee as "Younger Brother." These terms brought with them expectations of mutual obligation. Thus for Mohicans, the Moravian language was a familiar means of defining relations with those not necessarily related by blood. To be sure, fictive kinship terms meant different things to Mohicans and Moravians, but that both invested greatest significance in the fraternal relationship provided a common ground that facilitated the construction of new communities.

Evidence from the Moravian records suggests that the Mohicans of Shekomeko may have welcomed the possibility that a Christian bond between communities might alter the terms of relationship. In February 1744, a delegation from Stockbridge arrived in Shekomeko to announce the choice of a new Mohican sachem and ask whether the Shekomekoans "would live with them in friendship." The head men of Shekomeko sent the response,

"Yes, they would be their friends," and then they "preached the Savior to them, and said, 'if we all believe in the Savior, we do not need any embassies [*Gesandtshaften*], because we are good friends without them.'"[110] Perhaps some of the customs of diplomacy had become burdensome, and the Shekomekoans welcomed Christianity as a new means of maintaining peaceful relations. The comments of a Delaware man in the early 1750s reinforces the idea that some Indians found in the *Brüdergemeine* a means to maintain peace, the ultimate goal of diplomacy.[111] The man came to Abraham and told him that he wanted to live as the Brethren in Gnadenhütten lived, because he saw that "the Brethren were so blessed and happy, and they lived in love and peace with each other."[112]

Both the convergence of and the tensions between Mohican and Moravian traditions of fictive kinship language can be seen in the rich records left by the missionaries of a series of councils held in the summer of 1752 between the Shawnee and Nanticoke Indians, on the one side, and the "white and brown brethren" of Bethlehem and Gnadenhütten, on the other.[113] The Shawnees and Nanticokes, as emissaries of the Iroquois, were requesting that the Gnadenhütten residents move to Wyoming, where they would effectively serve as buffers between colonists and the Iroquois. The Delaware and Mohican Moravians of Gnadenhütten might have had little choice other than to accept the "invitation," but they did insist on their own terms. Specifically, they requested that they be allowed to settle some of the missionaries with them, insisting on a distinction between Moravians and other whites,

> But we do not want to have any other white people, but only the Brethren
> and the reason we want to have the Brethren with us is because they tell us
> quite often about our God and Savior. You have told us, that we should be
> able to continue on our good path and have our good thoughts as before
> and therefore we need the Brethren with us.[114]

"Brother Joseph" Spangenberg responded to the various speeches for the Gnadenhütten Brethren using the customary forms of Covenant Chain diplomacy, symbolically drying the sweat and wiping away the dust from the journey. After rehearsing the speeches of the Shawnee and Nanticoke chiefs, Spangenberg affirmed "as you have said so it is; the Brethren from Bethlehem and the Brethren from Gnadenhütten are one."[115]

Despite the fraternal language used at this council, both Mohican and European Moravians were already finding it increasingly difficult to imagine community across racial divisions. When Abraham was appointed to the position of captain by the Stockbridge Mohican chief sachem in 1753, he was brought into closer contact with other Indian peoples who looked upon the close relationship of Mohicans and Moravian missionaries with considerable suspicion. Likewise, other European colonists remained deeply suspicious of the Moravians' close alliance with Indian communities. The destruction of the Gnadenhütten community by French-allied Delaware and Shawnee Indians in November 1755, just months after the start of what would become known as the French and Indian War, aptly symbolized the dangers for both Indian and European Moravians of their interracial community.[116]

But for a time, in Shekomeko during the 1740s, there was a remarkable religious revival in which Mohican and Moravian religious beliefs and practices came into creative contact with one another, producing a vibrant new form of Christian practice that many Mohicans found to be an apt expression of inherited Mohican values and a remedy to some of the challenges posed by colonialism. In some respects, this revival had much in common with the far more studied revivals that have collectively come to be known—though not without dissenters—as the First Great Awakening.[117] Indian preachers like Johannes and Abraham traveled from village to village proclaiming the wonderful power of Jesus' blood. Late into the night, lay people testified to their friends, family, neighbors, and anyone who would listen about the transformation in their lives: they had given up drinking, they had been saved from sickness, they had been blessed with prosperity. Sometimes these new believers met with receptive audiences, but often they instead encountered scorn from those who believed the old ways were better.

But the revival among the Mohicans of Shekomeko differed in significant ways from the revivals that were spreading among their white neighbors. The most obvious difference, of course, was that for Mohicans, it was not simply a turn from one type of Christian profession to another but rather the adoption of a new religion, a new mythical narrative. Tschoop, Shabash, and the other Mohicans of Shekomeko had heard versions of the Christian story before the arrival of the Moravians—but always presented in a fashion that seemed to offer little and demand much. When Christian Rauch bumped into the two men in New York City, he told quite a different story, one that was not altogether foreign to the Mohicans. The rituals brought by Rauch and his missionary colleagues were not so unlike the feasts of thanksgiving and the invocations of the spirits that the Shekomekoans had inherited from their forebears: they conveyed power from spirits that could be applied in immediate and concrete ways in the supplicants' lives. And besides a narrative and course of ritual that offered some continuity with Mohican ways, the Moravian missionaries differed dramatically from their counterparts of other denominations in their mode of interacting with the Indians. Without this factor, the rest would have mattered little. Unlike virtually any other Europeans encountered by the Mohicans, Moravians happily lodged in Indian homes, partook of Indian meals, and expressed a deep affection for the Indian individuals they encountered.

Mohican men, of course, did not live in isolation. They were husbands and fathers, brothers and sons. The wives of Abraham and Johannes followed their husbands in baptism within a year. Many couples came forward together for baptism, although, occasionally, differing commitments to the newly emerging Christian community created or exacerbated family tensions. In the final analysis, roughly equal numbers of Mohican men and women came to identify as Christian, but a closer look reveals that they did so for quite distinct reasons and in distinctive ways. Men practiced Christianity within the traditional parameters of Mohican men's lives: as hunters, warriors, and diplomats. Women, not surprisingly, practiced Christianity in ways that corresponded with women's sphere of activity as mothers and as overseers of village and domestic affairs.

PART III

PRESERVATION

Chapter Seven

The Village Matriarch and the Young Mother

Six months after overseeing the baptism of the first Mohicans, Moravian leader Ludwig von Zinzendorf arrived in Shekomeko to check on the progress of the mission. The mercurial Count exclaimed excitedly about the "perfect palace of bark" constructed for his stay and then, a moment later, lamented that the Mohicans were "given to excessive drinking," yet "susceptible of good impressions." During the course of his visit, he and missionary Christian Rauch drew up a list of resolutions for the mission, including "to organize our Mohicans into a congregation," "to appoint native assistants in the infant congregation," and "to confer with Abraham, Isaac, Jacob, and John [Johannes] on our method of laboring among the heathen, and on its object, which is not the indiscriminate acquisition of large numbers, but the admission into the congregation of souls that have been renewed to life in Christ." The missionaries made good progress on their list: during Zinzendorf's visit, Abraham, Isaac, Jacob, and Johannes were appointed to positions as elder, server, exhorter, and teacher, respectively. Six other Mohicans were baptized, including Abraham's wife, who took the name Sarah, and Isaac's wife, predictably baptized Rebecca.[1]

The Moravians were not the only evangelists active among the Indians in the region. Just twelve days after Sarah was baptized, a young woman named Amanariochque from Pachgatgoch, a village just twenty miles from Shekomeko, listened as the missionary David Brainerd preached the Presbyterian gospel of salvation.[2] Brainerd's studies under John Sergeant of Stockbridge had done nothing to restrain his more enthusiastic bent, and so when he addressed his Indian audience, he delivered an emotional sermon on Job 14:14, causing listeners to "cr[y] out in great distress."[3] Although Brainerd fanned the flames of revival in Pachgatgoch, it was the Moravians who succeeded in establishing a mission there and baptized Amanariochque the following winter, bestowing the name Rachel on the young woman. And it was a Moravian missionary, Christian Friedrich Post, who sought Rachel's hand in marriage just weeks after her baptism.

Because of Sarah's and Rachel's marriages to prominent men—to the headman of Shekomeko and to a Moravian missionary—the already rich Moravian records are even more fruitful in tracing their lives. Sarah and Rachel lived out their lives as Indians and Christians, as wives and mothers. Temperamentally, Sarah and Rachel could not have been more different. Like her biblical namesake, Sarah was the matriarch, more advanced in years, devoted to her husband, her children, and her community. Rachel was just twenty-one at the time of her baptism, with a fiery temperament and a longing to be a mother. These women came to practice Christianity in distinctive ways. Like many of the men of Shekomeko, Sarah and Rachel found in Moravian Christianity a new source of spiritual power with which they tried to preserve inherited values. Their need for new spiritual resources testifies to the severe strains imposed by the increasing European presence, while their adaptation of Moravian Christian ritual testifies to their spiritual creativity.

SARAH

Sarah is one of the few individuals whose blood relatives are never mentioned in the Moravian records, suggesting either that she was originally from a more distant village or that her family had perished in one of the waves of smallpox to descend on the region, or possibly both. Sarah's marriage to Shabash (Abraham) in the late 1710s or early 1720s might well have cemented ties between the villages or even joined two villages together. Shabash was the grandson of Mammanochqua, who before her death in the early 1680s had attempted to ensure that the lands including Shekomeko remained under her family's control.[4] That Sarah took up residence in her husband's village (contrary to matrilineal traditions common among the Mohicans) provides further evidence of the precarious position of her home community.[5] Against the odds, by the time the Moravian missionaries arrived in 1740, Sarah and Shabash had probably been married for close to twenty years, and the couple had raised at least four children to adulthood.[6]

Sarah and Abraham raised their children in an uncertain world, a world with few relatives and precarious community ties. Given the demographic impact of colonialism, the social fabric of Shekomeko and surrounding communities must have been extremely fragile. Traditional cultural patterns that rested on kinship networks would have become virtually impossible to maintain. At the same time Sarah and Abraham were trying to build a new family and community, Abraham was struggling to secure his rights to his ancestral lands, which were increasingly being encroached upon by New York settlers. It was out of this frustration that Abraham had first considered Christianity and had traveled to Stockbridge to check out the mission there. And it was after another failed attempt at receiving satisfaction from the New York governor that he and Tschoop, his trusted companion, encountered Moravian missionary Christian Heinrich Rauch fresh off the boat from Europe.

Despite initial reservations, Abraham found the Moravian message and mission program appealing in some measure. Moravians offered access to new sources of spiritual power, few demands of cultural change (especially in comparison to the thorough cultural conversion expected at Stockbridge), and the prospect of a continued presence on ancestral lands. Sarah too came to find the Moravian message and manner appealing, though for different reasons—reasons that corresponded to (and sometimes challenged) traditional gender roles. Sarah sought individual fortitude, spiritual sustenance, and new tools of Christian ritual and Moravian social structures to bind together family and community.

The Moravian missionaries wrote little about their impressions of Sarah, but as she became active in the Christian community, they regularly recorded her activities. The first hint we have of Sarah's experience of Christian ritual comes from a diary entry by missionary Gottlob Büttner on the eve of a celebration of communion in December 1743, a year and a half after her baptism:

> She saw nothing with her eyes, but her heart believed so in the Saviour as if she had seen him and she had then such a feeling of it, that she thought that if any one should pull the flesh from her bones she would nevertheless abide with him, and said she, "I believe I should not have felt it neither, for my whole body and heart felt a power from his wounds and blood."[7]

If Sarah found resources of personal strength in Christian practice, she also sought means to reinforce community and kinship ties through her work as a member of the weekly meetings of missionaries and Shekomeko residents. Sarah exercised considerable authority in regulating behavior and overseeing the entrance of new members into the Christian community.[8] She strove in her work to establish a new foundation for community stability.

Sarah's family situation changed dramatically in the spring of 1747. That May, Sarah and Abraham were preparing for the birth of another child. It was an uncertain time to bring a child into the world, not only because Sarah was at least forty. The couple had arrived in the newly formed Christian-Mohican settlement at Gnadenhütten, Pennsylvania, having completed the 150-mile journey from Shekomeko while Sarah was eight months pregnant.[9] Abraham had been determined to remain in Shekomeko, unwilling to leave despite the continued refusal of the New York government to recognize his land claims and the increasing hostility of colonists towards Moravians and their native allies, that ensued with the outbreak of King George's War in 1744. The missionaries were banned from preaching in New York and, together with many Indians from Shekomeko and Pachgatgoch, they moved to Pennsylvania in 1746. It might well have been his wife's desire to have her unborn child baptized that finally persuaded Abraham to leave his home village.[10] Following the birth of their son, Sarah expressed her fear that the missionaries might refuse to baptize the child because the couple had initially remained behind in Shekomeko. She explained how much she had cried over the child and how greatly she desired that he might receive the Savior's grace. Missionary Martin Mack consented and baptized the child. He would be called Isaac.[11]

With her youngest safely baptized, Sarah began to worry about her older children. Two sons, Jonathan and Joachim, had recently left the Moravian community. The Moravians' banishment from New York made it eminently clear that an alliance with the Moravians counted for little in the colonial world. Jonathan and Joachim may well have thought it wise to investigate other native communities farther to the west. Whatever their reasons, Sarah was distraught, not knowing if and when her sons would return and fearing that their rejection of the Christian community might keep them from meeting again in the next world.[12] Unable to console his wife, Abraham pleaded with the European Sisters that they try to comfort her. Maria Spangenberg related to Sarah her own difficult experiences as a mother whose children had not accepted the Savior.[13] Sarah seemed to be somewhat relieved by Spangenberg's efforts and resigned to the reality that not all of her children would follow in her footsteps. Resigned to separation, Sarah was surely elated when Jonathan and Anna returned to the congregation and began building a house in February 1749. For the time, her family was reunited.

Several years later, Sarah would again be faced with trying circumstances, and this time she chose to follow family while attempting to maintain ties with the Christian community and especially with the power of the Savior's blood. In 1753, Abraham was appointed as captain of the Mohican nation by the sachem at Stockbridge and was called to move to Wyoming, Pennsylvania, to carry out his duties. Sarah did not want to leave the Brethren, but neither could she bear being separated from her husband.[14] Her daughter-in-law Anna faced the same painful decision in the winter of 1753–54. Clearly upset, Anna pleaded with Jonathan:

> My dear husband, decide soon what you want to do, and don't take long: I want to tell you what I want to do, I am not going with you to Susquehanna. If you want to go, you can. But I and my children want to stay with the congregation, for when I think about what the Savior did for us and for our children, it is impossible for me to resolve to go away from the congregation.

Anna attributed the well-being of her children to the Savior and feared that leaving the Christian community would jeopardize protection by the Savior. Jonathan promised to think over the matter while on his hunting trip and to have an answer for her when he returned. Anna anxiously awaited Jonathan's return, confessing to Esther, "Oh how often have I thought of him, especially during Christmas and New Year's week and I wished with my heart that he still feels some of that grace and blessing the Savior let us feel." Sarah too prayed for her son. When in the woods collecting firewood, she prayed to God to "have mercy on my husband and children." For the time being at least, Anna and Sarah's wish for Jonathan was granted: he decided to stay with the Brethren.[15] Sarah's relief that Jonathan decided to stay with the congregation was likely mixed with the sadness of her own impending departure. While the Christian congregation helped to cement new ties of community, particularly for women, it could also force painful choices when the multiple layers of Sarah's identity—as Mohican, wife, mother, and Christian—did not fit easily together.

As Sarah and Abraham set off for Wyoming in April 1754, the couple promised to "stay with the Savior and to tell others about him and his love whenever possible." In a letter sent later that year from Wyoming to her "dear sister" Maria Spangenberg, Sarah confessed the difficulty of living among non-Christian Indians but found that "the Savior still comes through to me" and that she continued to feel "what love I have for the Savior, because he was wounded and his blood shed that melts my heart and makes me happy." She prayed often for the Savior to "give me a drop of the blood that flows from his side." Finally, she asked that Spangenberg "remember me to the Savior."[16] Being separated from the Moravian community was clearly trying for Sarah, but she continued to find spiritual power through communion with the blood of Christ. The Savior seemed to function for Sarah in much the same way as a guardian spirit who offered protection in return for proper devotion.

On his deathbed in 1762, Abraham encouraged Sarah to return to the Moravians. Although eager to return, Sarah feared that the move would mean painful family decisions once again. She delayed returning for nearly a year, held back by her sons. Eventually, her older sons decided to move further west and urged her to join them. She refused, saying that she would rather go to the Brethren, but she urged, "Go where you will. I can't help you and I can't hold you back." Unable to compel her sons to stay with her, she turned to her teenaged daughter, Sarah, and, applying more than a little motherly guilt, pleaded, "You are my only daughter. You have heard my thoughts. What will you do? If you want to abandon me, you can do that. You have your freedom. I have raised you to adulthood and you would be sad if I should die in the woods at your side and be forever lost." The younger Sarah broke into tears and promised to follow her mother. The family was welcomed back into the congregation, and soon work was begun on a house for Sarah and her two children.[17]

One year later, in 1764, Sarah and Isaac were living in Philadelphia, where dozens of Moravian Indians had sought refuge during the frontier upheavals of Pontiac's Rebellion and the Paxton Boys incident, which followed on the heels of the French and Indian War. In this climate, no one trusted pacifist Christian Indians. In the cramped quarters of the Philadelphia Barracks, Sarah succumbed to smallpox in June 1764, and Isaac followed his mother in death several weeks later.[18]

At times, Sarah had found in the personal experience of the Savior's blood and in the support of the Moravian community a means of sustaining herself and her family, but her identity as a Christian Indian often left her in the impossible position of choosing one child over another, her faith over her family, her family over her faith.

Rachel

Rachel's life was more openly dramatic than Sarah's, yet she faced many of the same struggles of negotiating family and faith. Identified in the Moravian records as "Wampanosch" and a resident of Pachgatgoch, Rachel belonged to a community descended from coastal Algonquian refugees of the Pequot War.[19] The few short years of her life recorded in Moravian sources were filled with intense spiritual experiences, anxiety, and sorrow. Because Rachel married a missionary, her life is better documented than perhaps any of her sister villagers.[20] Like Sarah, Rachel drew heavily on the Moravian imagery of the blood and wounds of Christ. And she too directed her practice of Christian ritual to the ends of creating and preserving family.

At the time of her baptism, Rachel was twenty-one and already separated from her husband, Annimhard, a Mohican from Shekomeko who had another wife. We can't know for sure why the marriage was dissolved—perhaps the dynamics of the plural marriage were untenable, or perhaps the marriage had failed to produce children, or perhaps Annimhard had beaten his young wife.[21] Rachel seems to have been at once eager to break away from her own family, yet at the same time afraid to chart a new course. Among those attentive to David Brainerd's preaching, she then became one of the first from her village to be baptized by the Moravians.[22] Within weeks of her baptism, she was contemplating marriage to a white man, Christian Friedrich Post. Rachel was clearly a woman in search of a better life. There is little in the sources to suggest why Post and Rachel chose each other, but it seems that Post, who had a somewhat prickly and erratic character, was intent on marrying an Indian woman, and Rachel might have hoped marriage to a European man with an especially close relationship to the Moravians' God would produce the children she had been unable to conceive in her first marriage.[23]

The couple was engaged in early August 1743 and married later that month after much discussion about the matter in the missionary conferences. One matter for deliberation was whether Moravian custom should be followed, in which members of the congregation prayed during the consummation of the marriage. The missionaries agreed custom should be followed and appointed Büttner and Jannetje Mack to the task. But just four days after the betrothal, with the marriage still unconsummated, Rachel headed home to her mother in Pachgatgoch, apparently having second thoughts about her marriage to Post. Two weeks later, she returned, apologizing for her flight from Shekomeko. A month later, Rachel was still struggling with her marriage, confessing that she wanted to love her husband but could not.[24]

By December, Post's fellow missionaries were deeply concerned over Rachel's erratic behavior. Although she had returned to Shekomeko, she refused to consummate the marriage. The missionaries, perhaps prompted by Post, sought the help of the Savior through the lot. The answer came that it was time for the couple to consummate their union.[25] Although Rachel consented, Büttner had reason to believe that all was still not well. He was right, and Rachel was soon headed for Pachgatgoch. When she returned two weeks later, she refused to enter the mission house. Büttner sent his wife to speak with Rachel, and Post himself went to attempt to placate his wife. They inquired if she wanted to live alone and promised her her own house. But Rachel remained stubbornly silent. Other members of the congregation tried to appease her, but Rachel gave no answer and again ran away. When Büttner penned a worried letter to Bethlehem seeking advice, she had yet to return. At a loss, Büttner sent Post to Bethlehem bearing his letter and dispatched a member of the congregation to New York to bring back some cloth, hoping to win over the disgruntled bride. Two days later, Rachel returned to Shekomeko. One week later, on December 22, 1743, she moved into the missionaries' house. Nine months later, almost to the day, Rachel gave birth to a baby boy, named Ludwig Johannes, whom she called Hannes.[26]

Pregnancy seems to have settled Rachel's restless soul. A letter to her friend and spiritual mother Maria Spangenberg relates the joy she experienced at the prospect of becoming a mother.[27] She described for Spangenberg how she had once wept when she saw children at play in Shekomeko because she herself was childless. But now, she wrote, during worship services "my babe leaped in my womb," and she thanked "our Savior continually, that he has given me one." The letter implies that it was the Savior, working through Joseph Spangenberg, more than Post, who was responsible for the child Rachel was carrying. Wrote Rachel, "I never yet felt my heart so at the Lord Supper as this time. I can't express how it was with me when I received that Blood...and when Br. Joseph gave it to me, my heart, glowing and filled with the Sap of Life and thought, Muchree onewe onewe, onewe."[28] Doubt about the life-giving powers Rachel attributed to the blood of the Savior vanish when we read another letter to Maria Spangenberg, this one written in August of 1745. "O beloved Mother," wrote Rachel, "I was very poor [of spirit] in Bethlehem and while we [she and Post] were together in the cabinet and Brother Joseph prayed, I felt the great grace of the Savior flood my heart with blood."[29] It was probably on this occasion that Rachel conceived her second child. The sexual overtones of the letter are hard to ignore, yet again it seems that it was God's grace, mediated through Christ's blood and Spangenberg's prayer, that had bestowed a child on Rachel. Post, it seems, just happened to be present.

Like Sarah, Rachel found in the blood of Christ the ability to endure great suffering. In an account taken down by her husband, Rachel testified that when she experienced the blood and wounds of Christ, someone could pour scalding water over her without her noticing it. It was as though she "stood before God in his house" and could not tell whether she walked on the earth or floated in the air but felt the Savior and his angels sitting beside her.[30] Another letter dictated by Rachel in 1745 to the "Brethren and Sisters in Barbies [Berbice, Suriname]" offers further testimony to the life-giving properties Rachel found in Christ's blood. Rachel's eight-month-old Hannes died that year, and she had lost several siblings the year before, so she might well have felt an even greater pull to establish a new spiritual family, one that transcended the precarious bonds of biological kinship. She testified to the distant members of her new Christian family that the Savior had received her as his child and "washed my heart with his blood." Now that she felt the Savior's blood on her heart, she found that she was better able to love her husband, something she had clearly struggled with before. In concluding her letter, she professed her love for her distant

Brethren and Sisters, although "I don't know all your names." The Savior's blood was the means of establishing a new community—having been adopted by the Savior and enabled by his blood to love her new husband, Rachel now claimed membership in a community of Christian fraternity that transcended local boundaries.[31]

Rachel's letters offer testimony to the power she found in the Moravian practice of Christianity: the power to love a prickly husband, the power to conceive children, and the comfort of a new spiritual family. But they also testify powerfully to the very real and personal impact of colonialism. She had lost not only her son and three siblings but doubtless many other friends and neighbors as well. Moravian missionaries, including her husband, had been forbidden from preaching in all of New York. And when she traveled with several white Brethren, she met with taunts and jeers from colonists and accusations that the Moravians had forced her marriage to Post, that they "had given her a small bit of Paper to eat on which it was written 'that the Savior wo'd have it' which she was obliged to swallow."[32] On another occasion, as the tensions of war built in the colonies, her traveling party was assaulted by colonists who demanded of the missionaries, "What business have you with that Indian woman there....Ye plot with the Negroes and Indians."[33] The colonists clearly thought nothing good could come of such unions as Rachel and Post had chosen.

Things were little better at home in Shekomeko and Pachgatgoch. The communities were now divided between those who chose to stay behind to battle with creditors and encroaching white settlers and those who followed as the missionaries retreated to Pennsylvania. In September 1746, Rachel turned once again for solace to her "dear mother," Maria Spangenberg, who Rachel felt loved her "a great deal more than my own mother."[34] She confessed her sense of powerlessness: "I know and feel that I am a poor little creature and only the blood of our savior gives me wellness....Now I feel my heart [is] always more hungry and thirsty after the blood of our Savior." The more difficult life became, the stronger was her desire for sustenance from the Savior. In the same letter, she described for Spangenberg how she had a premonition that left her heart "very heavy." She pleaded with the Savior to identify the cause. Was it her husband's illness? No, said the Savior. Then what? "And then Joshua came home dancing and singing and it was as if my finger was cut off." Joshua, a friend from Pachgatgoch, had enlisted in the army that summer (against Moravian pacifist principles) and had been off fighting in Canada. He returned in early September and went on a drunken spree. Rachel experienced this threat to the solidarity of the Christian community as physical pain. She prayed for the Savior to help the wayward Joshua. Feeling uneasy, Rachel could not sleep, so she took the letter she had received from Maria and went to "the house of our

Savior." Unable to read, Rachel found that the mere physical presence of the letter cheered her considerably. In the meetinghouse with the letter, Rachel recounted, "It was just so as when the Savior gave me my Hannes, and I was so glad that I did cry."[35] The letter was a gift of Maria's presence from the Savior.

Finally, Rachel's thoughts turned to her young child, Maria, named after Spangenberg. It is here that the connections linking self, family, community, and Christian practice are most clearly and painfully evident. Wrote Rachel, "My child grows well and strong but it has a great cough. I wish our savior did make her well again. I can't help her at all. The Savior must do everything." Rachel felt powerless to ensure the health of her child and turned to the Savior, imagining that rather than breast milk, she fed her child from the Savior's wounds, "when I give my child suck and I think about the blood and wounds of our Savior I feel my heart sometimes very wet and so I think my child sucks the blood of our Savior and I feel the angels look after me and my child." She closed her letter with a prayer for her fellow villagers "that the Savior would give them a feeling of his blood and wounds in their hearts." She ended with an entreaty to Spangenberg: "You must think about me that he gives much grace....We are your poor children Rachel and Maria Post."[36] The next year, in December 1747, Rachel delivered a stillborn baby boy. Rachel and her young Maria both died the following day of an unnamed illness.[37]

Chapter Eight

Mohican Women and the Community of the Blood

The stories of Sarah and Rachel capture both the powerlessness and the empowerment experienced by many Indian women of Shekomeko and surrounding communities who sought help from the Moravian Savior. They demonstrate the spiritual creativity of native Christians, who enlisted new sources of spiritual power to strengthen the bonds of family and community and the ways that encroaching colonialism challenged the efficacy of tradition to sustain self, family, and community. Sarah followed her husband to baptism, perhaps hoping that the power of Jesus' blood would serve women's spiritual needs as well as men's. Childless from her first marriage, Rachel turned to Christ's blood and a European man she had difficulty loving to give her a child. Let down in some way by her own mother, Rachel found sustenance from her spiritual mother, Maria Spangenberg, whose strength she hoped to pass on to her own daughter, Maria. Fearing mother's milk alone was insufficient nourishment for her beloved child, she imagined she fed little Maria from the wounds of the Savior.

Sarah, Rachel, and others brought into existence an indigenous—and distinctly feminine—Christianity. While these women found new resources of spiritual power in Christian ritual, their need for such new sources testifies to the severe strains on native cultures: men's abuse of alcohol often translated into the abuse of women, and as the primary caregivers, women suffered especially from the loss of their children to disease. The dynamics of the colonial trade elevated men's status and challenged women's authority in their communities, a trajectory initially continued in the new mission as men like Tschoop joined the Christian community, seizing the opportunity to be freed of women's spiritual authority. Not surprisingly, then, some women were resistant to the mission program, perhaps perceiving it as a mechanism of disempowerment. But although men were generally the first to be baptized in a given family and although at least a few women actively opposed the mission, men and women came to make up roughly equal numbers of Mohican-Moravians, a fact that begs explanation. Sarah, Rachel, and other women of Shekomeko and surrounding villages, like their husbands, came to appreciate the Moravians first for their ability to observe native conventions of hospitality and subsequently for the new spiritual resources they offered, as well as the new networks of social support. The Moravians' blood and wounds theology together with their unique social arrangements provided a basis for the creative convergence of Mohican and Moravian religious practice.

The Christianity practiced by Indian women at Shekomeko and other towns expressed deeply rooted cultural values at the same time that it addressed the realities of a dramatically changed and changing world. Christianity was indigenized as it was literally incorporated through the rituals of consuming Christ's body and blood through communion, and through such human experiences as pregnancy, birth, and nursing. In the nascent Christian community of Indian and white Moravians, native women constructed new networks of kinship as brothers and sisters in Christ. When they felt incapable of caring for their children, they placed them in the care of their new European *geschwister* (siblings), as the members of the Moravian community were called. While Sarah and Rachel found new sources of power in Christian ritual and community, they also experienced the factionalizing power of Christianity, as the newly drawn lines between Christian and non-Christian sometimes bisected the very families and communities the women were struggling to hold together.

Women's practice of Christianity emerged in the wake of major cultural changes brought about by a century of contact with Europeans, changes with important consequences for spiritual and political power. The Moravian records provide glimpses into women's experiences of their changing roles. Women often spoke of feeling powerless to live the lives they wished to lead, and some women turned to Christian practice in part as a means of reclaiming spiritual power that had become increasingly difficult to secure. Yet women's experiences of the encounter with Christianity cannot be understood through simple categories of "tradition" or "assimilation." Mohican women engaged Christian practice and community to sustain, preserve, and often renegotiate their relationships with the human and the spiritual worlds.

WOMEN, POLITICS, AND SPIRITUAL POWER

Scholars have long debated whether men or women were more negatively affected by colonization, which sex had most to gain or lose by the introduction of Christianity. Although it may be impossible to answer these questions definitively, it is safe to say that men and women suffered in different ways. Evidence from a variety of sources suggests that pressures from colonialism had left women more vulnerable: their control over natural resources, communal ritual life, and family life all seem to have been on the wane.[1]

At the time of first contact in the early seventeenth century, the Mohican peoples of the middle Hudson River Valley were a horticultural, matrilineal, clan-based society. Economic activities were sharply divided along gender lines, with the men and women occupying largely distinct spheres. Women's sphere was the domestic—producing and processing food and clothing, raising children, and constructing homes. Men's activities often took them away from the village, whether to hunt, trade, or wage war and negotiate peace.[2] Anthropologist Kathleen Bragdon suggests that during the sixteenth and seventeenth centuries, the riverine peoples of southern New England tended to be less hierarchical than the coastal Algonquian peoples; women likely held considerable power.[3] This holds true in Mohican societies, as is suggested by the example of Abraham's grandmother and her effort to secure her land to her descendents. Records of land transfers in Mohican territory dating to the seventeenth and early eighteenth centuries frequently were signed by women, suggesting that women maintained substantial power in community affairs into the colonial period, even as the social structures of Mohican society were adapting to the colonial realities of disease, trade, and European settlement.[4] Women's work, like men's work, was changing. Women and men hired themselves out to Dutch neighbors for wage labor. Women made baskets, mats, and brooms for sale at nearby white communities.[5]

A few tantalizing bits of evidence from Shekomeko suggest that women continued to play an important role in the management of the community's resources. Some women owned considerable property, and women continued to be central to the production of wampum belts for use in diplomatic affairs. Wampum had long functioned as spiritual currency in southern New England. With the arrival of Europeans, wampum took on economic functions as well and fostered competition between lineages for control of the resource. Wampum played a central role in all ceremonial meetings with other peoples. It was the substance that backed up the words spoken by chiefs.[6] Hendrick Aupaumut, sachem of the Stockbridge Mohicans in the late eighteenth century, described the relationship between the diplomatic business of the sachem, wampum, and women:

> The Sachem is allowed to keep Mno-ti, or peaceable bag, or bag of peace, containing about one bushel, some less....In this bag they keep various Squau-tho-won, or belts of wampum, also strings; which belts and strings they used to establish peace and friendship with different nations, and to use them on many occasions, and passed as coin. In this bag they keep all belts and strings which they received of their allies of different nations. This bag is, as it were, unmoveable; but it is always remain at Sachem's house, as hereditary with the office of a Sachem; When they find the wampum will be fall short, besides what is kept in the bag, the Sachem and his counsel-ors would sent [sic] their runner to gather, or collect wampum from their women, which business they called mau-peen, or sitting into one place.[7]

This practice is evident in the Moravian records, which contain several references to women's involvement in the production and exchange of wampum. On at least two occasions, a baptized Mohican woman named Bathsheba played a role in preparing the wampum belts for use in official delegations.[8] Further evidence of women's roles in regulating wampum comes from Ruth's testament, which she drew up shortly before her death in April 1745. Among her possessions when she died were two belts of wampum, one large and one small. Her will specified that the larger belt be used to buy a dress for her burial and the remainder given to her daughters. The smaller belt was to be used to pay off her debts.[9] These examples suggest that women continued to play an important role in the distribution of resources.

Mohican women would also have been expected to provide food for guests of the sachem. According to Aupaumut in his history of the Mohi-can peoples, women "were to bring victuals to Sachem's to enable him to feed strangers;—for whenever strangers arrived at their fireplace they are directed to go to Sachem's house. There they stay until their business is completed."[10] There is at least some indication that this role had become burdensome in Shekomeko, where there were frequent visitors from Indian villages near and far. One line in the minutes from the mission conferences noted: "It was complained that Rebecca says nothing else to the visitors who come to her house than about the work and how they must help her if they want to eat at her house."[11] One missionary's report from Shekomeko in 1744 suggested that the residents were feeling burdened by so many visitors: "They all say the cause of their Present want is the many strangers and Brothers and Sisters which come so frequently to see them."[12]

Ruth's will also suggests just how extensively the women of Shekomeko were involved in the larger colonial trading network. At her death, Ruth left mats, wooden dishes, six spoons, six bags, five large and three small kettles, a mare, a yearling calf, a saddle, two bridles, one large and three small hatchets, four bowls, two chains for hanging kettles, a silk shirt, pans and bottles, two mortars, and the two pieces of wampum already mentioned.[13] Interestingly, at a time when married women had no rights to property in European colonies, the missionaries honored Ruth's will over the objections of Cornelius, one of the elder men of Shekomeko.[14]

Agricultural production in Northeastern Indian societies was traditionally the province of women. The Moravian records suggest, however, that both men and women in Shekomeko participated in planting, tending, and harvesting crops. Whether this was how things had always been done or the result of missionary involvement is difficult to determine. If the Moravians did set out to alter gender roles in regard to agricultural production, they did not write about it. But the mission diaries and conference records do make note of the missionaries helping Mohican men and women in the fields, whether fencing fields, plowing, planting, threshing, or harvesting. Although they are mentioned only rarely, domestic animals at Shekomeko were generally cared for by women. For example, Martha brought a complaint against Judith that her pigs were damaging her corn crops. Sarah was delegated by the committee to talk with Judith and recommend that she should either butcher the pigs or sell them.[15] In the course of Esther's long life with the Moravian community, she was noted as being interested in keeping chickens, and she picked berries, harvested corn, ran the guesthouse at Gnadenhütten, and applied for (and received) farmland at Gnadenhütten.[16]

Women played an important role in the management of spiritual and economic currency of the community: they created the materials that were used as collateral or confirmation of men's words. Without women's production—weaving the wampum into belts—a chief's words were worthless. When women created these belts, they signaled that the men acted on behalf of the community. Women's ability to collect and prepare food made it possible for community leaders to conduct business. At the same time, however, other evidence suggests that women's power was declining: anthropologist Ted Brasser concluded that increased warfare, diminishing supplies of game (which required men to travel farther to hunt), and land loss to colonial settlement all led to the diminishing importance of clans and lineages and to the rising importance of the nuclear family.[17] Further evidence of women's waning power is suggested by Johannes's desire to be free of his mother-in-law's religious authority. Significantly, this power was symbolized by the "idol" given to her by her grandmother, which was "made of leather in the shape of a man and adorned with wampum."[18]

For each Esther or Ruth who managed to secure some economic stability for herself, there were many women who struggled constantly against poverty. The challenges faced by Lea, a young woman from Pachgatgoch, would not have been uncommon to many native women. With three young children to care for and just days from giving birth to a fourth, Lea was abandoned by her husband. Nine months later, she was setting off to work in the woods, presumably collecting materials to make mats or brooms, because all of her corn had gone to pay her debts. That spring she received several supplies of corn from missionary Mack, but this could do little to alleviate her other problems: she was berated and struck by a neighbor, and on another occasion she was beaten by drunken men. Worst of all, when a merchant from nearby Woodbury came to collect on Lea's debts and she could not pay him, he seized two of her children and sold them into service to a neighboring white family. An effort was made by a party of Pachgatgoch residents to retrieve the children, but apparently without success.[19]

The Moravian sources provide evidence of women's subjective experiences of these changes: they are full of Indian women's expressions of feeling powerless, weak, and in need of sustenance and cleansing. Moravian descriptions of Mohican women's practice of Christianity are particularly revealing, for they provide evidence of a community in flux and the declining status of women. They also reveal the spiritual creativity of Mohican women as they adapted Christian practice to reclaim control over their lives. At first glance, Mohican women's expressions might seem simply to mimic European Moravian religious expression or to be a result of missionary license. But when these sources are read keeping in mind what we know of inherited Mohican culture, they emerge in an entirely new light. Christian practice enabled Mohican women to claim new sources of spiritual power when others were unavailable to them. This is especially clear when we read women's statements about their experience of communion in light of the rituals of the "mourning war."

The women of Shekomeko dictated scores of letters to the missionaries to be carried to loved ones in other communities. These letters reveal a pervasive sense of vulnerability and an inability to live the lives that the women wished. The letters often included an expression of desire for the blood of the Savior. Leaving aside for the moment what these women understood by "the blood of the Savior," their longing for ritual practice suggests that they understood their condition as a spiritual problem. For example, Jonas's wife (later baptized Bathsheba) confessed to her husband: "I have such a wicked heart, that I must always do evil even when I don't want to."[20] Another woman lamented that she felt she was unable to do the right thing, so she "wished she could taste the blood of the savior in her heart."[21] Similarly, Martha sent her greetings to her husband, Johannes (Tschoop), who was in Bethlehem at the time, confessing that her heart was bound to evil things and hoping that the Savior would "help that I can get another heart."[22]

These letters could be read as evidence that the women had internalized white colonial attitudes of Indian inferiority. Yet the letters do not so much express the displacement of native by European values as suggest the psychic suffering experienced by so many women when they were unable to live up to the cultural values that they embraced. They turned to Christian practice in the hope that they could gain the spiritual and physical strength they needed to be good women in their roles as mothers, wives, and community members.

Women were often drawn to Christian practice after they witnessed the transformation other women experienced, women who attributed that transformation to the power of Jesus's blood. When Isaac's sister visited the Shekomeko congregation and observed what she thought was a dramatic transformation, she too longed to experience the blood of the Savior.[23] The Bethlehem diarist recorded similar expressions from Delaware and Mohican women visiting Gnadenhütten. One Delaware woman reported that she knew little about Christianity before she visited Gnadenhütten, but now she heard how "she might get free from Sin and be saved; and now her Heart long'd much after that Blood." She and her husband were soon baptized. Also baptized that day was a thirteen-year-old Mohican girl who had recently arrived in town. The girl reported that "she could not bear any longer to be without our Saviors Blood and that particularly since she had seen Sophia...baptis'd in Gnadenhutten her heart long'd Day and Night after that Blood."[24] Women encouraged other women to turn to the blood and wounds for whatever help they needed. For example, Ziporra urged Martha that "she should stay close to the wounds so that she would get all that she needed."[25] Abraham and Sarah's daughter-in-law had been baptized in Stockbridge yet requested that the Moravians baptize her again, because "she had not felt or got anything" from her first baptism.[26] Women often felt empowered by their Christian practice, and they struggled to retain that feeling.

To many women of Shekomeko, the Moravian Savior was experienced as a powerful agent of change in their difficult lives. A hymn composed by Bathsheba and her husband reads simply: "You have sacrificed yourself. Let us be a little bee, so that we drink the juice of the bloody wounds so that we grow and become strong."[27] Justina similarly found strength in the Moravian Savior. In a dictated note, she confessed her weakness but also her thankfulness "to my Savior that he has been pleased to give me new Strength."[28] When circumstances called for extra reserves of strength and fortitude, at least some Mohican women turned to the blood of Jesus for assistance.

A recurring theme in women's experience of Christian practice was that of being transported and of leaving behind the difficulties of the world. Sarah had claimed the power to withstand her flesh being torn from her body. Rachel felt that she could be scalded with boiling water without noticing, feeling instead that she was floating in the air surrounded by angels.[29] Similarly, Esther reported to Sarah that she was sometimes so transported that "she did not know that she lived in this world." And when she emerged from this ecstatic state, she was miserable because "her mother often bothered her."[30] The constant theme in these women's experiences is one of being transported temporarily out of their everyday world and gaining the power to endure suffering, whether that suffering was the pain of physical torture or childbirth or the annoyance of a nagging mother.

At first glance, these expressions seem to be of a piece with Moravian expressions of piety, but upon closer examination, it appears that the imagery is altogether different from that commonly employed by European Moravians, whose writings tended to focus on mystical union with Christ. Mohican women's writings evoked instead practices associated with ritualized torture among many Algonquian and Iroquois peoples.

Understanding native women's descriptions of suffering stoically with the assistance of Christ's blood against the backdrop of mourning war rituals and the Moravian practice of communion suggests some intriguing possibilities about the intersection of gender, colonialism, and Christian ritual. The resonance of communion would have been slightly different for women than for men.[31] While women were traditionally less likely to be the victims of ritual torture, they were its directors. It was women's responsibility to balance the spiritual forces after the disruption caused by a death. Historian Theda Perdue's assessment of changing Cherokee gender roles might apply equally to the Mohican situation. The new motives for war introduced by the trade and by the French-English colonial rivalry "excluded women from the social and spiritual benefits that traditional warfare had brought them."[32] As Daniel Richter has shown, these same forces provoked the spiraling of mourning war practices among the Iroquois, rendering them far more deadly and socially destructive. Mohicans experienced many of these same pressures from colonialism, and so one source of spiritual power would have been less readily available to Mohican women.

The Moravian emphasis on the redemptive power of suffering and the transformative power of Christ's blood fused with Mohican cultural traditions to create a ritual practice fully Christian *and* Mohican. The Christian narrative became a revision of a deeply rooted Northeastern Indian narrative, a revision that maintained continuity with the past while also allowing them to leave behind practices no longer viable. In this new narrative, Jesus was a powerful warrior, one who, rather than being captured in battle, offered his body and blood willingly for the good of all, even the lowest and weakest. Through the practice of communion, participants could access the ritual power that came through the consumption of a powerful warrior without the costs of waging war. By participating in communion, Sarah and Rachel and other women laid claim to two types of spiritual power—that traditionally accorded women as they avenged the deaths of their kinsmen and that claimed by captive warriors who secured a chance at rebirth through stoic endurance of torture.[33] Consuming Christ's flesh might have functioned as a substitute for the traditional spiritual power available to women as active participants in the practice of war. In turn, this spiritual force was translated into the ability to suffer stoically.[34] Communion was thus one means of acquiring the spiritual power to sustain self in an environment increasingly hostile to Indian existence.

DOMESTIC LIFE: PRESERVING SELF AND FAMILY

The stresses of colonialism were felt particularly keenly in women's domestic relationships: disease and persistent poverty challenged women's ability to care for themselves and their families. Many women responded to these threats by drawing on resources offered by the Moravian missionaries—social, spiritual, and material—in an effort to preserve what was most important to them. While not always successful, their struggles, as recorded by the missionaries, help us appreciate not only how Mohican values found expression in Christian practice, but also how Christianity was transformed in the process of being inculturated in Mohican society.

In the century before the arrival of the Moravian missionaries, Mohican communities from the Hudson to the Housatonic Valleys suffered repeated onslaughts of epidemic disease.[35] By the Indians' own estimates, the epidemics had claimed 90 percent of their communities. Native healers were adept at treating external ailments—wounds, bruises, or other injuries—with a variety of plant-derived cures, but they could do little against the onslaught of the new pathogens. Other native cures, such as fasting, sweating, or purging, when used in the attempt to treat the new diseases often exacerbated the patient's condition.[36]

Disease was not only physically but also psychologically and socially devastating to native communities. Epidemic disease placed a tremendous strain on the spiritual and social resources of these communities. Cultural understandings about the nature and causes of illness shaped Mohican responses to the host of new pathogens brought by Europeans. Van der Donck reported that the Mohicans he encountered in the 1650s believed that all accidents, infirmities, and diseases were "sent by the devil"; if they had an internal complaint, they cried, "The devil is in me." To placate the spirit, the afflicted individual offered a sacrifice to the fire.[37] The presence of the evil spirit might be attributable to a person's failure to observe proper ritual practice or to the intervention of humans through the manipulation of spiritual forces.[38] Most Europeans dismissed such claims as devil worship or chicanery.[39] However understood, the increased incidence of disease undermined the social fabric by rendering native healers ineffective and by making community members feel particularly vulnerable to the spiritual forces. If good health signaled proper relationships between humans and the spirit world, ill health signaled a breakdown of communication between humans and the spirit world.

In the Moravian records, the grim statistics assume a human face. Abraham's grandmother, father, uncle, and sister all died in epidemics. In one year, Rachel lost one of her children and four other family members. Esther, another Shekomeko resident, lost at least four children to disease. Sarah and Abraham's son David and his wife, Sarah, lost three children in as many years.[40] There is some suggestion in the Moravian records that illness was indeed understood as a result of a personal failure, as when Ruth told Sarah that "she felt in her heart that she was sick as punishment because she knew how unfaithful she was to the savior."[41] However they explained ill health and death, many Shekomeko women turned to the missionaries and Christian practice for healing, and, when death seemed inevitable, for nursing care and hope for the next world.

For some women, Christian belief and practice became a means of confronting the destructive power of disease. A number of women either attributed their recovery to the power of Jesus's blood and wounds or, upon recovering, promised to be faithful to the Savior. For example, as Johannes's stepmother lay very sick in the early fall of 1743, she asked to be baptized. Missionary Büttner reported, "She feels again if she was not happy, and had not got that life in Jesus's Blood and she believed if she was to be baptized she could be helped."[42] Another woman, Eva, attributed her health to being close to the Moravian community. In a letter from Bethlehem to her friends and family who remained at Shekomeko and Pachgatgoch, she wrote that "in Shekomeko I was allways sick, but here I am very healthy."[43]

On occasion, then, Mohican women found the power of healing in Jesus' blood, but more often, all ministrations failed to cure ailing patients. When smallpox struck Gnadenhütten in the summer of 1746, claiming many, including Johannes, Rauch remarked that "the faithfullness which Brother and Sister Martin [Mack] have shewn to the sick Indian Brethren and Sisters, day and Night, is very great in their Eyes." Rauch observed that the love of the missionaries made a great impression and that it was "edifying when they see one go Home [die] with a Chearfull Heart, notwithstanding they love them so much."[44] In these instances, the nursing care offered by the missionaries provided some comfort and reminded the Indian community at the mission sites just how different the Moravians were from other whites they had encountered. And if the Mohicans found the nursing care of the Moravians particularly effectual, it might have been because it resonated with inherited Mohican values.[45]

The records give some indication that the Indians of Shekomeko and other surrounding communities continued to seek out both traditional cures and the ministrations of the missionaries. In December 1744, Sarah lay at death's door and requested to see Gottlob Büttner. The missionary was himself gravely ill with tuberculosis and was so weak that he had to be carried to Sarah. Büttner wrote in his journal that "we applied medicine and it did her good," after which they sang a Mohican hymn. Abraham arrived soon after and told Büttner that "a particular Circumstance had happened to her, by which means her pain would probably be assuaged, which our Savior accordingly brought about."[46] Unfortunately, the records provide no hint as to what sort of medicine was applied, what sort of circumstance had happened to Sarah, or to what powers Abraham attributed his wife's predicted recovery. The medicine may have been of European origin, but it seems just as likely that it was a native remedy. The Pachgatgoch diaries make frequent reference to the missionaries seeking medical assistance from native healers and to the continued use of the sweat lodge, which seems to have functioned for women and men both as a meeting place to discuss village affairs and as a method of healing.[47] These instances are telling, for they suggest the potential for cross-fertilization between Mohican and Moravian beliefs and practices: Moravians accepted Mohican healing traditions but attributed their efficacy to the Savior.

When neither traditional practices nor appeal to the Savior succeeded in restoring health, some Mohicans found comfort in the Moravian teachings about death. Missionary Rauch reported that the survivors of the 1746 smallpox epidemic were comforted because "they believe that they [the deceased] are with our Savior and [the survivors] have lost the fearfull Ideas of Death, which they have had all their life long."[48] Rauch may well have overestimated the extent to which Christian beliefs had supplanted traditional notions of death and the afterlife. More likely, there was some degree of melding of old and new. In the seventeenth century, van der Donck reported that the Mohicans he encountered believed that upon death, the soul separates from the body and "removes to a place toward the south, where the climate is so fine that no covering against cold will be necessary, and where the heat will never become troublesome." Further, they believed that it was only the good souls that would travel there, while the bad spirits would be forced to roam the woods at night.[49] If Rauch and van der Donck were both correct in their perceptions, it would suggest either that Mohican beliefs had changed considerably or, more likely, that many Mohicans, because of the conditions of colonialism, were more likely to judge themselves as among the bad souls who would face an uncertain fate after death. The many women who spoke of having a "wicked heart" or of being powerless were perhaps saying just this.

Moravian teachings coincided with inherited beliefs about life after death and offered a means of reclaiming the possibility of a good death. The Moravian theology of Christ's atonement for human sins provided consolation that even those who counted themselves sinners could enjoy an afterlife with their friends and family. A conversation between Jannetje Mack and a Mohican woman who had just lost her only remaining child to what she suspected was the work of a Delaware sorcerer suggests how this theology was presented to native parents. The woman asked Mack, "Do you believe that my child is now with your God?" to which Mack answered, "I do, because our God is a friend of the children." Sister Mack used the occasion to proselytize, "if your [*sic*] learn to know him, you may in eternity find your child with him; for he is not only *our* God but also *your* God and loves all men. He loved them so much, that he became a man and died for you and me, that we all might be saved if we receive him."[50] Indians sought assurances that the next world would be better than this and that family and friends would be reunited. As Gideon wrote to his daughter, Christina, who was living with the Single Sisters at Bethlehem, he found comfort in the thought of "what a blessed and happy Time this will be when we shall come together and meet one another there above, when we are gone home to our Savior for to live with him for ever."[51] A letter from Christina's sister, Johanna, expressed a similar sentiment: "I will always remain by our Savior and his open wounds and there I greet you *for there we meet.*"[52]

Just as we could hear in Nicodemus's description of the resurrection of bodies echoes of native southern New England cosmology, so too can we perceive in women's hopes for seeing the Savior in the next world evidence of the desire to maintain the connections between the generations of living and dead. The missionaries, of course, heard these deathbed utterances of evidence of the power of the Holy Spirit to melt heathen hearts. When the missionaries wrote that Abigail, who lay very sick, said she "was not fearful of dying because when she died she could go to the savior," she was not necessarily exchanging an inherited set of beliefs for those offered by the Moravians.[53] Rather, she had perhaps found in Moravian theology a means of revitalizing inherited traditions with a new vocabulary. Moravians went home to the Savior, while Mohicans traveled south to the land of the spirits.

The desire to ensure family ties beyond the grave often provided the impetus to baptism. The stepfather of a gravely ill thirteen-year-old girl first approached Büttner in late November 1742 and told him that the girl longed to be baptized. The next day, most of the village gathered in the mission house for the girl's baptism. The congregation sang several "blood verses" after which Jannetje Mack offered a prayer in Mohican, and while she prayed, Büttner baptized the girl, naming her Lazara, signifying the hope that she would soon be raised by the Savior. She died two days later, and her parents were both baptized just over a week later, together with six other couples.[54] Lazara's parents might well have hoped, as many other parents did, that baptism could ensure the family would be reunited in the afterlife. This might have been the sentiment that Jonathan (Abraham's son) and his wife, Sarah, conveyed to the missionary when they lost their prematurely born infant. "If we had seen it so," Jonathan reported, "and at the same time not known that it was our Saviors we should undoubtedly have been very Miserable about it." But he was comforted by the thought that "it's near to the wounds, and if we continue faithful to our Savior we shall see it again with him."[55]

Fear of separation from loved ones after death often prompted an interest in Christianity.[56] On their deathbeds, Mohican Christians exhorted friends and family to remain faithful. When Maria lay dying, she exhorted her husband and her parents not to grieve her death, for she was going to the Savior to "see and kiss his wounds" and if they remained devoted to the Savior, "then they would all come together again and remain eternally with our Savior, never more to die."[57] Similarly, when fatally ill in 1750, Abigail called her husband to her side and asked him to promise to remain faithful to the Savior so that they could meet again "in the side-hole." When her husband promised as she had requested, she replied that she could "now go peacefully to the savior and I will go soon." To those gathered, she added that she would "soon go into the little side hole and there I will...find my beloved Jannike, who I love so much and who spoke to me so often about the little Lamb."[58] Christian practice could provide extra assurance that one's spirit would not be condemned to walk abroad in the woods but would instead safely make the journey to a place where one could be reunited with family and friends.

Illness also brought neophytes to consider the physical and spiritual care of their loved ones after their death. When parents lost young children or faced death themselves, they were forced to make difficult decisions about the care of their surviving children. Just as Rachel had turned to the blood of the Savior in the hopes of sustaining her child, many parents sought spiritual and material help in caring for their children. The number of parents who literally gave their children over to the care of particular missionaries or sent them to the children's nursery at Bethlehem suggests just how difficult life in Shekomeko had become. Ruth was eight months pregnant and near death when she requested help in drawing up a will in April 1745. Ruth and her husband, Boaz, had been fighting for years, so the will was perhaps intended to ensure that she maintain control over the fate of her possessions from her husband or others who may have had different ideas. The child was stillborn, and Ruth died soon after. But her will poignantly conveys the dilemma of a mother trying to ensure her children's well-being in a changing world. Ultimately, Ruth chose to entrust her children to the care of the Spangenbergs in Bethlehem: "I have thought in my Heart, where I should bring my Children to, where they might be brought to our Saviour and their Souls be saved, I thought on all my Brethren and Sisters and Friends here in Shecomeco, but could not pitch upon any one with whom they could be, except Brother Spangenberg in Bethlehem: who I heartily intreat to bring my Children to our Saviour."[59] Unable to ensure her children's safe passage to adulthood, Ruth thought the best guarantee of a future for her children lay in missionary hands.

Ruth's case was scarcely unique. Scattered throughout the Moravian records are numerous references to other women who feared that they could not provide properly for their children's care. A number of them, like Ruth, entrusted their children to the care of the Moravians. Parents who clearly desperately loved their children were willing to part with them in the hopes that they would receive the care and instruction that would enable their children to survive. One letter from a young woman named Beata to Maria Spangenberg captures the desperation of a mother who had watched her other children die. Beata asked the congregation at Bethlehem to take her child "for she is sensible in her heart, that she can not bring it up for our Savior." She remembered how well her other child had been cared for by the congregation before going "home to our Saviour."[60]

The problem seems to have grown even worse at the new mission site in Gnadenhütten, to which many Shekomeko and Pachgatgoch residents had removed in 1746 after the Moravians were barred from preaching in New York. Esther, an active leader among the Christian Indian women, requested that her son Thomas be taken to Bethlehem and cared for there.[61] A letter from Joshua to the Spangenbergs in January 1747 entreated them to take care of his son at Bethlehem, because he was "very poor and cannot bring my Son into such a good Way."[62] Benjamin and Zippora made a similar request that year because, according to the missionary, they "see daily that they were unable to raise the child for the savior."[63] A year later, the couple again requested that a child—this time their daughter Salome—be cared for by the Brethren at the Bethlehem nursery.[64] Philip and Lydia twice asked that their children be cared for by the Brethren. On the second occasion, upon the birth of their daughter, Beata, they presented the girl to the childless Anna Rauch to raise as her own. The mission diarist noted Anna's delight, remarking strangely that "many would not have been as happy had they been given many 1000£."[65]

Whether or not the parents' central concern was raising children "for the savior," it is clear from these examples that many families suffered a severe crisis of confidence that they would be able to raise their children to succeed or even survive in the dangerous world around them. The extent of the social breakdown is suggested by the frequency with which children themselves requested they be given over to the care of the Moravians. When Joshua's parents received approval to send their son to be with the other children at Bethlehem, the young Joshua eagerly packed his things and prepared for the journey.[66] Philip and Lydia had petitioned the Moravians to care for two of their children. Their request to care for their son was apparently prompted by a beating they had given him for misbehaving. The child wept and addressed his parents (in the missionaries' rendering): "Dear Father and Mother: I have told you many times. Pray give my Body to Martin [Mack] I am sure he loves me better then you do. He will take care to bring me to the congregation. You don't bring me to the congregation and Martin understands it better then you how I can obtain a good heart."[67] The couple may have been ashamed of having struck their son and for that reason sought a place for him among the Moravians, whose views of childrearing were in keeping with traditional Mohican values toward children. Physical punishment was not traditionally a part of the Indian childrearing practices. In fact, from the era of first contact, many European commentators had remarked unfavorably on what they saw as overly indulgent childrearing practices among the Indians of the northeast, the result of which was a society that prized liberty over discipline.[68]

In fact, Moravian and Mohican ideals of childrearing arguably were more alike than were Moravian and New England styles. Moravians upheld the child as the ideal of faith, not a willful corrupt being whose will must be broken before salvation is possible, as was common among Anglo-Protestants.[69] Zinzendorf's theology, which held that Jesus's earthly life had sanctified all of human life, informed educational and childrearing practices. Although the mission records do not contain much commentary on Indian childrearing practices, it is clear that the missionaries were inclined to find marks of piety among children, as when the children asked to live among the Brethren. These examples were recorded as evidence that the Holy Spirit often planted the seed of piety in children, yet they testify as well to the severe strains on native families.[70]

The Moravian records suggest that many of the Mohican converts had lost faith in their ability to instill in their children the proper Mohican values. Some parents turned to the Moravians in the hopes that their children might be given the skills necessary for survival while also abiding by traditional Mohican ideals of childrearing. Shekomeko was a difficult place to raise a child, as was Gnadenhütten. The community's land resources were under constant pressure, and epidemic disease periodically blazed through the village, taking a toll especially on the very young and the very old. With the loss of elders went a store of social capital that had previously been enlisted in the project of rearing children. Families often lacked the social and material resources necessary to raise their children according to inherited ideals, so they often turned to the Moravian missionaries for assistance.

Poverty rarely promotes domestic harmony. And just as parents frequently struggled to be good parents in uncertain times, so husbands and wives strained to fulfill their obligations to one another. Little is known about Mohican marriage practices on the eve of the mission era, but the Moravian sources provide some hints about marriage customs and the changes prompted by increasing contact with Europeans.[71] The available evidence suggests that the nuclear family had grown in significance while the lineage or clan had weakened since the mid–seventeenth century. Van der Donck had observed Mohican villages in which sixteen to eighteen families—presumably including members of a single lineage—lived together around individual hearths within longhouses that sometimes reached a hundred feet in length. The precipitous decline of population caused by disease and the increasingly great distances hunters had to travel for their quarry rendered such arrangements less practical. Increasing contact with colonial European society would also have exerted pressure in favor of the nuclear, patriarchal family structure. The sketch of Shekomeko in 1745 by Moravian missionary Johannes Hagen offers visual evidence of this trend: of the sixteen dwellings, all seem to be single-family houses, with only Abraham's being somewhat larger. At the time, the population of Shekomeko was estimated at about one hundred, or about six people per home, suggesting that residences were arranged by nuclear family unit. By the beginning of the mission era, the longhouse served primarily as the chief's residence and the site of ceremonial observances.[72]

The rearrangement of social space no doubt reflected change in gender relations; husbands and wives would have become increasingly dependent on one another, perhaps opening the door to greater dissatisfaction. The mission records, particularly the conference minutes, contain ample evidence of the struggles between husbands and wives. Of course, the conference minutes—like the court records that have been the staple of social histories—present a distorted view of reality, as domestic harmony is rarely fodder for discussion.

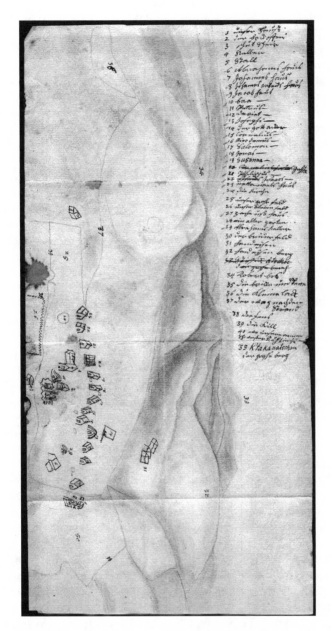

Figure 6 Sketch of Shekomeko, by Johannes Hagen, 1745. #1 & #24 mission house and church, #6 Abraham's house, #7 & #8 Johannes's house and workshop, #14 Burial ground, #15 Cornelius's house, #20 Jephta's house. 112/7/1 Courtesy of Moravian Archives, Bethlehem, Pennsylvania.

The Indian men and women who served on the committee were to meet individually with all community members and report back to the committee on everything from their spiritual state to marital relations to plans for hunting or harvesting. These meetings served as a forum to discuss both family and community problems. The conferences generally functioned in support of existing leadership structures; Abraham, Cornelius, and Sarah, for example, were all regular committee members.[73]

The records of the weekly conferences contain frequent references to the challenges facing husbands and wives. In some cases, one spouse had been driven from the home by regular quarreling and sometimes by physical abuse. And while women were sometimes responsible for bringing alcohol into the community, they also bore the brunt of the violence it so often incited.[74] Scarcity of food—whether caused by shrinking hunting territories, depleted game reserves, failed crops, or alcohol-induced languor—caused tensions. Differing degrees of commitment to the Christian community also produced tensions between husbands and wives. Somewhat surprisingly, very few of the problems brought before the conference seem to be the result of missionary attempts to impose a new morality of marriage on villagers. Rather, the minutes call attention to the difficulties average men and women had in securing domestic harmony. In fact, the conferences likely took on some of the functions of communal regulation once the province of the leadership within a lineage or clan. The conferences were at once a potentially divisive force in the community, and a significant venue for native leadership.

Moravian missionaries harbored ideals regarding the definition of marriage, but for the most part, they were not especially heavy handed, in keeping with their early mission policy of emphasizing inner transformation rather then external, cultural change. Rather, the problems were discussed at the conferences, where the Indian delegates brought forward any issues they had discovered in the course of their visiting in the community, and the committee members decided on a course of action. On the one hand, the weekly conferences were clearly a new institutional structure imported by the missionaries, but the way they were constituted and operated prevented them from being a simple instrument of Moravian will. Indeed, the missionaries often deferred to villagers' judgment. For example, when Jonas came to a conference for advice about what he should do if his unbaptized wife returned to him, the missionary turned the tables and asked him what he wanted to do.[75]

Moravian missionaries occasionally intervened in Indian marriages, sometimes serving as mediators between quarrelling spouses and at other times pressing for conformity to a Christian model of marriage. In one early meeting of the missionaries, it was resolved that they should call a meeting with the

Indian congregation in order to acquaint them with the "order of the congregation," particularly "in relation to matchmaking either among themselves or through others."[76] Presumably this meant that Indian marriages would be considered by the elders of the congregation and submitted to the lot as well for the Savior's approval.[77] The records contain numerous references to debates about proposed marriages at the Workers' Conferences, which contained both white and Indian members. For example, in 1751, Benjamin was noted as casting the decisive vote on his sister Esther's marriage.[78]

One of the most notable cases of missionary involvement in arranging marriages (besides the marriage of Rachel to the missionary Friedrich Post) involved Maria, the much sought-after eighteen-year-old daughter of Gideon and Martha, the head couple of Pachgatgoch. She was considered as a wife for Post and subsequently for Jonathan, one of Abraham's sons. Then Umpachenee of Stockbridge expressed interest. Apparently, Umpachenee, whose wife Hannah had died two years earlier, was seeking a wife, and perhaps because of the preexisting kinship ties between the two prominent families—Gideon and Umpachenee were cousins—a marriage with Maria would reconfirm ties between the two communities.[79] At an August 1743 conference that included native leaders Abraham, Isaac, Jacob, Gideon, Cornelius, and Johannes as well as six missionaries, Gideon reported that the "the Captain from Westenhook," wanted to marry his daughter, Maria, but that he and his daughter would "abide by the advice of the Brethren" if they disapproved. The next day, the minutes show the resolution "Gideon and Maria must be asked how the issue stands in her [Maria's] heart." Another entry from that meeting suggests that the missionaries made it clear how they felt, with Büttner noting, "We think it is not good because she is so young and he so old, and especially because it is against the apostolic rule that a believer and an unbeliever marry."[80] At another conference two months later, the missionaries resolved not to interfere.[81] But then in December, conference minutes note that "the captain" from Stockbridge was angry with Büttner "because he had hindered his marriage with Maria of Pachgatgoch."[82] On the one hand, the missionaries seem to have intervened and prevented a marriage that likely would have served an important political function. On the other hand, Gideon and Martha apparently expressed their willingness to submit to the guidance of the Brethren. Gideon and Martha's other daughter, Christina, moved into the Single Sisters' house in Bethlehem in 1752, and perhaps the family saw this arrangement as confirming the relationship between the Indian and white Moravians.[83]

The case of Jonathan's marriage provides a bit more detail about the missionaries' involvement in marital affairs. As the son of Abraham and Sarah and an early convert, Jonathan quickly rose to a prominent position in the community, often serving as interpreter and conducting services. In a February 1743 letter to Anton Seiffert, Büttner requested advice about Jonathan, among other matters. He thought it was best that Jonathan should find a wife from among the Indian congregation but expressed his willingness to defer to Seiffert's opinion.[84] In August 1743, the White Workers Conference put the question of Jonathan's marital status to the lot, a process they repeated that day for all of the unmarried mission residents. The primary candidate for Jonathan at the time was Maria, but the Savior seems to have responded that Jonathan's marriage should wait and perhaps that Maria was not the proper choice (it was in the same meeting they were considering Umpachenee's desire to marry Maria). The missionaries continued to propose different combinations to the lot, eventually meeting with the Savior's approval for a match between Jonathan and Anna, a woman from Wechquadnach related to both the Stockbridge sachem and to Gideon of Pachgatgoch.[85] Three months later, the match was approved by the Indian and White Workers Conference, at which point Sarah set off to seek the approval of Anna's parents.[86]

In the presence of Jonathan and Anna's lineages and with over one hundred people gathered, the couple was officially engaged on December 26, 1743, an event celebrated with a lovefeast.[87] The missionaries submitted possible dates and locations for the wedding to the lot, and the answer came from the Savior that they were to be married on January 3, 1744, in Anna's home village of Wechquadnach, near present-day Sharon, Connecticut. And so on that day, missionaries Büttner and Mack bundled onto a sleigh for the fifteen-mile journey from Shekomeko. Büttner preached a sermon and presided over the ceremony.[88] Although the ceremony incorporated Moravian customs, the process, which the Moravians understood to be guided by the Savior, was remarkably in keeping with Indian customs, and the end result reinforced rather than strained community bonds. If van der Donck's observations held true nearly a century later, it was Mohican custom that "when the parties are young and related, the marriage usually takes place upon the counsel and advice of their relatives, having regard to their families and character."[89] Jonathan and Anna's marriage linked the leading families of Wechquadnach, Pachgatgoch, Shekomeko, and Stockbridge; it added the additional support of a new fictive kinship of native and Euro-American Christian brethren.

The Moravian missionaries also became involved in marital affairs when one party was suspected of having extramarital relations. At first glance, this would seem to be a case of the missionaries imposing European sexual mores on Indian society. Most Algonquian cultures allowed for the dissolution of a marriage initiated by either partner. Sexual relations were generally permitted before marriage and outside of a marriage, particularly by men whose wives were nursing children and observed strict abstinence during this time.[90] But interestingly, when the Moravians became involved, it was generally at the request of a member of the Indian congregation. For example, Isaac was suspected of having an extramarital relationship with Susanna, an unmarried woman.[91] Isaac and his wife Rebecca do not seem to have had any young children at the time, and so it seems unlikely that his alleged relationship with Susanna was a traditionally sanctioned extramarital relationship. In this case, missionary intervention seems to have come when Rebecca brought forward a complaint, suggesting that even if such relationships might have been acceptable in the pre-mission era, Rebecca no longer wished to tolerate her husband's behavior, and in this she found support from the missionaries. In another instance, the missionaries supported Magdalena in demanding better treatment from her husband, Zacheus, who was excluded from services in December 1742 for quarreling with his wife. In 1744, Zacheus was suspected of having an affair with Bathsheba. The missionaries consulted with the various parties, and for a time, Zacheus and Magdalena's relationship seems to have improved, but by March 1745, Magdalena regretted having returned to her abusive spouse.[92] Mohican women turned to the network of missionaries for help in renegotiating their marriages on terms they found more agreeable.

The very real impact of colonialism can be seen in the desperation of Shekomeko resident Maria when her husband Joseph proved an unproductive hunter, apparently due to the effects of alcohol. She confessed to the missionaries that she had "evil thoughts" and that she had asked her husband "how it would please him if she cut their child's throat because he wasn't a better provider."[93] Maria attributed their marital difficulties to her husband's drinking, a judgment Joseph shared. In another conference just a week later, Joseph reported to Isaac that he was "always so angry when the brethren told him he led a wicked life. He had therefore always become so drunk he wanted to go away from Shekomeko and take another wife and then come back to Shekomeko and run Maria off."[94] Wherever the cycle started—with drinking, with missionary intrusion, or with a shortage of food—it is clear that some Mohican families were caught in a devastating cycle of dysfunction.

Marital tensions sometimes escalated from harsh words to physical violence.[95] The mission records rarely provide much detail as to the cause of the violence, but they do note its incidence; from what can be gleaned, it seems that most instances arose when the partners failed to live up their partners' expectations. Several couples made frequent appearances in the records because the husband had beaten his wife.[96] Boaz and Ruth are perhaps representative. The couple seems to have been caught in an endless cycle: Boaz complained that Ruth often refused to feed him when he returned home, to which Ruth responded that she didn't want to feed him because he was always angry. Eventually, Ruth had enough and left her husband, apparently without objection from the missionaries.[97]

It is difficult to discern just how the various couples understood their marital troubles, but one entry in the Gnadenhütten diary is suggestive. In speaking with Anna Rauch, Bathsheba spoke of her marital troubles with her second husband, Joshua. She explained that "the enemy had given her much trouble, and had tried to lead her away from her husband," but she was able to resist when she remembered "she was married before the Congregation."[98] The missionaries generally referred to Satan as "the enemy," and Bathsheba's use of the term here suggests perhaps that Mohicans and missionaries shared the view that spiritual forces could work to upset social relations. Interestingly, Bathsheba attributed her ability to resist to the power of the community.

Differing levels of commitment to the Christian community sometimes caused domestic tensions and became the subject of conference discussions. The conference minutes record a number of instances in which unbaptized wives ran away from their husbands. Jonas's unbaptized wife ran away from him following a Christian service. When Jonas consulted with the missionaries in January 1743 who asked whether he should receive his wife back if she returned, he answered that he would: he could not be angry at her because "she must do the devil's will so long as she does not have the blood."[99] Nascapamuth, baptized in Shekomeko on December 26, 1742, and given the name Petrus, experienced personally the factionalizing power of Christianity. We do not know the exact nature of the marital problems between Petrus and his unbaptized wife, whether they were preexisting or whether Petrus's baptism was the wedge between them. Yet he was reported to have been quarreling with his wife and urging her to be baptized. The unnamed woman apparently held firm, for in March 1745, Petrus lamented to the missionaries the difficulties of a mixed marriage, that is, the difficulty of being a Christian married to an unbaptized woman.[100] Cornelius, the "Old Captain" of Shekomeko, met with resistance from his unbaptized wife regarding Christianity: he reported at a conference that his wife had told him "if she heard anyone speaking about the Savior, so it would be funny to her because her heart would be dead to it."[101] On one occasion, Ruth was beaten by her husband because she came home late from a communion service.[102]

The marital strains experienced by many couples at Shekomeko and other villages may well have been a symptom of changing gender roles and changing dynamics within marriage brought in turn by changing social and economic circumstances. When a woman resented her husband's expectations, she may have been registering a sense of loss—the breakdown of the larger kinship networks would have robbed women of some of the important mechanisms of social support, leaving them to feel underappreciated or undercompensated. The presence of the Moravian missionaries, particularly the women, came to be an important means by which Mohican women sought to construct new networks of social support.

REBUILDING COMMUNITY

Sarah and Rachel's close relationship with Maria Spangenberg calls attention to the importance of the active presence of European women at the Moravian missions, arguably the single most important factor in the Moravian missionaries' success in gaining an audience among native women. In this, the Moravian mission program stood in dramatic contrast to Anglo-Protestant missions, in which an unmarried man labored alone (as typified by David Brainerd) or in which the missionary's wife functioned primarily as a provider of comfort for the missionary rather than as a helpmeet in his mission work (as typified by John Sergeant and his wife Abigail at Stockbridge).

It was no accident that women played a central role in the Moravian missionary project. In fact, it was a natural development from the Moravian choir system instituted by Zinzendorf, by which peer groups worshipped, lived, and worked together. In Bethlehem, women directed the labor and the spiritual life of their peers. It was expected that qualified women would be needed in the missions to minister to the particular needs of the native women.[103]

One of the first tasks for men who wanted to serve as missionaries was to find a wife to work with them, a decision that was often left to the lot. Rauch, Pyrlaeus, Büttner, Mack, Hagen, and Shaw were all married within months of each other just as they began their missionary work.[104] Moravian mission work was significantly advanced when Martin Mack—recently assigned to establish satellite mission sites at other villages near Shekomeko—married Jannetje Rauh, daughter of Johannes Rauh, the farmer who boarded Rauch during the tense early months of his mission. Jannetje had grown up in close contact with her Indian neighbors and had acquired some degree of proficiency in Mohican.[105] Mack could not have made a better selection.

Mack's early visits to the villages of Pachgatgoch and Potatik testify to the importance of his wife's presence in gaining and keeping an audience for the missionaries. When the Macks arrived at Pachgatgoch in the midst of a snowstorm, they were welcomed into the village chief's home. Most remarkable to the chief (later baptized as Gideon) was the Macks' willingness to be lodged in Indian homes. The Macks adhered to native customs of hospitality, no doubt the result at least in part of Jannetje's familiarity with native ways.[106] And in Potatik, when Mack first gained permission to preach, it was his wife who interpreted, much to the surprise of an Englishman in the audience who had come to satisfy his curiosity about the Moravian preacher. The observer asked an Indian man what he thought of Jannetje, to which the man answered, "She believes what she says, she believes in the Saviour and has felt his blood. I've never heard any man speak with so much assurance." When the man asked other villagers whether they understood Jannetje, they answered, "Yes, perfectly well."[107] Jannetje and her female colleagues were often the crucial link in forging connections with native peoples, particularly women.

Again and again, European Moravian women impressed native women with just how different they were from other Europeans they had encountered. For example, one Indian woman from Shamokin in Pennsylvania reported of her visit to Philadelphia, where she had been hosted by Moravians; she had "liked the Brethren there, especially the women," and she could not believe "with what great love she had been received by our People in Philadelphia but particularly that the women had kissed her." It made such a great impression, she said, because she "had never before been treated in that manner by white people."[108] A greeting sent by Bathsheba of Shekomeko suggests that she too placed the Moravians in an altogether different category from other Europeans. She wrote: "I greet Brother Joseph. I wish to stay with the Brethren and not go among the white people."[109] The women of Shekomeko discovered that the Moravian God and his messengers were different from other Europeans they had encountered.

The missionary Sisters distinguished themselves by involving themselves in the lives of the village women, nursing the sick, counseling and consoling the parents of sick children, and teaching girls to read. Their work was facilitated by the communal organization followed by the missionaries at Shekomeko. The missionaries all lived in one house, enabling women to be involved in duties other than housekeeping. Minutes from the missionaries' House Conference in November 1742 spelled out the details of the wives' duties. Margaretha Büttner and Jannetje Mack were to alternate responsibilities: each would cook one week while the other taught school for the girls and paid visits to the Indian women. The wives were encouraged to improve their own reading and writing skills so that they could serve more effectively as teachers. In addition, the Sisters were to spin as much cloth as much as possible for Johannes Rauh as a means of earning an income.[110] Most importantly, the Sisters were instructed to "devote themselves this whole week to visiting with the Indian women and getting to know them so that in 8 days they can give a reliable report in the conference."[111] Language skills would be crucial to their task, and Jannetje Mack was not the only one to gain proficiency in Mohican. In November 1743, Büttner noted in the mission diary that his wife "spoke for the first time in Indian to the single sisters" after only three months at the mission site.[112]

Bonds between Mohican and European women formed when they shared in the common experiences of women's lives. For example, when Sister Sensemann gave birth to a son, the missionary diarist reported, "our Indians were elated to have a little brother, and they all kissed him."[113] When David's wife Sarah was about to go into labor, she requested that Jannetje Mack come to spend the night with her for what proved to be a difficult labor.[114] And when Salome of Shekomeko was in advanced pregnancy and her husband was away, the missionaries appointed a European Sister to live with her and care for her.[115]

Some of the women of Shekomeko and the surrounding villages developed a close connection with the white Sisters. Jannetje was especially beloved among the Indian Sisters. When the Macks were readying to leave Shekomeko for a visit to Bethlehem, the Indian Sisters pleaded that Jannetje stay behind, at least until Büttner and his wife returned.[116] And when Martin Mack came to Shekomeko in November 1745 without his wife, the women immediately asked "for my Anna [Jannetje], if she was not also here." When he told them she was not with him, "some of them began to weep because my Anna did not also come to visit them."[117]

Mohican women found a degree of sisterhood with the wives of the Moravian missionaries. Just as Rachel had found maternal nurturing in her relationship with Maria Spangenberg, so many Mohican women turned to their white sisters in the mission community for support and comfort for themselves and, often, care for their children. In the choir system established by the Moravians, a number of Indian women like Sarah found new support for their authority within the community. Indian women were named as helpers, sacristans, and disciples in the emerging Christian community. They stood as sponsors, or godparents, of newly baptized children. In these capacities, they performed special roles at lovefeasts and communion services. They served in the conferences that decided on important community matters. The Moravian mission structures thus provided new opportunities for women's leadership at a time when clans and lineages were declining in influence. But as Sarah's experience suggests, these new roles were not always welcomed by all members of the community.

Some women found solace in Sarah's counsel, while others bristled at her authority. During one conference in the spring of 1745, Sarah reported on her conversation with a sick unbaptized woman from Pachgatgoch. The unnamed woman had remained behind in Pachgatgoch when many villagers had moved to Shekomeko but now felt drawn to the Christian community. In a poignant image, the woman likened the Christian community to a grove of chestnut trees and herself to a lone tree.[118] Not all villagers, however, saw Sarah's role in such a positive light. Rebecca, who with Sarah was among the first women to be baptized, resented that she was expected to confess the state of her heart to Sarah. She complained to the missionaries that she could not understand why Sarah should be her confessor and expressed disdain for the conferences.[119] Sarah's daughter-in-law, a woman from Stockbridge, was reported to have "a great enmity" toward Sarah, although no further explanation was given.[120]

Sarah's authority was not limited to other women. On one occasion, Sarah and Abraham reported that Isaac had recently spent an entire day at a nearby tavern and in his drunken state had threatened to shoot Johannes, all the while spouting derogatory words about the missionaries. The couple queried the missionary whether they should speak to Isaac on their own or together with the missionary. After putting the question to the lot, the missionary answered that the Savior wished them to speak with Isaac alone. One suspects that the missionary sensed his involvement would only heighten tensions.[121]

Sarah's frequent service on this committee might well have functioned to support the role she would have held by tradition as wife of the headman of the village. Women in native societies had traditionally maintained oversight of domestic village affairs. What to European observers often looked like the absence of a formal legal code was in fact the operation of powerful moral suasion that shaped behavior through public praise and scorn.[122] The social upheaval of the decades prior to the founding of the Moravian mission at Shekomeko created a space for different forms of moral regulation that came to be filled by the weekly conferences.

The women of Shekomeko and the surrounding communities were often slower to turn to the Christian practice introduced by Moravian missionaries, in part because it was perceived as a possible threat to women's religious power. In time, the distinctive Moravian mission policies, particularly the central role of women missionaries, exerted an appeal for Mohican women. European-Moravian women served as nurses and teachers to Mohican women and sometimes even as parents to the children of couples who had lost confidence in their ability to care for their children. In Christian practice, focused on contact with the blood and wounds of Christ, Mohican women found new resources of spiritual power they could enlist in the service of simultaneously upholding and renegotiating inherited traditions regarding gender roles. They sought to restore health to their bodies, and when that failed, they turned to the blood and wounds of Christ to enable them to endure suffering. Communion functioned in traditional native ways as the means of transferring spiritual power, but it also introduced a new ideology that made suffering meaningful. In addition, Mohican women turned their Christian practice to the ends of preserving family and restoring community bonds. Although Christianity often proved empowering to these women, the fact that they were searching for new sources of power is testimony of the disruptive force of colonialism. And while women sought to strengthen social ties of family and community through a shared Christian practice, these efforts could also lead to new fractures.

The Moravians' distinctive mission facilitated the indigenization of Christianity at Shekomeko and the surrounding Mohican communities. Native men and women found new sources of spiritual power in the blood and wounds of Christ and creatively adapted Christian practice to meet the particular challenges of colonialism. Ironically, the qualities of the Moravian missionaries that appealed to Mohican men and women rendered them suspect within the broader Euro-American community, so the Indians who cast their lot with the Moravians ultimately became even more vulnerable to abuse and mistreatment in colonial society.

PART IV

PERSECUTION

Chapter Nine

The Dying Chief and the Accidental Missionary

August 1751 was a busy month in Stockbridge. Umpachenee had been ailing since the spring, and a constant stream of visitors arrived to pay their regards to the dying leader. Among the visitors were Moravian missionaries and several Indian residents of Pachgatgoch. The Stockbridge pulpit had been empty since John Sergeant's death two years earlier. A new missionary was to be installed: the famed Jonathan Edwards was officially to assume leadership of the mission. Like Sergeant's ordination at Deerfield sixteen years earlier, Edwards's installation became an occasion for official diplomatic business as well: a party of Massachusetts officials arrived in town from Boston, anticipating negotiations with New York Mohawks, nearly a hundred of whom were expected any day to discuss the possibility of joining the Stockbridge experiment.

The full story of this busy month only emerges when the Stockbridge and Moravian sources are considered in tandem.[1] For instance, Edwards preserved the notes for the sermon he preached on the occasion of his installation, but only from the Moravian sources do we learn that a large party of Pachgatgoch Indians and a Moravian missionary were in attendance for the occasion. And only from the Moravian sources do we learn that after Sergeant's death, the Stockbridge Indians requested a Moravian minister to come fill his spot.[2] Another sermon preached by Edwards that month likely memorialized the recently deceased chief, yet Edwards did not bother to mention the chief's death in a lengthy letter to the Speaker of the Massachusetts House of Representatives detailing the events of the week. But it is only from the Moravian mission diaries that we learn of the chief's decline and the remarkable networks of kinship and friendship that bound Stockbridge so closely to the surrounding Indian communities, even across denominational affiliations.

Word of the chief's illness reached the Moravian missionary Joachim Sensemann in May 1751, when he encountered Umpachenee's son on the road near Pachgatgoch. The chief's son informed the missionary that he was looking for a doctor to provide medicine for his father; he was likely seeking Umpachenee's cousin, Gideon, chief of Pachgatgoch and a renowned healer. On hearing the news, Sensemann immediately set out for Stockbridge to call on the sick chief. Following Sensemann on his rounds during this visit makes eminently clear the ties of kinship and diplomacy that spread across the landscape, reaching to Pachgatgoch, Gnadenhütten (near Bethlehem in Pennsylvania, where most of the Shekomeko residents had resettled), and beyond, a network that remains almost entirely invisible in the Stockbridge records.

Umpachenee and the Moravian missionaries had initially regarded each other with considerable caution, but over the years, particularly as the chief's relationship with John Sergeant deteriorated, both parties warmed. Umpachenee's regular visits to the Moravian-affiliated Indian communities at Shekomeko and Pachgatgoch provided him with a glimpse of a different model of Christianity and, perhaps even more significantly, a different model of Indian-white relations. During one diplomatic mission to the governor of New York, undertaken with Abraham of Shekomeko, the Mohican delegation lodged with white Moravian brethren, and Umpachenee was astounded by the hospitality they received, exclaiming that he would never forget the experience.[3] On another occasion, during a visit to Pachgatgoch, Umpachenee joined the Moravian missionaries for a Sunday dinner and so charmed the missionaries that they invited him to return the next day for tea.[4] Now, as the chief lay dying, Sensemann took the opportunity to pay his regards and call on the other Stockbridge residents he had come to know over the years of his service.

As he approached the mission town, Sensemann encountered a Stockbridge resident named Paul Umpeatkow who had once sought to relocate to Shekomeko, where some of his relations lived and where he said he hoped to hear about the blood of the Savior.[5] Umpeatkow warmly welcomed the missionary and invited him into his house for a meal. Refreshed, Sensemann continued on to see the sick chief, Umpachenee. He bore with him greetings from the Brethren in Bethlehem, Gnadenhütten, Wechquadnach, and Pachgatgoch. Sensemann concluded the visit by evoking for Umpachenee "the Savior and his wounds and how he loved poor sinners."[6] After the brief meeting, Sensemann made the rounds in the community, visiting many Indian houses—most of which counted among their kin former residents of Shekomeko now residing in Gnadenhütten.

Sensemann's first stop was at Wilhelm's house, where he received a warm welcome from Wilhelm's wife, who despite being sick, offered Sensemann a drink to refresh himself and apologized that her husband was not at home. From there, Sensemann continued on to pay a visit to Eva's family. Originally from Stockbridge, Eva had followed her husband Nicodemus to Gnadenhütten (it was Nicodemus who had inspired the Moravian missionaries with his colorful metaphors). Sensemann reported that the whole family rejoiced to see him, and apparently he was right: two years later the family had resettled with the Moravians in Gnadenhütten, moving in with the recently widowed Eva.[7]

From there, Sensemann proceeded to visit Ludwig Anton's sister and other members of her lineage. Ludwig Anton was a sometime resident of Gnadenhütten, the son of a Mohawk man from Wyoming and a Mohican woman.[8] Not finding the woman at home, Sensemann continued on to Bartholomew's house, where he visited with his wife, Elizabeth, a Shawnee woman.[9] Next, it was on to the house of Bartholomew's brother Benjamin, where he also found Moses, chief of the Mohican community of Wechquadnach, who now resided principally at Gnadenhütten.[10] Bartholomew, Benjamin, and their sister Anna were originally from Wechquadnach, and all had been baptized by the Moravians.[11] The siblings belonged to the same lineage as the chief sachem at Stockbridge, and Anna's marriage to Abraham's son Jonathan linked the Stockbridge, Shekomeko, and Wechquadnach communities.[12]

After leaving Bartholomew's house, Sensemann was called to Noah's lodge, where he visited with many members of Ruth's lineage. Ruth was the long-suffering wife of Boaz, who upon her death had entrusted her two daughters to the care of the Spangenbergs at Bethlehem. Sensemann found the family to be "a people not without feeling" and lamented that they had "fallen into Presbyterian hands" and currently lacked a minister. That evening, Sensemann was called on by Jephta's son, another Shekomeko villager. The son asked Sensemann to pass on a message to his father, now at Gnadenhütten, inquiring whether his father wanted to go to Gnadenhütten or Stockbridge next. The son offered to send a horse for him.[13]

The next day, Sensemann caught up with most of those who had been absent on his first visit. Wilhelm came to visit, eager to talk about his spiritual state. Sensemann encouraged him with talk of the Savior, assuring him that "the Savior wanted to make him right blessed so that the others could look at him and see that he belonged to the Savior and the Congregation."

Next, Sensemann visited with Paul and his family, talking with them about the Savior's love. The family gave him a gift of two pounds of maple sugar before Paul and Sensemann set out to pay another call on Umpachenee. They found the chief very sick. Since Umpachenee believed he wouldn't have the chance to visit his Moravian friends, he asked the missionary to pass on his greetings.[14]

After taking leave of the chief and his wife, Sensemann was given a tour of the mission school by Umpeatkow. The school was meant to house twelve students, but they had all returned to their own homes. When Sensemann asked why, Umpeatkow explained that they did not have enough to eat and that they were not provided with sufficient clothing to keep them warm during the cold winter months. Although they did not meet any of the Stockbridge students, they did meet a few of the Mohawk Indians who had arrived the previous fall on the promise of room, board, and an education in English ways.[15] After one last visit with one of Abraham's sons (it might have been either David or Jonathan, as both of the Shekomeko leader's sons had married Stockbridge women), Sensemann finally set off again on his journey, accompanied for a time by Umpeatkow. The missionary dutifully passed on Umpachenee's greetings to the other settlements: the Gnaden-hütten diary noted a few weeks later that they had received greetings from the Brethren in Pachgatgoch, Wechquadnach, "and especially from the Governor in Westenhook [Stockbridge] who had visited in Bethlehem and Gnadenhütten two years earlier, but who now lay deathly ill."[16]

The ailing chief did not improve over the summer, and there was a steady stream of visitors from surrounding communities visiting Umpachenee to pay their last regards. At one point the word went out that "the old King Aron," as the Moravians sometimes called him, had died.[17] But when Mora-vian missionary Abraham Büninger got word that he was still alive, he set off from Pachgatgoch with Gideon and a party of other Pachgatgoch residents. They arrived on July 30 to find Umpachenee very weak and barely able to recognize his visitors.[18] Gideon told him who they were and why they were there, at which Umpachenee revived a bit. He was glad for their visit, saying that he thought much about his friends in Pachgatgoch, Bethlehem, and Gnadenhütten. He thought "always about the Savior and his wounds, and that He had died for him and spilled his blood."[19]

The following day, Thursday, August 1, Gideon and Büninger visited with Umpachenee, who was now so weak that he was unable to speak. Many were sick in Stockbridge at the time, and Gideon and Büninger would spend much of the day and evening visiting among the different houses, offering the sick comforting words about the Savior and his wounds. Gideon translated for Büninger, since many of the Stockbridge residents did not understand En-glish well. In between rounds of visiting, Büninger and Gideon made time to

Figure 7 Portrait of Jonathan Edwards, by Joseph Badger. Courtesy of Jonathan Edwards College, Yale University, bequest of Eugene Phelps Edwards.

attend the Fast Day sermon preached by Jonathan Edwards in anticipation of his installation as Stockbridge minister the following Thursday. Büninger had encouraged the Pachgatgoch visitors to attend the sermon.[20] And so a sizable Moravian party filed into the meetinghouse to take their seats among the Stockbridge Indians, the dozen or so Mohawks, and the English residents of the community. Surely, Edwards was aware of the Moravian presence in the pews, but unfortunately he left no record of the visitors.

Edwards did, however, leave a manuscript of the sermon he preached that day, drawn from a chapter in Acts, in which the Apostle Paul receives a vision from God of a Macedonian standing and praying, "Come over into Macedonia and help us." The text, preached Edwards, showed "what great need poor sinners as they are by nature stand in of Help." The Macedonian was like "a miserable captive in the hands of Satan" or, in words that likely struck home that day as the village chief lay dying, like one who was "sick with a very terrible and wicked disease, like one that is bitten by a serpent that is full of deadly poison." In this state, Edwards preached, the Macedonian "could not help himself," for he "was poor and had no money." But God had provided for those who lived in darkness, calling on ministers to propagate the saving word of the gospel. The future was bright for those who heeded the word of the Gospel: God was "able to rise up their Bodies at the End of the world [and] make both Soul and body Happy and Glorious to all Eternity." In conclusion, Edwards exhorted his audience to "pray for God's Blessing on the minister that He may have wisdom and Grace and that God would assist Him in his work." If his ministry is blessed, "you will not only be happy yourself but it will have a tendency to the Good of other Indians." But if they went "on in drunkenness and other wickedness," they would be "the Devil's people" for whom God reserved "a worse Place in Hell than those that never heard the Gospel preached."[21] Unfortunately, the usually prolific Moravian missionary seated in the pews did not bother to comment on the sermon, nor did Edwards comment on the response of his new flock or the presence of visitors.

One week after the Fast Day, on August 8, Edwards was officially installed as the new minister at Stockbridge, to serve both the Indian and white populations. Two days later, Umpachenee drew his last breath.[22] And presumably, when Edwards stood in the pulpit one Sunday that August and preached on 2 Corinthians 4:18—"look not on the things that are seen, but the things that are not seen; for the things that are seen are temporal, but the things that are not seen are eternal"—it was intended as an exhortation to the Stockbridge Indian community to "improve" the death of their leader, to take the lessons of his death to heart. "All the things of this world are but for a time and will come to an End," warned Edwards, "the time soon comes when men die and return to dust." In this world, fortunes are ever changeable, but in the next world there would be no alteration.

Edwards, in his classic revivalist style, then spelled out in great detail the two possible fates all would face after death: eternal happiness or eternal torment. In his sermon, Edwards dwelled far longer on the latter, not, he assured his audience, in order "to trouble and afflict you" but rather "so you mayn't come to this Place of Torment." Justice would prevail in the next world, righting the wrongs of this world, in which "sometimes wicked men greatly Prosper…and good men meet with great Sorrow and trouble," where one day one was a "conqueror [of] men and another day a poor Captive." In another world, "all things shall be set to rights." In words that must have held special appeal to the beleaguered Stockbridge Indians, Edwards promised that "there will be no Enemies no more death or sickness. There will be Life forever and no more death. There shall be health and [no] more sickness. Peace and no war. There shall be Love and Friendship and no more Enemies. Joy and Pleasure and no more sorrow or Pain. Joyful singing and no more groaning and weeping." Edwards did not allow his congregation to savor sweet visions of heaven for long. The last half of the sermon was devoted to imagery worthy of his most famous revival sermon, "Sinners in the Hands of an Angry God." In Hell, the wicked would be cast into a fire, and "though they shall burn in the fire yet they shall never die," unlike men in this world, who, when thrown into a fire they "quickly die and the fire burns 'em up and then they feel the Pain no more." But those cast into hell would suffer forever in body and soul: "their Heads, their Bodies their Hearts and Bowels and all their flesh and Bones shall be full of fire and yet they shall never die."[23] By the time Edwards finished, the Stockbridge Indians may well have entertained second thoughts about having given their approval to hiring the stern revivalist.

If they did, they would not have had long just then to contemplate these matters. Likely joining the Indians at the meetinghouse that Sunday were members of a group appointed by the Massachusetts General Assembly (who had arrived on the same day Umpachenee died) on a mission to treat with the Mohawks to encourage more of their number to settle at Stockbridge.[24] Earlier in the summer, the Massachusetts commissioners for Indian affairs had stopped in Stockbridge on their way to Albany for a council to renew the Covenant Chain linking New York, Massachusetts, Connecticut, and South Carolina, and the Six Nations. They had hoped to meet with the Mohawk chiefs prior to the larger council and come to an agreement whereby the remainder of the population at the Mohawk castles (as central Indian villages were often called by the English), Canajoharie, and Tionderoga would join those who had already settled at Stockbridge the previous fall. Massachusetts officials, for their part, acted with the same motivations they had when the mission to the Mohicans was launched. All eyes were on the Mohawks as the great diplomatic prize and a key element in securing British interests. In terms of trade and war, Mohicans were no longer important players; they were safely in the British interest; what were once Mohican lands had sprouted dozens of new English settlements.

Figure 8 "King Hendric, a Mohawk Indian." Courtesy of Williams College Archives and Special Collections, Williamstown, Massachusetts.

Edwards's long letter to Speaker of the Massachusetts House of Representatives Thomas Hubbard recounting the developments in the Mohawk affair betrays the same sentiment.[25] There is scarcely a mention of his new congregation of Stockbridge Mohican Indians. It is clear, however, that Edwards deemed the success of the Mohawk mission to be of the utmost importance to British interests in North America. The successful wooing of the Mohawks would be a victory not only for the British Crown but also for true religion, dealing a blow against "Romish" religion. If the mission to the Mohawks failed, Edwards feared—as his grandfather Stoddard had in his 1723 sermon—that God would use the Indians as an instrument to punish the unfaithful New Englanders. Stoddard had asked then, "Is it not a Shame to us to be backward to promote the true religion?"[26]

The commissioners had not been able to negotiate with the Mohawks in Stockbridge on their way to Albany in June, as the Mohawk chief Hendrick and most of the heads of families had returned to their home country.[27] At the request of the commissioners, Edwards accompanied the party to Albany where he was able to meet with chiefs Hendrick and Nicholas, in his words, "using arguments with them to persuade them to endeavor to get as many of their chiefs as they could to come to Stockbridge, and give opportunity to the commissioners to discourse fully with them about this great affair." Hendrick answered that it was necessary, "according to their manner, first to have some time of consideration, and to hold a council among themselves," but that they would send word to Stockbridge within twenty days. True to their word, Nicholas arrived in Stockbridge near the end of July and gave word that the rest of his people would arrive in about a week. And so on August 13 "a great train," as Edwards called it, of nearly ninety Mohawks arrived in town, including Hendrick and twelve other chiefs, seven in all from Canajoharie and six from Tionderoga.[28] Having grown increasingly frustrated with fraudulent New York patents on Mohawk lands, Hendrick and his community were considering shifting allegiance from New York to Massachusetts, hoping that they might have better assurances of secured land.[29] It was a similar calculation to that made by Housatonic Mohican leaders decades earlier.

The company of Mohawks stayed in Stockbridge for just over a week meeting with Stockbridge Mohicans, negotiating with the appointed Massachusetts committee, and, for at least one afternoon, listening to a lecture by Jonathan Edwards in which he presented the history of the work of God's redemption of sinners.[30] Edwards, like his grandfather Stoddard before him, lamented that "altho 'tis about 140 years since the white People came over here there are but few of the poor Indians have been thoroughly Instructed to this very day." Instruction in reading was particularly important in order access the Bible, something the Indians would not find among the French who, Edwards warned, "pretend to teach the Indians religion but they won't teach 'em to read," refusing "to open the Bible to the Indians."[31]

Despite Edwards's efforts, it was clear that the negotiations were not going entirely smoothly. The Mohawks began their address to the Massachusetts representatives by reminding them "how the English had failed of those things, that they had encouraged them with the hopes of heretofore." Now they desired that "nothing might be said but what should stand, and be made good." In the end, the Mohawk chiefs presented a belt of wampum signifying their "compliance with the proposal which had been made of sending their children here." Perhaps exaggerating the reach of their influence, the Mohawks concluded by assuring the committee that "now they opened the door for all nations that they might come and bring their children hither to be instructed; and that they gave this belt as a confirmation that they would not only send their own children, but would do what in them lay to persuade other nations to do the same."[32] This was precisely what Massachusetts officials had hoped for: securing greater safety for Massachusetts borders by drawing more Indian nations into the Covenant Chain of friendship that had subsisted between English and Iroquois since the 1670s.

Despite the seemingly happy resolution of the council, Edwards was worried. It was customary according to Covenant Chain protocol for the promises of both sides to be confirmed with presents, and the offering of the Massachusetts representatives that day was particularly pathetic. Edwards knew that the French were offering stiff competition: while they could not compete with Britain's trade terms, the French were "indefatigable in the endeavors they use," including "extraordinary provision" for the Indians to "draw all those nations over to them and engage them in their interest." The Mohawks were even more peeved than Edwards, and some of them left in disgust.[33] Two years later, Hendrick would declare the Covenant Chain broken, a pronouncement that shook the British imperial authorities, and set off a course of events leading to the Albany Conference of 1754, which in turn prompted Benjamin Franklin to propose the Albany Plan of Union, the first (and failed) attempt at colonial union.[34] The local events at a mission outpost were part of a much larger web of relations.

One final event of this busy month deserves mention, for it suggests that Edwards was attentive to the local context when he stepped into the Stockbridge pulpit. One Sunday that August, Edwards ascended the pulpit and delivered a remarkable sermon to the gathered Mohican and Mohawk Indians. The pews were filled. Perhaps as many as 150 congregants gathered for the first celebration of communion for the new pastor and flock. Edwards had chosen his text for the occasion carefully. The text for the sermon was Psalms 1:3, "He shall be like a tree planted by the Rivers of Water." The doctrine: "Christ is to the heart of a true saint like a river to the roots of a tree that is planted by it." It is worth quoting the sermon at length:

As the waters of a river run easily and freely so the love of Christ. [He] freely came into the world, laid down his life and endured those dreadful sufferings. His blood was freely shed. Blood flowed as freely from his wounds as water from a spring. All the good things that Christ bestows on his saints come to 'em as freely as water runs down in a river. The chief and most excellent things that Christ bestows are the influences of his Spirit on their hearts to enlighten and sanctify and comfort. These all come freely from Christ like the waters of a River. Christ willingly gives his people that look to him and trust in Him light and life in their souls. There is an abundance of Water. Christ is like a river in the great plenty and abundance of his love and grace.... The tree that spreads out its roots by a river has water enough—no need of rain or any other water. So the true saint finds enough in Christ. Great plenty of water enough to supply a great multitude of persons with drink to satisfy all their thirst, to supply the roots of a multitude of trees. So [it is] for all the saints. [The] water of a river don't fail, [it] flows constantly, day and night. Waters that run upon the [ground from the] showers of rain or melting of snows soon dry up. But [not so the water of a river.] Little brooks dry up in a very dry time. But the waters of a great river continue, running continually and from one age to another and are never dry. So Christ never [leaves] His saints that love Him and trust in Him.... He never leaves off to take care. The grace of Christ in the heart shall alwaies continue. Christ never will take away his spirit from them. That inward life and comfort that Christ gives the hearts of his saints shall continue to all eternity. When the death comes, that comfort and Happiness shall continue. When the end of the world comes yet their comforts shall be like a river that shall not be dried up. The soul [of the saint] is joined to Christ and they are made one. As the water enters into the roots, so Christ enters the heart and soul of a godly man and dwells there. The spirit of Christ comes into the very heart of a saint as water to the roots of a tree.... Water gives life and keeps it alive, makes it grow, makes it grow beautiful, fruitful. A tree planted [by the river] is green in time of great drought when other trees wither. So the soul of a true Saint in time of affliction. At death. At the end of the world.[35]

Everything about Edwards' sermon suggests that he believed his new pastorate called for new methods of preaching and pastoring. The imagery of the sermon seems designed to resonate with the presumed sensibilities of his audience and with the rich, metaphorical cast of Indian rhetorical styles. The emphasis on the neverending love of Christ suggests that Edwards recognized he faced a congregation in need of love, comfort, and solace. The emphasis on the freely flowing blood of Christ suggests that Edwards may indeed have spoken with visiting Moravian missionaries or possibly that his Indian congregants asked Edwards as part of the interview process whether he would tell them about the blood of Christ. Edwards repeated and elaborated the metaphor of Christ as a river from which all who thirst might drink the waters of salvation.

The events of that month marked the end of one era and the beginning of another. At the time of his death, Umpachenee might have been quite encouraged at the continuing growth of the Stockbridge Indian community, particularly with the impending arrival of dozens of Mohawks from Canajoharie and Tionderoga, promising as it did greater attention from colonial officials. The poor treatment the Stockbridges regularly received from the town's English residents and from the colonial government had made it all too clear that the Mohicans were not held in high regard. Delivering, or at least facilitating, an alliance with the more powerful tribes to the west would become a key part of Mohican diplomacy in decades ahead. The accounts Moravian missionaries left behind of their visits to Stockbridge depict the extent and the strength of the ties that bound Stockbridge residents to the larger Mohican world, while also shedding light on the troubled state of the Stockbridge mission.

The installation of the renowned revivalist and theologian Jonathan Edwards as missionary might have been cause for hope among the Stockbridge Indians that the irregular dealings would soon be remedied. His various sermons preached that month made it clear that Edwards would not shy from teaching the harsh doctrines of Calvinism to his new flock. But they also demonstrated that Edwards believed the Indians to be included among the elect, something that Sergeant seemed to have become more and more doubtful about over the course of his tenure as missionary.

A decade later, the fate of the Stockbridge Indian community once again was in flux. Edwards had left his position to take up the presidency of Princeton, only to die soon after of a smallpox inoculation. This time, the Stockbridge community would go even longer without a replacement. And most telling of all was a petition submitted by a contingent of Stockbridge's white population to the Massachusetts General Assembly seeking permission to transact all town affairs separately from the Indians. Although the separation was not officially enacted until 1774, Stockbridge was well on its way to becoming a New England town, like many others with a marginalized Indian population.[36]

Chapter Ten

Indian and White Bodies
Politic at Stockbridge

The events of that August in 1751 marked the end of one era and the beginning of another. The years leading up to Umpachenee's death saw the birth of a new community that came to be known as the Stockbridge Indians. This community, composed of settlers from Mohican, Housatonic, and Shawnee villages, laid claim to the mantle of Mohican identity even as they increasingly lived in English-style houses and engaged in English-style husbandry. Where once Mohicans had played a key role as brokers in the fur and wampum trade, they were now established as traders in culture. Stockbridge residents studied English, the principles of the Christian religion, and English patterns of subsistence, all of which were enlisted in the task of cementing alliances with neighboring peoples. In acquiring these skills, the Stockbridges did not understand themselves to be relinquishing their Mohican-ness, neither did they seek to become English. Rather, they had simply entered into a new type of exchange.

During the last fifteen years of Umpachenee's life, the Stockbridge Indians were remarkably successful in these dual tasks: they drew a critical mass of new settlers to Stockbridge, and in their intertribal diplomacy they often cast Christianity as a new bond that could serve to reaffirm ancient ties that had once been articulated with the language of fictive kinship. While not all of the Indian communities they approached in this way acknowledged Christianity as the grease that kept the chain of friendship from rusting, the

Stockbridges' diplomatic efforts were arguably largely responsible for sparing Stockbridge from attack during the wars of the 1740s and 1750s. Ironically, at Stockbridge, where the missionary program was meant to build
a new Christian civilization over the grave of Indian culture, Christianity
served as a means of preserving native institutions and transforming them
to suit new circumstances.

But as we learn from Umpachenee's interactions with the Moravian missionaries, the Stockbridges were often frustrated at the terms of the cultural
trade. No matter how far the Stockbridge Indians traveled on the path to
"civility," they repeatedly encountered new barriers to full protection under
colonial law. Indeed, the English expected complete transformation of the
Indians in emulation of English "civility," and yet they also needed them to
remain Indian, for they depended on the Stockbridge Indians to maintain
native ways of warfare and diplomacy in the service of protecting and expanding the edges of the British empire.

The Stockbridges proved not to be as sectarian as Massachusetts officials would have liked, and many were drawn to the Moravian gospel of the
blood and wounds of Christ. Even if relatively few Indian settlers left Stockbridge for Shekomeko, many more posed difficult questions to Sergeant
and Massachusetts officials prompted by the different type of relationships
between Indian and white they witnessed at Shekomeko. The links between
the Stockbridge Indians and the Moravians are virtually invisible in the
Stockbridge records. These sources, although silent on the Indians' religious lives, are quite vocal in response to the Moravian mission project. The
response of John Sergeant, his clerical brethren, and colonial civil officials
to the Moravians reveals much about how New England religious identity
intersected political and cultural identities.

At a critical time when Anglo-Protestant clergy were divided over the
meaning of the recent religious revivals, the Moravians became an important
example against which revivalist ministers defended their own orthodoxy,
as anti-Moravian tracts from the 1740s make clear. The nature of the attacks
is revealing: what was most troubling about the Moravians to these pro-
revival ministers was their effectiveness at communicating with the socially
marginal and their emphasis on Christ's love rather than the importance of
obedience to God. Religious and civil leaders alike feared that the Moravians' success in establishing close relationships with the Indians threatened
the security of colonial society. Although not explicitly articulated, it is clear
that a major concern for critics of the Moravians was that they had decou-
pled Christianity and European—particularly British—civility.

With the onset of King George's War, the Moravians became even more
suspect, for their richly liturgical worship smacked to Anglo-Protestants of

"papism," and their facility in winning adherents among the Indians seemed further evidence of their affinity to the Catholics, whose Jesuit priests were widely acknowledged to be far more successful missionaries than the English. The Moravians' commitment to pacifism was feared to be a screen for allegiance to the French and French-allied Indians. Moravian pacifism implicitly challenged the union of Christianity with British interests. The responses of Stockbridge Indians, Anglo-Protestant clergy, and civil magistrates to the Moravian mission project reveal much about the intersection of religious, cultural, and national identities during this crucial era.[1] The struggles over identity can also be seen in the life and writings of Stockbridge's second missionary, Jonathan Edwards.

The challenges Edwards faced when he stepped into his various roles as missionary to the Indians, agent for the British colony, and preacher to the English congregation prompted him to take different and sometimes contradictory stances on the relationship of one's cultural or national identity to the state of one's soul. In many respects, Edwards was a man of his times, and he shared in the assumption of British cultural superiority to the Indians, believing English civility was the necessary foundation for the Indians' development as Christians. Yet at the same time, Edwards witnessed the ill treatment of the Stockbridge Indians at the hands of the English (and particularly the Williams family, members of which had spearheaded the effort to remove Edwards from his Northampton pulpit), leading him to downplay the idea of a national covenant between God and New England. Especially from the pulpit, both to English and Indian, Edwards stressed that national identity granted no special access to Christ's saving work.[2] Edwards's sermons, treatises, and letters from these years provide another window onto the changing understandings of identity in colonial British America.

For both the Indians and the English, the decades of the 1740s and 1750s saw the emergence of a new sense of identity. The Stockbridges' claims to identity as Mohican did not rest on adherence to what others (including later anthropologists and ethnohistorians) deemed characteristic of Indianness: their mode of dress or subsistence or their religious rituals. Rather, the Stockbridges affirmed a continuity of identity that transcended blood and material culture and rested instead in the nature of their relationships with other peoples. Their relationships at Stockbridge did indeed come to define the community's identity: again and again, the Stockbridge Indians discovered that they would not be guaranteed equal protection under the laws of the town and the colony. The de facto existence of distinct codes of justice created pressure toward a racialized construction of identity, one that the Stockbridges often resisted.[3]

GATHERING COMMUNITY

In January 1735, Umpachenee and Konkapot worried about the prospects of the upcoming council of the River Indian confederacy called to consider the mission proposal. The council grudgingly decided to give the mission a chance and to see how association with the Christian God and the opportunity to learn the tools of English culture served Mohican interests, but the decision clearly had not been an enthusiastic endorsement, as evidenced by the Housatonic leaders' fears of a plot on their lives. From the earliest days of the mission, the Housatonic Mohicans actively sought to attract new settlers to the community. Their success is evidenced by the growth of population and the shift of the tribal seat of the Mohican confederacy to Stockbridge in the 1740s. In building the new community, Stockbridge leaders relied on longstanding diplomatic methods—sending embassies to visit communities near and far, affirming old relationships, and forging new ones. Now, however, the Stockbridge Mohicans presented Christianity as a means of reinforcing traditional ties while forging new ones with powerful English allies, an appeal that sometimes worked and sometimes met with polite rejection. The records of various councils and embassies between the Stockbridges and other Indian communities reveal the consistency of the Stockbridge agenda and signal the emergence of a new corporate identity that rested on the embrace of Christianity as a means of forging new alliances and reinforcing traditional fictive kinship ties.

On the eve of the mission era, the Housatonic Mohicans belonged to a larger regional alliance of River Indians, which included the Mohicans proper of the Hudson River valley, Highland (or Wappinger) Indians, and the Housatonic Mohicans. There were clearly ties of kinship and alliance that bound Housatonic and Hudson River Mohicans, but while there may have been a chief sachem who represented these allied communities at official dealings, he did not have coercive power over any of the constituent bands.[4] So despite the apparent disapproval of the larger confederacy, Umpachenee and Konkapot struck out on their own when they accepted John Sergeant and the mission project.

In the early years of the mission, the two men spent considerable time away from Stockbridge attempting to win over other communities and to persuade them to cast their lot with the growing community at Stockbridge. They traveled to the nearby Mohican villages of Kaunaumeek, Wechquadnach, and Shekomeko, and as far away as a Shawnee settlement on the Susquehanna River in Pennsylvania and Mohawk communities on the far side of Albany. When Sergeant traveled with them, they introduced him as their elder brother, signifying Sergeant's advisory role.[5] With their interest sparked by visits from Stockbridge residents, a steady flow of curious visitors arrived to check out the happenings at the mission. Some eventually relocated to Stockbridge; those who chose not to were perhaps hopeful of being able to remain at their home villages or believed that the mission required too much in the way of cultural change. Others, like Abraham of Shekomeko, cast their lot with other missionaries.[6]

Already in the summer of 1735, Stephen Williams reported that several families from the Hudson River had expressed interest in the mission, and several had already moved to Housatonic.[7] By the following January, Sergeant claimed that he regularly had an audience of eighty to ninety Indians when he preached at Umpachenee's longhouse. About half of those in attendance were "strangers" visiting from elsewhere in the valley, from the Hudson River area, and sometimes from as far away as the Susquehanna River.[8] The appeal for newcomers seemed to be the same as for the initial settlers: the promise of secured land and instruction in the English cultural ways that would help them to navigate their way in a rapidly changing world, and assistance in fending off the dangers of alcohol.[9] By the spring of 1740, Sergeant reported in his diary that the Stockbridge community had increased to 120 residents, including eighteen full church members.[10]

The case of Kaunaumeek is instructive. There was regular contact between the Housatonic village and the Stockbridge Indians beginning in 1736, if not earlier. The village was headed by a man named Aunauwauneekheek. The chief, whom Sergeant described as a "a rational and judicious man," paid regular visits to Stockbridge seeking to "inform himself further" about the Christian religion, seeking schooling for his only child, a daughter, and eventually receiving baptism in 1738 together with his daughter and another prominent chief named Wautaunukumeett.[11] Although Aunauwauneekheek himself never settled at Stockbridge, he was a regular attendee at Sergeant's sermons, and by 1744, most of the village's population had relocated to Stockbridge, perhaps in part because of the mission but also for greater safety as war loomed.[12]

At the same time that Stockbridge leaders campaigned among neighboring Mohican communities to draw new settlers to the mission, they actively sought to create or reaffirm ties with non-Mohican Indian peoples. Stockbridge leaders presented Christianity as a mechanism of alliance with Shawnee, Abenaki, and Mohawk peoples. In all of these, the Stockbridge Mohicans attempted to extend their reach and bring more distant Indians into alliance, usually to secure a neutrality agreement in case of renewed war between England and France. And like their efforts to draw new settlers to Stockbridge, their broader campaign met with mixed results. When King George's War broke out in 1744, the neutrality agreements that the Stockbridges had settled with French-leaning Indian communities crumbled.

Mohican relations with the Shawnee long predated the mission era. Mohicans referred to the Shawnee as their younger brother, memorializing the Mohican role in securing a new residence for the Shawnee when they were forced out of their native homelands. Ever since, the Shawnee had called the Mohicans their elder brothers and promised "obedience to them, which they still acknoledged to this day."[13] The Shawnee-Mohican relationship seems to have been regularly reaffirmed through marriages and grants of land. The Kaunaumeek chief Aunauwauneekheek's wife, for example, was a Shawnee woman from a Susquehanna community.[14] It had been Aunauwauneekheek's suggestion that prompted Sergeant to undertake a tour to the Susquehanna to promote the Stockbridge mission. In 1739, Aunauwauneekheek informed Sergeant that he wished to visit the Shawnee communities on the Susquehanna—presumably including his wife's native village—bearing the Christian message.[15] Aunauwauneekheek's message to the Shawnee does not survive, but Sergeant recorded the Shawnee response, as relayed by the Kaunaumeek chief in May 1739. The wampum belts brought in response affirmed the fraternal relationship between the Shawnee and the Mohicans. The Shawnee promised that when they "have found out any good thing," they would "hold it fast" and teach their children. The Shawnee concluded by thanking the Stockbridges for their advice: "You told me drinking was not good. I regard your words. I now leave it off; you shall not find your brother drunk any more."[16]

Encouraged by the Shawnees' response, Sergeant resolved to take a trip to their village, "to open a way if possible for the introducing Christianity among them," which he embarked on during the summer of 1741.[17] In sending Sergeant, the Stockbridge Mohicans perhaps hoped both to impress the missionary (and by extension the colonial Massachusetts government) with their ties to Western Indians and to impress the Shawnee with their alliance with powerful colonists. Sergeant carried with him belts of wampum that served as a letter of introduction from the Stockbridges. "Brother," said the Stockbridges, "this is our Teacher; we have brought him with us, thinking perhaps he may open your Eyes a little, that you may see the Way to eternal Life. We wish you would hear him. He is our elder Brother." The message invoked "the Priviledge of an elder Brother to teach his younger Brother if he knows any Thing that is Good." The Stockbridges told the Shawnees they came because "I dislike our way of living, our Father above does not approve of it, we weary out his Patience." Although the Mohicans did not spell out what they meant by "our way of living," presumably they meant the use of alcohol and the general breakdown of social structures that many Indian communities suffered at this time. And so the Stockbridges urged the Shawnee to accept the Christian religion "if you pity your Body & Soul."[18]

The Susquehanna Shawnee saw things differently. They affirmed their historic relationship with the Mohicans, and they agreed that there was "a father above," but they asserted that Indians had one way of honoring that father and whites another, and "both are acceptable to Him." They believed that "Christianity need not be the Bond of Union between us." The Shawnee gave an additional reason: "As for your teacher, I cannot understand him. If I could understand him, it might be well to hear him, but he speaks in an unknown Tongue."[19] Clearly, the Shawnee were not persuaded by the Mohican experiment that Christianity and instruction in English needed to be the basis for continuing their alliance.

In the midst of the various councils with the Shawnee, the Mohicans sought to affirm a neutrality agreement with the communities of Norridgewock (eastern Abenaki) and St. Francis (western Abenaki) at a council held in Stockbridge in 1740.[20] During the various colonial wars of the late seventeenth and early eighteenth centuries, the Abenakis had struck fear among the English settlers of the frontier regions in Maine and western Massachusetts, striking devastating blows.[21] Now, in 1740, with another war brewing between the French and English, a council was held in Stockbridge between the Stockbridge Mohicans, the Wappinger, and Schaghticoke Indians on the one hand and the St. Francis Indians on the other. The Stockbridges delivered two belts of wampum to the St. Francis with the following message:

> Brother we have always lived in strict alliance with you, by leagues of friendship long ago enter'd into by our Forefathers; and we have been wont from time to time to consult and advise with one another upon affairs of importance, and to communicate our determinations to each other. We depend upon it therefore, you will be willing to hear us.

Perhaps appealing to the St. Francis's Catholicism, the Stockbridges affirmed: "Brother at Wtanshekaunhtukko. By this we may know, that we are Brethren, because we have one Father in Heaven, the Lord of all. Let us have a tender regard to our families." In pursuing their own interests, the St. Francis Indians had generally allied with the French, a tie that became stronger as the English pushed further into Abenaki territory in the early decades of the eighteenth century.

The last item of the Stockbridges' address is particularly interesting. They called on the St. Francis to stay out of any French-English conflicts for the sake of self-preservation: "We only destroy ourselves by meddling in their wars.... Let us only sit and look on, while they engage in war. Don't let any of our people assist your allies in their wars. But while they fight, let us sit and smoke together."[22] Although the Stockbridges were unable to secure the St. Francis Indians' neutrality, the connection between the two tribes was likely an important factor in preserving Stockbridge from attack when war finally erupted in 1744.[23]

The Stockbridges had little more success with the Mohawks. Tensions had simmered between England and France during the early part of the 1740s, and on the eve of renewed hostilities, in May 1744, the Stockbridges and the Mohawks held a council at Stockbridge. Although John Sergeant did not specify which Mohawks were in attendance, it was likely the Canajoharie Mohawks, led by Hendrick—the same Hendrick who would briefly consider taking up residence at Stockbridge six years later.[24] The two parties promised to remain neutral in case of war. In their address to the Mohawks, the Stockbridges blended the traditional ceremonial customs intended to clear the way for open communication with the addition of a shared commitment to Christianity as a further bond between the once warring peoples.[25]

The Mohican speaker began the proceedings by addressing the Mohawks as "Uncle," in keeping with fictive kinship designations: "Uncle I live a poor and Miserable people at Muhekun (Hudson's River) I had to raise up out of the Dust where should I get wisdom. I now stand up here where our Fore Fathers used to hold their Consultations. I cleanse your Ear that you may distinctly hear me, and your heart, that you may well understand what I say." Several additional opening statements followed, each recalling the time when Mohawk and Mohican forefathers took council with each other "under a pleasant shady tree." Now the fire had gone out and needed to be rekindled, so the Mohicans symbolically swept the ground clean and covered up the bones of Mohawk warriors who had "left their bones scattered in every place." The Stockbridges premised their deference to the Mohawks on the basis of the Mohawks' longer engagement with Christianity.[26]

Finally, the Stockbridges came to the central issue of securing a neutrality agreement: "Uncle I ask you a question. I hear you have agreed with the French Mohawks to sit still in case of a war between their Friends and ours. You well know how that matter is I desire you to tell me what we are to do in that Affair. If you say we must sit still we will sit still. If we see those Indians help their Friends we must help ours." In other words, the Stockbridges would remain neutral so long as the French-allied Mohawks remained aloof but would fight with the English if the Mohawks entered the war. "Uncle," concluded the speaker, "let us hear and obey the word and Commandments of our Lord which are taught us by our Ministers that we may meet together in Heaven, and there continue our friendship forever." Christianity was a new element of Indian diplomacy, and the language of millennialism aptly expressed the frustrated hopes harbored by Stockbridge leaders just a decade into the experimental alliance with the English.

In their response, the Mohawks confirmed Christianity as one basis of their bond to the Mohicans: "Cousin. You say we have been long instructed and you but a little while. It is very true and we greatly rejoyce to hear that you have likewise embrac'd the Christian Faith, it is indeed a very great happiness that we are assured of a better and more durable life after this [illegible] and miserable life shall have an end." Like the Mohicans, and the British sponsors of missions for that matter, the Mohawks saw their commitment to Christianity as a central piece of their alliance with the English. They concluded by praying to the "God from whom all good does come to give us grace to follow it and to unite us both together with our friends the English in Faith and Friendship that we may not only hold our hands link'd fast together in this life but that we may be all happy together in the life to come forever."[27] The neutrality agreement did not last long. French-allied Mohawks joined the fighting, and soon the Mohicans of Stockbridge and the Canajoharie Mohawks were drawn into the conflict as well, fighting on the English side. Whether or not it was the result of Mohican diplomacy, Stockbridge community was spared direct attack during the ensuing war.[28]

One further aspect of the document deserves mention: in the heading, John Sergeant noted that the meeting took place in Stockbridge. What then to make of the Mohican speaker's assertion that "I live...at Muhekun's River"? The speaker's words suggest a continuity of identity: the settlers at Stockbridge claimed the mantle of the Mohican confederacy whose leadership traditionally had been located along the Hudson River. Stockbridge had become "Muhekun's River," a shift confirmed by the move of the tribal chief to Stockbridge in late 1743 or early 1744.[29] The move of the chief sachemship to Stockbridge confirmed that other Mohican peoples recognized the Stockbridge leaders as authorized to carry out the diplomatic agenda of the larger Mohican community.

During the 1730s and 1740s, the Indians who came to settle at Stockbridge were engaged in a process of negotiating their identity, forging a new identity as the Stockbridge Indians, and redefining relationships with other Indian communities and nations while also exploring the possibilities and limitations of their new identity as Christian Indian farmers in a New England town. Early Stockbridge leaders embraced the mission program, but for quite different reasons than those that motivated Massachusetts religious and civil officials. Instruction in Christianity, literacy, and English style husbandry, it was imagined, would bind English and Indian together in a mutually beneficial partnership. But even as the Stockbridge Indians served faithfully alongside the English in King George's War, Indian presence in British colonies became yet more precarious. The Stockbridges were not above suspicion, and the Shekomeko Mohicans fared even worse due to their affiliation with the pacifist Moravians. English colonial responses to

Moravians and their Indian associates reveal much about the emerging Anglo-Protestant sense of identity.

ANGLO-PROTESTANT IDENTITY

At precisely the time when the Stockbridge community had become the head of the Mohican confederacy, partly on the strength of ties with English colonists, that tie was being frayed both by the impending war between England and France and by the Stockbridges' increasing familiarity with Moravian Christianity. Ultimately, many Stockbridge residents felt the pull of Moravian religious practice, with its familiar grammar of spiritual efficacy and the emphasis on Jesus' blood. Yet despite ties of kinship and the draw of Moravian religion, few Stockbridges cast their lot with the Moravians, in part because they judged that their community's interest lay in an alliance with the more powerful New Englanders. Exploring Stockbridge Mohican interactions with the Moravians offers a means of triangulating the Stockbridge Indians' political and religious aims as an emerging community. Investigating Anglo-Protestant responses to the Moravians in turn reveals much about the development of English colonial identity and the extent to which that identity depended on maintaining firm social and racial barriers.

John Sergeant and other Massachusetts officials welcomed the growing importance of Stockbridge, believing it would help spread the gospel to other tribes and provide a means of more firmly attaching the Indians on the borders of Massachusetts to British interests. In a 1746 letter, Sergeant reported that there was land enough at Stockbridge for three times as many Indian settlers and that the new settlers could be attracted with the promise of an education and with the prospect of becoming a means of propagating the gospel among the far tribes.[30] Sergeant had not counted on competition from the Moravians.

At first, Sergeant welcomed the contact with his Moravian counterparts, perhaps hoping for collegial relations in their common missionary endeavor. But the more he learned of the Moravians and, perhaps most importantly, the greater the pull Moravian missions exerted on members of Sergeant's flock, the more wary he became. In an early letter to Stephen Williams, Sergeant wrote that he "did much scruple the account Tennant gives of his [Zinzendorf's] doctrines," believing they were "too absurd and ridiculous to be held by any man of Learning and sense, such as I suppose the Count is." Sergeant's willingness to credit Zinzendorf over the provocative revivalist Gilbert Tennent is evidence perhaps of Sergeant's Old Light leanings and possibly reflects a disposition to respect Zinzendorf's status as part of the aristocracy.[31] In any case, Sergeant reported that he had struck up a correspondence with the Moravian missionaries "near Hudson's River" who did "not appear to entertain such silly notions." Sergeant agreed that Count Zinzendorf wrote in "a peculiar and enthusiastic manner" but thought that he seemed to have "right notions of the manner of conversion in Adult sinners, at least he plainly eno' supposes a deep conviction to be the antecedent of it."[32] But as he came to know his Moravian neighbors and their Indian proselytes, Sergeant began to reconsider his initial estimation.

Umpachenee and the others who settled at Stockbridge believed that education in English ways was indispensable for their survival in a changing world. But Umpachenee had feared from the beginning that the English might not apply the same standards of justice to Indians as to colonists, and the incessant land disputes that arose at Stockbridge would eventually prove Umpachenee right. Time and again, government committees considered Stockbridge Indian petitions, and while they often acknowledged the legitimacy of the complaints, they countered that righting the wrong would mean considerable inconvenience to the English party.[33] Add to this Sergeant's low esteem for Indian capacities and the Anglo-Protestant mission strategy that emphasized the necessity of biblical literacy and doctrinal proficiency before one had a hope of experiencing God's grace, and it is not surprising that Umpachenee was intrigued by the Christianity preached by the Shekomeko residents who testified to the transformative powers of Christ's blood.[34]

Sergeant was well aware of Umpachenee's dissatisfaction, which he generally attributed to his "natural haughtiness" rather than justifiable concerns. In October 1739, for example, Sergeant reported that Umpachenee was "increased in his wickedness, giving himself up to drinking, talking against me and Captain Williams and in general against the English."[35] The following spring, when Sergeant declared a day of public fasting, he reported that "the Lieutenant cavell'd as he has a disposition to find fault with everything" and seemed "bent to do all the mischief he can." In fact, the chief seems to have been raising a question about the biblical authority for fast days.[36] By late March 1740, Sergeant was considering excommunicating the chief.[37] When the Moravian missionaries came on the scene, they found a ready audience in Umpachenee and other disaffected Stockbridge Indians.

The first recorded contact between the Stockbridge Indians and the Moravian missionaries came in October 1742, when a delegation of eighteen Stockbridge Indians—presumably including Umpachenee—arrived in Shekomeko together with Sergeant and a minister from nearby Sharon, Connecticut, on what Sergeant likely viewed as a recruiting trip. At the Moravians' invitation, Sergeant preached in Mohican to a large gathering of Indians at Abraham's house.[38] Sergeant apparently left on good terms and extended an invitation to the Moravian missionaries to pay a visit at Stockbridge. Christian Rauch accepted the invitation and appeared in

Stockbridge together with a contingent of Shekomeko and Pachgatgoch residents in the late winter of 1743. He found many of the Stockbridge residents at their sugar houses and took the opportunity to tell them of the saving power of Christ's blood. Later, in Sergeant's house—and in the minister's presence—a Stockbridge Indian resident announced: "The Breth'n in Shecomeco spoke much of a New Heart. They had heard their minister 8 years together, and to this Hour he had never told them, how they should get it." Apparently, many Stockbridges were intrigued by the message, for just a few months later Büttner reported that the majority of the baptized Indians from Stockbridge arrived in Shekomeko to hear more. Büttner attributed their interest to the fact they had "a Dissenter as Preacher who is a stone dead man."[39]

Stockbridge Indian leaders found much to recommend Moravian Christianity, including a sense of protection in a hostile world and a spiritual confidence, precisely the appeal that many Shekomeko residents had found in the Moravian blood and wounds theology. Büttner reported a conversation overheard by Johannes between the "Indian Governor" of Stockbridge (perhaps Umpachenee) and Sergeant in which the governor asked Sergeant why he was so afraid of the French and proceeded to answer his own question: "You must certainly not have the true Faith nor the right God, for if you had, He is Strong, and can help." The governor said mockingly, "I think you don't believe on him in your Heart and therefore you are so afraid; If you was good Friends with ye Great God, you must necessarily believe that he wo'd protect you."[40]

Over time, there developed a mutual respect and friendship between the Stockbridge Indian leaders and the Moravian missionaries. In December 1744, Umpachenee arrived in Shekomeko accompanied by ten other Stockbridges in order to attend the burial of a young tribesman. The Moravian missionaries assisted at the burial, and the Shekomeko Indians used the occasion to preach a message that seemed tailored specifically to the Stockbridges, warning that "all Knowledge and Understanding is nothing unless one has Experienced the Blood of Jesus, and loves him, yea, that every one is and must be a Servant of Sin, till the Blood of Jesus has destroyed the Power of Sin." The visitors stayed at least a week and so would have had plenty more opportunities to hear the distinctive Moravian gospel. Umpachenee stayed behind after the others left, accepting the missionaries' invitation to join them for several meals. On Umpachenee's final day in town, Büttner invited the chief to the mission house for a cup of hot tea to prepare him for his cold journey home. The missionary reported on the meeting in a long letter to Moravian bishop August Spangenberg, describing the chief as a "prudent and clever man" who proved himself to be a "very good friend" of the Brethren. Over the course of their meals together, Umpachenee called attention specifically to the appeal of the Moravians' non-dogmatic ways.[41]

Umpachenee was clearly not the only Stockbridge resident to find the Moravian message appealing. The Shekomeko and Pachgatgoch records provide evidence related to several other regular visitors from Stockbridge. Many of the references are simply that—records of visits by Stockbridge residents to their friends or family members. A few Stockbridge Indians, however, appear regularly and for one reason or another, the Moravian missionaries recorded their visits in substantial detail. Paul Umpeatkow was a Stockbridge resident and landholder who visited Shekomeko regularly and reported his views of Sergeant and the Stockbridge experiment to the Moravian missionaries. He would also serve as Moravian missionary Sensemann's host during his 1751 visit to the dying Umpachenee.[42]

According to Büttner, Umpeatkow was "a clever, witty and learned Indian" who had been baptized in Stockbridge around 1737 and had often served as Sergeant's interpreter. Paul had family ties at Shekomeko—he was married to the sister of a Shekomeko resident named Nathanael.[43] Over the years, Umpeatkow had apparently become frustrated with Sergeant, and in April 1743 he sought permission from the Moravians to settle in Shekomeko. When asked why he wished to move, Umpeakow answered, "Here you speak Jesus's words and so my heart says to me as well, and I feel everything you say, and this I have never heard so long as I have been taught. Our teacher says nothing of the blood and there my heart feels nothing." When he had tried to ask Sergeant about the "new heart," the missionary became "so anxious and fearful" that he responded with irritation, "Oh Paul, you know well that I do not know what more you want." Paul pleaded with the Moravians to accept him, telling them he couldn't stand to live with his heart in Shekomeko and only his body in Stockbridge.[44] Büttner responded first by telling Umpeatkow that it was not the missionaries' decision to make, because the land belonged to the Indian brothers. Although there is no record of the Shekomeko Indians' response, the missionaries expressed their disapproval on the grounds that Paul needed to provide for his family in Stockbridge.[45] Umpeatkow's affection for the Moravians put him on shaky ground with Sergeant, who threatened to excommunicate him.

John van Guilder, the son of a Dutch father and a Mohican mother, was another frequent visitor in Shekomeko. In August 1743, Büttner recorded an interchange between van Guilder and Sergeant in which the missionary asked van Guilder if he had been in Shekomeko to hear the Moravians' preaching and what he thought of it. Van Guilder reportedly answered, "I think they preach the Truth, right better than ye; when I hear them it is always so with me that I feel they speak downright to the matter that must be in the Heart, but on the contrary, ye always go around about way." Further, he likened Sergeant to a bad husbandman, charging that "you let your People go and have no care of them, if they Love god or if they perish."[46] One appeal of the Moravian message for Stockbridge residents was clearly the sense of spiritual empowerment it bestowed.

As the Moravian mission at Shekomeko came to exert a greater pull on local Indians, John Sergeant became more wary of his competitors and attempted to entice Mohicans baptized by the Moravians to settle instead at Stockbridge by emphasizing the promise of land and education. According to an account by a Wechquadnach resident baptized by the Moravians, Sergeant had promised the men that they would "be better instructed than in Shekomeko" and that they would "have a good piece of land also." The new boarding school Sergeant intended to open in the spring would equip students to "get a good Maintenance." Most importantly, Sergeant insisted, "the Doctrine in Shecomeco was good for nothing," and the Moravians "spoke of nothing else but of Jesus's Blood & of the heart." Sergeant took out his Bible and read several chapters, hoping to show "that Neither Blood nor Heart stood there." Sinners are not saved by Jesus's blood, insisted Sergeant, but "by the Election of God." The path to salvation did not begin with the heart, Sergeant maintained; rather "one must learn to read, and then when one understands, one must act accordingly."[47] Although Sergeant's words might well have been substantially altered in the process of transmission and translation, the sentiment captured in the Moravian records is eminently believable, as it fits squarely with those expressed in Sergeant's own writings.

Many of the Stockbridge Indians, like Umpachenee and Umpeatkow, found much to recommend in the Moravian form of Christianity, and many used their experience with the Moravians to press for changes in the religious program at Stockbridge. The extensive kinship ties linking Stockbridge, Shekomeko, and Pachgatgoch facilitated the exchange of knowledge about the different missionary programs offered by the Congregational and Moravian missionaries. While Umpachenee and Umpeatkow both remained in Stockbridge, the Moravian records provide at least a few instances of Stockbridge residents relocating to Shekomeko.[48] Sergeant believed, with good reason, that the growth of the Stockbridge mission community was hindered by competition from the Moravians, remarking "It is probable, we should have had more of them before now, if there had not come some Moravian Preachers among some of them near to us." While Sergeant initially had reserved judgment of the Moravian ministers, by 1747 he had little good to say of "the Converts they have made," whom he found to be "Enthusiastick and bigotted."[49]

Sergeant was no New Light supporter of revivalism, and so it is not surprising that he should have been critical of what he saw as the Moravians' religious "enthusiasm," especially when those Stockbridges who had contact with the Moravians tended to question Sergeant's authority and theology. More surprising is the depth of the vitriol directed at the Moravian missionaries by prominent defenders of the revivals, such as Gilbert Tennent, Samuel Finley, and Joseph Bellamy, who redirected the criticism they had faced and turned it against the Moravians.[50] Ironically, Finley, Tennent, and other pro-revival ministers charged the Moravians with religious enthusiasm, accusing them of playing to the heart to the neglect of the head, precisely the slur they had been trying to defend themselves against. Their attacks, largely directed at Zinzendorf, presaged legal restrictions on the Moravians' missionary activity and suggest that doctrine was less at issue than preserving social boundaries. Old Light critics of the revivals found New Lights overly presumptuous in their judgments of the spiritual states of others, especially ministers. But even New Lights became concerned when Indians displayed the sort of spiritual assurance that was the hallmark of the New Lights. Although the revivalists and the Moravians were perhaps all equally guilty of enthusiasm, there was indeed an important difference: Anglo-Protestant revivalists reached the emotions with hellfire preaching that warned of God's wrath. By contrast, the Moravians did the same by preaching Christ's love. Finley and Tennent's tracts both react against the Moravians' emphasis on the love and nearness of Christ, which they perceived as a threat to the social order, potentially leveling distinctions between male and female, Indian and white.

What makes this fear all the more palpable is the language used by both authors: both compare the Moravians to wild animals and wild Indians to emphasize what they see as the Moravians' deceptive methods of evangelism. The author of the preface to Tennent's tract, which was endorsed by six prominent Massachusetts ministers, accused the Moravians of "insinuating themselves into the Affections of the Weak and Unstable, and creeping into Houses, in order to lead captive silly Women." Finley borrowed this language for his sermon, elaborating, "They go ravening after Souls, as Wolves, and use cunning like Foxes. They take sculking methods, creeping into Houses, and lead Captive silly Women."[51] Tennent feared the consequences of preaching Christ's love to women, Indians, and the uneducated, asking, "Do not they take special Care to apply to young Persons, Females, and ignorant People who are full of affection?" The Moravians, Tennent charged, used "smiles and soft Discourse about the Love of Christ" to insinuate their way into the affections of the weak but kept their heretical doctrines secret until their victims were already ensnared.[52] In the battle for true religion, the Moravians did not fight fairly, and Tennent feared that those souls captured by the Moravians would be beyond redemption.

Moravians further threatened the social order by challenging patriarchal authority in various ways: worshipping in peer groups and thus "neglecting Family Prayer," appointing women (and presumably others of "weak affections," such as Indians) to religious offices "without any Authority from the Word of God," and sending out missionaries "without human Learning." Just as the Moravians paid little attention to the proper ordering of the social realm, so too they upset the order of the Trinity, "confining their Addresses, almost wholly, to the Second Person of the sacred Trinity," stressing the son's love for sinners rather than the necessity of obedience to God the Father. The Brethren spoke of the saving power of the blood and wounds of Christ to the neglect of "his active obedience to God." All of these teachings, the signers of the preface believed, were "subverting the Souls of our People." One implication was that Indian converts who learned Christianity from the Moravians could scarcely be expected to submit themselves to their English "fathers." The Moravians proved a useful foil against which the New Lights could defend their orthodoxy.[53]

Attacks on the Moravians often directly or indirectly called attention to Moravian missionary successes, revealing substantial discomfort with the Moravian emphasis on the fraternity of believers rather than obedience to divine authority. Finley, like Tennent, called attention to what he saw as the deceptive nature of the Moravian evangelism, focusing particularly on the Brethren's spiritual confidence and deceptive tactics. In his sermon *Satan Strip'd of his Angelick Robe,* Finley aimed to demonstrate that the Moravians were not true claimants to the revivals but were instead dangerous enthusiasts. The Moravians claimed to feel Christ's presence constantly and have "no Heart-Condemnings or down castings thro' Challenges of Conscience, or Sorrow, Darkness, or Desertion, but constant Peace and Comfort." This was a sure sign of delusion: "they that are unacquainted with Desersion, are surely unacquainted with CHRIST, for he was deserted."[54] The Moravians were simply too happy.

When he took occasion to comment on the Moravians in a letter to a Scottish evangelical friend, Jonathan Edwards found, like Tennent and Finley before him, that they were but one example of "counterfeits of vital experimental religion" to flourish in recent years. He was certain that their theological "absurdities" would lead only to "sin, folly, absurdity, and things to the highest degree reproachful to Christianity."[55] The Moravians, implied Edwards, had failed to learn the painful lessons of the revivals.[56]

Compared to the lay and legal responses to the Moravians that erupted with the onset of King George's War in the summer of 1744, the clerical rejoinders were relatively subdued, focusing primarily on Moravian doctrine and methods. Tennent and Finley's tracts, both published in 1743, fanned the flames of anti-Moravian sentiment among English settlers in

New England and New York, especially as France and England headed toward war once again. The Moravian records contain accounts of numerous clashes between the missionaries and their English neighbors. The suspicions first articulated by the Moravians' clerical opponents grew into a widespread hysteria that the Moravians were "papists" whose close relationship to the Indians would facilitate attacks against British colonists. The lay response—and the legislation passed in Connecticut and New York that was directed specifically against the Moravians—suggests a popularization of the initial clerical response. The Moravians were dangerous because they did not see English civility as a prerequisite to Christianity. In particular, they stressed the Savior's love for sinners more than sinners' obligation of obedience to God and his ministers and magistrates on earth, thus threatening the patriarchal (and racial) order.

The complaints of English colonists against the Moravians fall into two frequently intertwined categories: fear of Moravian allegiance to Rome and fear of Moravian alliance with the Indians. Everywhere, the Moravians were suspected of being papists. The contest for empire among England, France, and Spain that had preoccupied the nations for the better part of two centuries was a contest for true religion as well as worldly riches. The Moravians' rich liturgy seemed all too Catholic in the eyes of their Anglo-Protestant neighbors, enough so that many assumed that they were in league with the French.

The Moravians' close relationship with the Indians only further confirmed their likeness to the French, whose Jesuit missionaries were generally more successful at winning native adherents. When Christian Rauch went on a scouting trip to Mohawk territory in January 1743, he found that "it was common talk every where that we were papists." Many suspected the Moravians' missionary work was simply a ruse intended to disguise their true aim of going to "war with them [the Indians] against the other inhabitants and help deliver the land into the hands of the Spaniards."[57] That same year, missionaries Christoph Pyrlaeus, Joseph Shaw, and Martin Mack were arrested in Kent, Connecticut, for preaching without a license, in violation of the recently passed legislation aimed explicitly at the Moravians. Their two-week stay in New Milford, where they stood trial, proved to be a local spectacle, drawing both curious onlookers and impassioned detractors.[58]

The Moravians' spiritual assurance appealed to their Indian audiences but incensed their English neighbors. Pyrlaeus reported that as the missionaries came into town, the gathered crowd "raved violently" against the Brethren, and they would have "liked to have torn us to pieces with their Teeth." With disdain, Pyrlaeus reported, "I have never in all the world come across people who had so loose a tongue in speaking of & disputing about spiritual matters as in this province." Pyrlaeus's opinion was little better of the Anglican service the three missionaries were obliged to attend. The sermons, Pyrlaeus complained, were "read off page by page, & were as dry & dead as any piece of old rotten wood."[59]

The antipathy was mutual, and the Anglican priest charged that Moravian methods of instructing the Indians were "erroneous, dangerous and papist-like."[60] He feared that Moravians made "ignorance the Mother of Religion as the Romans do." Further, Moravians were sly in their dealings with potential converts by seeking to "raise their Affections without first having a good foundation in teaching them the principles of Religion." Mack also raised suspicions when he told his examiners that they had no authority to question him, that he obeyed only God. The audience took this to mean that Mack's allegiance lay with the Church of Rome.[61] The parries back and forth soon prompted a melee: "It was not very long before he [the Anglican] had become so entangled, & displayed his ignorance & stupidity so clearly to all the hearers...that every one would rather himself have taken up a lance against him." The missionary was relieved when "a 7 day baptist did this, sparing me the trouble & continued the discussion, which a New Light finally ended by requesting Mr. Brown to relate how & when he had been converted." The missionaries were eventually fined and released, but the incident was not the end of their troubles.[62]

A year later, tensions between the Moravians and the surrounding settlers had been ratcheted up a notch by the imminent war with France. Rumors circulated widely that the Brethren were Catholic and in alliance with the French, from whom they had allegedly received a shipment of guns and powder.[63] So great was the general fear of the Moravians that churchgoers in Sharon, Connecticut, brought loaded guns to services to protect against attack by the Moravian Indians at nearby Pachgatgoch.[64] About the same time, a group of thirty Connecticut men descended on a group of Moravian Indians out in the fields near Wechquadnach, demanding to know whether they were friends or enemies. Moses, the leader of the Christian Indian community in the village, responded with a rebuke to the militia captain, asking whether his minister taught the congregation to kill Indians. When the captain answered no, Moses retorted, "Much less are we taught so."[65] The men left, somewhat reassured, but before long, several Moravian missionaries were arrested, this time by New York officials.

Early in the summer of 1744, a New York constable arrived in Shekomeko bearing a warrant ordering missionaries Büttner, Sensemann, and Shaw to appear before a board of justices the following day. Charges included the Moravian missionaries' failure to appear for militia exercises or to swear oaths of loyalty, both contrary to Moravian religious convictions.[66] The justices had received numerous complaints about the Moravians, including the charge that they were encouraging the Indians to murder whites. At the trial held in Filkintown before Justice Henry Beekman, numerous witnesses were called to testify against the Moravians. The testimony betrays deep-seated fears of "papism" and racial mixing. One witness claimed that the Moravians were observed to worship images by candlelight behind locked doors. Questions also emerged about Post's marriage to Rachel, the Indian woman from Pachgatgoch. An onlooker at the proceedings jumped in to ask whether it was lawful for a white man to marry an Indian woman, pulling out a Bible to prove the contrary. One of the Brethren responded that it was lawful because both she and her husband were believers—"whereupon war was proclaimed." The gathered crowds swung their hats in the air and shouted; one man was heard to yell, "We have no need of any farther Witness, they are Romans. They are our Enemies."[67] Post's marriage to an Indian woman challenged the equation of true Christian faith with English civility.

Two days after the Moravians were dismissed by a somewhat miffed Justice Beekman, who found the Moravians less of a threat than did their riled neighbors, Governor Clinton of New York issued a letter requesting the Moravian missionaries to appear before him to explain their affiliation with the Mohicans of Shekomeko. He had heard that a "great number of Indians" had assembled at Shekomeko and that "four or more moravian Priests are with them," whose behavior had given him "just Cause of Suspicion that they are seducing those Indians from their obedience to His majesty."[68] In August, missionaries Gottlob Büttner and Joseph Shaw appeared before the governor in New York to answer questions about their affiliation with the Indians. One examiner challenged the missionaries' right to preach to the Indians, noting that they already had a "very Worthy Minister which Preaches to them at Albany if they would take so much trouble to go and hear him." The examiner also questioned the Moravians' credentials: "It is a fine thing when such Men as you pretends to Teach the Indians, the one is a Carpenter, the other a Baker and the other a wool weaver. Fine People to Preach."[69]

Tensions mounted throughout the summer. In September, Governor Clinton issued a decree forbidding proselytizing activity by unlicensed ministers. The law began, "Whereas an Invasion hath been lately attempted against his Majesties Kingdom and Government in favour of a Popish pretender." The purpose of the law was to prevent "the Ignorant and unwary from being led way by Jesuetical and other pretences of Vagrant Teachers." Further, "no Vagrant Preacher Moravian or Disguised Papist shall preach or teach in publick or private without first taking the oaths appointed by this act and obtaining a License from the Governour or Commander in Chief." Moravians were clearly the target of this act, for Quakers and members of almost every other sectarian group were explicitly exempted from the requirement of obtaining certification.[70]

One final scene captures the intensity of sentiment against the Moravians. Having been banned from preaching in New York, the Moravian missionaries retreated to Bethlehem. As they made their way to Pennsylvania, a small party of missionaries including Friedrich Post and his Indian wife, Rachel, were arrested in Esopus, New York. There they were met by a justice who cried out, "Hei, Hei, Hop! You must not go a mile farther, else I put you presently in Prison." He continued to rant, "Ye Dogs, Ye Traitors, Ye Pack of Hores and Rogues. Ye go yonder to make a gang....Ye plot with ye Negroes & Indians." The gathering crowd, according to Mack, "raged so much, that they continually stamped on the Ground and call'd us Traitors, Deceivers."[71]

The Moravians' message of Christian fraternity appealed to many Indian peoples who were increasingly surrounded by English settlers. Moderate Anglo-Protestant clergy like John Sergeant found the Moravians guilty of enthusiasm. Missing the irony, revivalist ministers such as Gilbert Tennent leveled precisely the charges against the Moravians that they had faced from anti-revivalists: that they played on people's emotions and devalued study as preparation for the ministry. Both groups were perhaps equally guilty of religious "enthusiasm," but they differed in their understanding of the relationship between Christian profession and cultural identity. The revivalists feared Moravian influence with the socially marginal; challenging the Moravians reaffirmed their commitment to a patriarchal interpretation of Christianity that stressed obedience to the divine Father.

Clerical hostility to the Moravians paled in comparison to the lay response, particularly after the eruption of King George's War. English settlers in towns neighboring the Moravian missions were sure that the Moravians' distinctive religious practices marked them as Catholic, and the Brethren's close connection with the Indians seemed further confirmation that they were somehow in league with the French. With an eye on the safety of their borders, colonial legislatures in Connecticut and New York passed laws to restrict Moravian work among the Indians. These fervent responses among the British settlers in the northern colonies offer powerful testimony of the extent to which British, Protestant, and white identity had become inseparable. Further insights into the hardening of racial and cultural lines come to us from a somewhat unlikely source: the letters, sermons, and Jonathan Edwards.

JONATHAN EDWARDS, THE STOCKBRIDGE INDIANS, AND THE POLITICS OF IDENTITY

That busy month of August 1751 chronicled in chapter 9, saw Jonathan Edwards wearing many different hats: pastor to the Stockbridge Indians, overseer of the Stockbridge Indian schools, and promoter of colonial British interests. By the time Edwards was installed as the new missionary in 1751, the promise of the mission was seriously in doubt. Mohicans had discovered that the bar of acceptance in New England society was continually raised just out of their reach. The promise made to Umpachenee back at the Deerfield conference in 1735, that Indians would receive the same treatment and same application of colonial law as the English, had proven depressingly hollow. Petitions by Stockbridge Indian residents to the General Assembly protesting unfair land dealings were often met with some acknowledgment of their legitimacy but rarely with justice. The upheavals of King George's War had demonstrated that Christian identification and loyal service to British imperial interests did not raise the Stockbridges above the suspicion of nervous English settlers. Stockbridge Indian ties with the Moravian-affiliated Mohicans fueled English fears.

During his tenure at Stockbridge, from his official installation in August 1751 until he was offered the post as president of Princeton in the fall of 1757, Jonathan Edwards ascended the pulpit hundreds of times to preach to the Stockbridge Indians; he also wrote dozens of letters to government and mission society officials in the effort to defend Indian interests against abuse. Edwards does not seem to have developed any close relationships with the Stockbridge Indians, but this might be said of the whole of his life, not just his Stockbridge years. Yet Edwards was profoundly affected by his experience at the mission, contrary to the popular and scholarly image of the reclusive scholar too busy producing his masterworks to be overly concerned with the daily affairs of the mission. Perhaps unexpectedly, despite the nearly constant battles, his post at Stockbridge may well have been his most rewarding ministry.

Edwards faced new challenges in his role as minister to Indian and white congregations at the far reaches of the Massachusetts settlement, and these challenges—whether consciously or unconsciously—prompted reflection on the nature of identity. Edwards's Stockbridge-era writings not only provide insight into the great theologian's life and thought, they also serve as a case study in the ways that encounters with New England's native peoples challenged New England ways of thinking. In his detailed letters to government officials and mission benefactors, Edwards defended Indian rights and was himself forced to question his assumption that English civility guaranteed greater access to true religion. Whereas Edwards, like many of his fellow ministers, understood New England society to be in a special, covenanted relationship with God, in his sermons to the Stockbridge Indians, Edwards was prompted to deemphasize the importance of nationality and stress that Christ died for Indian and English alike.[72] But when Edwards looked beyond Stockbridge to the national level and considered

New England–Indian relations in the light of British imperial interests—as we see in his dealings with the Mohawks—Edwards continued to associate English civility with Protestantism.

There was little reason to think that Edwards would develop a good relationship with his Indian congregation. He was not an especially warm person, and the regular duties of a minister to comfort, console, and counsel his flock did not come easily to him.[73] In the case of his Indian congregation, the barriers to personal communication were even greater: Edwards did not speak Mohican, and he believed Indian culture to be in need of fundamental reformation. Nonetheless, Edwards came to find a satisfaction in his new post that he had not expected. Edwards's relief is detectable in a note to his father, in which he reported that "the Indians seem much pleased with my family." "Here, at present," he declared, "we live in peace; which has of long time been an unusual thing with us."[74] The circumstances of his departure from Northampton and the political struggles at Stockbridge strained Edwards's relationship with his English congregations—both experiences left him feeling abused, misunderstood, and unappreciated.[75] By contrast, the relationship to his Indian congregation seemed far simpler: these were clearly people, Edwards believed, in need of the saving light of the gospel. They were poor and abused and in need of an advocate.

Edwards arrived in Stockbridge straight from the traumatic controversy that had cost him his job at Northampton. Over the years, Edwards had become uncomfortable with the practice of open communion instituted by his grandfather and predecessor, the much-beloved Solomon Stoddard. Communion, in Stoddard's view, was a converting ordinance, a chance to experience God's grace that could bring the individual toward true conversion, whereas Edwards believed that only those who had already had a true conversion experience could rightfully partake in it. Edwards's decision to change admission practices to require a profession of faith met with near-universal opposition. The controversy affected Edwards in a deeply personal way, leaving him feeling monumentally unappreciated and fearful that his parishioners, with his own Williams relations at the forefront, had willfully turned their backs on the gospel.[76] When a vote was called among church members, only nineteen of 600 voted in Edwards's favor, and so on June 22, 1750, Edwards found himself without a job.[77]

Meanwhile, the missionary post at Stockbridge had been vacant since John Sergeant's death in July 1749. Ephraim Williams, Abigail Sergeant's father and Edwards's kinsman, was now effectively in control of the mission: the New England Company granted him funds to complete the boarding school that Sergeant had first proposed in 1743, but it had remained unfinished at the time of his death, stalled by the disruptions of war. Williams was also charged to head the committee to find a permanent successor for Sergeant.

Williams and his family (especially Abigail, whose marriage prospects living in Stockbridge must have looked quite grim) favored the young and eminently eligible Ezra Stiles (who went on to be president of Yale) for the position, but Stiles begged off when he realized that his theology would come in for close scrutiny, possibly revealing his liberal leanings.[78] Much to the dismay of the Williams family, Edwards soon became the frontrunner, winning the favor of the Indians and the schoolmaster, Timothy Woodbridge, who was no friend of the Williamses. Raising the central issue of the communion controversy, Ephraim Williams Jr. objected that Edwards "was a very great Bigot, for he would not admit any person into heaven, but those that agreed fully to his sentiments." He did, however, see one advantage to Edwards's presence—the value of his property was sure to rise with the presence of the renowned evangelist.[79] With a "chargeable" family of ten children, Edwards felt that his options were limited, so he welcomed the invitation to be considered for the position.[80] Edwards made the forty-mile journey westward from Northampton to Stockbridge in the early months of 1751 to audition before his prospective congregation. In April, Indian and English residents of Stockbridge, together with a council of local ministers, cast their votes, and Edwards was selected to the post. The commissioners for Indian affairs endorsed the choice and summoned Edwards to Boston "so they may have opportunity to confer with him upon the terms of his Settlement."[81]

When Edwards formally assumed his duties as missionary in the summer of 1751, there were roughly 250 Housatonic Mohicans and a handful of Mohawk Indians in residence. About half of the Indian residents had been baptized, of which forty-two were communicants. The English population had swelled to thirteen families. Fifty-five Indian students regularly attended Timothy Woodbridge's school. The boarding school, begun during John Sergeant's tenure with the intention of more quickly "raising" the students to become "a civil industrious and polish'd people," was under the management (or mismanagement, as Edwards came quickly to believe) of Captain Martin Kellogg, the rather undependable longtime friend of the Williams family and survivor of the Deerfield raid.[82] What might have appeared from the outside to be a burgeoning young New England town was in many regards a shambles. As the Moravian missionary Sensemann had discovered upon his visit in May 1751, Stockbridge Indian parents had withdrawn their children from the mission school for want of adequate provision.[83] Barely six months into his appointment, Edwards was deeply distraught by the state of the mission, writing that he expected "nothing by perpetual dissensions, undermining, and counterworking of one another among the inhabitants of the town, which probably will soon bring all to the ground." Edwards laid the blame at the feet of the Williams family. "It is enough," he confessed, "to make one sick."[84]

The Indians shared Edwards's contempt of the Williamses, harboring, he wrote, "a very ill opinion" and "the deepest prejudice" toward Ephraim Williams, "he having often molested 'em with respect to their lands and other affairs, and, as they think, done very unjustly to 'em."[85] Edwards complained to the commissioners about Williams's increasingly erratic and antagonistic behavior, reporting that Williams had embarked on a campaign to set the Indian children against him by telling them that Edwards's previous people "had thrown him away" and the "poor Stockbridge Indians" had been willing to take him but would be better off sending him away in exchange for a "good minister." According to Edwards, Williams went so far as to ply the children with wine in an unsuccessful effort to get them to sign a petition against him.[86]

Edwards attempted to bring order to the schools by hiring the twenty-four-year-old ministerial candidate, Gideon Hawley, to instruct the Mohawk children. He was, according to Edwards, a "young man of uncommon prudence and steadiness of mind, spirit of government, and faculty of teaching."[87] Not surprisingly, the move did not sit well with the Williams faction, which now included Joseph Dwight, recently married to the widowed Abigail Sergeant. Dwight had supported Edwards during the communion controversy and had settled in Stockbridge at Edwards's invitation, but now he became a firm opponent. In a fury one day, Dwight accosted Hawley at the schoolhouse and "continued him under his chastisement for three hours" in the presence of the Mohawk children in an effort to force his resignation.[88] The lines of the conflict were thus drawn: Woodbridge, Edwards, Hawley, and most of the Stockbridge and Mohawk Indians on one side, and the Dwight/Williams families (including Kellogg) on the other.[89]

For a time, the Williamses prevailed, and Kellogg remained. When Kellogg died in the fall of 1753, Joseph Dwight assumed control of the school.[90] With her new husband as overseer, Abigail expected to be put in charge of the girls' school, for which Hollis had sent additional funds, a prospect that Edwards found quite troubling.[91] A volley of claims and counterclaims was fired off to the General Court and to the commissioners from the time of Sergeant's death until the spring of 1754, when the mission's primary benefactor, Isaac Hollis, settled the matter by affirming Edwards's control over the mission.[92] One of the petitions against the Williams faction was signed by forty-one Stockbridge Indians, including Umpachenee, Konkapot, Ebenezer Poohpoonuk, and Paul Umpeatkow.[93]

The decision came too late to salvage the Iroquois presence in Stockbridge—contingents of Mohawks had begun leaving in the spring of 1753, leaving only about ten in residence by late summer. From the beginning, according to Edwards, Mohawk parents objected to the "confused state that they observed things to be in: their children much neglected, no regular school maintained, nor those measures taken for the instructing their children which they had observed the English thought necessary in teaching their own children."[94] All save one lone Mohawk student who lived with Edwards were gone by sugaring season in early 1754. Edwards laid the blame squarely on the shoulders of Joseph and Abigail Dwight and Captain Martin Kellogg, whom he accused of "murdering the Mohawk affair themselves with cruel hands."[95] Although Edwards was unable to salvage the Mohawk presence, he did find consolation in the apparent loyalty he had won of both Stockbridge and Mohawk Indians, which he surely counted as a moral victory over his opponents. The Indians' support counted for much to a minister who had been dismissed by his last congregation.[96]

Edwards's writings on the larger implications of the Mohawk affair reveal him to be very much a man of his times: securing the allegiance of the powerful Iroquois to the British interest would be crucial to the victory of "true religion" over what he saw as the anti-Christian religion of the French. Although he disagreed with Sergeant's widow and her allies' conduct of the Mohawk affair, he agreed with his predecessor's estimation of the importance of a Mohawk alliance. The Mohicans had once seemed to hold the key to New England's future, but in the wake of King George's War, the military allegiance of the Stockbridge Indians was of relatively little importance to British imperial aims. The Iroquois, however, remained central to British interests. Near the end of his life, John Sergeant had set his sights on bringing Mohawk settlers to Stockbridge, concerned at once for the salvation of Mohawk souls and for the safety of the colony's borders.

Sergeant likely first broached the possibility to the Mohawks of their settling in Stockbridge when the Stockbridge Indians met in a council with a delegation of Mohawks in June 1744 to secure a neutrality agreement.[97] He made at least one visit himself to Mohawk country in 1746 and in 1748 or 1749 extended an invitation to the Mohawks to settle in Stockbridge.[98] In writing to potential benefactors in Britain, Sergeant emphasized the importance of winning Indian allies. One of Sergeant's English benefactors described the place of Indian missions in the imperial struggles, arguing the wisdom of securing the tribes of "Heathen Indian Natives" who resided "in the vast Wilderness behind the British Settlements in New England . . . to the Interest of the British Nation, and to the Knowledge and Love of Christianity." If treated well and given proper instruction, these Indians could be of "vast Service to the Crown," especially in case of renewed war with France.[99] Sergeant was successful in his efforts, although it was not until after his death that the first contingent of about fifty Mohawks from Canajoharie and Tionderoga arrived to settle in Stockbridge in the fall of 1750.[100]

Edwards, too, was convinced of the utility of securing Mohawk allegiance and feared Massachusetts was doing too little toward that end.[101] It was not simply a matter of worldly interest. Embracing the providentialism of his Puritan forefathers, including his own grandfather Stoddard, Edwards believed that New Englanders were duty-bound to their God to bring the gospel to the Indians. Even more, he believed that neglect of this duty spelled disaster for the colony. As Edwards saw it, the English had "not only greatly failed of their duty in so neglecting the instruction of the Indians" but had been "extremely impolitick," leading "the whole British America into very difficult and dangerous circumstances." He lamented the paltry mission efforts in New England, speculating that God "will make them [the Indians] a sore scourge to us as a just punishment of our cruelty to their souls and bodies, by our withholding the Gospel from 'em, defrauding them of their goods, prejudicing them against Christianity by our wickedness; and killing of multitudes of them, and easily diminishing their numbers with strong drink."[102] Greater attention to Indian souls would ensure greater prosperity for New England.

Later, as the French and Indian War dragged on and the British were suffering regular defeats, Edwards turned to the logic of the jeremiad, as many of his Puritan forebears had also done in times of war: "God is indeed frowning upon us everywhere: our enemies get up above us very high, and we are brought down very low.... God is making us, with all our superiority in numbers, to become the object of our enemies' almost continual triumphs and insults."[103] Edwards was distraught by the successes of the French in winning Indian allegiance, for " 'tis evident the French are now exerting themselves in an extraordinary manner to draw all those nations over to them." To compete with the French, the English would have to do more to instruct the Indians in "true protestant religion" and "useful knowledge," which were "the only remaining means that divine providence hath left in our power" to secure the Indians "in the British interest."[104] Throughout his tenure at Stockbridge, Edwards continued to view the state of the mission and the outcome of battles during the French and Indian War as signs of God's pleasure or displeasure with New England.

Edwards's belief in the necessity of imparting "civility" to the Indians alongside Christianity is further confirmed in his defense of original sin, written and published during his tenure at Stockbridge. Pointing to the "multitudes of nations" of North and South America, Edwards asked, "What appearance was there when the Europeans first came hither, of their being recovered, or recovering, in any degree from the grossest ignorance, delusions, and most stupid paganism?"[105] Edwards believed that the Indians suffered not only from "those corruptions of Heart which are naturally in the Hearts of all mankind" but also from the "heathenish barbarous brutish Education" that resulted from "those opinions and customs which they have long lived in."[106] The heathen world, believed Edwards, was held captive by Satan, and missionaries were Christ's army, sent to liberate those held under Satan's sway.[107]

Thus Edwards, like most English proponents of mission work, believed that "civilization" and Christianity were inseparable and that a thorough reformation of Indian culture was necessary in order for Christianity to take root, and this conviction is apparent in his plans for the mission. Along with the gospel, mission residents would be taught the basics of reading, writing, and arithmetic together with English husbandry and domestic arts. Proper instruction in basic verbal and mathematical literacy would serve, Edwards believed, "the more speedily and effectually, to change the taste of Indians, and to bring them off from their barbarism and brutality, to a relish for those things, which belong to civilization and refinement."[108]

In laying his plans for the education of Indian youth, Edwards operated on the assumption that "all children are capable of being informed, and having an idea of these things." Although Edwards believed Indian culture to be lacking in many respects, he believed that Indian children had an equal capacity to learn. With the proper education, Edwards believed, the Indians would "renounce the courseness, and filth and degradation, of savage life, for cleanliness, refinement and good morals." While Edwards may have been exemplary at the time in believing that Indians were not inherently inferior, he did share the common view that Indian languages were "ill-fitted for communicating things moral and divine, or even things speculative and abstract." In order to join the ranks of "people possessed of civilization, knowledge and refinement," the Indians would have to give up their "barbarous" tongue for English.[109]

Edwards proposed novel educational techniques for teaching his Indian charges, for he was frustrated by the failure of traditional methods of rote memorization to engage the Indian children he instructed once a week.[110] Students were generally taught to repeat words only, without learning the ideas behind them. As a solution, Edwards proposed to teach by using stories. By emphasizing biblical stories, Edwards believed, "a child's learning will be rendered pleasant, entertaining and profitable.... His lesson will cease to be a dull, wearisome task, without any suitable pleasure or benefit."[111] Edwards saw stories as a means to engage the minds of children in a way that teaching by rote simply could not.

There is no external evidence of Edwards's work as a teacher and no way of knowing to what extent he employed these theories of education during his time at Stockbridge. Nonetheless, in his teaching philosophy there are echoes of his preaching style. Edwards attempted to suit his method to his audience, and in so doing he proposed a radical notion of education. Edwards viewed Indian cultures as barren, but his educational philosophy reflects his conviction that humans are fundamentally equal, differing only in circumstance and environment, a belief that emerges most clearly in his Stockbridge sermons. In his sermons to Indians and English alike, Edwards consistently downplayed the importance of nationality and emphasized instead the importance of the individual's relationship with God, a trajectory that arguably began with the change in his view of the church that culminated in the communion controversy.[112] A closer look at Edwards's Stockbridge sermons provides further evidence of an increasing discomfort with assertions of anything other than an individual covenant between God and the believer.

Through the battles with the Williams family, the coming and going of the Mohawks, and the renewal of war on New England's borders, Edwards ascended week after week to the pulpit to preach to his Indian congregation, averaging three appearances per month in the pulpit throughout his Stockbridge years. By far, the majority of these sermons to the Stockbridge Indians were new compositions, though he likely drew on his vast body of notes and prior sermons in writing them.[113] Edwards clearly had his new audience in mind as he penned new sermons for his Stockbridge congregation.[114] Stockbridge schoolmaster Gideon Hawley recalled that to the Indians, Edwards was "a plain and practical preacher" whose delivery was "grave and natural." He refrained from displaying "any metaphysical knowledge in the pulpit" and took care to use sentences that were "concise and full of meaning."[115] Hawley's observations are borne out by the manuscripts.

Although he never learned the Mohican language, Edwards attempted to employ the English language in a way that would reach straight to the experience of his auditors. The Stockbridge sermons rest on the power of images and stories, freed of the complicated syntax of his Northampton sermons. Edwards was trying to reach not only the heads of his Indian listeners but also their hearts. In his sermons to the Stockbridge Indians, Edwards emphasized that Christ died not for the English alone, as they might have been inclined to infer from popular sentiment among colonists, but for some of all nations. To his English congregants and his readers, Edwards preached the absolute necessity of God's regenerating grace, whether one was born English or Indian. The sermons tell us not only of the workings of Edwards's mind and the shift in rhetorical style necessitated by a change in audience. With a bit of teasing, the sermons also prove a valuable source for Indian history, for embedded within the sermons are clues to the Indians' experience at Stockbridge during these years.[116]

When Edwards's Indian sermons are compared to those preached to his English congregations, whether at Northampton or Stockbridge, their distinctiveness is immediately apparent.[117] His rhetoric, style, and application of doctrine were transformed to suit what he perceived to be the needs of his congregation. For his Indian sermons, Edwards drew most often upon the New Testament with a heavy reliance on the gospels of Matthew and Luke.[118] The content of these sermons suggests why Edwards may have found New Testament texts particularly appealing in preaching to the Indians. Drawing on the parables of the New Testament, Edwards preached of sowers of seed, of fishermen, of ground too dry for a seed to take, of trees fed by rivers that never ran dry, and of briars and thorns that impeded a traveler's way. It is clear in his earlier Northampton sermons that Edwards understood the power of story and imagery; yet in his Indian sermons, this imagery becomes all the more pronounced, as he radically simplified his syntax.[119]

What is most intriguing about Edwards's Stockbridge sermons is neither the style nor the doctrine but rather the application of doctrine. Edwards's experience among the Stockbridge Indians led him to emphasize the encouraging aspects of Calvinist doctrine more in his sermons to the Indians than to the English of Stockbridge. On one occasion, Edwards depicted Christ as one who "delighted in the thoughts of saving poor sinners before ever the world was made," because he had formed a covenant with God to save sinners.[120] He preached standard Calvinist fare, but he balanced the exhortations to abandon sin with assurances that Christ was ready to serve as shelter for all who came to him, of whatever nation or rank. And so when Edwards preached to his Indian congregation on the total depravity of humanity, he often taught that they were no worse than the English. Similarly, when he preached unconditional election, he emphasized that Christ died for members of all nations and all social ranks. Edwards affirmed English cultural superiority, but he rejected any idea that this superiority was innate. Rather, he affirmed that the English had simply benefited from longer exposure to the gospel; so, Edwards informed the Indians, "we do no more than our duty in it for it was once with our Forefathers as 'tis with you." God had shown his mercy by sending others to bring the gospel to the English. The moral of Edwards's story was that "we are no better than you in no respect only as God has made us to differ and has been pleased to give us more Light and now we are willing to give it to you."[121]

The requirements for salvation would be the same for Indian and English: acceptance of God's word as presented in the Bible. "There is forgiveness offered to all nations," Edwards preached, for Christ "did not die only for one nation"; he made clear "his design of making other nations his People," even those that "had been Heathens."[122] Christ offered himself "readily and freely" to suffer for sinners, "let 'em be who they will of what nation soever they are."[123] In a baptismal sermon, Edwards preached, " 'tis the will of Christ that all nations shall be taught." Christ recognized "no difference" among the nations; Christ had "died for some of all / all need / all alike."[124] The offer of salvation is open to all: "For God is a merciful God and would have all men saved and come to the knowledge of the truth." But even as Edwards downplayed the difference between English and Indian, he accused the French of denying Indians full access to the gospel. "The French," he preached to the Mohawks, "they pretend to teach the Indians religion but they won't teach 'em to read," for they were afraid if the Indians should learn to read, they would discover "that these ways are not agreeable to the Scripture," and so the French "keep [the Bible] safe shut up."[125]

Edwards used quite different imagery to express the same theological point in his famous sermon, *Sinners in the Hands of an Angry God,* delivered in Enfield, Connecticut, in 1741, and in a sermon delivered to the Stockbridge Indians a decade later.[126] The doctrine in both sermons is the same: God is a just and merciful God. But whereas in the Enfield sermon, the sinner dangles as a spider held over the pit of hell with the flames of God's wrath lapping at the fragile thread, suspended only by God's mercy— a point easily missed amidst the fire and brimstone—in his Stockbridge sermon, a bleeding Christ stands at the door of the sinner and knocks. No matter their sins, Edwards preached, "He invites you all men and women, young and old. You that have been the greatest sinners, drunkards, quarrellers, Lyars. If any of you have been guilty of fornication adultery murder or whatever wickedness." However great the sin, "the great Saviour the King of Heaven and Earth" is now "come to your door." All that was needed was "to let Him in."[127] The implication of the difference in imagery is notable: in the Enfield sermon, God would be just in unleashing his wrath, whereas in the Stockbridge sermon, Christ *wants* to save sinners, even though they are justly deserving of damnation.

How to account for the difference in Edwards's application of doctrine? At Stockbridge, Edwards witnessed as the resident Indians were antagonized by the same family that had led the charge against Edwards in Northampton. This fact most certainly served to strengthen Edwards's sympathy for the Indians and his commitment to protecting their interests. Edwards used his pulpit to counsel the Stockbridge Indians and offer comfort during difficult times. For example, in a sermon preached in August 1753, at the height of the controversy over the management of the mission schools, Edwards warned his listeners that sometimes it is necessary "to wait till we get to another world before we have our reward."[128] One particularly poignant sermon preached in August 1756, in the midst of the French and Indian War, captures Edwards's empathy for the plight of his Indian congregants, many of whom were discovering that despite their loyal service in fighting alongside the British, they were rarely granted the same protections or rewards as their white neighbors.[129] "You that are poor you that have but few Friends," urged Edwards, "if any of you are weary of sin, if you are weary of seeing so much wickedness in the world" or "weary of seeing others drunk, weary of contention," then do not "walk in the ways of drunkness [*sic*] and do the works of darkness" but instead "chose [*sic*] heaven as your house.... Trust in Christ. "Edwards promised that in heaven, the saints would find "bounty without deformity...friends and no enemies...and nothing but peace and love and no contention," something both Edwards and the Stockbridge Indians found elusive in this world.[130] Another sermon delivered in the midst of war suggests that morale was particularly low among the Stockbridges. Edwards encouraged his congregants to seek God's mercy, and then refuted potential—or real?—objections, all of which are poignant and telling indicators of the state of the Indian congregation. The list included the following objections: "I love my sins so that I don't know how to forsake 'em;...I have sinned so much already that I think God won't hear me," and finally, "I have prayed in times past and I don't see it does any good. I am not better but worse." It would seem that at least some members of his congregation were questioning the efficacy of the Christian God. Edwards's response was to assure his congregation of God's love and mercy and to offer guidance as to how to pray to God. Most importantly, Edwards encouraged his congregation not to lose hope: "God commands us to pray alwaies and never be discouraged." Though it may seem fruitless, counseled Edwards, all of this was part of a divine plan: "Sometimes he makes men wait long when he all the while intends to hear 'em to do 'em good."[131] In other words, the Indians were long-suffering, and circumstances were sufficiently trying for them to be discouraged.

If Edwards often offered comfort to his Indian congregation, he did not spare them the hard doctrines of Calvinism. As he marched through the history of human relations with God in his sermons to the Indians, he explained that since the Fall, "men naturally have the image of the devil in their souls" and therefore are given to "sin and wickedness."[132] In a catechism to Indian children, Edwards warned, "every body as they are at first are not good...all are born with wicked hearts."[133] In the sermon that most likely marked Umpachenee's death, Edwards was at no loss to describe what awaited sinners in hell: "They shall be cast into a furnace of fire," where their souls would burn in hell until the Day of Judgment.[134] He warned them, too, that access to the gospel brought greater obligations: "You had better know your duty more than others and God has done more for you than others and therefore if you don't do your duty you will have a better place in Hell than the Heathen that never heard of Jesus Christ."[135] But Edwards balanced these harsh bits of Calvinist doctrine with assurances that sinfulness was the natural state of *all* humanity and therefore that Indians had as good a chance of being saved as any others who had heard the gospel.

At Stockbridge, Edwards was plagued by some of the same fears he had faced throughout his life—that his ministrations as bearer of the word of

God were going unheeded and that at least some of his flock were not granting him the proper respect he felt he deserved as Christ's messenger. A number of sermons from 1755 suggest that attendance at meetings had been slack and that he felt he was going unheeded as Christ's messenger. In a sermon delivered in March 1755, Edwards warned that those who hear the gospel, yet refuse to believe, have a worse spot in hell reserved for them than those who had never heard the gospel. From the text Matthew 10:14–15, Edwards drew the lesson, "they that will not harken to them that Christ sends to preach the Gospel, it will be worse for 'em at the day of Judgment than for the worst sort of them that never had the gospel offered to 'em."[136] On another occasion, Edwards reminded his congregants that "tis kind and friendly in ministers and not what they should at all dislike, when ministers warn sinners of their dangers of God's wrath" and on another, cautioned "they that are going on in their sins should consider what they will do hereafter when God comes to call 'em to account."[137] Edwards was perhaps facing pressure from his Indian congregation to preach the gospel more along Moravian lines. A report by the Indian commissioners at the time confirmed the strain between Indian and English residents of the town, noting with relief in January 1755 that "the fears that were Entertained of their [the Stockbridges] defection are much abated."[138]

The few original sermons that Edwards composed for his English congregation at Stockbridge betray quite a different sentiment than those to the Indians.[139] Edwards's sermons to the English were often castigatory, upbraiding his parishioners for having not made good use of the fine gospel preaching they had been provided and reminding them that they were incapable of achieving salvation on their own.[140] There was no mistaking that parts of his sermon preached to the Mohawks in August 1751 were aimed at the white representatives in the audience, as when he declaimed, "Since the white people came over the seas and have settled in these parts of the world they have not done their duty to you. They have greatly neglected you."[141] He also took occasion to remind the well-to-do among his English audience, "Those that obtain the [highest] degree of worldly wealth and honour and enjoy the most pleasure in their carnal enjoyments can retain them but for a moment all suddenly vanishes away like a vapor that is dissipated by the winds."[142] Even his sacramental sermons, occasions on which Edwards usually described the great love of Christ to humans, Edwards railed at his English audience, "I will tell you who they be that eat unworthily." Edwards then proceed to explain "why such as eat and drink unworthily are guilty of murdering the body and shedding the blood of Christ."[143] And in one lecture to the English children at Stockbridge, Edwards warned, "I had rather go into Sodom and preach to the men of Sodom than preach to you and should have a great deal more hopes of success."[144] Edwards seems to have been frustrated that those who had had benefit of English civility had not proven themselves to be worthier Christians when it came to their treatment of their Indian neighbors.

In his sermons to the Indians, Edwards wrestled with questions of national identity. On the one hand, his commitment to the idea of a Protestant empire remained firm, as he warned the Mohawks in particular that "true religion don't consist in worshipping the Virgin Mary." On the other, Edwards challenged the idea of a national covenant when he assured his Indian congregants that "the English are no better than you" and that "Christ died not for one nation, but for some of all nations."[145] Interestingly, while he preached to both Indians and English that nationality conferred no inherent advantages or disadvantages, he spun that message quite differently depending on the audience. Edwards preached to the Indians that they too were among the elect. To his English congregants, Edwards preached the absolute necessity of God's regenerating grace whether one was born English or Indian. Edwards's experiences at Stockbridge became one more piece of evidence in his campaign against the inroads of Arminianism, the heresy of human ability.

Had not Edwards experienced firsthand the racial politics of the Stockbridge mission, and had it not been his old antagonists the Williams family spearheading the alienation of Indian lands in Stockbridge, he might have taken his defense of *The Great Christian Doctrine of Original Sin* in quite a different direction. Read in the context of what we know of Edwards's relationships with his Indian and white congregations at Stockbridge, his treatise appears in a new light. In this treatise, while the American Indians, together with other examples of "pagan" peoples, serve as examples of the absolute necessity of divine revelation in acquiring knowledge of "true religion," the conclusion Edwards wished his readers to draw was that all humanity would be in a similar state were it not for the grace of God. Europeans had not shown a lesser tendency toward sin. Rather, God's grace had been more readily available.

At the end of his treatise, Edwards underscored what he saw as the ethical implications of the doctrine of original sin. Far from resulting in "an ill opinion of our fellow-creatures," thereby promoting "ill-nature and mutual hatred," as his opponents argued, the affirmation of the doctrine of original sin would in fact induce a welcome humility. By contrast, to disown "that sin and guilt, which truly belongs to us," in Edwards' view, leads only to a "foolish *self-exaltation* and *pride.*" Acceptance of the doctrine would have the salutary effect of teaching "us to think no worse of others, than of ourselves," and convincing people that "we are *all,* as we are by nature, *companions* in a miserable helpless condition." This, in turn, "tends to promote a mutual *compassion.*" If the doctrine of original sin is abandoned in favor of faith in human reason, then sin becomes a matter of choice, and so one is free to believe "that the generality of mankind are very wicked, having made themselves so by their own free choice, without any necessity: which is a way of becoming wicked, that renders men truly *worthy of resentment.*"[146] In a strange way then, the treatise *Original Sin* became a call to human fellowship rooted in a conviction of equality. Had it not been for his mission experience, Edwards might not have emphasized in *Original Sin* the equality in human depravity to the extent that he did.

Edwards's vast corpus of writings from his tenure at Stockbridge reveals tensions in his thinking about the relationship between the state of one's soul and the state of one's citizenship. In one important respect, Edwards's writings differ little from those of other Anglo-Protestant missionaries: they provide precious little information about the lives of the Stockbridge Indians. A few tantalizing clues suggest, however, that Edwards gained considerable respect from his Indian congregation and that this was in large measure due to his efforts to defend their interests and his willingness to take them seriously as catechists.

Edwards's writings rarely reference Indian individuals—individual Stockbridge Indians are mentioned by name fewer than twenty times. His letters include several references to his interpreter, John Wauwaumpequunaut, whom he described as "an extraordinary man on some accounts; understands English well, [is] a good reader and writer and is an excellent interpreter. And perhaps there was never an Indian educated in America that exceeded him in knowledge, in divinity, [and] understanding of the Scriptures." Later that year, Edwards submitted a request to the commissioners for Indian affairs to increase the provision for Wauwaumpequunaut to alleviate the "insufficiency of his salary to support his family," for he had been so constantly engaged in his work as interpreter and usher that "he can't hunt nor yet follow husbandry."[147] That there is so little information on this man with whom Edwards must have spent a considerable amount of time underscores some of the differences of the Moravian and New England missions.

A number of other Stockbridge Indians are mentioned by name in Edwards's account book, in which he primarily recorded books borrowed and lent. Here Edwards recorded having performed eight marriages of Indian couples and having paid "Hannis" for his services as interpreter.[148] A few more hints of Edwards's relationship with his Indian congregation emerge from his sermon notes. One of his first sermons preached at Stockbridge was a "lecture before the sacrament" in January 1751, indicating that he officiated at communion from the beginning of his service as missionary and, more importantly, that he recognized Indians as full church members.[149]

Among the papers left by Edwards are a collection of professions of faith, written in Edwards's own hand but each slightly different. Except for the names Cornelius and Mary Munneweaunummuck signed to the bottom of the longest profession, nothing would signal that these were Indian individuals. Their profession begins, "And I do now appear before God and his People solemnly to give up my self to God to whom my Parents gave me upon my Baptism having so far as I know my own Heart chosen Him for my Portion and set my Heart on Him as my greatest and sweetest Good," and ends, "I profess universal forgiveness and good will to mankind and promise to be subject to the Government of this Church during my abode here."[150] Because it is so formulaic and written in Edwards's hand besides, the professions could perhaps be dismissed as having little to tell us. But, given that Edwards was willing to lose his job for his insistence on a profession of faith, we can safely assume that he did not treat these professions as merely *pro forma* recitations. He must have been persuaded that Cornelius and Mary's testimony, though scripted, was an apt representation of their inner lives. While this does not tell us anything at all about what it meant to Cornelius and Mary, it does suggest that there had been a significant exchange between the candidates and Edwards on the subject of Christian belief and practice.

Other evidence suggests that this exchange left its imprint on the Stockbridge Indian community long after Edwards's death in 1758. Hendrick Aupaumut, the Stockbridge Indians' chief sachem in the late eighteenth and early nineteenth centuries, came to be an eloquent advocate of a Christianity that challenged rather than reinforced the rising barriers between Indian and white in America. Although Aupaumut was born in the same year Edwards died, he seems to have developed a friendship with Edwards's son, Timothy. Several letters survive from Aupaumut to the younger Edwards. "My friend," he wrote in one, "I should be thankful if you would lent me a Book. The Authors [*sic*] is your Father—Concerning Affections or if you han't such—wish to have the other mention—the Will."[151] Whether he read the treatises, or what he thought of them, we will never know, but a speech likely delivered by Aupaumut in 1795, with its mention of disinterested love, suggests that the theology of Edwards and his New Divinity disciples had had some influence. John Sergeant Jr. recorded in his diary part of a speech by the tribal speaker to the Quaker missionaries who had recently arrived to work among the Brotherton Indians: "Brothers we thank the great spirit above that he has put it into your hearts to come this long journey to make us this friendly visit.... Brothers, we heartily thank you for the many tokens of your disinterested love and friendship towards us poor Indians."[152] Aupaumut's long career, glimpsed briefly in chapter 12, suggests that Edwards's message of equality, hinted at in *Original Sin*, became an important element of native Christian theology, one used to challenge the increasingly racialized definitions of American and Christian identity in the United States.[153]

It had been during Umpachenee's life that a new identity as the Stockbridge Mohicans emerged. The Indian community at Stockbridge attracted new settlers with the promise of education in English ways, which they hoped would be the means of entering into a relationship with the English on more equal terms. The Stockbridge Indians viewed Christianity as a new means of reinforcing traditional fictive kinship ties between peoples. But the Stockbridges were repeatedly disappointed as they found the bar for admission to New England society again and again raised just beyond their reach. The vitriolic responses of Anglo-Protestant clergy and English settlers to the Moravian missionaries and their Indian affiliates provide clues as to just why this was so. The intensity of the attacks on the Moravians reveals the extent to which Christianity was linked with English civility and, increasingly, with whiteness.

Precious little about the religious lives of the Stockbridge Indians during the tenure of Jonathan Edwards can be reconstructed from the available sources, but the trove of sources left by Edwards provides some surprising insights into the relationship between the pastor and his congregation. When he arrived to fill the missionary post at Stockbridge, Edwards differed little from other Anglo-Protestant missionaries in his desire to "reduce" the Indians by introducing the gospel alongside English "civility." Edwards's dismissal from Northampton and his battle at Stockbridge for control of the mission pushed his thinking in new and surprising directions. The Stockbridge Indians were constantly on the defensive, seeking to secure equal protection under provincial and town laws, but rarely did they meet with justice. In his sermons to the Indians and the English, Edwards began to question the idea of a federal covenant between God and his people and deemphasized the importance of nationality, even while his public writings during the French and Indian War revealed the persistence of Puritan providentialism.

The mission at Stockbridge had been founded with the ostensible purpose of introducing "Christian civility" to the Indians, thus lessening the cultural chasm between English and Indian. Ironically, with some exceptions, both Indians and whites emerged from the experience with a starker sense of their differences. The terms of the bargain were not quite what either party had anticipated. The next chapter steps back to take a wider view, measuring the state of affairs in the 1750s against the original hopes and aspirations of the missionaries and the Mohicans that had brought the Stockbridge and Shekomeko missions into being. The final chapter returns to biography, following two sons of the missions from their birth at Stockbridge and Shekomeko through the early nineteenth century. The lives of Hendrick Aupaumut of Stockbridge and Joshua of Shekomeko reveal the very real consequences of the early histories of the two communities.

CONCLUSION

Chapter Eleven

Irony and Identity

By the 1760s, the land between the Hudson and Housatonic River Valleys was no longer the land of the Mohicans. English, Dutch, and German colonists arranged themselves into villages, towns, and counties where Mohicans had once hunted, fished, and farmed, raised their families, lived and died. Some things, however, had not changed. Disease, white land hunger, and alcohol continued to plague the remaining Mohican communities. The hopes that had brought Mohicans and missionaries together had proved illusory. Ebenezer Poohpoonuc's dream that worship of the Christian God would enable Mohicans to "greatly increase and multiply" like the English had not been fulfilled. Umpachenee's hope that the acquisition of literacy would secure Mohican lands from the grasp of the English and ensure the fair treatment of the next generation also went unfulfilled. Abraham's faith that the blood of Christ would cure the ravages of alcohol could not bring it to pass for all those who suffered. Nor could Rachel's imagining that she was nursing her child on the blood of the Savior ensure her child's survival. Likewise, the English design of "reducing" the Indians to civility had met with mixed results. And the Moravian hope of creating a new community of Indian and white Brothers and Sisters in Christ had been hindered by constant persecution and hostility from suspicious neighbors, both English and Indian.

Evaluating the fate of mission communities is a tricky business. Missions can be studied for what they tell us of the fate of Indian groups or about the development of Euro-American society. But missions also provide ideal conditions for studying the process of religious adaptation. Cultural encounter transformed not only the missionized but also the missionaries. All parties had entered the mission with hopes and aspirations rooted both in their history and in their perception of present circumstances, but none were able to achieve quite what they had intended. Nonetheless, there is more to the story than disappointed hopes and fractured visions. All participants brought with them to the mission a set of religious beliefs and practices that would be challenged and transformed through the encounter with others.

Mohicans and missionaries alike strove to bring their belief systems into accord with changing circumstances. Initially, each group had found both religious and political utility in the mission, but their assessment of this utility waxed and waned, leading in turn to periodic reevaluations of their commitment to the mission. It was through these choices that each group continued to shape its identity. Those choices reflect an attempt to maintain a continuity with the past while charting a viable course for the future. Mohicans, Moravians, and Congregationalists all made such choices, but the constraints on each were quite different. The range of choices was most severely restricted for those who wielded the least power in colonial society. Conversely, those who held the greatest political power possessed the greatest number of options, including the possibility of constructing a future that effectively excluded the other residents of the Housatonic River Valley. Thus, the Mohicans, Moravians, and Congregationalists were quite different people in 1760 than they had been in 1730, a result of both the choices and the constraints that arose from their interactions with one another. The transformations that occurred at Stockbridge and Shekomeko during these decades are symbolic of larger shifts in colonial society, with important implications for the Revolutionary Era and beyond.

The English settlers of Stockbridge and the Massachusetts government could and would extricate themselves from their commitment to the mission once the political utility of that commitment had waned. Some of the contentions at Stockbridge stemmed from problems inherent in the design of the mission. For example, Sergeant's proposal to have model English families contained no provisions to determine how the children of these model families and the children of the first Indian settlers would be accommodated with land. Higher fertility and infant survival rates among the English meant that the Indian population would be outnumbered within little more than a generation. Also, the relative strength of Massachusetts meant that its religious and civic representatives were forced to concede little to the Indian settlers in the early phase of the mission, leaving little room for negotiation. Consequently, Sergeant and other supporters clung to a program that sought to "civilize" the mission residents by exterminating Indian culture and inculcating English habits not only of worship but also of dress and husbandry. Ironically, even while the English sought to replace savage ways with civil ones, they depended on the Indians to remain Indian when it came to war. First in King George's War and then in the French and Indian War, the English turned to the Stockbridge Indians for their expertise in Indian warfare tactics, although the loyal service of the Stockbridge Indians in multiple colonial wars was not rewarded with gratitude and acceptance into New England society.

As it had become clear that the Mohicans would not become just like New England men and women, the English settlers became more committed to the idea of a community devoid of Indians. With little to fear from the small band of loyal Indians, English settlers showed little compunction about displacing those people their government had, just decades earlier, professed to save. Nothing speaks more clearly of this commitment to an Indian-free Stockbridge than the increasingly vociferous and ultimately successful effort of the English population to establish separate Indian and white townships.[1]

The efforts to transform Stockbridge into a typical New England town did not go unopposed. During his tenure at Stockbridge, Jonathan Edwards sought to forestall what he saw as increased worldliness and neglect of true religion, as manifested in the bungling of the mission project in particular and colonial Indian affairs in general. Edwards, like Sergeant, expected a radical transformation in the Indian converts. But his experiences as pastor to the Stockbridge Indians prompted him to reflect on the relationship between national or cultural identity and the state of one's soul, with some important theological implications. In his sermons to the Stockbridge Indians, Edwards downplayed the importance of national identity, stressing instead the inherent equality of humans, who all stood in need of God's saving grace.

Although Edwards was never able to straighten out mission affairs at Stockbridge to his satisfaction, his dedication to the project resulted in an important, if unintended, consequence for the Stockbridge Indians. Together with Stockbridge schoolmaster Timothy Woodbridge, Edwards defended the rights of the Indians to receive what had been promised them—protected lands and a Christian education. Combined with the original structure of the mission, which granted the Stockbridge Indians their own township in New England fashion, the result was to delay the alienation of Mohican lands. Although these were not easy years, the Mohicans of Stockbridge were able to remain on their tribal lands significantly longer than the Mohicans at Shekomeko, most of whom had left the area by the early 1750s. Despite the endless contentions and the perpetual quest of English settlers after Mohican lands, the Indian residents remained at Stockbridge so long as they had land and a say in the town governance. With their lands nearly depleted by the time of the Revolution, most Stockbridge Indians opted to leave, accepting the invitation of the Oneidas to settle with them in upstate New York in 1783.[2]

Joining their fates to Christian missionaries and becoming a Christian people did not resolve some of the most insidious problems brought on by European colonization, yet it did provide the occasion for the formulation of a new identity that enabled the Mohicans of Stockbridge to live in the new world emerging around them. This new identity as the Stockbridge Indians was rooted in a Mohican past, but it also pointed toward a new future. Ironically then, the mission that was specifically aimed at eliminating "Mohican-ness" in some ways facilitated the survival, or rather the recreation, of that identity.

The Stockbridge Indians continued the practices of their forebears who had maintained an intricate web of alliances rooted in trade and diplomacy. These ties became the basis for forging new communities when populations were thinned by disease or warfare. The settlers at Stockbridge were able to draw the remnants of the declining Mohican and Housatonic villages to the mission site; within a decade of its founding, the seat of the Mohican nation had moved from its traditional Hudson River location to Stockbridge. This development was further encouraged by a mission policy that sought to bring as many prospective converts as possible to live at Stockbridge, on the premise that conversion was likelier if the Indians were assembled into a compact settlement, far from the influence of non-Christian Indians. The Stockbridge Indians invoked their Mohican heritage and cast themselves as cultural brokers, not only consolidating Mohican and Housatonic peoples but also reaffirming and expanding intertribal ties. They expanded traditional fictive kinship ties to incorporate their English allies, fighting alongside their English "brothers" in King George's War and the French and Indian War and attempting to hold the English to their kinship obligations.

Along the way, the Stockbridge community emphasized particular elements of their pre-mission past as the basis for a continuity of identity: principles of exchange, cultural mediation, and preservation of a land base took precedence over continuity of religious or subsistence practices. For a time, this agenda seemed to coincide with Congregational mission policy: both Sergeant and Stockbridge leaders valued population growth at Stockbridge and acquisition of English cultural currency. The intersection of these goals facilitated the creation of a new body politic, one with the power to carry the Stockbridge Mohicans through the many difficult years and removals ahead. Today the Stockbridge-Munsee Band of Mohicans persists, and their reservation in Shawano County, Wisconsin, thrives.[3]

The story that emerges here is a local one, but one with substantially broader implications. The formation of a new identity as the Stockbridge Indians, fashioned out of the material of Mohican tradition, new Christian ideas, and English cultural practices, challenges the overly simplistic narratives of accommodation and resistance that have long dominated the historiography of Indian-white relations. The Stockbridge Indians were not alone in this project: across New England—indeed throughout the colonies—native peoples were engaged in reshaping and redefining their identity. Declining populations and increased alienation of Indian lands prompted consolidation of Indian communities and the forging of new, more broadly defined identities. It also challenges essentialized notions of identity that see "Indian" and "Christian" as mutually exclusive categories.[4] The Indians of Stockbridge saw themselves as no less Mohican than their forefathers. In fact, more and more, the Stockbridge Indians assumed a leading position as spokesmen for the larger Mohican community.

The Mohicans of Shekomeko did not fare as well as their Stockbridge neighbors. Without a reserve of land sanctioned by colonial authorities, Shekomekoans faced more immediate pressure to cede their lands than did the Mohicans of Stockbridge. Their affiliation with Moravian missionaries aroused fears of their loyalty in times of war. Alone, the Mohicans of Shekomeko had been unable to oppose the encroachment of European settlers on their lands, as Abraham's experience testifies. And although the Moravian missionaries despised the treatment their Indian affiliates met with at the hands of colonists, they could do little to protect Mohican lands. But the Mohicans of Shekomeko did find in their alliance with the Moravians a place of psychic refuge.

During the early years of the mission, Shekomeko showed signs of becoming a vibrant and self-sustaining community of Christian Mohicans. In the daily life of the mission, Christianity was well on its way to being indigenized. The emergent community was both thoroughly Christian and thoroughly Mohican. Converts found in the language of the blood and wounds of Christ a powerful resonance with their own lives as Mohicans. Many traditional practices—from feasts to funerals—gained new life when inflected with Moravian theology. Jesus became in the Mohican imagination a keeper of the game and a powerful *manitou* who offered his protection to his petitioners. Women turned to the Moravian blood and wounds theology to preserve self, family, and community at a time when the forces of colonialism threatened to tear them apart. Men and women found support for waning authority in Christian offices.

But Christianity was not simply an overlay on top of Mohican traditions. Moravian theology gave redemptive significance to suffering, while Moravian ritual practice provided access to new sources of spiritual power that provided comfort if not always solutions to problems. Beyond new ritual forms, Moravian Christianity provided consolation for beleaguered souls, relief from suffering, and the love of a powerful and sympathetic Savior. It also offered a model of a relationship with whites that held out the promise of equality. Because the Moravians themselves had long been outsiders to political and social power, they were little inclined to hold the acquisition of European habits as a prerequisite to the Christian life, so Mohican life was spared a systematic assault by the Moravian Brethren.

New religious beliefs and practices imbued Mohican existence with new meaning. But what seemed to be the emergence of a new religious tradition, one that melded Mohican experience with a Christian message of suffering and redemption, was ultimately cut short by the force of demographics and colonial politics. Mohican populations, suffering from perpetually high mortality rates, were rapidly overtaken by European settlers. Arguably, these demographic trends were exacerbated by the Shekomekoans' affiliation with the Moravians, who made few friends among their English neighbors. Whenever war erupted, Moravian missionaries and their Indian associates came under suspicion of "papism" and alliance with the French.

By late 1745, the Mohicans of Shekomeko faced the difficult choice of remaining on their native soil or following the exiled missionaries to Pennsylvania. Those who joined the missionaries faced separation from family and friends and the pain of leaving their homeland. Those who stayed also faced separation from loved ones as well as increasing pressure on their lands, harassment for payment of debts, and little hope of emerging from a cycle of poverty. Remaining on their homelands did not prove a viable option—it quickly became clear to those who stayed behind that the pressures on their lands were too great and that they lacked colonial allies able to protect their interests. By the early 1750s, most of the Mohicans of Shekomeko and the surrounding villages had followed the Moravian missionaries to Pennsylvania. A few remained behind, determined to live out their lives on their homelands, while a few joined the settlement at Stockbridge. Those Mohicans who followed the Moravian missionaries to Pennsylvania did not face an easy road. The Moravians continued to be regarded warily by other colonists, and neither they nor the Indians affiliated with them enjoyed a respite from persecution: within years of their relocation, the French and Indian War erupted, and the Pennsylvania backcountry became the principal theater of war.

The middle decades of the eighteenth century were years of change for the Moravians, just as they were for the New Englanders and Mohicans. The Moravians arrived in America with an abundance of enthusiasm and a cadre of missionaries eager to save Indian souls and unite European colonists under a common profession of Christianity. It was the zeal of the

Moravian leader Zinzendorf and the energy of the first generation of members in the Renewed Church of the Unity of the Brethren that had fueled Moravian missions. Such states of religious enthusiasm and renewal have always proven difficult, if not impossible, to sustain. The Moravian settlers at Bethlehem prospered, and the more they prospered, the greater the pressure was to conform to the norms of the surrounding colonial society—and the more the missionary impulse waned. One simple fact amply illustrates the transformation of the missionary spirit of the Moravians: there are few individual missionaries from the first two decades of the Moravian missions in America who stand out in the annals of history: the missions at this time were very much a communal affair. But after 1760, the year the General Economy was dissolved, a much smaller proportion of the community volunteered for missionary work. Those who devoted their lives to mission work, such as David Zeisberger and John Heckewelder, were now the exception rather than the rule, and they bore the burden of carrying on the community's commitment. This transition arguably pushed these and other Moravian missionaries to reflect more consciously and publicly on their role as missionaries, which in turn brought an even greater change in the Moravian mission strategy.[5]

Over the course of the eighteenth century, Moravian missionaries became more interested in Indian cultures. Zeisberger and Heckewelder both systematically recorded and published their observations of Indian cultures, a stark departure from early Moravian missionaries, who scarcely mentioned Indian customs at all. Although these writings have earned the later Moravians a reputation as kindler, gentler missionaries and the gratitude of modern students of Indian culture, the shift in Moravian mission culture arguably marks the emergence of a sense of distinct racial identities that had been largely absent in the early Moravian missions. This development is confirmed by the shift in Moravian mission policy, which came more and more to resemble that of their Anglo-Protestant counterparts, stressing the importance of stamping out heathen ways and introducing the arts of European civilization.

The Moravian mission diary from the 1803 visit of Hendrick Aupaumut and a delegation of Stockbridge Indians to the Delaware mission community stands in dramatic contrast to early Moravian missionary writings. Gone are the accounts of proclaiming the blood and wounds of Christ to visitors. Instead, the diarist Benjamin Mortimer took careful stock of the Stockbridges' progress toward civility, noting approvingly, "The men plow their lands, most of the women spin, some can knit and do all the other domestic work which is usually performed by their sex." Rather than hunting, they produced crops for the market, including "wheat, Indian corn, cattle, and part of the wool of their sheep." They managed their own flour and sawmills and orchards that generated upwards of a thousand barrels of cider a year. Mortimer was particularly impressed that the delegation traveled with a collection of books, that they took the time to write letters home, and that they asked about buying an almanac from the Moravians, as they had forgotten theirs at home. In sum, the diarist noted with a touch of envy, "in all the improvements of civilized life, they appear to be much farther advanced than our converts here."[6]

Gone, too, was the disdain that earlier Moravian missionaries had harbored for other Protestants. Wrote Mortimer, "The best of all was, these Mahikkans were mostly Christian Indians.... They had not, like all the strange Indians in these parts, trinkets of silver, or other metal, attached to their noses, ears, hair and garments. On the contrary, they were plain in their apparel, & cleanly in their persons like our brn here; & well dressed." This, believed Mortimer, was "as things should be," for when "the heathen have once the grace to be converted to knowledge of a Saviour, they ought gradually to be taught to relinquish the life of savages."[7] Gone from the Moravian missionary sources is talk of the blood and wounds of Christ, and in its place are measurements of the markers of civilization: barrels, bushels, and books. The Moravians' distinctive mission practices had brought them under constant suspicion in the early years of their missions. The shift in policy, in which a few remarkable individuals took the place of a corps of missionaries, allowed the Moravian community to maintain a sense of continuity with its original purpose while enabling them to fit more comfortably into the broader colonial society. Sixty years after the inauguration of the Moravian missions, the Brethren had come to embrace the Anglo-Protestant missionary model: Indians must be "civilized" in order to be properly Christianized.

Mortimer's remarks reveal much about the transformations in Moravian mission strategy that had occurred by the early nineteenth century. Much in America had changed as well. By turning now to the stories of Hendrick Aupaumut and Joshua, sons of Stockbridge and Shekomeko, we can trace the very real consequences of the early mission histories in the lives of individual Mohicans. Their lives, though unique, reveal much about the place of Indians in the emerging American nation. Aupaumut's story testifies to the limits of Anglo-Protestant mission policy: even those Indians who embraced the "civilizing" project were ultimately barred by their race from a place in Euro-American society. And Joshua's story makes clear that those Indians who engaged in indigenizing Christianity, thus challenging emerging racial identities of Indians and whites risked their lives.

Chapter Twelve

The Cooper and the Sachem

The lives of individual men and women form the heart of this book: Umpachenee, Shabash and Tschoop, Sarah and Rachel, John Stoddard and Jonathan Edwards: their stories put a human face on the familiar narrative of European colonization and Indian displacement. Their lives also complicate that narrative, prompting us to rethink the role of religion in the encounter of Indian and European. The focus on the Mohican communities of Stockbridge and Shekomeko allows for an in-depth look at two very different mission projects. From the midst of the stories, however, it is sometimes difficult to step back to see the broader contexts and long-term ramifications. The lives of two sons of the missions—one raised at Shekomeko, the other at Stockbridge—provide that perspective. Their lives followed very different—sometimes intersecting—trajectories, a result of the divergent early histories of the two missions. Despite the differences, both men were engaged in the struggle to determine how best to live as a Mohican in a rapidly changing world. Both men drew on the Christianity introduced at the mission sites and adapted it in ways that resonated with Mohican tradition.

Joshua was born in 1741 in the Mohican village of Wechquadnach and raised in Shekomeko. Hendrick Aupaumut was born in 1758 in Stockbridge, just months after the death of Jonathan Edwards. Both were born to prominent families, became leaders of their communities, and lived into the early nineteenth century. Both identified as Mohican and Christian, and both could read and write, often assisting the missionaries in translating Christian texts and interpreting at official meetings. During their youth, the communities of both men were forced from their homelands westward, eventually ending up among the diverse Indian communities on the White River in Indiana at the same time that Tenskwatawa, better known as the Shawnee Prophet, and his brother Tecumseh were rallying the Indians of the region to fight against encroaching American settlement. Both men opposed the Prophet's campaign, but for quite different reasons—reasons that reflect the particular heritage of their respective communities—and with quite different results.

JOSHUA

The names of many of Joshua's relatives will already be familiar to readers. Joshua's parents were among the first to be baptized by the Moravian missionaries—his father in September 1742 and both his mother and his grandfather several months later.[1] Joshua's maternal grandfather was Cornelius, the "old captain" of Shekomeko, whose family was closely tied to Abraham's.[2] Young Joshua was also identified as nephew of Benjamin Kokhkewenaunaunt of Stockbridge, who had become chief sachem of the Mohicans by 1750.[3] Joshua's father, also known as Joshua, was an important leader in the Shekomeko community, likely serving as "runner" whose responsibilities included delivering important diplomatic messages on behalf of the village chief. The senior Joshua's extensive travels with Moravian missionary leaders and his skill as a preacher suggest an extension of his role as runner.[4] Until his death in 1775, the elder Joshua was an active hunter, canoe builder, and diplomat. He also collaborated on a number of Mohican-language hymns and a translation of the Passion story into Mohican.[5] The younger Joshua followed in his father's footsteps, becoming an able canoe builder and hunter, cooper and musician, interpreter and diplomat.

Young Joshua was only five in 1746, when his family undertook what proved to be the first of many removes, leaving Shekomeko for what they hoped would be a more peaceful existence in Pennsylvania. The Moravian missionaries had been barred from preaching in New York since 1744, the victims of both a volatile religious climate in the aftermath of the revivals of the early 1740s and the renewed war between England and France. Neighboring English settlers had taken to toting their guns to church on Sundays for fear of attack by the Moravian-affiliated Indians. With the missionaries gone, Shekomeko residents faced increasing pressures on their lands and became more vulnerable than ever to the abuses of unscrupulous creditors. Joshua's family was among the first group to set out for Bethlehem in

April 1746. Within the year, a new mission settlement was begun, called Gnadenhütten, or "tents of grace," thirty miles from the Moravian headquarters at Bethlehem. Gnadenhütten was geographically and strategically central, located near the confluence of the Mahoning Creek and the Lehigh River and on the main routes to the south and west. The mission community nestled between the Delaware and Susquehanna Valleys had little hope of escaping the new war on the horizon. The French and Indian War was the first of the imperial conflicts to start on American soil, and it began in the Pennsylvania backcountry in May 1754. More than simply an imperial struggle between Britain and France, the conflict was an expression of long-festering tensions between the Indian and white occupants of the region, leaving Gnadenhütten particularly vulnerable to attack by Delaware Indians, who considered the mission Indians too friendly with Anglo-Americans, and white settlers, who were often indiscriminant in their hatred of Indians.[6]

The pattern established in this first move from Shekomeko to Gnadenhütten would be repeated again and again: when fighting broke out between the French and English (and later between the Americans and the British), the Indians affiliated with the Moravians became suspect for their pacifism. And the Indians who opposed the British presence suspected the Moravians (Indian and white) of furthering British encroachment, a claim not entirely without merit. With each new eruption, the Moravian mission community sought refuge further west, usually landing right in the next major theater of war.

The milestones in Joshua's life—baptism, marriage, the birth of his children—were punctuated by tragedy. War, disease, and forced migration intruded frequently into Joshua's life. The mundane, the joyous, and the tragic all appear in the pages of the Moravian mission records. "Little Joshua" sent greetings to his grandfather, Cornelius; six-year-old Joshua repaired his shoes in anticipation of the journey to Bethlehem to join the Young Boys' choir; at eight years, Joshua was baptized; at fourteen, he was admired for his ability to write.[7] At fourteen, while the French and Indian War heated up around them, Joshua and his father took to the woods, narrowly escaping the Munsee attack on the Gnadenhütten mission, in which eleven missionaries were killed, prompting the Christian Indian community to move closer to the Moravian headquarters at Bethlehem for protection.[8] At seventeen, he requested admission to communion; at eighteen, he barely escaped an angry mother bear whose cub he has just killed; at twenty-one, he led religious services for a hunting party in the woods.[9]

Joshua's twenty-third year, 1764, was an eventful one. Late in 1763, the Ottawa chief Pontiac attracted Indians from the Ohio and Great Lakes region with a vision of expelling the British from Indian country by attacking forts and frontier settlements.[10] The raids provoked frontier rage against all Indians, and Joshua's community was soon forced to take refuge in Philadelphia under armed protection. There, at the Philadelphia Barracks, life continued. Joshua played the spinet for curious onlookers, including the Pennsylvania governor.[11] He married Sophia, the baptized daughter of the Munsee Delaware chief, Papunhank, who had recently been baptized by the Moravians.[12] He watched as nearly half of the refugee community (including Abraham's widow, Sarah, and their son, Isaac) succumbed to smallpox and other pathogens in the course of their yearlong asylum. Together with his father and father-in-law, he scouted for a new home for the mission community along the Susquehanna. Six months later, the Indian congregation, now composed of Mohicans and Delawares, moved near the site of Papunhank's village, Wyalusing, establishing a new mission, optimistically named Friedenshütten, meaning "tents of peace."[13]

In 1765, settled into their new home at Friedenshütten, Joshua and Sophia welcomed their first child into the world, a girl they named Anna. During their time at Friedenshütten, the couple would have two more daughters, Bathsheba and Salome, named after Joshua's mother and stepmother, and a son. Soon after the birth of his son in September 1769, Joshua set out on several hunting trips to supply his growing family. The infant boy died a few days after Joshua returned from a successful hunt. Just months later, Joshua read to a gathering from the Mohican New Testament that his father had helped to prepare. At Easter, Joshua and others sang hymns about the Passion of Christ, perhaps including some composed by his father.[14] In the 1768 Treaty of Fort Stanwix, the Iroquois had ceded much of the Pennsylvania backcountry to the British, ensuring a flood of white settlers to the region and prompting thoughts of another move westward.[15] By the time Joshua and Sophia's second son, Nathanael, was born in August 1773, the mission community had been reestablished on the Muskingum River in Ohio, in a settlement also named Gnadenhütten. Just months before the twenty-fifth anniversary of his own baptism, Joshua lost little Nathanael.[16] Another daughter, Sophia, arrived in July 1774, followed by two more children in 1777 and 1779, both of whom died within two weeks of their birth. Adding to the string of tragedies was the death of Joshua's father in 1775.[17]

In the midst of these family joys and tragedies, war swirled around the Gnadenhütten community. The Indian congregation, having moved west in hopes of being free of white settlers clamoring for their lands, found instead that they had stepped into the next major imperial conflict. Most Indian peoples in the region, including the majority of Shawnee, Delaware, and Miami as well as more southern tribes, were now firmly set against the newly independent Americans, resenting the incursions of white settlers who ignored treaties and pushed beyond the agreed upon line of settlement. Only small pockets of support could be found for the Americans among the many Indian communities, their support rooted less in affection than in a pragmatic desire to avoid war with the powerful emerging nation. These communities sought to maintain their independence while also maintaining tribal ties with their Christian kin at Moravian missions. The Moravian Indians' affirmations of neutrality fell on deaf ears.[18]

Backwoods American settlers suspected the Christian Indians of colluding with enemy Indians, while the British suspected both the Moravian missionaries and Moravian Indians, including Joshua, of spying for the Americans.[19] In September 1781, a group of British-allied Delaware and Shawnee Indians headed by the Wyandot (Huron) chief known as the Half-King, led the Christian Indians of Gnadenhütten 125 miles to the Sandusky River, allegedly for their own protection, while the missionaries Zeisberger and Heckewelder together with Joshua were held for questioning by the British at Detroit on charges of treason.[20]

Ironically, Joshua's arrest on charges of spying for the Americans may have saved him from being killed by the Americans. In February 1782, the Christian Indians were near starving at "Captive's Town," so roughly a hundred of them returned to Gnadenhütten to salvage what they could of the crops they had been forced to leave standing the previous fall. While there, an American militia led by David Williamson raided the mission town, claiming that the Indians had participated in raids on American settlements in Pennsylvania. They gathered the Indians together and told them to prepare to die the next day. The condemned Indians spent the night singing hymns, and the next day, the militia led the Indians two by two into houses they had designated as slaughterhouses. Among the nearly one hundred men, women, and children killed and then scalped were two of Joshua's teenaged daughters, Anna and Bathsheba, both allegedly killed with a cooper's mallet, most likely the one their father had used to practice his trade. It was only chance that Joshua's life was spared: he was probably away from the village delivering a message for the missionaries who had been recalled to Detroit days earlier.[21] Just months after the Gnadenhütten massacre, Joshua's wife Sophia gave birth to the couple's last child, a son named Christian.

By the 1790s, after several more moves—from Ohio to Michigan and back to Ohio—Joshua and a small contingent of missionaries and Indian settlers accepted the invitation of Delaware chiefs to settle on the White River in Indiana at a village called Woapicamikunk.[22] Still, they were not far enough to escape the reach of white settlers and the disease and alcohol that were their constant companions. In the space of just one year, Joshua lost his wife and his three remaining children. It is not altogether surprising, then, that when his youngest son, Christian, lay dying in 1801,

Joshua brought him to see a native healer, but to no avail. Christian died in April 1802, and his daughter Salome died the following month.[23] All ten of Joshua's children had preceded him to the grave. At some point in the midst of these tragedies, Joshua took to drinking and apparently boasted (as reported by a missionary), "if, after the heathen manner, he wanted to make use of the dream of his youth, he could also do evil, for in his vision a bird had appeared unto him and said: 'I am a man-eater, and if you wish to feed me, you need but point out to me some one, and then I will put him out of the way.' "[24] His claim was taken seriously, and in 1803 he was accused of killing a child by means of sorcery.[25]

Joshua's experiences, while devastating, were certainly not unique. For many Indians and whites, the world of the early nineteenth century seemed a world turned upside down. New religious movements and practices burst forth, giving voice to a pervasive sense of dislocation and uncertainty. Joshua witnessed at least two of these movements, one with fatal consequences. For the first, business took him to Cincinnati during the summer of 1802. When he returned to Indiana, he reported on a strange phenomenon that had gripped the whites in the settlements along the Ohio and Miami Rivers. By Joshua's account, people "fell into a faint and lay as if dead for 2 or three hours. When they again regained consciousness they said to the other people: 'We must be converted from our ungodly life, otherwise we will all be lost, for in the state we are in at present we will not reach heaven.' "[26] Joshua had just witnessed some of the early revivals of the great camp meetings that had started in Kentucky the previous summer, launching what came to be called the Second Great Awakening.[27]

A few years after observing the ecstatic religious practices among the white settlers, Joshua would hear of another man who fell down as if dead and returned to the living committed to reforming himself and his community. In April 1805, in a village not far from the Delaware settlement where Joshua lived, a Shawnee man from whom nobody had expected much fell into a stupor. Even as the preparations for his burial proceeded, Lalawethika awoke and reported the amazing experiences he had had conversing with the Master of Life. The Creator had led him to a fork in the road: one path led to paradise and the other to eternal misery. Faithful Shawnee who renounced the alcohol and the other trade goods of Europeans would be granted admission to paradise. The Prophet, who now called himself Tenskwatawa, would be the "Open Door" signified by his name, instituting rituals of religious renewal. He called on all of the Indians in the area to return to old-style religion, to relinquish all ties with whites, and to forswear all use of European goods or services. In return, he promised long life to his believers, the restoration of an Indian-centered world, and death to unbelievers. The Prophet's message spread quickly along the White River and beyond, giving voice as it did to the sense of loss many Indians felt while also presenting a glimmer of hope that they could bring about a reversal of fortunes. The desperate straits of native peoples, believed Tenskwatawa, were caused by a magic poison in the possession of certain individuals. In order that further evil be avoided, the possessors of the poison must be discovered and executed.[28]

By February 1806, a witch-hunt was on, and the Moravian missionaries rightly suspected that Joshua, the only remaining Indian Brother living at the mission, was likely to be targeted because of his connection to the missionaries and the prior accusations. Joshua had apparently reaffirmed his commitment to Christianity; when a follower of the Prophet confronted him, charging that baptism signified a pact with the devil, Joshua responded: "You don't need to pity me. The rather, pity yourself that you are still so blind and ignorant that you prefer to believe the lies of the heathen teachers to the Word of God which we have." Just two days later, Joshua was summoned to appear at a sacrificial feast to be held by the Prophet.[29] He was out of town at the time, but several weeks later, a party returned for Joshua and brought him before the special council called to investigate witchcraft. A Delaware woman and a Delaware chief, both of whom had connections to the Moravians, preceded Joshua to the flames.[30] The chief denied possessing any poison, but under pressure he accused Joshua. He later recanted his accusation, but Joshua was doomed.[31]

On March 18, 1806, at the age of sixty-four, Joshua was struck on the head with a hatchet and then thrown to the flames. The missionaries took comfort in the report that Joshua "had said a great deal at the place of murder that the savages could not understand. It is quite likely that he prayed to the Saviour in German." They also found it miraculous that his body was reportedly scarcely singed after two hours, prompting the gathered Indians to stoke the fire even hotter. Not until the following morning was Joshua's body reduced to ashes.[32]

Joshua had lived his life on the border between two worlds, and it proved a dangerous place to be. He identified as both Christian and Mohican at a time when the racial lines between Indians and whites were becoming ever more sharply drawn. Several months after his death, the Moravian missionary Abraham Luckenbach remembered Joshua as he preached (whether in Mohican or Delaware is not clear) on the verse "Come unto me all ye that are heavy laden, I will give you rest," using a translation prepared by Joshua.[33]

HENDRICK AUPAUMUT

Joshua's Stockbridge counterpart, Hendrick Aupaumut, also identified as Christian and Mohican, and he too resisted the nativism of the Shawnee

Prophet's movement, but his path from youth in Stockbridge to old age in Indiana had not been quite so treacherous. The important differences between the two men's lives can be traced in large part to the early histories of the Shekomeko and Stockbridge missions. Much less is known about Aupaumut's early years than Joshua's, a reminder of the differences between Anglo-Protestant and Moravian missionaries. It is only once Aupaumut rose to prominence as a sachem and began producing texts of his own—letters, translations, and a tribal history—that he appears in the documentary record.

During his youth, Aupaumut would have absorbed the lessons of tribal leadership from his elders. The constants of Stockbridge leadership included a commitment to Christianity, education, and faithful service alongside British (later American) troops.[34] When Aupaumut narrated his people's history from the vantage point of the late eighteenth century, he highlighted migration, piety, and facility with neighboring cultures as the central features of Mohican heritage. The ancestral Muhheakunnuk peoples were "more civilized than what Indians are now in the wilderness," living in large towns and worshiping "one Supreme Being who dwells above, whom they style Waun-theet Mon-nit-toow, or the Great, Good Spirit, the author of all things in heaven and on earth."[35] When famine forced Mohican ancestors to seek a new home, the people moved east until they came upon the "great waters or sea, which are constantly in motion," which reminded them of "Muhheakunnuk our nativity." During the hard journey, they "lost their ways of former living and apostasized." By narrating a past in which proto-Christian virtues were espoused, Aupaumut transformed the Mohican acceptance of a Christian missionary into a decision to restore ancient values abandoned by other Indian peoples.[36] Aupaumut mythologized the founding of the mission, linking it to an ancient Muhheakunnuk past, thereby confirming the Stockbridge Mohicans as the true heirs of the tribal legacy.

Aupaumut's account of Muhheakunnuk history carefully establishes that his people abided by Christian precepts long before Europeans arrived in the New World. Further, it suggests that the move westward to the Oneida lands in New York in 1780, far from being a departure, was in fact a *return toward* the ancient homeland, toward ancient values. Aupaumut was thus able to acknowledge the current strains on Mohican culture and present the introduction of Christianity as a means of reviving rather than supplanting ancient Mohican ways.

As sachem of the Stockbridge Mohicans in the decades surrounding the turn of the century, Hendrick Aupaumut translated history into policy; he drew from his understanding of Mohican history to chart the future of his people. In the decisive decade of the 1790s, Aupaumut did what he could to cement the dependence of the Western Indian confederacy and the United States on Mohican service as intermediaries, promoting selective adaptation of Christianity and the "arts of civilization" to Indian neighbors while exhorting American officials to fulfill the obligations of kinship. Aupaumut successfully presented himself to Indian Commissioner Timothy Pickering in 1791 for the role of brokering a peace between the nascent American republic and the Western Indians who resented the U.S. government's claim to Ohio Indian lands by right of conquest. To both Indians and whites, Aupaumut promoted a vision of a virtuous republic composed of independent white and red nations united by a common devotion to "the great and good spirit." Ultimately, the peace efforts failed, and in 1794 the United States called off its negotiations with the western Indians. Warfare quickly escalated, and the western tribes suffered severe losses at the hands of the American army. Aupaumut's diplomatic services were no longer needed, for the demographic and military force of the Americans obviated the need for negotiations—they could simply impose their will.[37]

Never again would Aupaumut stand so squarely in the spotlight of American diplomatic affairs, but he did not abandon his mission. Over the next decades, Aupaumut continued to propose Mohican service as intermediaries to various parties. And even more than before, Aupaumut promoted his vision of a virtuous republic in which independent Indian communities lived peacefully side by side with white followers of the Great Spirit. He pursued this mission by calling on the United States to honor its debt to Mohicans while promoting the Stockbridge way of indigenized Christianity to neighboring tribes. More than ever, Aupaumut was convinced that Indians must regain self-sufficiency and revive ancient values—not through a return to traditional practices but rather through the embrace of Christianity and the "arts of civilization." This strategy is evident in his address to a gathering of Stockbridges on a day of public thanksgiving in December 1793 at which he reminded his people that "through the goodness of God, we have been carried throu all the Tryals we have experienced in the year passed" and that they now "have been allowed to sit together in love and peace and partake of the bounty of heaven." Most importantly, the Stockbridges could celebrate their independence and be thankful "not in eating the food we might have obtained from the white people, our neighbours which was our state of dependence in the Country from whence we came, but we have now been fed by the labour of our own hands. This is matter for thankfulness." Self-sufficiency was no longer possible through hunting, so Aupaumut extolled settled agriculture and husbandry as the best path for cultural preservation.[38] The invocation suggests the value of European husbandry lay not in "reducing" Indians to a state of "civilization," as both missionaries and government officials had imagined, but in providing a means to remain an independent people.[39] What Aupaumut valued most—and what he hoped to promote among other Indian communities—was self-sufficiency, for he knew well that dependency brought abuse. Aupaumut presented just this strategy to the various communities he visited in 1803, including the Moravian mission at Goshen, Ohio, and Woapicamikunk in Indiana.

Aupaumut's speech to the Delaware at Goshen reveals the extent to which native and Christian traditions had been woven together. Aupaumut addressed the gathered Delawares as "Grandfathers and Brothers," signifying at once the traditional fictive kinship relationship between the Mohicans and Delawares as well as "their spiritual relation in Christ."[40] First, Aupaumut extended his thanks to the Delawares for their hospitality "during our stay here by the side of your fire place," which he took to signify "that you still retain the friendship that was established between your ancestors and ours." The Mohicans were glad to find the Delawares prospering "by the goodness of the great good Spirit above," which enabled them to have "the gospel preached to you constantly, a good land to improve, a forest around you abounding with all kinds of game, and fish in the waters." The Stockbridges clearly did not understand their Christian profession as a radical break from the Mohican past, but neither was it simply an overlay atop Mohican tradition, as Aupaumut encouraged the Delawares to "hold fast the religion of our blessed Lord and Saviour Jesus Christ." Jonathan Edwards would likely have been pleased, had he been able to hear the Stockbridge Indians' address to their Delaware kin. Aupaumut exhorted the Delawares "to keep good courage in the Lord; for he is a Friend that loveth always; he sticketh closer than a brother to those who believe in his name. There is nothing better for us all than to have Him for our friend, & to keep his commandments, which are not grievous."[41]

From Goshen, the party of Stockbridge Mohicans continued on their way to the White River, where they intended to meet with other Delawares, Miamis, and Shawnee communities. Their purpose, as Aupaumut explained to the Moravians at Goshen, was

> to renew their ancient covenants of friendship with them; to recommend wherever they came, the maintaining of perpetual peace and friendship, both among themselves, and with the white people; to advise them to keep their lands, and learn to live by the cultivation of them; to propose the acceptance of missionaries to preach the gospel and schoolmasters to teach their children to read and write, if such should be sent to them; and to exhort them to refrain from the use of spiritous liquors.

Their other aim was to secure a tract of land "given to their forefathers many years ago by the Miamis or Twechtwees, and where a few of their nation have ever since resided. Thither they intend to retire, in case they should ever deem it advisable to quit their present place of residence at New Stockbridge."[42] Even as highly "civilized" Indians, Aupaumut's community had discovered, they could not count on the British, or later American, government to honor its promises to protect the Christian Indians' land, and so Aupaumut and his counselors were trying to ensure they would always have a home. It was a fine line that Aupaumut and the Stockbridge Indians were attempting to walk. They advocated self-sufficiency through education in white ways; they extended native bonds of fictive kinship to Indians and whites through Christian fraternity; they resisted nativism, whether espoused by whites or Indians. Aupaumut's work on the White River, particularly his response to the Shawnee Prophet, shows just how different his and Joshua's paths were.

It is only through the records describing the Stockbridge delegation's visit to Woapicamikunk that we learn of the only certain face-to-face meeting between our two mission sons, Joshua and Aupaumut—the scene that opened this book. When Aupaumut arrived at the White River in April 1803 and delivered a speech to the Delaware Indians, Joshua served as his interpreter. Aupaumut had advised the Delaware to follow the Stockbridge model as the best way to hold onto their lands and become a "a wise people," happy "indeed in this life and the life to come." If they did not follow the Stockbridge path, Aupaumut warned, they would "become extinct from the earth."[43] When he heard of Joshua's death several years later, Aupaumut reported in a letter to John Sergeant Jr., "By his [the Prophet's] accusations the Deleware burnt Tatepokqseet their great Sachem and his Nephew called Patterson, and one aged woman, likewise our friend Josewah, the Interpreter."[44]

Joshua's death likely fueled Aupaumut's determination to counter the Prophet's influence. Writing from the White River in 1808, Aupaumut explained that he was working to "cut off the Prophets influence." If the Prophet was not silenced, Aupaumut believed, "the price will be we shall war with one another merely for one man's deadly poisonous tongue."[45] Several years earlier, Aupaumut had rebuffed another Prophet, likely the Seneca Handsome Lake, by making the case for pragmatic pluralism. When messengers of the Prophet arrived at New Stockbridge, New York, preaching rejection of white ways, Aupaumut responded by explaining to the Prophet that at New Stockbridge, "we give liberty to our young men and women to go and hear the Ministers of the gospel any where" and also "to hear and see the ancient way of worship of your forefathers." All were free to follow what they believed was right: "We don't respect this party or that but we love them all alike," Aupaumut asserted. Pluralism and tolerance were the best guarantees of Indian survival. "If you and we use both these means," urged

Aupaumut, then "when one fails the other may stand; but if you, and we depend only upon one instrument; and neglect all the rest, when this fails you and I must come to ruin."[46] This was a classic expression of the Mohican way as it had come to be articulated at Stockbridge: facility in the cultures of whites and Indians would be the key to the Mohicans' survival, a philosophy that helped the Stockbridges endure many future disappointments and obstacles on the long path to relative security today in Wisconsin, where the community continues to embrace Aupaumut's commitment to education and the preservation of Mohican identity.

Chapter Thirteen

Epilogue: Real and Ideal Indians

Aupaumut's message of pluralism and tolerance delivered to the Seneca Prophet's messengers is not quite the end of the story. Before his death, Aupaumut despaired that perhaps his people's chosen path of cultural mediation could not ensure their survival as an independent community within the American republic, as he had so fervently hoped. Revolutionary promises of liberty and democracy had proved not to apply to Indian peoples. For the most part, tribal and colonial peoples had settled into essentialized definitions of identity that affirmed a vast chasm between Indian and white. Something of Aupaumut's despair survives in a remarkable address delivered by the sachem in 1819 to the "Sachems and the head men of the remnant of the Children of Abraham, Isaac, and Jacob commonly called Jews, at or about Jerusalem." The address was delivered by Aupaumut on behalf of "the Chiefs of the remnants of the Muhheakunnuk nation" on the occasion of a visit by the Reverend Levi Parsons, an American missionary raising funds to travel to the Holy Land to convert the Jews.[1]

The message was intended to affirm Mohican kinship with the descendents of the original chosen people, a kinship made more poignant by their common status as diaspora peoples. The Stockbridges, living since the 1780s on Oneida land in New York, had recently learned that their planned removal to the White River in Indiana had been thwarted by the federal government's suspect purchase of the land without the knowledge or consent of the Stockbridges. Aupaumut's diplomatic skills had helped to secure confirmation of the Miami grant from President Thomas Jefferson in 1808. But as the Stockbridges had often discovered before, assurances meant little. A few months before Parsons' visit, the New Stockbridge community observed a fast day to mark their disappointment and to remember the chiefs who had gone to Washington to express their grievances and to pray "that the Lord would dispose the great men of the United States to return their lands to them."[2] This latest betrayal would have been fresh in Aupaumut's mind as he prepared the tribe's address to the Jews seeking kinship with a wandering people. Aupaumut's disappointment with how his people had been treated can be heard in his address to the Jews.

In the name of the chiefs, Aupaumut presented the missionary Parsons with a donation of $5.87, two gold ornaments, several baskets, and a lantern with an inscription that read, "This to illumine the streets of Jerusalem. Jerusalem is my chief joy." Then Aupaumut delivered his remarkable address, a written copy of which was presented to Parsons to carry to the Jews. By way of introduction, Aupaumut recounted for his Jewish correspondents his people's history. He told how his forefathers had worshipped the Great Spirit with sacrifices until one day eighty-four years ago a white man by the name of John Sergeant, father of their present minister, arrived at their fireside as "one of the messengers of the great and good Spirit" and instituted new practices. From Sergeant they learned that "jesus Christ was sent into this world to save poor sinners that he was crucified and had again rissen from the dead and had gone into the heaven." Aupaumut wished to inform his Jewish brethren that the Mohican nation was "siting [*sic*] at the front door to the house" with their friends, the Unnannaumpauh, "commonly called Indians" sitting to the west. Having recounted a bit of Mohican history, Aupaumut turned to Jewish history. He had learned from the Bible that "all nations in the world descend from one man and woman," and that Jesus, a member "of the Jewish Tribe," came to die for all, so, wrote Aupaumut, "we can call you brothers and address you as such." Aupaumut had devoted his career to extending the ties of fictive kinship to peoples near and far, and with this address he affirmed his people's fraternity with the Jews.

This world might not hold much promise for Jews or for Indians, but Aupaumut had hopes for the next. Aupaumut looked forward to the fulfillment of biblical prophecy, when "you are to return from different parts of the world to the country of your ancestors" and to a day when there would be "no distinction between the different Tribes, wheather white, red or black." Aupaumut concluded with an exhortation: "If you and Annunnaumpauh or Indians would be faithfull to the end, truly worship the great and good spirit, we shall meet and see each other at the great day of Jesus when you and all the faithfull Gentiles will be received into heaven or Wohwekoiyewwonkunnuhneh uhtauk mauth chaick annemenauwonkun, or when there is full of peace and joy and consummate happiness."[3] This world had shown little favor to the Jews and Indians, but Aupaumut had hopes for the next.

Aupaumut went to his grave in 1830 with little reason to be hopeful about his tribe's prospects in this world. But a quarter century after his death, and after numerous moves and battles with state and federal officials, the Stockbridges finally secured land in Shawano County, Wisconsin, where the Stockbridge-Munsee Band of Mohican Indians thrives to this day, devoted now—as in the eighteenth and nineteenth centuries—to preserving Mohican tradition and community, pursuing a pluralistic education, and, for many, cultivating their Christian faith.[4] Despite their survival today, most Americans likely believe that the "Last of the Mohicans" has long since perished.

Joshua's community was not so fortunate. The Shekomeko Mohicans' association with the Moravian missionaries arguably accelerated the pressures that forced them to leave their homelands nearly forty years before the Stockbridge Mohicans left Massachusetts. By the time of Joshua's death, there was no distinct community of Moravian Mohicans. Those who remained among the Moravians had largely blended, like Joshua, into Delaware communities. Uncounted others left the Moravian fold to join other Indian communities, some perhaps to join the Stockbridges, others likely to join the multi-tribal Indian settlements of the Ohio region.

Mohicans living in Shekomeko in the 1740s and on the White River in the early 1800s found few friends. But beginning in the 1820s, when the descendents of the Shekomeko Mohicans had been long buried or become widely dispersed and the Stockbridge Mohicans were once again in search of a home, the earliest Shekomeko converts were on the verge of gaining international fame. Once the Moravians had been reviled as "papists," but they were soon to be embraced as heroes by the nascent Anglo-Protestant mission to the world. And Johannes and Abraham, feared and reviled during their lifetimes by their colonial English neighbors, in death came to provide inspiration to new generations of missionaries fanning out across the globe, their story the subject of several missionary tracts.[5]

One such tract, published in Dublin in 1824 under the title, *Tschoop and Shabasch, Christian Indians, of North America,* bore on the cover an engraving of the two men, standing proudly, clad in toga-like garments, deep in conversation and gesturing toward a man sleeping peacefully by their side. Presumably, the image depicts Tschoop's account of Christian Rauch's arrival at Shekomeko, familiar from chapter 5: "When he had finished his discourse, he lay down upon a board, fatigued by the journey, and fell into a sound

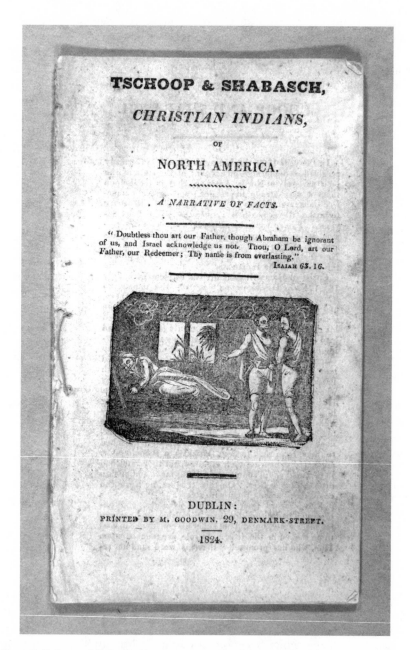

Figure 9 *Tschoop and Shabasch, Christian Indians of North America* (Dublin: M. Goodwin, 1824). Courtesy of American Antiquarian Society, Worcester, Massachusetts.

sleep. I then thought, what kind of man is this? There he lies and sleeps. I might kill him and throw him out into the wood, and who would regard it? But this gives him no concern."[6] Although one of the men in the image totes an axe at his waist, the impression is of primitive nobility rather than of savagery. Something like palm trees can be glimpsed through the window of the cabin, subtly inviting the prospective missionary on an exotic adventure.

Johannes's life was featured in another missionary tract, this one published by the American Sunday School Union, entitled *Tschoop: The Converted Indian Chief,* which drew on Moravian sources to construct his biography. The pamphlet tells of his rejection of heathen ways and embrace of Christianity, which he faithfully professed until he succumbed to smallpox. Interestingly, both of these tracts chose not to use the Mohican men's Christian names, preferring their more Indian-sounding names.[7] The names, together with the cover graphic of the 1824 tract, depicting the two men in decidedly non-Anglicized attire, suggest an important shift in Anglo-Protestant missionary thought from the eighteenth century. The goal would still be "civilization," but now native culture was depicted as inherently noble. This nobility, however, was easily corrupted by contact with the bad elements of white society. Virtuous missionaries would travel the seas to reach pagan prospective converts before they were tainted. In America, this same logic facilitated Indian removal by casting it as a humanitarian endeavor to save Indians from the harmful influences of white society.[8]

Few readers today stumble upon these crumbling missionary tracts, but millions have encountered a romanticized and stylized Tschoop in the form of Uncas and Chingachgook, the noble Mohicans depicted in James Fenimore Cooper's Leatherstocking Tales. For his most famous volume of the series, *The Last of the Mohicans,* published in 1826, Cooper drew heavily on Moravian missionary sources, finding inspiration in the lives of the earliest converts, including Johannes and Joshua Sr.[9]

Nearly a century after his death, the missionary tracts and the literary success of Cooper's works generated a stream of pilgrims to Johannes's grave in God's Acre, the Moravian burial ground in Bethlehem, Pennsylvania. The 1842 missionary tract directed readers to visit the grave, marked by a marble tombstone (funded in part by contributions raised by the Young Men's Missionary Society), bearing the inscription:

In Memory of Tschoop, a Mohican Indian, who, in holy baptism, April 16, 1742, received the name of JOHN; One of the first-fruits of the mission at Shekomeko, and a remarkable instance of the power of divine grace, whereby he became a distinguished teacher among his nation. He departed this life in full assurance of faith, at Bethlehem, August 27, 1746.

There shall be one fold and one Shepherd. John x.16.[10]

Throughout the second half of the nineteenth century, Tschoop's grave drew thousands of visitors who wished to pay tribute to the "Last of the Mohicans." At the same time, Bethlehem's Moravian past was on its way to being romanticized as part of a quaint "Pennsylvania Dutch" past.[11] Real Indians had been largely removed from view, but the fame of idealized Indians continued to grow.

Abbreviations

At a Conference	*At a Conference Held at Deerfield in the County of Hampshire, the twenty seventh day of August 1735* (Boston, 1735)
Description of the New Netherlands	Adriaen van der Donck, *Description of the New Netherlands* (1655; repr. Syracuse, NY: Syracuse University Press, 1968)
Fliegel *Index*	Carl J. Fliegel, *Index to Records of the Moravian Mission among the Indians of North America* (New Haven: Research Publications, Inc., 1970)
Gospel Ministers	Nathaniel Appleton, *Gospel Ministers Must Be Fit for the Master's Use, and Prepared to Every Good Work, if They Would Be Vessels unto Honor* (Boston: S. Kneeland and T. Green, 1735)
Historical Memoirs	Samuel Hopkins, *Historical Memoirs Relating to the Housatonic Indians* (Boston: S. Kneeland, 1753)
History of the Mission	George H. Loskiel, *History of the Mission of the United Brethren among the Indians of North America,* trans. Christian Ignatius La Trobe (London: Brethren's Society for the Furtherance of the Gospel, 1794)

History, Manners, and Customs	John Heckewelder, *History, Manners, and Customs of the Indian Nations Who Once Inhabited Pennsylvania and the Neighbouring States* (1820; repr. Philadelphia: Historical Society of Pennsylvania, 1876)
HNAI	*Handbook of North American Indians,* ed. William C. Sturtevant (Washington: Smithsonian Institution, 1978)
JEC	Jonathan Edwards Collection, Gen. MSS 151, Beinecke Rare Book and Manuscript Library, New Haven, Connecticut
JHRM	*Journals of the House of Representatives of Massachusetts, 1715–1766,* 43 vols. (Boston: Massachusetts Historical Society, 1919–1973).
MAB	Moravian Archives, Bethlehem, Pennsylvania
Mass. Archives	Massachusetts Archives Series, Massachusetts State Archives, Boston, Massachusetts
Memorials of the Moravian Church	William C. Reichel, ed., *Memorials of the Moravian Church,* vol. 1 (Philadelphia: J. B. Lippincott & Co., 1870)
MHS	Massachusetts Historical Society, Boston, Massachusetts
NEC	New England Company Records, New England Genealogical and Historical Society, Boston, Massachusetts
NEC Letterbooks	*Letterbooks, 1688–1761 of the Company for the Propagation of the Gospel in New England.* University of Virginia Library, Charlottesville, Virginia (microfilm edition)
NEQ	*The New England Quarterly*
NYCD	E. B. O'Callaghan, ed., *Documents Relative to the Colonial History of the State of New York,* 15 vols. (Albany: Weed, Parsons, and Co., 1853–87)
RMM	Records of the Moravian Mission among the Indians of North America (New Haven, Conn., [1978]), microfilm, 40 reels, from original materials at the Archives of the Moravian Church, Bethlehem, Pa. Citations

given as reel/box/folder/item/page. Not
all sources have an item or page number.
Unless otherwise noted, all originals are in
German, and all translations are my own.

Stiles Papers
Ezra Stiles Papers, 1727–1795. MS Vault
Stiles. Beinecke Rare Book and Manuscript
Library, New Haven, Connecticut

White River Mission
Lawrence Henry Gipson, ed., *Moravian Mission
on the White River: Diaries and Letters, May 5, 1799,
to November 12, 1806,* trans. Harry E. Stocker,
Herman T. Frueauff, and Samuel C. Zeller
(Indianapolis: Indiana Historical Bureau, 1938)

WMQ
The William and Mary Quarterly, 3rd series

Works
The Works of Jonathan Edwards, 25 volumes
to date (New Haven: Yale University
Press, 1957–), Perry Miller, John E. Smith,
Harry S. Stout, general editors.

Zeisberger's History
Archer Butler Hulbert and William Nathaniel
Schwarze, eds., *Zeisberger's History of the Northern
American Indians in Eighteenth-Century Ohio, New
York and Pennsylvania* (Columbus: Ohio State
Archaeological and Historical Society, 1910)

Notes

Chapter 1. Introduction

1. The standard term used in ethnohistorical literature has been *Mahican,* derived from the Dutch *Mahikander,* an approximation of the indigenous term, usually rendered as *Muhheakunnuk.* I have chosen to use *Mohican* throughout, as it is the designation used by the tribe today and as it is the more familiar term.

2. "Extract from the Indian Journal, being the 6th Speech that was delivered to the Delaware Nation residing at Waupekummekut, or White River, on the 15th day of April, 1803," printed in *Massachusetts Missionary Magazine* (April 1804): 467–71.

3. Lion G. Miles, "Red Man Dispossessed: The Williams Family and the Alienation of Indian Land in Stockbridge, Massachusetts, 1736–1818," *NEQ* 67, no. 1 (March 1994): 46–76.

4. Entry dated April 10, 1803, *White River Mission,* 222–23.

5. W. R. Ward, *The Protestant Evangelical Awakening* (Cambridge: Cambridge University Press, 1992).

6. *White River Mission,* 412. See also Goshen Diary, August 5, 1805, 19/172/5/10 RMM.

7. On the tribal history of the Stockbridge Mohicans from Aupaumut's time, see James W. Oberly, *A Nation of Statesmen: The Political Culture of the Stockbridge-Munsee Mohicans, 1815–1972* (Norman: University of Oklahoma Press, 2005).

8. Linda Colley, *Britons: Forging the Nation, 1707–1837* (New Haven: Yale University Press, 1992); Nancy Shoemaker, *A Strange Likeness: Becoming Red and White in Eighteenth-Century America* (New York: Oxford University Press, 2004); and John Sweet, *Bodies Politic: Negotiating Race in the American North, 1730–1830* (Baltimore: Johns Hopkins University Press, 2003).

9. For a useful synthesis of the transatlantic trade in culture and commodity, see Alan Taylor, *American Colonies* (New York: Viking Press, 2001), 301–37.

10. For a recent summary of the colonial economy, see Jon Butler, *Becoming America: The Revolution before 1776* (Cambridge: Harvard University Press, 2000), 50–88.

11. Colin G. Calloway, ed., *After King Philip's War: Presence and Persistence in Indian New England* (Hanover, NH: University Press of America, 1997); and Daniel R. Mandell, *Behind the Frontier: Indian Communities in Eighteenth-Century Massachusetts* (Lincoln: University of Nebraska Press, 1996). Pennsylvania became home to many refugee Indian populations, including Delaware, Shawnee, and Iroquois, sometimes mixed in the same community. See, for example, the essays in William A. Pencak and Daniel K. Richter, eds., *Friends and Enemies in Penn's Woods* (University Park: Pennsylvania State University Press, 2004).

12. Andrew F. Walls, *The Cross-Cultural Process in the History of Christianity: Studies in the Transmission and Appropriation of Faith* (Maryknoll, NY: Orbis Books, 2002).

13. Mark Noll, *America's God: From Jonathan Edwards to Abraham Lincoln* (New York: Oxford University Press, 2002), 33; and Thomas Kidd, *The Protestant Interest: New England after Puritanism* (New Haven: Yale University Press, 2004).

14. See especially Gregory Evans Dowd, *A Spirited Resistance: The North American Indian Struggle for Unity, 1745–1815* (Baltimore: Johns Hopkins University Press, 1992).

15. In talking about preserving "traditional" Mohican values, I do not intend to suggest that tribal designations like "Mohican" are static categories. By Mohican culture I mean that which is expressed by those who identify as Mohican.

16. The emphasis on imperialism and Indian resistance to imperialism is not surprising, given that many of these scholars began their work as the Vietnam War dragged on. Much excellent, if sometimes polemical, scholarship has come out of this line of inquiry. Seminal works include Robert F. Berkhofer Jr., *Salvation and the Savage: An Analysis of Protestant Missions and American Indian Response, 1787–1862* (Lexington: University of Kentucky Press, 1965); Francis Jennings, *The Invasion of America: Indians, Colonialism, and the Cant of Conquest* (Chapel Hill: University of North Carolina Press, 1975); Henry Warner Bowden, *American Indians and Christian Missions: Studies in Cultural Conflict* (Chicago: University of Chicago Press, 1981); and James Axtell, *The Invasion Within: The Contest of Cultures in Colonial North America* (New York: Oxford University Press, 1985).

17. Anthony F. C. Wallace launched the study of revitalization movements with an article in *American Anthropologist* 58 (1956): 264–81, and his subsequent book, *The Death and Rebirth of the Seneca* (New York: Alfred A. Knopf, 1969). Several works have followed in the same rich vein, including Dowd, *A Spirited Resistance* and *War under Heaven: Pontiac, the Indian Nations, and the British Empire* (Baltimore: Johns Hopkins University Press, 2002); Joel Martin, *Sacred Revolt: The Muskogee Struggle for a New World* (Boston: Beacon Press, 1991). On resistance specifically to Christianity, see Neal Salisbury, "Red Puritans: The 'Praying Indians' of Massachusetts Bay and John Eliot," *WMQ* 31 (1974): 27–54; and James P. Ronda, "'We Are Well as We Are': An Indian Critique of Seventeenth-Century Missions," *WMQ* 34 (1977): 66–82. On Christianity as a form of resistance, see Elise M. Brenner, "To Pray or to Be Prey: That is the Question: Strategies for Cultural Autonomy of Massachusetts Praying Town Indians," *Ethnohistory* 27 (1980): 135–52. Notable exceptions include James P. Ronda, "Generations of Faith: The Christian Indians of Martha's Vineyard," *WMQ* 38 (1981): 369–94; John Webster Grant, *Moon of Wintertime: Missionaries and the Indians of Canada in Encounter since 1534* (Toronto: University of Toronto Press, 1984); Harold W. Van Lonkhuyzen, "A Reappraisal of the Praying Indians: Acculturation, Conversion, and Identity at Natick, Massachusetts, 1646–1730," *NEQ* 63 (1990): 396–428; and the work of Kenneth M. Morrison, whose essays are collected in Morrison, *The Solidarity of Kin: Ethnohistory, Religious Studies, and the Algonkian-French Religious Encounter* (Albany: SUNY Press, 2002).

18. Jean and John Comaroff, *Of Revelation and Revolution: Christianity, Colonialism and Consciousness in South Africa*, 2 vols. (Chicago: University of Chicago Press, 1991). Mary Louise Pratt, *Imperial Eyes: Travel Writing and Transculturation* (Routledge: New York, 1992), 4; and Bernd C. Peyer, *The Tutor'd Mind: Indian Missionary-Writers in Antebellum America* (Amherst: University of Massachusetts Press, 1997).

19. James H. Merrell, *The Indians' New World: Catawbas and Their Neighbors from European Contact through the Era of Removal* (Chapel Hill: University of North Carolina Press, 1989);

Colin G. Calloway, *New Worlds for All: Indians, Europeans, and the Remaking of Early America* (Baltimore: Johns Hopkins University Press, 1997); Mandell, *Behind the Frontier;* Jean M. O'Brien, *Dispossession by Degrees: Indian Land and Identity in Natick, Massachusetts, 1650–1790* (New York: Cambridge University Press, 1997); and Ann Marie Plane, *Colonial Intimacies: Indian Marriage in Early New England* (Ithaca, NY: Cornell University Press, 2000).

20. Douglas L. Winiarski, "Native American Popular Religion in New England's Old Colony, 1670–1770," *Religion and American Culture* 15 (2005): 147–86; David J. Silverman, *Faith and Boundaries: Christianity and Community among the Wampanoag Indians* (New York: Cambridge University Press, 2005); and Jane T. Merritt, "Dreaming of the Savior's Blood: Moravians and the Indians' Great Awakening in Pennsylvania," *WMQ* 54 (1997): 723–46 and *At the Crossroads: Indians and Empires on a Mid-Atlantic Frontier* (Chapel Hill: University of North Carolina Press, 2003).

21. Barry O'Connell, ed., *On Our Own Ground: The Complete Writings of William Apess, A Pequot* (Amherst: University of Massachusetts Press, 1992); Hilary E. Wyss, *Writing Indians: Literacy, Christianity, and Native Community in Early America* (Amherst: University of Massachusetts Press, 2000); Joanna Brooks, *American Lazarus: Religion and the Rise of African-American and Native American Literatures* (New York: Oxford University Press, 2003); Kristina Bross, *Dry Bones and Indian Sermons: Praying Indians in Colonial America* (Ithaca, NY: Cornell University Press, 2004); and Laura M. Stevens, *The Poor Indians: British Missionaries, Native Americans, and Colonial Sensibility* (Philadelphia: University of Pennsylvania Press, 2004).

22. Axtell, *Invasion Within.* One important exception is Sergei Kan's study of Russian Orthodox and Presbyterian missions to Alaskan natives. Kan, *Memory Eternal: Tlingit Culture and Russian Orthodox Christianity through Two Centuries* (Seattle: University of Washington Press, 1999).

23. Kenneth S. Greenberg, ed., *The Confessions of Nat Turner and Related Documents* (New York: St. Martin's Press, 1996), 26.

24. In a letter to his friend and former Stockbridge teacher Gideon Hawley, Edwards conveyed news of the imminent attack. JE to Hawley, October 9, 1756. *Works,* vol. 16, pp. 690–91. The sermon on which Ebenezer's handwriting is preserved was preached in October 1756, but there is no indication of the specific date. Psalms 27:4, October 1756, JEC. The Franklin quotation appears in his book *The Way to Wealth,* a collection of sayings culled from his *Poor Richard's Almanac* published in 1758.

CHAPTER 2. THE RIVER GOD AND THE LIEUTENANT

1. In this deed, Umpachenee is named as Sunkewenaugheag. Harry Andrews Wright, ed. *Indian Deeds of Hampden County* (Springfield, MA: 1905), 116–18.

2. See Shirley W. Dunn, *The Mohicans and their Land, 1609–1730* (Fleischmanns, NY: Purple Mountain Press, 1994), appendix A, and *The Mohican World, 1680–1750* (Fleischmanns, NY: Purple Mountain Press, 2000), appendix A.

3. Evan Haefeli and Kevin Sweeney, *Captors and Captives: The 1704 French and Indian Raid on Deerfield* (Amherst: University of Massachusetts Press, 2003), 99, 115. On Solomon Stoddard, see Paul R. Lucas, "'An Appeal to the Learned': The Mind of Solomon Stoddard," *WMQ* 30 (1973): 257–92.

4. On the "River Gods," see Kevin Sweeney, "River Gods and Related Minor Deities: The Williams Family and the Connecticut River Valley, 1637–1790," Ph.D. dissertation, Yale University, 1986; and Gregory H. Nobles, *Divisions throughout the Whole: Politics and Society in Hampshire County, Massachusetts, 1740–1775* (Cambridge: Cambridge University Press, 1983).

5. Sweeney, "River Gods," 153–59.

6. Nobles, *Divisions throughout the Whole,* 19–23.

7. Clifford K. Shipton, *Sibley's Harvard Graduates, Biographical Sketches of Those who Attended Harvard College,* vol. 5 (Boston: MHS, 1937), 96–119. The following depiction of John Stoddard is based on Nobles, *Divisions throughout the Whole,* 28–31; and Sweeney, "River Gods," ch. 4.

8. Stoddard's half-sister, Eunice Mather, was the daughter of Esther Warham Mather Stoddard and the wife of John Williams. Haefeli and Sweeney, *Captors and Captives,* 11–33. For the experiences of the Williams family, see John Demos, *The Unredeemed Captive: A Family Story from Early America* (New York: Alfred A. Knopf, 1994).

9. Haefeli and Sweeney, *Captors and Captives,* 1, 113–15, 212–14; "Stoddard's Journal," *New England Historical and Genealogical Register* 5 (1851): 21–42; and Demos, *The Unredeemed Captive,* 112–19.

10. Timothy Woodbridge to Ephraim Williams Jr., July 21, 1748, Misc. Mss. vol. 37, p. 18, Williams College Archives, Williamstown, Massachusetts; and Sweeney, "River Gods," 333–412.

11. Covenant Chain diplomatic protocol was based on the rites of the Iroquois Great League of Peace, which had been established among the Five Nations on the eve of European colonization. Daniel K. Richter, *Ordeal of the Longhouse: The Peoples of the Iroquois League in the Era of European Colonization* (Chapel Hill: University of North Carolina Press, 1992), 134–42. There has been considerable scholarly debate about the nature of the Iroquois "empire." Francis Jennings, *The Ambiguous Iroquois Empire: The Covenant Chain Confederation of Indian Tribes with English Colonies* (New York: W. W. Norton, 1982); and the essays collected in Richter and James H. Merrell, eds., *Beyond the Covenant Chain: The Iroquois and Their Neighbors in Indian North America, 1600–1800* (Syracuse, NY: Syracuse University Press, 1987).

12. The later petition was passed in the House of Representatives on June 29, 1722. The charge of the Commissioners to the Albany Treaty was recorded on July 5, 1722. *JHRM,* vol. 3, p. 193, vol. 4, pp. 68–69.

13. Stoddard, *Question Whether God is not Angry with the Country for doing So little toward the Conversion of the Indians?* (Boston, 1723), 6, 8, 9. The senior Stoddard did not always preach benevolence toward Indian peoples: two decades earlier, on the eve of the Deerfield attack, Solomon Stoddard had urged Massachusetts Governor Joseph Dudley to allow soldiers to be "put in a way to hunt the Inds. with dogs." Solomon Stoddard to Joseph Dudley, October 21, 1703, quoted in Demos, *Unredeemed Captive,* 12.

14. *Historical Memoirs,* 2. As early as February 1724, Stoddard proposed that a chaplain be stationed at Fort Dummer (on the site of present-day Brattleboro, Vermont) to serve the Indians and English who traded at the fort. Egbert Smyth Coffin, "Fort Dummer," *Proceedings of the Massachusetts Historical Society,* 2nd ser., vol. 6 (March 1891): 370.

15. Stoddard, *Question Whether God is not Angry,* 6, 8.

16. Stephen Williams recorded Umpachenee's age as 38 in 1734. *Gospel Ministers,* iii. Shirley Dunn cites 1768 testimony of Joseph Van Guilder that in 1738, Umpachenee was over sixty years old, which would make him at least seventy-three at the time of his death. Dunn, *Mohican World,* 365. The older age makes sense for a number of reasons. Moravian mission records of 1751 note the illness and death of "Der Alte König" (the old king). Pachgatgoch Diary, July 12, August 4, 1751, 114/4 RMM. On the other hand, Umpachenee sent his eight-year-old son Etoakaum to board with John Sergeant in New Haven during the winter of 1734–35. *Historical Memoirs,* 16.

17. For reference to Umpachenee as "king," see note 16. The Moravian records usually refer to Umpachenee as "Captain" and occasionally as "Governor." See, for example, Pachgatgoch Diary, May 27, 1751, 114/3 RMM; and Gnadenhütten Diary, June 16, 1747, 117/2 RMM. Anthropologist Philip Colee dismisses claims that Umpachenee was a major sachem and speculates instead that he was tribal speaker. Colee, "The Housatonic-Stockbridge Indians, 1734–1749," Ph.D. dissertation, SUNY Albany, 1977, 166–67. Ted J. Brasser speculates that Umpachenee became chief sachem sometime in the 1740s. Brasser, *Riding on the Frontier's Crest: Mahican Indian Culture and Cultural Change* (Ottawa: National Museums of Canada, 1974), 34. On English attempts to understand native leadership categories through English terminology, see Nancy Shoemaker, *A Strange Likeness: Becoming Red and White in Eighteenth Century North America* (New York: Oxford University Press, 2004), 345–60.

18. Skatekook, which lay at the confluence of the Green and Housatonic Rivers, between what is now Great Barrington and Sheffield, is to be distinguished from Scaghticoke, one of the originally Mohican villages along the Hudson River, and Scaticook ("Pachgatgoch" in the

Moravian records), which lay at the confluence of the Ten Mile and Housatonic Rivers near Kent, Connecticut. The names all derive from "P'ska'tikook," meaning "at the river fork." Brasser, *Riding on the Frontier's Crest*, 65–66, 68.

19. However, at least one historian has suggested that Etowaukaum's title was more a fiction created by hopeful whites than a reflection of actual status among the Mohicans. Eric Hinderaker, "The Four Indian Kings and the Imaginative Construction of the First British Empire," *WMQ* 53 (July 1996): 491.

20. Dunn, *Mohican World*, 365.

21. Electa F. Jones, *Stockbridge, Past and Present: Or, Records of an Old Mission Station* (Springfield, MA: Samuel Bowles and Company, 1854), 20–22.

22. Jones, *Stockbridge, Past and Present*, 15; and Brasser, *Riding the Frontier's Crest*, 11.

23. *History, Manners and Customs*, xxxv, xxxix.

24. *NYCD*, vol. 5, p. 663. Francis Jennings traces the change in 1643 of the metaphor from a rope to a chain binding Dutch and Mahicans. A rope symbolized a non-aggression pact, while a chain symbolized a pact of mutual assistance. Jennings, *Ambiguous Iroquois Empire*, 54.

25. Francis Jennings, *Ambiguous Iroquois Empire*, 48–50; Brasser, "Mahican," in *Handbook of North American Indians*, ed. William C. Sturtevant, vol. 15, *Northeast*, ed. Bruce G. Trigger (Washington: Smithsonian Institution, 1978), 202–3, and *Riding on the Frontier's Crest*, 12–14; and Allen W. Trelease, *Indian Affairs in Colonial New York: The Seventeenth Century* (Ithaca, NY: Cornell University Press, 1960), 46–48, 228–30. For an alternative view, see William Starna and José Antonia Brandão, "From the Mohawk-Mahican War to the Beaver Wars: Questioning the Pattern," *Ethnohistory* 51 (Fall 2004): 725–50; on the relocation to the Connecticut River area, 739.

26. Richter, *Ordeal of the Longhouse*, 134–36; and Brasser, *Riding on the Frontier's Crest*, 22.

27. See, for example, James Merrell, *The Indians' New World: The Catawbas and Their Neighbors from Contact through the Era of Removal* (Chapel Hill: University of North Carolina Press, 1989).

28. *NYCD*, vol. 3, p. 27. "Western Corner" here most likely refers to the Westenhook Indians. Westenhook seems to have been coined to refer to the northwestern corner of Connecticut but later came to mean the area to the west of the Housatonic River. Two tracts along the Housatonic were sold to traders from New York in 1685, and another such transaction occurred in 1706. On Mohican land ownership in the Housatonic area, see Dunn, *Mohican World*, 68–76; Brasser, *Riding on the Frontier's Crest*, 22–23; and *NYCD*, vol. 5, pp. 266–67, 387.

29. 1701 speech by the River Indians suggests such an alliance. *NYCD*, vol. 4, p. 902.

30. Brasser, *Riding on the Frontier's Crest*, 23, 30.

31. Dunn, *Mohican World*, 70–75.

32. There is no record of the identities of the other members of the Mohican party. *NYCD*, vol. 5, pp. 661–65.

Chapter 3. Covenants, Contracts, and the Founding of Stockbridge

1. The literature on New England missions is vast. Among the most important works are James Axtell, *The Invasion Within: The Contest of Cultures in Colonial North America* (New York: Oxford University Press, 1985); Charles L. Cohen, "Conversion among Puritans and Amerindians: A Theological and Cultural Perspective," in *Puritanism: Transatlantic Perspectives on a Seventeenth-Century Anglo-American Faith,* ed. Francis J. Bremer (Boston: MHS, 1993), 233–54; Richard Cogley, *John Eliot's Praying Towns before King Philip's War* (Cambridge: Harvard University Press, 1999); Harold W. Van Lonkhuyzen, "A Reappraisal of the Praying Indians: Acculturation, Conversion, and Identity at Natick, Massachusetts, 1646–1730," *NEQ* 63 (1990): 346–68; Daniel R. Mandell, *Behind the Frontier: Indians in Eighteenth-Century Eastern Massachusetts* (Lincoln: University of Nebraska Press, 1996); Douglas L. Winiarski, "Native American

Popular Religion in New England's Old Colony," *Religion and American Culture* 15 (Summer 2005): 147–86; and David J. Silverman, *Faith and Boundaries: Colonists, Christianity, and Community Among the Wampanoag Indians of Martha's Vineyard, 1600–1871* (Cambridge: Cambridge University Press, 2005).

2. There is a substantial literature devoted to the Mohicans and the Stockbridge Indians. Ted J. Brasser, *Riding on the Frontier's Crest: Mahican Indian Culture and Cultural Change* (Ottawa: National Museums of Canada, 1974); Patrick Frazier, *The Mohicans of Stockbridge* (Lincoln: University of Nebraska Press, 1992); Daniel Mandell, "Behind the Frontier: Indian Communities in Eighteenth-Century Massachusetts," Ph.D. dissertation, University of Virginia, 1992; Philip S. Colee, "The Housatonic-Stockbridge Indians: 1734–1749," Ph.D. dissertation, State University of New York at Albany, 1977; Colin G. Calloway, *The American Revolution in Indian Country: Crisis and Diversity in Native American Communities* (Cambridge: Cambridge University Press, 1995), ch. 3; and Shirley W. Dunn, *The Mohicans and Their Land, 1609–1730* (Fleischmanns, NY: Purple Mountain Press, 1994), and *The Mohican World, 1680–1750* (Fleischmanns, NY: Purple Mountain Press, 2000). Other important works dealing with seventeenth-century Mohican history include Allen W. Trelease, *Indian Affairs in Colonial New York: The Seventeenth Century* (Ithaca, NY: Cornell University Press, 1960), 46–48; Bruce G. Trigger, "The Mohawk-Mahican War (1624–1628): The Establishment of a Pattern," *Canadian Historical Review* 52 (1971): 276–86; and William Starna and José Antonio Brandão, "From the Mohawk-Mahican War to the Beaver Wars: Questioning the Pattern," *Ethnohistory* 51 (Fall 2004): 725–50.

3. There is considerable scholarship on the ways that native peoples in French and Spanish colonial settings adapted European cultural tools to serve their own ends. On the Spanish colonies, see especially Inga Clendinnen, *Ambivalent Conquests: Maya and Spaniard in Yucatan, 1517–1570* (New York: Cambridge University Press, 1987); Sabine MacCormack, *Religion in the Andes: Vision and Imagination in Early Colonial Peru* (Princeton: Princeton University Press, 1991); Erick Langer and Robert H. Jackson, eds., *The New Latin American Mission History* (Lincoln: University of Nebraska Press, 1995); and Nicholas Griffiths and Fernando Cervantes, eds., *Spiritual Encounters: Interactions between Christianity and Native Religions in Colonial America* (Lincoln: University of Nebraska Press, 1999). On the French context, see Kenneth M. Morrison, *The Solidarity of Kin: Ethnohistory, Religious Studies, and the Algonkian-French Religious Encounter* (Albany: SUNY Press, 2002). On Indians and Catholicism more broadly, see Christopher Vecsey, *The Paths of Kateri's Kin* (Notre Dame: University of Notre Dame Press, 1997).

4. Nancy Shoemaker, *A Strange Likeness: Becoming Red and White in Eighteenth-Century North America* (New York: Oxford University Press, 2004); Daniel K. Richter, *Facing East from Indian Country* (Cambridge: Harvard University Press, 2001); and John Wood Sweet, *Bodies Politic: Negotiating Race in the American North, 1730–1830* (Baltimore: Johns Hopkins University Press, 2003).

5. *Gospel Ministers,* 27.

6. Laura M. Stevens, *Poor Indians: British Missionaries, Native Americans and Colonial Sensibility* (Philadelphia: University of Pennsylvania Press, 2004), 50–61; and John Canup, *Out of the Wilderness: The Emergence of an American Identity in Colonial New England* (Middletown, CT: Wesleyan University Press, 1990).

7. The rest of Hakluyt's justifications mostly related to bolstering England's flagging trade, reinvigorating its navy, and putting a check on Spanish ambitions. Richard Hakluyt, *Discourse of Western Planting,* 1584.

8. Nathaniel B. Shurtleff, ed., *Records of the Governor and Company of the Massachusetts Bay in New England,* vol. 1 (Boston, 1853), 17.

9. *Winthrop Papers, 1498–1649,* vol. 3 (Boston: MHS, 1929), 149.

10. John Winthrop, "Reasons to Be Considered…," in *The Puritans,* ed. Perry Miller and Thomas H. Johnson, rev. ed. (New York: Harper and Row, Publishers, 1968), 73.

11. Francis Jennings, *The Invasion of America: Indians, Colonialism, and the Cant of Conquest* (Chapel Hill: University of North Carolina Press, 1975).

12. Axtell, *Invasion Within,* 131–33.

13. Kristina Bross argues that Puritan evangelization efforts emerged when they did in response to various crises that challenged the Puritan sense of purpose. Bross, *Dry Bones and Indian Sermons* (Ithaca, NY: Cornell University Press, 2004), 11, 27.

14. Michael Winship, *Seers of God: Puritan Providentialism in the Restoration and Early Enlightenment* (Baltimore: Johns Hopkins University Press, 1996), 24–25; and Richard Slotkin and James K. Folsom, eds., *So Dreadful a Judgment: Puritan Responses to King Philip's War, 1676–1677* (Middletown, CT: Wesleyan University Press, 1979), 3–5.

15. Kellaway, *New England Company*, 171–80.

16. Mary Rowlandson's famous narrative of her captivity among the Indians during King Philip's War exemplifies the suspicion many colonists harbored toward Christian Indians. Bross, *Dry Bones*, 146–48.

17. *Historical Memoirs*, 165.

18. Edmund S. Morgan, *Visible Saints: The History of a Puritan Idea* (New York: New York University Press, 1963), 137–38.

19. William Kellaway has detailed the difficulties of recruiting suitable candidates. Kellaway, *New England Company, 1649–1776 Missionary Society to the American Indians* (New York: Barnes and Noble, 1962) 76–77, 231–32. Missionaries were generally drawn from the bottom third of their college class. Axtell, "Preachers, Priests, and Pagans: Catholic and Protestant Missions in Colonial North America," in *New Dimensions in Ethnohistory: Papers of the Second Laurier Conference on Ethnohistory and Ethnology*, ed. Barry Gough and Laird Christie (Ottawa: Canadian Museum of Civilization, 1983), 73–74.

20. On the praying towns, see Cogley, *John Eliot's Praying Towns*. For the fate of New England Indians in the wake of King Philip's War, see especially James D. Drake, *King Philip's War: Civil War in New England, 1675–1676* (Amherst: University of Massachusetts Press, 1999), 101–4, 136–39; Mandell, *Behind the Frontier*, 24–47; Jean M. O'Brien, *Dispossession by Degrees: Indian Land and Identity in Natick, Massachusetts, 1650–1790* (Lincoln: University of Nebraska Press, 1997), 60–70; and the essays in Colin G. Calloway, ed., *After King Philip's War: Presence and Persistence in Indian New England* (Hanover, NH: University Press of New England, 1999).

21. Perhaps more than any other New England missions, those established by the Mayhew family among the native residents of Martha's Vineyard resulted in a greater degree of native leadership. These communities benefited from the natural barriers the islands provided, which served to slow English encroachment. See James P. Ronda, "Generations of Faith: The Christian Indians of Martha's Vineyard," *WMQ* 38 (1981): 369–94; and Silverman, *Faith and Boundaries*. Douglas L. Winiarski has studied the development of the native Christian community in Plymouth County. See Winiarski, "A Question of Plain Dealing: Josiah Cotton, Native Christians, and the Quest for Security in Eighteenth-Century Plymouth County," *NEQ* 77 (2004): 368–413.

22. Harry S. Stout, *The New England Soul: Preaching and Religious Culture in Colonial New England* (New York: Oxford University Press, 1986), 175.

23. For further discussion of changing demographics and land distribution politics in colonial New England, see Richard L. Bushman, *From Puritan to Yankee: Character and the Social Order in Connecticut, 1690–1765* (Cambridge: Harvard University Press, 1967); Kenneth A. Lockridge, *A New England Town: The First Hundred Years* (New York: Norton, 1970); Philip J. Greven, *Four Generations: Population, Land, and Family in Colonial Andover, Massachusetts* (Ithaca, NY: Cornell University Press, 1970); and Patricia Tracy, *Jonathan Edwards, Pastor: Religion and Society in Eighteenth-Century Northampton* (New York: Hill and Wang, 1979), ch. 4.

24. Three missionaries were sent into the field to serve Forts George, Dummer, and Richmond. The New England Company was far more active in the eastern regions of the colony.

25. The missions were a result of a stipulation in a wealthy Scottish benefactor's will stating that his estate could not be used to fund mission efforts until the Society funded three missionaries to "foreign Infidel countries." These missions marked the first efforts by the SSPCK in America. Kellaway, *New England Company*, 186–87.

26. Joseph Sewall, *Christ Victorious over the Powers of Darkness, by the Light of His Preached Gospel* (Boston: Samuel Kneeland, 1733), 17.

27. *Historical Memoirs*, 3. Stephen Williams makes precisely the same argument in his letter of June 25, 1735, quoted in *Gospel Ministers*, vii–viii.

28. Benjamin Colman to William Grant, December 25, 1733. Benjamin Colman Papers, MHS.

29. Kellaway, *New England Company*, 62, 269.

30. *JHRM*, vol. 12, pp. 94–95.

31. *Gospel Ministers*, vii; and *Historical Memoirs*, 3.

32. Historian Shirley Dunn persuasively argues that Mohican ties to the Housatonic region date back at least to the mid–seventeenth century. Dunn, *Mohican World*, 59–64.

33. These issues will be discussed in greater detail in the subsequent chapters on Shekomeko. The Moravian sources provide for a more complete discussion of ritual in general and health and healing in particular. On Algonquian religions, see Neal Salisbury, *Manitou and Providence: Indians, Europeans, and the Making of New England 1500–1643* (New York: Oxford University Press, 1982); Calvin Martin, *Keepers of the Game: Indian-Animal Relationships and the Fur Trade* (Berkeley: University of California Press, 1978); William S. Simmons, *The Spirit of the New England Tribes: Indian History and Folklore, 1620–1984* (Hanover: University Press of New England, 1986); and Kathleen J. Bragdon, *Native Peoples of Southern New England, 1500–1650* (Norman: University of Oklahoma Press, 1996).

34. John Sergeant observed that the Indians once held "pawwaws" in high esteem, but now "they confess they have no Power over Christians." *Historical Memoirs*, 24.

35. On Mohican connections with St. Francis Abenaki, see Colin G. Calloway, *The Western Abenakis of Vermont, 1600–1800: War, Migration, and the Survival of an Indian People* (Norman: University of Oklahoma Press, 1990), 86. On Mohican connections with the Miami, see Brasser, *Riding on the Frontier's Crest*, 3, 25. On Aupaumut's history, see Electa F. Jones, *Stockbridge, Past and Present: Or, Records of an Old Mission Station* (Springfield, MA: Samuel Bowles and Company, 1854), 17.

36. For example, in 1729, the Mohican chief Ampamit's brother requested to have his sister's son put in school and "Brought up to Learning." March 29, 1729, *NEC Letterbooks*, University of Virginia Library, Charlottesville, Virginia (microfilm ed.). This was still in practice among the Mohicans in the late eighteenth century. Hendrick Aupaumut, "A Short Narration of My Last Journey to the Western Contry," *Historical Society of Pennsylvania Memoirs* 2 (1827): 87. This practice is well documented among the Iroquois and seems also to have been common among the Mohicans. Daniel K. Richter, *Ordeal of the Longhouse: The Peoples of the Iroquois League in the Era of European Colonization* (Chapel Hill: University of North Carolina Press, 1992), 111–12.

37. When Konkapot, Umpachenee, Umpachenee's brother, and Ebenezer traveled to New Haven in May 1735 to fetch the boys, Sergeant reported: "I entertain'd these Men with as much Respect, and Kindness, as I could; shew'd them our Library, and the Rarities of the *College;* with which they seem'd to be well pleas'd; and behav'd themselves, while they were there, well, and with much Decency." *Historical Memoirs*, 16, 27.

38. *Historical Memoirs*, 28.

39. Wnahktukook was generally known by the English as Housatonic, and residents of the village were among the first settlers at Stockbridge, established just to the north of the village. The area of the Housatonic was referred to by the Dutch as Westenhook, apparently a corruption of the native name, meaning "western corner." In the Moravian records, Stockbridge is commonly referred to as Westenhuc or some variation of Wannachgoattegock. Brasser, *Riding on the Frontier's Crest*, 66. See for example, Shekomeko Diary, October 5, 1742, 1/111/1 RMM.

40. *Gospel Ministers*, iii; *Historical Memoirs*, 2; and Kellaway, *New England Company*, 199; entry dated May 31, 1734, NEC Letterbooks. See for example, Shekomeko Diary, October 5, 1742, 1/111/1 RMM.

41. Sergeant's journal, April 20, 1735, quoted in *Historical Memoirs*, 48–50.

42. *Historical Memoirs*, 2.

43. *Gospel Ministers*, iv.

44. *Historical Memoirs*, 20.

45. *Historical Memoirs*, 21.

46. According to Shirley Dunn, Corlaer was living at Weatuck (near present day Salisbury) by 1714 and had moved west of the Hudson to Greene County by the mid 1740s. Dunn, *Mohican World*, 126, 128, 129, 140, 149. Either he or some relation of his settled at Stockbridge, as Metoxen became a prominent name at Stockbridge.

47. Umpachenee and Konkapot requested the presence of the ministers. Three attended: Stephen Williams, Samuel Hopkins, and Jonathan Ashley. *Gospel Ministers*, 6.

48. "Extract from the Indian Journal, being the 6th Speech that was delivered to the Delaware Nation residing at Waupekummekut, or White River, on the 15th day of April, 1803," printed in *Massachusetts Missionary Magazine* (April 1804): 467–71.

49. A few weeks later, Timothy Woodbridge rode to Skatekook to Umpachenee's longhouse to observe what he thought would be "a proper Search into the Matter" of the recent deaths. Woodbridge was surprised to witness instead a divining ceremony that lasted through the night and was intended to reveal the identity of the alleged sorcerers. It is unclear whether they were asking why the Housatonics are like the English or why the Housatonics like the English. "Capt. Cunkapot and Lieut. Umpicheney to Nehemiah Bull," February 5, 1735, Ayer Collection, Vault box MS 205, Newberry Library, Chicago, Illinois.

50. *Gospel Ministers*, vi–vii.

51. "Extract from the Indian Journal," 467–71.

52. The Schaghticokes were a community of Indians on the Hoosic River northeast of Albany formed in the wake of King Philip's War and including New England Algonquians, Western Abenakis, and Mahicans. Richter, *Ordeal of the Longhouse*, 136.

53. Joseph Dwight would ultimately marry Abigail Williams Sergeant after John Sergeant's death. Israel Williams was one of the sons of William Williams, who had married Solomon Stoddard's daughter, Christian Stoddard. Mary C. Crawford, *Among Old New England Inns* (Boston: L. C. Page and Company, 1907), 56. For the Williams family relations, see Kevin Sweeney, "River Gods and Related Minor Deities: The Williams Family and the Connecticut River Valley, 1637–1790," Ph.D. dissertation, Yale University, 1986, 747–55.

54. Among the native participants were members of the Caughnawaga Mohawks, together with Abenakis, Pennacooks, and others. On the French side, the raid represented one prong of the imperial war that came to be known as Queen Anne's War. The French aimed to unsettle the English and push back their line of settlement so that they could retain firm control over trade in the Champlain Valley. Indian participation in the raid stemmed from their resentment over English encroachment and population loss due to disease and warfare. Raids like the one on Deerfield were an important source of captives who could be adopted or turned over to the French in exchange for valuable trade items. Evan Haefeli and Kevin Sweeney, *Captors and Captives: The 1704 French and Indian Raid on Deerfield* (Amherst: University of Massachusetts Press, 2003).

55. Stephen Williams's sister, Eunice, was adopted among the Caughnawaga, eventually marrying a Mohawk man. She steadfastly refused to return to New England. John P. Demos, *The Unredeemed Captive: A Family Story from Early New England* (New York: Oxford University Press, 1994); Haefeli and Sweeney, 239–40, 264, 269, 284; and *At a Conference*, 2.

56. For most of the colonial era, the Five Nations of the Iroquois leaned toward English allegiance. The Caughnawaga (Kahnawake) Mohawks were an important exception. Starting in 1676, many left their homelands in what is now upstate New York to join the Jesuit mission in New France, near Montreal. Since the Grand Settlement of 1701, the Iroquois League had been officially neutral, agreeing to refrain from attacking the Indian allies of the French or the English. Richter, *Ordeal of the Longhouse*, 214–25; and Haefeli and Sweeney, *Captors and Captives*, 268–69. A speech by Massachusetts representatives to the Caughnawagas at a 1751 meeting in Albany recounted the recent history, recalling the friendship established in 1724 at Albany and

renewed at Deerfield in 1735, on the occasion of Sergeant's ordination. The covenant ensured free trade. "A Journal of the Commissioners of the Province of the Massachusetts," July 4, 1751, Mass. Archives, vol. 38A, pp. 160–66.

57. *At a Conference,* 2–3. Covenant Chain rites were based on the condolence ceremonies of the Iroquois Great League of Peace and were employed in British-Iroquois conferences to reaffirm the alliance first established in the 1670s. For a discussion of the history and historiography of the Covenant Chain, see Daniel K. Richter and James H. Merrell, eds., *Beyond the Covenant Chain: The Iroquois and Their Neighbors in Indian North America, 1600–1800* (Syracuse, NY: Syracuse University Press, 1987), 5–8. For an early challenge to the idea of Iroquois dominance, see Francis Jennings, *The Ambiguous Iroquois Empire: The Covenant Chain Confederation of Indian Tribes with English Colonies* (New York: W.W. Norton, 1984).

58. *At a Conference,* 7–8.

59. Ebenezer Hinsdale was the "Father" in question. Hinsdale was another survivor of sorts of the Deerfield raid—he had been born on the return journey of his mother from captivity. Haefeli and Sweeney, *Captives and Captors,* 259–60; and *At a Conference,* 2, 8, 9.

60. *At a Conference,* 5, 6.

61. Wauntaugaweet, Naunaunecannutt, and Ampamit's son joined Umpachenee and Konkapot as the Housatonic Mohican leaders in attendance. *At a Conference,* 4, 10, 16.

62. On reciprocity and leadership, see Bragdon, *Native Peoples of Southern New England,* 132–22; and *At a Conference,* 11.

63. See Ann Marie Plane, *Colonial Intimacies: Indian Marriage in Colonial New England* (Ithaca, NY: Cornell University Press, 2002), 99–102. The Moravian records provide evidence of one case in Connecticut in which a creditor took two of a woman's children when she was unable to pay her debts. Pachgatgoch Diary, December 6, 1753, 3/114/8 RMM.

64. *At a Conference,* 14–15.

65. Thomas S. Kidd, *The Protestant Interest: New England after Protestantism* (New Haven: Yale University Press, 2004), 12.

66. *Gospel Ministers,* 3, 21, 25.

67. *Gospel Ministers,* 13, 19.

68. *Gospel Ministers,* ii, 25.

69. Ebenezer Pemberton, *A Sermon Preach'd in New-Ark* (Boston: Rogers & Fowle, 1744), 17.

70. *Works,* vol. 7, p. 208.

71. Hawley arrived at Stockbridge in 1752 to teach the Mohawks who had settled there. When the Mohawks left, Hawley began at Oquaga, but returned to Stockbridge at the outbreak of the war. He eventually served the rest of his career as missionary among the Mashpee Indians. Journal entry dated February 11, 1757. Gideon Hawley Manuscripts, American Congregational Library, Boston.

72. *Historical Memoirs,* 5; reports dated August 16, 1734, September 29, 1734, NEC Letterbooks. On Edwards's salary, see Patricia J. Tracy, *Jonathan Edwards, Pastor* (New York: Hill and Wang, 1979), 157.

73. Sergeant's valedictory address, delivered in 1729, was an obsequious tribute to his university mentor, Edwards. John Sergeant, *A Valedictory Oration* (1729; repr. New York: Henry W. Turner, 1882).

74. *Historical Memoirs,* 5, 6.

75. *Historical Memoirs,* 20, 31.

76. *Historical Memoirs,* 8.

77. *Historical Memoirs,* 8, 20.

78. Frazier, *Mohicans of Stockbridge,* 20.

79. *Historical Memoirs,* 8–9.

80. *Historical Memoirs,* 18.

81. *Historical Memoirs,* 35, 42; and Sergeant to Stephen Williams, November 28, 1735, NEC Letterbooks.

82. *Historical Memoirs,* 11, 18.

83. Some of those in attendance were likely residents of Shekomeko and Pachgatgoch, villages that would accept Moravian missionaries a few years later. *Historical Memoirs,* 37, 38.

84. Sergeant's stay was only a week this time, but the following year, Sergeant and Woodbridge spent six weeks living with the Housatonics—Sergeant went first to Konkapot's house and Woodbridge to Umpachenee's for three weeks before switching. *Historical Memoirs,* 26–28, 52.

85. *Historical Memoirs,* 24.

86. *Historical Memoirs,* 19.

87. *Historical Memoirs,* 10. On native perceptions of literacy, see James Axtell, "The Power of Print in the Eastern Woodlands," in his *After Columbus: Essays in the Ethnohistory of Colonial North America* (New York: Oxford University Press, 1987), 86–99.

88. Sandra Gustafson, *Eloquence is Power: Oratory and Performance in Early America* (Chapel Hill: University of North Carolina Press, 1999); and Kathleen J. Bragdon, "Vernacular Literacy and Massachusett Worldview, 1650–1750," in *Algonkians of New England Past and Present,* ed. Peter Benes (Boston: Boston University Press, 1993).

89. Letter from Sergeant to Stephen Williams, quoted in *Gospel Ministers,* vii; and *Historical Memoirs,* 67.

90. *At a Conference,* 10.

91. *NYCD,* vol. 5, p. 663.

92. *Historical Memoirs,* 54.

93. Letter signed by eleven Stockbridge Indians, including Umpachenee and Poohpoonuc. July 17, 1736, quoted in *Historical Memoirs,* 56–57.

94. Axtell, *Invasion Within,* 131–78.

95. David Hackett Fischer writes about the conservative impulse that often characterized new colonial settlements. Fischer, *Albion's Seed: Four British Folkways in America* (New York: Oxford University Press, 1989), 55–57.

96. Quoted in Kellaway, *New England Company,* 269–70.

97. *JHRM,* vol. 12, pp. 94–95.

98. Belcher to Sergeant, January 20, 1736, quoted in *Historical Memoirs,* 44.

99. *At a Conference,* 15.

100. *JHRM,* vol. 13, pp. 19, 215.

101. All quotations that follow from Conference with the Housaatunnock Indians, February 21, 1736, Mass. Archives, vol. 29, pp. 309–16.

102 Report of Conference with House in Council Chambers, August 7, 1736, Mass. Archives, vol. 29, pp. 324–32.

103. Sergeant's journal, dated April 20, 1736, quoted in *Historical Memoirs,* 48–50.

104. Sarah Cabot Sedgwick and Catherine Sedgwick Marquand, *Stockbridge, 1739–1974* (Stockbridge: Berkshire Traveller Press, 1974), 24; and Mass. Archives, vol. 31, pp. 202–5.

105. Many similar "exchanges" over subsequent years would chip away substantially at Stockbridge landholdings. Lion G. Miles, "Red Man Dispossessed: The Williams Family and the Alienation of Indian Land in Stockbridge, Massachusetts, 1736–1818," *NEQ* 67, no. 1 (March 1994): 46–76; and *Historical Memoirs,* 58.

106. Jones, *Stockbridge, Past and Present,* 64.

107. In the newly surveyed town, Sergeant and Woodbridge each received a hundred acres, and additional tracts were reserved for the four model families. *Historical Memoirs,* 47; and *Acts and Resolves, Public and Private of the Province of the Massachusetts Bay* (Boston: Wright and Potter, 1869–1922), vol. 12, pp. 245–46.

108. *Historical Memoirs,* 44, 47.

109. For a more complete discussion of Hannah Edwards, see Kenneth P. Minkema, "Hannah and Her Sisters: Sisterhood, Marriage, and Courtship in the Edwards Family in the Early Eighteenth Century," *New England Historical and Genealogical Society* 146 (1992): 35–56.

110. He signed his letter, "your great admirer and passionate lover." Sergeant to Hannah Edwards, July 28, 1735, 28/1528, JEC.

111. Sergeant to Hannah Edwards, February 3, 1736, JEC; John Sergeant to New England Commissioners, likely February 1736, quoted in Sedgwick and Marquand, *Stockbridge, 1739–1974*, 19.

112. Sergeant to Hannah Edwards, September 20, 1736, 28/1528, JEC.

113. Sergeant to Hannah Edwards, February 28, 1737, 28/1528, JEC.

114. Sergeant to Hannah Edwards, April 22, 1737, 28/1528, JEC. Edwards eventually married at the relatively advanced age of thirty-five.

115. "In a Letter from a Friend in the Country," *Boston Post Boy*, September 3, 1739. Quote from *Historical Memoirs*, 78, emphasis in original.

116. Sergeant diary, May 21, 1739, Stiles Papers.

117. "In a Letter from a Friend."

118. Jones, *Stockbridge, Past and Present*, 59.

119. *JHRM*, vol. 17, p. 31.

120. Sergeant, diary entry dated July 1, 1739, Stiles Papers.

121. Mandell, "Behind the Frontier," 140; and Miles, "Red Man Dispossessed," 49–55.

122. Sergeant diary entries dated August 5, October 10, 21, 28, November 29, 1739, February 5, 10, 17, March 27, 1740, Stiles Papers.

123. John Sergeant, *A letter from the Revd Mr. Sergeant of Stockbridge, to Dr. Colman of Boston* (Boston: Rogers and Fowle, 1743); and *Historical Memoirs*, 113.

124. John Sergeant to Benjamin Colman, August 1, 1743, Benjamin Colman Papers, MHS.

125. Sergeant to Colman, August 1, 1743.

126. *Historical Memoirs*, 127–30.

127. John Sergeant to Stephen Williams, Housatunnuk, May 14, 1739, Ayer MS 800, Newberry Library, Chicago, Illinois.

128. For the Stockbridge Mohicans' military service, see Frazier, *Mohicans of Stockbridge*, chs. 6, 10, 12, and 16. On their involvement in the Revolution, see Calloway, *American Revolution in Indian Country*, ch. 3.

129. At the time of Sergeant's death in 1749, there were 218 Indian residents; 129 were baptized, and 42 were communicants. *Historical Memoirs*, 143.

CHAPTER 4. THE CHIEF AND THE ORATOR

1. Shabash would be baptized as Abraham. He appears in the Moravian records as Shabash, Shawas, and Mamanetthekan but most commonly as Abraham. Gnadenhütten records, April 5, 1753, 6/119/1/9 RMM. "Tschoop" was apparently a rendering of "Job." His native name was Wasamapah. He appears most commonly in the Moravian records by his baptismal name, Johannes.

2. Missionary Christoph Pyrlaeus described the two men's roles in his history of Moravian missionary work, written sometime after 1751. He described Abraham (Shabash) as "an honored chief among his people" and Tschoop (Johannes) as "an orator in his language." Pyrlaeus, "Historical Account of the Indian Mission Work, 1739–1751," 26/221/21, p. 10–11, RMM. On the role of tribal speaker, see *History of the Mission*, pt. I, pp. 135–36.

3. This sketch of Shabash's life is drawn from several memoranda located in the Moravian Archives, 3/113/5 RMM, including item 2, Büttner, Memorandum [Eng.], September 1743; item 3, Gottlob Büttner, statement, n.d.; item 4, Abraham, Memorandum [Eng.], October 16, 1743; item 6, Büttner to Noble, October 16, 1743; item 7, Abraham to Noble, n.d.; item 8, Abraham, Petition to the Partners of the Little Nine, October 17, 1743; and item 11, Abraham to Martinus Hoffmann [Eng.], October 10, 1743. Also Abraham to Martinus Hoffman [Eng.], October 10, 1743, 3/113/5/11, RMM. For further discussion of these land transactions, see Isaac Huntting, *History of Little Nine Partners of North East Precinct and Pine Plains, New York, Duchess County* (Amenia, NY: Charles Walsh & Co., 1897), 3–20, 135; and Dunn, *The Mohican World, 1680–1750* (Fleischmanns, NY: Purple Mountain Press, 2000), 231–36. The Moravian

missionaries attempted to help Abraham with his land troubles, believing he had been unfairly dealt with by the Little Nine Partners and New York officials. See Gottlob Büttner to Anton Seiffert, December 9, 1743, 1/111/8/7 RMM.

4. The evidence is suggestive but not conclusive about his grandmother's status. Robert Steven Grumet identifies an Esopus woman sachem named Mamanuchqua as appearing in New York colonial documents. Grumet, "Sunksquaws, Shamans, and Tradeswomen: Middle Atlantic Coastal Algonkian Women during the 17th and 18th Centuries," in *Women and Colonization: Anthropological Perspectives,* ed. Mona Etienne and Eleanor Leacock (New York: Praeger, 1980), 43–62. See also, *NYCD,* vol. 13, pp. 507, 572; and Lawrence H. Leder, *Livingston Indian Records, 1666–1723* (Gettysburg: Pennsylvania Historical Association, 1953), 65–68. Shirley Dunn suggests that Abraham's grandmother may have been a woman identified as Mamanequanaskqua, an heir of Sauwachquanent, son of Aepjen, chief sachem of the Mohicans in the mid–seventeenth century. Dunn, *Mohican World,* 241.

5. The trustees were "Tatamshon und Wommpepawachen." Tatamshon (also Tataemshatt, Tattaemshaet) was the father of Catharickseet, later known by the Moravians as the "old captain" and baptized as Cornelius. Memorandum, September 1743, 3/113/5/3 RMM.

6. There may have been an additional brother. The Moravian records identify Blackfish as Abraham's brother. Blackfish was a captain or chief at Pachgatgoch and later resided at Shamokin, a refugee Indian community in Pennsylvania. Gnadenhütten Diary, January 12, 1752, 5/117/3 RMM.

7. Memorandum, September 1743, 3/113/5/3 RMM.

8. Shabash is identified as Maumauntissekun by Sergeant. Sergeant diary entry April 14, 1739, Stiles Papers.

9. John Sergeant, diary entry dated May 21, 1739, Stiles Papers. The description of Stockbridge in 1739 is drawn from "In a Letter from a Friend in the Country, dated Aug. 21, 1739," *Boston Post Boy,* September 3, 1739. Agriculture was primarily women's work in most Northeastern Indian societies. Kathleen J. Bragdon, *Native People of Southern New England, 1500–1650* (Norman: University of Oklahoma Press, 1996), 179–81.

10. Sergeant diary entry June 17, 1739, Stiles Papers.

11. *History of the Mission,* pt. II, p. 14.

12. *History, Manners, and Customs,* 199.

13. Memorandum, September 1743, 3/113/5/2 RMM.

14. Clarence E. Beckel, ed., *Marriage Records of the Bethlehem Moravian Congregation, 1742–1854,* vol. 2 (Bethlehem, PA: Bethlehem Public Library, 1936), 4.

15. *History of the Mission,* pt. II, p. 7; Shekomeko Diary, July 16, 1740, 1/111/1; "Gottlob Büttner's Trial" [Eng.], August 13, 1744, 2/112/3/5 RMM.

16. Martin features prominently in Jon Sensbach, *Rebecca's Revival: Creating Black Christianity in the Atlantic World* (Cambridge: Harvard University Press, 2005).

17. Shekomeko Diary, July 16, 1740, 1/111/1 RMM.

18. *History of the Mission,* pt. II, p. 8.

19. *History of the Mission,* pt. II, p. 65.

20. The warrior was Hendrich, who was baptized by the Moravians and given the name Michael. Shekomeko Diary, December 12, 1742, 1/111/1 RMM. Michael's tattoo is described in *History of the Mission,* pt. II, p. 189. The original can be found in the Bethlehem Diary, 1758, vol. 19, 60–64, MAB.

21. On the place of a serpent in the cosmology of Algonquian peoples, see Bragdon, *Native People of Southern New England,* 143, 188–89.

22. For a description of Tschoop's injury, see Pyrlaeus, Historical Account, 29/221/21, p. 7 RMM.

23. Shekomeko Diary, July 16, 1740, 1/111/1 RMM.

24. *History of the Mission,* pt. II, p. 14. There is a similar letter in the mission records. Johannes [Tschoop] to the Bethlehem Congregation, Shekomeko, January 5, 1744, 34/319/1/5 RMM.

25. *History of the Mission,* pt. II, pp. 7–12. Shekomeko Diary, July and August 1740, 1/111/1 RMM. Loskiel's account differs somewhat from that in the Shekomeko diary, which is in Gottlob Büttner's hand and was clearly written later, as under the September 1740 entry it states that Rauch lived with Rauh for two years.

26. Shekomeko Diary, August 1740, 1/111/1 RMM.

27. Rauch quoted in *History of the Mission,* pt. II, pp. 12–13.

28. Shekomeko Diary, August 1740, September 1740, June 1741, and January 1742, 1/111/1 RMM.

29. The Holy Spirit was understood as feminine by the Moravians. On Moravian theology, see Craig D. Atwood, *Community of the Cross: Moravian Piety in Colonial Bethlehem* (University Park: Pennsylvania State University Press, 2004), ch. 2; and Gary Steven Kinkel, *Our Dear Mother, the Spirit: An Investigation into Zinzendorf's Theology and Praxis* (Lanham, MD: University Press of America, 1990).

30. Moravian missiology held that the Holy Spirit must first prepare the hearts of sinners. Thus, Moravian missionaries tended to see themselves as the occasion and not the agent of native conversions.

31. Rauch to Zinzendorf, December 1741, 26/221/4/5 RMM. See also Shekomeko Diary, February 7, 1741, 1/111/1 RMM.

32. This letter was dictated by Tschoop and likely taken down by Gottlob Büttner. It is impossible to know the exact process by which this document came into existence or the extent to which it accurately reflected Tschoop's words. The original (item 1 in the same folder) is in very broken English, lending further weight to Tschoop's authorship. If the missionaries were trying to spin Tschoop's words, they would have written it in their native German. The second version (item 2) is in more standard English. In the interest of readability, all quotations are from the second version. Tschoop to Zinzendorf [Eng.], December 19, 1741, 34/319/1/2 RMM. Moravian missionaries commonly took down letters dictated by Mohicans and delivered them to friends and family at other mission locations. This became especially common once the first wave of Shekomekoans moved to Bethlehem in the spring of 1746.

33. Tschoop's letter to Zinzendorf [Eng.], December 19, 1741, 34/319/1/2 RMM; Johannes's letter to Bethlehem, January 5, 1744, 34/319/1/5 RMM.

34. Tschoop's letter to Zinzendorf [Eng.]. The prominence of Tschoop's mother-in-law would seem to be confirmed by a work of local history that claimed "the Indians at the foot of Indian Mountain were idolaters" and that "they had an Idol which they worshipped as God, and committed to the care of an old squaw." Dyer, the author, was relying on an early account by Cotton Mather Smith. Edward Dyer, *Gnadensee, The Lake of Grace* (Boston: Pilgrim Press, 1903), 20–21.

35. Craig Atwood, *Community of the Cross,* 37–38; and Peter Vogt, "Zinzendorf und die Pennsylvanischen Synoden 1742," *Unitas Fratrum* 36 (1994): 5–62. See also Jacob John Sessler, *Communal Pietism among Early American Moravians* (New York: Henry Holt and Company, 1933), ch. 2.

36. Quoted in Sessler, *Communal Pietism,* 40.

37. The description in the Shekomeko diary is cursory, as is that in the official record of the synods, published by Benjamin Franklin as *Zuverlässige Beschreibung der Dritten Conferenz der Evangelischen Religionen Teutscher Nation in Pennsylvania* (Philadelphia: B. Franklin, 1742). The following account is drawn largely from two documents, "An Acct of the baptism of our Br. Gottlieb and Maria, husband and Wife, the first Fruits of the Delaware Indians" [Eng.], April 15, 1745, 34/319/5/1 RMM; and "Relation of the Baptism of three Indian Girls" [Eng.], 34/319/5/4 RMM.

38. Atwood, *Community of the Cross,* 158–60. At the conclusion of a 1749 baptismal ceremony at Gnadenhütten, in Pennsylvania, to which many Shekomeko residents had relocated, the congregation sang:

> "o most beloved side Hole dear,
> Thou has much empty Space
> The foremost Row of Chambers there,

Have still some vacant Place;
Draw therefore 'till that dearest Hole
Is of brown hearts quite full, quite full
And all have found their safe Place there
Who thereto destin'd are."

"Extract from the Bethlehem Diary" [Eng.], June 4, 1749, 26/211/19/1 RMM.

39. "Acct of the baptism of our Br. Gottlieb and Maria."

40. "Relation of the Baptism." For another reference to exorcism, see Gottlob Büttner to Anton Seiffert, December 13, 1742, 1/111/7/8 RMM.

41. On shamans, see Bragdon, *Native People of Southern New England*, 203–4.

42. "Relation of the Baptism."

43. *Zuverlässige Beschreibung der Dritten Conferenz*, 47–48.

44. Shekomeko diary, February 11, April 16, 1742, 1/111/1 RMM. Sarah and Rebecca were baptized August 11, 1742, Rachel on December 12 of the same year. Shekomeko Diary, August 11, 1742, 1/111/1 RMM.

45. These events will be discussed in greater detail in chapter 10. They are also described in *History of the Mission*, pt. II, pp. 55–68.

46. Büttner to Seiffert, June 23, 1744, 2/112/2/3 RMM.

47. On Johannes' move to Bethlehem, see Shekomeko Diary, August 12, 1745, 34/111/1 RMM. On Johannes's death, see Beckel, ed., *Bethlehem Church Register*, vol. 1, p. 84 and Pyrlaeus, Historical Account, 29/221/21, p. 15 RMM. On Moravian theology regarding death, see Craig Atwood, "The Joyfulness of Death in Eighteenth-Century Moravian Communities," *Communal Societies* 17 (1997), 39–58.

48. On land as the reason for Abraham's reluctance to move, see David Bischoff's Diary, Shekomeko, May 30, 1746, 3/113/1 RMM.

49. See especially Shekomeko Diary, June 16, 25, 1745, and June 24, 25, 1746, 1/111/1 RMM.

50. Abraham and his family arrived on April 22, 1747; Isaac was born on May 6 and baptized two days later. Gnadenhütten Diary, April 22, May 6, 8, 1747, 4/116/1 RMM.

51. Gnadenhütten Diary, January 12, 1752, 5/117/3 RMM.

52. For a summary of these events, see *History of the Mission*, pt. II, p. 151. See also, Jane Merritt, *At the Crossroads: Indians and Empires on a Mid-Atlantic Frontier, 1700–1763* (Chapel Hill: University of North Carolina Press, 2003), 157–59. For a discussion of the duties of a captain, see *Zeisberger's History*, 100–101. The Iroquois had been seeking for some time to settle allied Indians in this area. In 1745, Abraham had decided not to move to Wyoming out of fears that it lay on the war path of the Flat-heads (Catawbas) and that the Indians there lived immoral lives. For Abraham's view of the move, see Shekomeko diary entries dated, May 30, June 1, and June 16, 1745, 1/111/1 RMM. Abraham felt he must go, although he feared the conditions there would not be conducive to a Christian community. Gnadenhütten Diary, March 2, 1754 5/118/1 RMM. On Abraham's new status, see notes from a conference between the Delaware and Mohicans, April 5, 1753 6/119/1/9 RMM.

53. Nain Diary, December 2, 1762, 7/125/3 RMM.

54. Meniolagomekah Diary, June 13, 1763, 6/124/4 RMM.

55. James Sullivan et al., eds., *The Papers of Sir William Johnson* (Albany: SUNY Press, 1921–1965), vol. 10, p. 853.

CHAPTER 5. MORAVIAN MISSIONARIES OF THE BLOOD

1. *History of the Mission*, pt. II, p. 14.

2. In this version, Tschoop's account of his meeting with Rauch is identified as part of a letter he addressed to a Delaware Indian audience. Rufus Rockwell Wilson, *Rambles in Colonial Byways*, vol. 2 (Philadelphia: J. B. Lippincott Co., 1906), 148–49.

3. *History of the Mission,* pt. II, p. 14.

4. Peter C. Mancall, *Deadly Medicine: Indians and Alcohol in Early America* (Ithaca, NY: Cornell University Press, 1995).

5. Michael D. McNally, *Ojibwe Hymn Singers: Hymns, Grief, and a Native Culture in Motion* (New York: Oxford University Press, 1999), 13–15.

6. Quoted in Paul A. W. Wallace, *Conrad Weiser: Friend of Colonist and Mohawk* (1945; repr. Lewisberg, PA: Wennawood Publishing, 1996), 144. On the community at Shamokin, see James Merrell, "Shamokin, 'The Very Seat of the Prince of Darkness': Unsettling the Early American Frontier," in *Contact Points: American Frontiers from the Mohawk Valley to the Mississippi, 1750–1830,* ed. Andrew R. L. Cayton and Fredrika J. Teute (Chapel Hill: University of North Carolina Press, 1998), 16–59.

7. See, for example, the comments recorded by Lutheran leader Henry Muhlenberg. *The Journals of Henry Melchior Muhlenberg,* trans. Theodore G. Tappert and John W. Doberstein (Philadelphia: Evangelical Lutheran Ministerium of Pennsylvania and Adjacent States, 1942–58), vol. 1, p. 168.

8. All of these comments formed part of Brainerd's report sent from Crossweeksung in 1744 to the offices of the Scottish Society. David Brainerd, *Mirabilia Dei Inter Indicos* (Philadelphia: William Bradford, n.d.), 208–15.

9. *History of the Mission,* pt. II, pp. 12–13.

10. *Memorials of the Moravian Church,* 65.

11. The literature on the Moravians and their mission program is rapidly growing. Church histories include J. E. Hutton, *History of the Moravian Church* (London: Moravian Publication Office, 1909); and J. Taylor Hamilton and Kenneth G. Hamilton, *History of the Moravian Church: The Renewed Unitas Fratrum* (Bethlehem: Moravian Church in America, 1967). General studies include Jacob John Sessler, *Communal Pietism among Early American Moravians* (New York: Henry Holt and Company, 1933); Gillian Lindt Gollin, *Moravians in Two Worlds: A Study of Changing Communities* (New York: Columbia University Press, 1967); Beverly Prior Smaby, *The Transformation of Moravian Bethlehem from Mission to Family Economy* (Philadelphia: University of Pennsylvania Press, 1988); and Craig D. Atwood, *Community of the Cross: Moravian Piety in Communal Bethlehem* (University Park: Pennsylvania State University Press, 2003). Histories of the Moravian mission program among the Indians of North America include Loskiel, *History of the Mission;* John Heckewelder, *A Narrative of the Mission of the United Brethren among the Delaware and Mohegan Indians, from its Commencement, in the Year 1740, to the Close of the Year 1808* (Philadelphia: McCarty and Davis, 1820); *History, Manners, and Customs;* and Hermann Wellenreuther and Carola Wessel, eds., *The Moravian Mission Diaries of David Zeisberger, 1772–1781,* trans. Julie Tomberlin Weber (University Park: Pennsylvania State University Press, 2005). Recent scholarship on Moravian mission work includes Stefan Hertrampf, *"Unsere Indianer-Geschwister waren lichte und vergnügt": Die Herrnhuter als Missionare bei den Indianern Pennsylvanias, 1745–1765* (Frankfurt am Main: Lang, 1997); Carola Wessel, *Delaware-Indianer und Herrnhuter Missionare im Upper Ohio Valley* (Tübingen, 1999); and Jane T. Merritt, *At the Crossroads: Indians and Empires on a Mid-Atlantic Frontier, 1700–1763* (Chapel Hill: University of North Carolina Press, 2003). Amy C. Schutt's recent book promises to make an important contribution to the field, but it was published too late to incorporate its insights into the present work. Schutt, *Peoples of the River Valleys: The Odyssey of the Delaware Indians* (Philadelphia: University of Pennsylvania Press, 2007).

12. W. R. Ward, *The Protestant Evangelical Awakening* (Cambridge: Cambridge University Press, 1992). The literature on the era of revivalism is vast. Among the most important works are Jon Butler, "Enthusiasm Described and Decried: The Great Awakening as Interpretive Fiction," *Journal of American History* 69 (1982): 305–25; and Harry S. Stout, "Religion, Communications, and the Ideological Origins of the American Revolution," *WMQ* 35 (1977): 519–41. A recent reconsideration of the era of revivalism is Mark R. Noll, *The Rise of Evangelicalism: The Age of Edwards, Whitefield, and the Wesleys* (Downers Grove, IL: Intervarsity Press, 2004). The following account is drawn from Hamilton and Hamilton, *History of the Moravian Church,* pt. 1;

Smaby, *Transformation of Moravian Bethlehem,* ch. 1; Sessler, *Communal Pietism,* ch. 1; and John R. Weinlick, *Count Zinzendorf: The Story of His Life and Leadership in the Renewed Moravian Church* (1956; repr. Bethlehem: Moravian Church in America, 2001), 16–101.

13. There is substantial debate over the true extent of the continuity between the fifteenth-century followers of the martyr Jan Hus and the community of Herrnhut that formed on Zinzendorf's Saxony estate in the 1720s.

14. Gollin, *Moravians in Two Worlds,* 4; and Ward, *Protestant Evangelical Awakening,* 120, 126.

15. Hamilton and Hamilton, *History of the Moravian Church,* 41; and Ward, *Protestant Evangelical Awakening,* 129.

16. For an early internal history of the missions, see George Neisser, *A History of the Beginnings of Moravian Work in America,* trans. William N. Schwarze and Samuel N. Gapp (Bethlehem, PA: Archives of the Moravian Church, 1955). On the Moravian missions among African slaves, see Jon Sensbach, *A Separate Canaan: The Making of an Afro-Moravian World in North Carolina, 1763–1840* (Chapel Hill: University of North Carolina Press, 1998) and *Rebecca's Revival: Creating Black Christianity in the Caribbean World* (Cambridge: Harvard University Press, 2005). For an early history of the Greenland mission, see David Crantz, *History of Greenland Including a Description of the Country and its Inhabitants* (London: Brethren's Society for the Furtherance of the Gospel among the Heathen, 1767).

17. Augustus Gottlieb Spangenberg, *An Account of the Manner in which the Protestant Church of the Unitas Fratrum, or United Brethren, Preach the Gospel, and Carry on their Missions among the Heathen* (London: H. Trapp, 1788), 60, 61, 64.

18. For a survey of early Moravian mission work in North America, see Wellenreuther and Wessel, eds., *Moravian Mission Diaries of David Zeisberger,* 51–71. Aaron Fogelman has challenged the traditional interpretation of the failure of the mission in Georgia, which in Moravian historiography is generally attributed to conflict with other colonists over the Moravians' refusal to take up arms against the Spanish. Fogelman attributes the dissolution of the community to internal conflict. Gottlob Büttner's diary suggests that Moravians did meet with at least some hostility for their pacifism. His diary tells of being questioned by a deckhand on a boat as he was sailing to New York whether he would fight against the Spanish. Büttner answered that he would not, because it was against his religious principles, to which the man answered, "There are no principles on a ship." Büttner responded, "We have them, and the Bible is our rule on a ship as well as on land." The ship's mate retorted, ending the conversation: "The Bible was his rule too, but he would as easily kill all the Spaniards as eat peas." Büttner's diary, September 29, 1741, 26/211/5/1 RMM. Aaron S. Fogelman, "The Decline and Fall of the Moravian Community in Colonial Georgia: Revisiting the Traditional View," *Unitas Fratrum* 48 (2001): 1–22. See also Weinlick, *Count Zinzendorf,* 93–101.

19. *History of the Mission,* pt. II, pp. 7–8.

20. On the founding of Bethlehem, see J. Mortimer Levering, *A History of Bethlehem, Pennsylvania, 1741–1892* (Bethlehem, PA: Times Publishing Company, 1903), 59–79; and Atwood, *Community of the Cross,* 115–39.

21. For discussions of the economy at Bethlehem, see especially Katherine Carté Engel, *Pilgrims and Profits: The Interplay between Religion and Economic Life in the Eighteenth-Century Mid-Atlantic* (Philadelphia: University of Pennsylvania Press, forthcoming), Gollin, *Moravians in Two Worlds,* 138–47; and Atwood, *Community of the Cross,* 118–26.

22. An early expression of Zinzendorf's mission theology is found in his instructions to missionaries sent to Russia, in 1736. Zinzendorf, "Instruktion für die zu den Samojeden gesandten Brüder," in *Texte zur Mission,* edited and with an introduction by Helmut Bintz (Hamburg: Friedrich Wittig Verlag, 1979), 39–42.

23. John Webster Grant has argued that when missionaries wielded substantial secular power, then they were able to demand more in terms of cultural change, leaving little room for the indigenization of Christianity. John Webster Grant, *Moon of Wintertime: Missionaries and the Indians of Canada in Encounter since 1534* (Toronto: University of Toronto Press, 1984), ch. 11.

24. Zinzendorf, in *Memorials of the Moravian Church*, 116, 117. In his tract *Christenings Make Not Christians*, Williams wrote, "I know it to have been easier for my selfe, long ere this to have brought many thousands of these Natives, yea the whole country, to a far greater Anti-Christian conversion then ever was yet heard of in *America*." He renounced the task however, crying, "Woe be to me, if I call light darknesse or darkness light…woe be to me if I call that conversion unto God, which is indeed subversion of the soules of Millions in *Christendome*, from one false worship to another." Williams, "Christenings Make Not Christians," in *The Complete Writings of Roger Williams* (New York: Russell and Russell), vol. 7, pp. 36, 37.

25. Zinzendorf, quoted in *Memorials of the Moravian Church*, 124.

26. Spangenberg, *An Account*, 50–51. When Christian Rauch recalled his travels in Mohawk country in 1743, he noted that his purpose was to "make known to them the Slaughter'd Lamb, or at least to learn their language." "Brother Rauch's Journal," n.d., 29/221/4/1 RMM.

27. Reichel identifies this trip as having taken place in 1743, but it was in fact 1742. Zinzendorf went on to explain that the time had not yet come because the Jews were yet to be converted: "For it is believed in our Church that the Conversion of the Jews, and of all Israel must needs go before, ere the proper Conversion of the Heathen can go forward." Zinzendorf, in *Memorials of the Moravian Church*, 64, 116.

28. Quoted in Wellenreuther and Wessel, ed., *Moravian Mission Diaries of David Zeisberger*, 52.

29. Vernon Nelson et al., eds., *The Bethlehem Diary, Volume II, 1744–1745*, trans. Kenneth G. Hamilton and Lothar Madeheim (Bethlehem: Moravian Archives, 2001), March 7, 1745, p. 239.

30. Spangenberg, *An Account*, 50–51.

31. Pachgatgoch (Scaticook), near present-day Kent, Connecticut, was headed by Gideon Mawehu, who was identified by the Moravians as being *Wampano*, a term simply meaning "easterner" in Algonquian languages. Most likely, the community was a refugee community of Pequots. The Moravian records identify Mawehu as a cousin of Umpachenee, one of the Housatonic Mohican founders of the Stockbridge community. The Pachgatgoch community was closely tied with the Indian community at Derby, Connecticut. On the history of the Pachgatgoch Indians, now known as the Schaghticokes, see Paulette Crone-Morange and Lucianne Lavin, "The Schaghticoke Tribe and English Law: A Study in Community Survival," *Connecticut History* 43 (Fall 2004): 132–62. Potatik (or Potatuck) was a village near Woodbury, Connecticut.

32. Martin Mack diary [Eng.], January 29, 1743, 1/111/3/3 RMM.

33. Martin Mack diary [Eng.], February 4, 5, and 6, 1743, 1/111/3/3 RMM. The Moravian missionaries' willingness to lodge with the Indians raised suspicions among their English neighbors, as Mack reported on a visit to New England. He reported of the curious English settlers who came to investigate: "They were amaz'd and asked me why I would not lodge in their Houses, but rather among the Indians. I answer'd I am not sent to you but to them." "Mack's Journey to New England" [Eng.], March 4, 1743, 1/111/3/4.

34. "A Short Account of Br. John Martin Mack & Christian Froelick's Journey to Wayomick & Hallobank" [Eng.], April 1745, 217/12/3 RMM.

35. *History of the Mission*, pt. II, p. 37. For a references to the missionaries helping villagers with agricultural work, see Shekomeko Diary, September 7, 1743, 1/111/1 RMM; and Rauch Diary, [Eng.], April 18, 1744, 2/112/19/3 RMM. On one occasion Gottlob Büttner reported that when he was unsuccessful at hunting, he turned to studying the Mohican language instead. Büttner Diary, November 19, 1742, 2/112/5/3 RMM.

36. During the particularly harsh winter of 1744, missionary Joachim Sensemann reported that nearly all the Indian brethren and sisters were abroad, working for wages among whites. In his report, he listed all of the supplies needed from Bethlehem, including coffee, sugar, a new grindstone, quills, garden seeds, books, a summer cap, and leather for mending shoes. Sensemann to Büttner, February 21, 1744, 30/223/3/2 RMM.

37. On the economic arrangements of Bethlehem in the early decades, particularly the regulation of property, the religious meaning of work, and the division of labor, see Engel, *Pilgrims and Profits*, ch. 1; and Gollin, *Moravians in Two Worlds*, 138–47, 156–68.

38. Shekomeko Diary, January 1, 1742, August 17, September 4, 1742, January 14, February 13, April 30, 1743, 1/111/1 RMM; and Loskiel, *History*, pt. II, p. 37. Pyrlaeus married Susanna Benezet June 29/July 10, 1742. Mack and Büttner were married on the same day, September 3/14, 1742. Büttner married Margaretha Bechtel. Shaw married Maria Jones of Philadelphia March 27/April 7, 1743. Sensemann was already married when he joined the Shekomeko community. Shekomeko Diary, January 14, 1743, 1/111/1 RMM. Clarence E. Beckel, ed., *Marriage Records of the Bethlehem Moravian Congregation* (Bethlehem, PA: Bethlehem Public Library, 1936), vol. I, pp. 1–6. Beckel provides old and new style dates, following Julian and Gregorian calendars. Britain did not adopt the new style until 1752.

39. Shekomeko Diary, August 8, 24, 1743, 1/111/1 RMM. For a discussion of Post's marriage prospects, see Büttner Diary, February 21, 1743, 1/111/2/1 RMM. Rachel's story will be featured in chapter 7 below.

40. By 1759, Gollin observes, missionaries constituted the single largest occupation, employing 36 percent of the male labor force. Missionary wives and children were also removed from the income-generating labor force, meaning that the entire community at Bethlehem depended for its survival on the labor of a third of the entire population. Gollin, *Moravians in Two Worlds*, 159–60. Of the core missionaries serving at Shekomeko, only Pyrlaeus had received a university education. The Moravians' lack of education became a point of contention with their English neighbors. When several of the missionaries were arrested in New York in 1744, the examining magistrate pronounced: "It is a fine thing when such Men as you pretends to Teach the Indians, the one is a Carpenter, the other a Baker and the other a wool weaver. Fine People to Preach." (Punctuation added for clarity.) Shaw to Seiffert and Böhler [Eng.], August 11, 1744, 2/112/4/2 RMM.

41. The records of the White Workers' Conference contain a wealth of information about the daily lives of the missionaries. White Workers' Conferences from 1742–1744, 1/111/6/2 and 1/111/6/3 RMM.

42. "Extract from the Instructions or Rules for such of the United Brethren as are used as Missionaries or Assistants in propagating the Gospel among the Indians," 34/315/3/7 RMM.

43. Gottlob Büttner to Anton Seiffert [Eng.], October 1742, 26/211/5/5 RMM.

44. "A Short Acct of Br. Martin Macks Journey to Checomeco" [Eng.], November 1745, 28/217/12b/2 RMM. For further examples, see a letter from an unidentified Brother Petrus, probably Peter Böhler, to his "Brethren at Skatticock," September 1755, 4/115/5/14; and Shekomeko Diary, November 2, 1745, 1/111/1 RMM. See also Nathanael Seidel's greeting to the residents of Gnadenhütten, October 4, 1751, 5/117/2 RMM.

45. Johannes Hagen to Indian Christians, October 7, 1742, 26/211/17/1 RMM. See also Shekomeko Diary, May 22, 1745, 1/111/1 RMM.

46. Spangenberg Diary, November 6, 1744, 30/223/6/1 RMM. Pyrlaeus also compared Johannes to Luther in his history of the mission. Pyrlaeus, "Historical Account of the Indian Mission Work, 1739–1751," 26/221/21, p. 15 RMM.

47. Shekomeko Diary, November 25, 1742, 1/111/1 RMM.

48. "A Short Account" [Eng.], August 23, 1746, 34/319/5/3 RMM. Jonas was a cousin of Jonathan (Abraham's son) and the brother of a Stockbridge resident. Büttner to Spangenberg, December 19, 1744, Shekomeko, 26/211/5/7 RMM.

49. Shekomeko Diary, October 18, 1744, 1/111/1 RMM.

50. Shekomeko Diary, March 5, 1745, 1/111/1 RMM.

51. Martin Mack diary [Eng.], entries dated February 4, 5, and 6, 1743, 1/111/3/3 RMM. Mack was in Shamokin at the time visiting with Andrew Montour and scouting possibilities of a future mission. Mack's diary entry dated September 13, 1745, 28/217/12b/1 RMM.

52. Shekomeko Diary, May 22, 1745, 1/111/1 RMM.

53. Büttner to Spangenberg, [Eng.], December 19, 1744, Shekomeko, 26/211/5/7 RMM. The original in German can be found in 2/112/6/11 RMM. The son killed his cousin while under the influence of alcohol. After this incident, Martha was pressed by the missionaries

to choose whether she would "follow the murderer or the Brethren." Conference, March 17, 1745, 2/112/15/1 #11 RMM.

54. It should be noted, however, that these conferences were composed of an equal number of missionaries and native leaders. Cornelius was chosen by the Shekomeko community as overseer of external affairs on January 25, 1743. He was appointed judge April 11, 1743, and requested to be released from the office June 28, 1743. He registered his complaints about the deceased Ruth's children on April 26, 1745. Shekomeko Diary, 1/111/1 RMM.

55. Indian Workers Conference, January 1, 1745, 2/112/5/3 RMM.

56. Zinzendorf, quoted in *Memorials of the Moravian Church,* 54.

57. Weiser reported on his trip with Zinzendorf to Shamokin, where the Count bungled his efforts to inaugurate a mission. Of the Count, Weiser wrote, "He is hotheaded and likes to give orders, the Indians on the other hand won't take orders in the least and consider a dictator nonsensical." Weiser had tried to tell "the Count that it would have been more fitting if he had made himself agreeable to the Indians and lodged with them, put up his tent by their Huts: I defended the Indians as well as I could and blamed him severely. But he flew into a rage, flung at me that I was a traitor and had deserted him in this savage place and as good as betrayed him. But his blood soon cooled again." Wallace, *Conrad Weiser,* 136, 141.

58. Mark Noll provides an overview of the revival era in Noll, *Rise of Evangelicalism,* 50–135.

59. Two of the best works on Whitefield are Harry S. Stout, *The Divine Dramatist: George Whitefield and the Rise of Modern Evangelicalism* (Grand Rapids, MI: Eerdmans, 1991); and Frank Lambert, *"Pedlar in Divinity": George Whitefield and the Transatlantic Revivals, 1737–1770* (Princeton: Princeton University Press, 2002). For a table of Whitefield's American preaching tours, see Lambert, *Inventing the "Great Awakening"* (Princeton: Princeton University Press, 1999), 117.

60. Edwards, *Life of Brainerd, Works,* vol. 7, p.176. The Shekomeko diary reports that visitors from Pachgatgoch arrived in Shekomeko in October 1742, together with a contingent from Stockbridge including about twenty Indians and their minister, John Sergeant. Shekomeko Diary, October 5, 6, 1742, 1/111/1 RMM. Mack's account of his first visit to Pachgatgoch and other villages can be found in Martin Mack Journal, January 26–February 18, 1743, 1/111/3/3 RMM.

61. *History of the Mission,* pt. II, p. 45.

62. *History of the Mission,* pt. II, p. 54.

63. Tatemy served as interpreter for David Brainerd and maintained occasional ties with the Moravians. Brainerd, *Mirabilia Dei Inter Indicos,* 10–14.

64. See especially Gregory Evans Dowd, *A Spirited Resistance: The North American Indian Struggle for Unity, 1745–1815* (Baltimore: Johns Hopkins University Press, 1992).

65. This idea of the familiarity and difference of the missionary message is drawn from Grant, *Moon of Wintertime,* ch. 11.

66. It was this attempt, Max Weber famously argued, that had the opposite effect of desacralizing time and work instead. Weber, *The Protestant Ethic and the Spirit of Capitalism* (1903).

67. This account of Moravian piety is drawn from Atwood, *Community of the Cross,* 77–112.

68. For a discussion of the Moravian use of the lot, see Elizabeth Sommer, "Gambling with God: The Use of the Lot by the Moravian Brethren in the Eighteenth Century," *Journal of the History of Ideas* 59 (1998): 267–86.

69. *The Journals of Henry Melchoir Muhlenberg,* trans. Theodore G. Tappert and John W. Doberstein (Philadelphia: Muhlenberg Press, 1942), vol. 1, p. 154.

70. Atwood, *Community of the Cross,* 99; and Atwood, ed., *Zinzendorf's Pennsylvania Journey,* 56–57, 82–83.

71. "Martin Mack's Journal of his Journey to Shomoko," October 11, 1745, 217/12b/1 RMM. Another example can be found in the Shekomeko Diary, December 25, 1745, 1/111/1 RMM.

72. It is impossible to construct a thorough portrait of Mohican religion on the eve of the mission era. Such concepts as *manitou*, however, appear to have been universal throughout northeastern Indian societies. On the cosmology of the Ninnimissinouk neighbors of the Mahicans, see Kathleen J. Bragdon, *Native People of Southern New England, 1500–1650* (Norman: University of Oklahoma Press, 1996), 184–99.

73. Aupaumut's account of ancient Mohican ways likely shows the influence of a Christian worldview, but it is instructive in demonstrating that Christianity was not perceived as a radical break from tradition. Aupaumut, in Electa F. Jones, *Stockbridge, Past and Present: Or, Records of an Old Mission Station* (Springfield, MA: Samuel Bowles and Company, 1854), 18.

74. Shekomeko Diary, April 17, 1746, 1/111/1 RMM.

75. *Historical Memoirs,* 11.

76. The additional conjectural details of bear hunting ritual are derived from Robert A. Brightman, *Grateful Prey: Rock Cree Human-Animal Relationships* (Berkeley: University of California Press, 1993), chs. 3 and 4.

77. Bragdon, *Native People of Southern New England,* 186

78. *History, Manners, and Customs,* 212.

79. Brainerd, *Mirabilia Dei Inter Indicos,* 213–14

80. Hostility toward Moravian missionaries from other colonists will be discussed at greater length in chapter 10.

81. The "Sifting Time" has traditionally been understood as a period of spiritual excess in the 1740s from which the Moravian Church later attempted to distance itself. Atwood argues that it was neither the aberration nor the watershed that has been claimed but rather that this interpretation served an important apologetic function by trying to bring the Moravian Church within the mainstream of Protestantism. Atwood, *Community of the Cross,* 11–19. 102, 147. On the Sifting Time, see also Paul Peucker, " 'Blut auf unsre Grünen Bändchen': Die Sichtungszeit in der Herrnhuter Brüdergemeine," *Unitas Fratrum* 49–50 (2002): 41–94.

82. Shekomeko Diary, March 13, 1743, 1/111/1 RMM.

83. Atwood, *Community of the Cross,* 148–52, 203–8.

84. All quotations from the Litany of the Wounds are from Craig Atwood's translation in *Community of the Cross,* 233–338.

85. Gnadenhütten Diary, February 26, 1748, 116/3/1 RMM.

86. Atwood, *Community of the Cross,* 173–200.

87. Nikolaus Ludwig Zinzendorf, *Sixteen Discourses on Jesus Christ our Lord. Being an Exposition of the Second Part of the Creed. Preached at Berlin, by the right Reverend, Lewis, Bishop of the Ancient Brethren's Churches. Translated from the High Dutch* (London: J. Beecroft, 1751), 4.

88. Joseph Bellamy to Mr. David Brainerd, March 7, 1743, Letters to Joseph Bellamy from Aaron Burr, David Brainerd, etc, and other papers concerning Mr. Bellamy, 1739–1787 [Microform], Collections of the Presbyterian Historical Society, Philadelphia, Pennsylvania.

89. See for example, Gilbert Tennent, *Some Account of the Principles of the Moravians* (London, 1743), 19, 35, 36. These controversies will be discussed more fully in chapter 10.

90. For a discussion of Moravian mysticism, see F. Ernest Stoeffler, *Mysticism in the German Devotional Literature of Colonial Pennsylvania* (Allentown: The Pennsylvania German Folklore Society, 1950), especially ch. 4, "Mysticism among the Moravians."

91. For instance, "The Delaware would not eat rabbits or ground hogs, nor kill rattlesnakes, for fear that they might be related to them. The rattlesnake they acknowledged as grandfather and observed a prohibition on killing them. If the sanction was violated its relatives would soon find out and organize an uprising against humans. Further, they acknowledged fire to be the father of all the Indian tribes." *History, Manners, and Customs,* 211–12, 251–54. *History of the Mission,* pt. II, pp. 40, 42; Bragdon, *Native People of Southern New England,* 190–91; and Charles C. Trowbridge, "Account of Some of the History, Manners and Customs of the Lenee Lenaupaa or Delaware Indians," appendix to C. A. Weslager, *The Delaware Indians: A History* (New Brunswick, NJ: Rutgers University Press, 1972), 473–500.

92. "Journal of Christian Henry Rauch's Journey to the Mohawks, January and February 1743" [Eng.], 130c/1, MAB.

93. Christian Rauch, journal entry dated March 23, 1744, 2/112/19/3 RMM.

94. As suggested above, this may not have been purely idealism but rather a reflection of the Moravians' lack of any power of compulsion over the Indians.

95. Mack to Brother Antony in Bethlehem [Eng.], January 30, 1743, 1/111/3/3 RMM.

96. Johannes to "Meine Liebe Brüder und Schwester," 34/319/1/13 RMM.

97. Gnadenhütten Diary, January 13, 1751, 5/117/2/1 RMM.

98. Martin Mack diary [Eng.], January 30, February 5, 1743, 1/111/3/3 RMM.

99. Martin Mack diary [Eng.], February 8, 1743, 1/111/3/3 RMM.

100. Büttner diary, June 6, 1743, 1/111/2/4 RMM.

101. *History of the Mission*, pt. II, p. 50. The original can be found in the records of the White Workers Conference, August 12, 1743, 1/111/6/3 RMM. The minister in question, whom Loskiel wrongly identifies as Anglican, was the Congregational minister of New Milford, Daniel Boardman.

102. "Zeugniße von den braunen Geschwistern in Gnadenhütten," April 9, 1753, 34/319/4/1 RMM. On singing to spirit helpers among contemporary Cree hunters, see Brightman, *Grateful Prey*, 104–6.

103. Gnadenhütten Diary, July 1, 1748, 4/116/3/1 RMM.

104. Gnadenhütten Diary, April 24, 1748, 4/116/3/1 RMM.

105. The classic work on dreams in Native American cultures is Anthony F. C. Wallace, "Dreams and the Wishes of the Soul: A Type of Psychoanalytic Theory among the Seventeenth-Century Iroquois," *American Anthropologist* 60 (1958): 234–48. See also Jane T. Merritt, "Dreaming of the Savior's Blood: Moravians and the Indian Great Awakening in Pennsylvania," *WMQ* 54 (October 1997): 723–46. On dreams and visions in colonial America, see Carla Gerona, "Imagining Peace in Quaker and Native American Dream Stories," in *Friends and Enemies in Penn's Woods: Indians, Colonists, and the Racial Construction of Pennsylvania*, ed. William A. Pencak and Daniel K. Richter (University Park: Pennsylvania State University Press, 2004), 62; and Mechal Sobel, "The Revolution in Selves: Black and White Inner Aliens," in *Through a Glass Darkly: Reflections on Personal Identity in Early America*, ed. Ronald Hoffman, Mechal Sobel, and Fredrika J. Teute (Chapel Hill: University of North Carolina Press, 1997), 163–205.

106. "A short account," 34/319/5/3 RMM.

107. Gnadenhütten Diary, December 27, 1747, 4/116/4; and January 6, 1748, 4/116/3/1 RMM.

108. Gottlob Büttner [Eng.], August 18, 1743, 1/111/2/7 RMM; and Büttner Diary, August 18, 1743, 26/211/5/1 RMM.

109. Gnadenhütten Diary, January 1, 1748, 4/116/3/1 RMM.

Chapter 6. Mohican Men and Jesus as *Manitou*

1. Johannes to the Bethlehem Brethren, 34/319/1/13 RMM.

2. *History of the Mission*, pt. II, p. 77.

3. Daniel Richter discusses the meaning of this practice extensively in *The Ordeal of the Longhouse: The Peoples of the Iroquois League in the Era of European Colonization* (Chapel Hill: University of North Carolina Press, 1992), 33–36, 66–71 and "War and Culture: The Iroquois Experience," *WMQ* 40 (1983): 528–59. John Steckley has written provocatively and persuasively about the ways in which Jesuit missionaries used Iroquois and Huron torture practices as a basis for conveying Christian themes. Steckley, "The Warrior and the Lineage: Jesuit Use of Iroquoian Images to Communicate Christianity," *Ethnohistory* 39 (1992): 478–509, on stoic suffering, 491–94.

4. Johannes reported to the missionaries that Abraham was opposed to the proposed move to Wyoming, on the west branch of the Susquehanna, because it lay on a major thoroughfare between warring Iroquois and Catawba ("Flathead") peoples and he did not want

his people to be caught up in the hostilities. Shekomeko Diary, May 30, 1745, 1/111/1 RMM.

5. In Moravian missionary David Zeisberger's description of this practice, a man from the family that had lost a member presented a belt of wampum to the captain of the village, signifying that the captain should organize a raid to secure captives. When the captain was successful, he would place the belt of wampum around the captive's neck, which meant the captive would be adopted into a family. Upon his successful return, the captain was given the belt in payment. Given the association of women with the production of wampum, it seems likely either that Zeisberger mistakenly believed that a man had the responsibility for ordering a raid or that by the eighteenth century, practices had changed such that it had become the province of men and that the ritual retained elements that suggested it had once been under women's direction. *Zeisberger's History*, 101–8.

6. *The Jesuit Relations* contain a number of references to Mohicans being tortured and killed by Iroquois. See, for example, Rueben Gold Thwaites, *The Jesuit Relations and Allied Documents: Travels and Explorations of the Jesuit Missionaries in New France, 1610–1791* (Cleveland: Burrows Bros. Co., 1896–1901), vol. 53, pp. 137, 149, 159, which includes documents from 1669–1670 from lower Iroquoia. For a lengthy description of one such instance of torture, see vol. 52, pp. 251–67.

7. *Description of the New Netherlands*, 99–101; *History, Manners, and Customs*, 217–19; and *Zeisberger's History*, 102–8.

8. For a review of the question of anthrophagy among the Iroquois, see Richter, *Ordeal of the Longhouse*, 303–4n11, n12.

9. Shekomeko Diary, October 2, 1743, 1/111/1 RMM.

10. Christian Rauch, April 7, 1744, 2/112/1/3 RMM. An English version can be found under the same date at 2/112/19/3 RMM.

11. Gnadenhütten Diary, July 7, 1753, 5/117/4 RMM.

12. Gnadenhütten Diary, February 9, 1748, 4/116/3/1 RMM.

13. *Description of the New Netherlands*, 64.

14. Van der Donck may well have translated any Mohican reference to spirit as "devil." *Description of the New Netherlands*, 96, 97, 102.

15. *Zeisberger's History*, 83–84. Although the larger thesis of his book is problematic, Calvin Martin's discussion of the nature of the relationship between Algonquian Indian hunters and their game is especially helpful. Martin, *Keepers of the Game: Indian-Animal Relationships and the Fur Trade* (Berkeley: University of California Press, 1978), 33–39. His account of the reasons behind overhunting in the fur trade era has been widely criticized. See especially Shepherd Krech, ed., *Indians, Animals, and the Fur Trade: A Critique of Keepers of the Game* (Athens: University of Georgia Press, 1986).

16. The mission diary from Pachgatgoch recorded that the men were preparing to go on a hunt and were meeting in the sweat lodge, preventing the missionary from holding services. The diarist added no additional commentary—no lament about the continuation of primitive ways. If they had found such practices abhorrent or anti-Christian in some way, there likely would be some evidence of efforts to stamp them out. Pachgatgoch diary, November 25, 1750, 3/114/2 RMM.

17. Shekomeko Diary, December 14, 1745, 1/111/1 RMM.

18. Jonathan made these remarks one month after his baptism. Shekomeko Diary, November 9, 1742, 1/111/1 RMM. See also entry for November 14, 1742. A longer description of this exchange can be found in Gottlob Büttner to Anton Seiffert, January 28, 1748, 1/111/7/6 RMM.

19. Büttner's Diary, February 26, 1743, 1/111/1/#3b RMM. Several examples suggest the attribution of success to Jesus continued in the 1750s. Gnadenhütten Diary, October 26, 1750, 5/117/1 RMM. In 1752, Joshua believed the twenty deer and two bears captured by his hunting party had been sent by Jesus. Pachgatgoch Diary, December 6, 1752, 3/114/7 RMM.

20. *Zeisberger's History*, 84.

21. See especially Gregory Evans Dowd, *A Spirited Resistance: The North American Indian Struggle for Unity, 1745–1815* (Baltimore: Johns Hopkins University Press, 1992), 9–16; and William S. Simmons, *Spirit of the New England Tribes: Indian History and Folklore* (Hanover, NH: University Press of New England, 1986), 59–60.

22. *History, Manners, and Customs,* 211.

23. Hymn #20, "Probe einem Gesang-Bücher," 35/331/3 RMM.

24. This form of communication might have added to the Mohicans' esteem for the Moravians' spiritual power. Loskiel noted that when some Indians witnessed as someone read from a book or paper, "some imagine that a spirit speaks secretly to the reader, dictating whatever he wishes to know. Others think that the paper, when written upon, can speak to the reader, but so as to be heard by no one else." *History of the Mission,* pt. I, p. 23. More generally, see James Axtell, "The Power of Print in the Eastern Woodlands," *WMQ* 44 (April 1987): 300–309. The mission diaries contain frequent references to letters being carried from one community to another and being read aloud to the recipients. Many of these dictated messages survive in the mission records. The largest collection is in 35/319 RMM. Two mentions of the process of dictating the letters can be found in Mack's Diary, [Eng.], February 25, 1744, 2/112/1/2 RMM; and Shekomeko Diary, July 24, 1746, 1/111/1 RMM.

25. "Letters from a Couple of Brethren in Shekomeko" [Eng.], March 31, 1746, 34/319/2/4 RMM; "Christian Indians in Bethlehem to Shekomeko and Pachgatgoch" [Eng.], June 1, 2, 1746, 34/319/2/8 RMM (the original German can be found at 34/319/2/7 RMM); Gnadenhütten Diary, February 9, 1748, 4/116/3/1 RMM.

26. "Gnadenhütten Christian Indians" [Eng.], May 21, 1746, 34/319/2/6 RMM. The German can be found at 34/319/2/3 RMM.

27. Little is known about Mohican healing practices. For discussions of neighboring Delaware medicine, see C. A. Weslager, *Magic Medicines of the Indians* (Somerset, NJ: Middle Atlantic Press, 1973). The literature on the impact of disease on Native Americans is vast. See especially the recent article by David S. Jones that challenges the virgin soil thesis, arguing instead that impoverishment was the greatest cause of increased susceptibility to European pathogens. Jones, "Virgin Soils Revisited," *WMQ* 60 (2003): 703–42. See also Henry F. Dobyns, *Their Number Become Thinned: Native American Population Dynamic in Eastern North America* (University of Tennessee Press, 1983), 15, Table 1, "Probable Epidemic Episodes of Smallpox among Native Americans in North America, 1520–1898." See also Ann F. Ramenofsky, *Vectors of Death: The Archaeology of European Contact* (Albuquerque: University of New Mexico Press, 1987); and Alfred W. Crosby, "Virgin Soil Epidemics as a Factor in the Aboriginal Depopulation in America" *WMQ* 33 (1976): 289–99.

28. *Description of the New Netherlands,* 106. According to van der Donck, the Mohicans explained the diffidence of the chief spirit by explaining that he had a beautiful goddess with him in the sky and thus he couldn't be bothered to interfere with human affairs.

29. Dowd, *Spirited Resistance,* 30; Neal Salisbury, *Manitou and Providence: Indians, Europeans, and the Making of New England, 1500–1643* (New York: Oxford University, 1982), 35; and James Axtell, *The Invasion Within: The Contest of Cultures in Colonial North America* (New York: Oxford University Press, 1985), 16–17.

30. Hymn #24, "Probe einem Gesang-Bücher," 35/331 RMM.

31. Letter dated December 25, 1744, 34/319/1/8 RMM.

32. Büttner's Diary [Eng.], September 23, 1744, 2/112/19/5 RMM. See also entry under the same date in the Shekomeko Diary, 1/111/1 RMM.

33. Gnadenhütten Diary, January 20, 1751, 5/117/2/1 RMM.

34. On Moravian ideas of death generally, see Craig D. Atwood, *Community of the Cross: Moravian Piety in Colonial Bethlehem* (University Park: Pennsylvania State University Press, 2004), 194–99; and Renate Wilson, "Reflections on the Training and Medical Resources of Physicians in Foreign Missions: The Moravians in North America," paper presented at the "Self, Community, World: Liberal Arts and Moravian Education" conference, Moravian College, Bethlehem, Pennsylvania, April 21, 2006.

35. Shekomeko Diary, January 25, 1744, 1/111/1 RMM.

36. This theme will be taken up more thoroughly in part 3. Diary of Joseph and Maria Spangenberg, November 16, 1744, 223/6/1 RMM.

37. Atwood, *Community of the Cross,* 88.

38. Peter C. Mancall, *Deadly Medicine: Indians and Alcohol in Early America* (Ithaca, NY: Cornell University Press, 1995), 63–84.

39. *Zeisberger's History,* 117–18, 140. For another example, see Joseph Shaw to Peter Böhler, 223/4/2 RMM.

40. Johannes sustained permanent injuries in a fire while intoxicated. Christoph Pyrlaeus, "Historical Account of the Indian Mission Work, 1739–1751," 29/221/21 RMM. Jephta, an older Shekomeko man, lost his wife to alcohol in April 1744. Later that year, a drunken fight broke out in Shekomeko, leaving one dead of a gunshot wound. Büttner diary, December 6, 1744, 2/112/19/6 RMM; and Joseph Shaw to Peter Böhler, 223/4/2 RMM.

41. There are numerous references in the Moravian records to the problem of alcohol at Stockbridge. See, for example, Shekomeko Diary, April 29, 1744, May 25, 1746, 1/111/1 RMM. References to the problem of alcohol in Stockbridge can be found in Shekomeko Diary, April 29, 1745, 1/111/1 RMM. Sergeant's diary also suggests that alcohol continued to be a disruptive influence in Stockbridge. Sergeant's Diary, Stiles Papers. For the use of alcohol to alienate Indian lands in Stockbridge, see Lion Miles, "The Red Man Dispossessed: The Williams Family and the Alienation of Indian Land in Stockbridge, Massachusetts, 1736–1818," *NEQ* 67 (1994): 46–76.

42. Of course we don't know whether the man used the word *devil* or whether this was Heckewelder's choice. If it was in fact *devil,* it might be that the man saw both the devil and alcohol as imported by Europeans. *History, Manners, and Customs,* 264, 265.

43. Büttner's Diary [Eng.], August 19, 1744, 2/112/19/5 RMM. A shorter version of the encounter in German can be found in Shekomeko Diary, August 19, 1744, 1/111/1 RMM.

44. For Zinzendorf's account of Tschoop's conversion, see *Memorials of the Moravian Church,* 129.

45. Tschoop's letter to Zinzendorf, December 19, 1741, 34/319/1/1 RMM.

46. Abraham recounted to Friedrich Post that he had been drunk at the coast together with Jacob, Jonathan, David, and Samuel. Friedrich Post Diary, August 9, 1746, 3/113/1/5 RMM.

47. *Memorials of the Moravian Church,* 145.

48. Quoted in *History of the Mission,* pt. II, p. 100.

49. Shekomeko Diary, March 20, 30, 1745, 1/111/1 RMM; and Johannes Hagen diary [Eng.], March 20, 1745, 2/112/8/2 RMM.

50. In separate incidents, Michael's intoxicated son had to be restrained all night, and Joseph was restrained by Cornelius during a drunken disturbance. Shekomeko Diary, April 10, 28, 1743, 1/111/1 RMM. More detailed accounts are found in Büttner's diary. Büttner diary, April 10, 1743, 26/211/5/1 and 1/111/2/4 RMM.

51. *Memorials of the Moravian Church,* 55–57.

52. Six other Shekomeko residents (including the wives of Abraham and Isaac) were baptized that same day. Shekomeko Diary, August 11, 1742, 1/111/1 RMM. On the meaning of *diener* (sacristan), see Vernon Nelson, Otto Dreydoppel Jr., and Doris Yob, eds., *The Bethlehem Diary, Volume II, 1744–1745,* trans. Kenneth G. Hamilton and Lothar Madeheim (Bethlehem, PA: Moravian Archives, 2001), 383.

53. Kathleen Bragdon challenges the traditional understanding of "redistributive" chiefs that see the chief's function as managing resources. " 'Redistributive' chiefs," writes Bragdon, "do not 'manage' the flow of staples, but rather extract agricultural tribute to 'finance' their own political activities." Bragdon, *Native People of Southern New England, 1500–1650* (Norman: University of Oklahoma Press, 1996), 46–49.

54. At this early point in Moravian missionary work, cultural transformation was not central to their mission project, and their silence on the issue could mean that traditional ceremonies continued, unremarked by the missionaries for any number of possible reasons: the missionaries might have understood such ceremonies to be examples of Christian worship prompted

by the Holy Spirit. Or perhaps the missionaries understood the ceremonies as secular affairs, although this seems unlikely.

55. The next day another lovefeast was held, again at Abraham's house; following the meal, two more Shekomekoans received baptism. Shekomeko Diary, December 25, 26, 1742, 1/111/1 RMM.

56. His father was Tataemshat, known as "Goose," a Mohican sachem from the Catskills. Gadrasachseth's mark appeared on deeds dating back to 1704 selling land along the Housatonic (near future Stockbridge) and Salisbury, Connecticut, also along the Housatonic River. Tataemshat had served as guardian for Manhat's children (Abraham's mother and uncle). Memorandum, September 1743, 3/113/5/3 RMM; and Shirley W. Dunn, *The Mohican World, 1680–1750* (Fleischmanns, NY: Purple Mountain Press, 2000), 351.

57. Nicodemus was a Pharisee and a leader in his community who became a follower of Jesus. Residents of Pachgatgoch were generally identified by the Moravians as "Wampanosch," derived from the term meaning "easterner." Wampano Indians should not be confused with the Wampanoags of eastern Massachusetts, although the derivation of the term is the same.

58. Moses's wife was also baptized and given the name Miriam. Another couple was baptized, taking the names Joseph and Mary. Others baptized included Philip and Lydia, Johannes's wife Martha, Joshua's wife Salome, Zaccheus and Magdalena, and Jacob's wife Rachel. Shekomeko Diary, December 12, 1742, 1/111/1 RMM.

59. The diarist used the term *Freunde,* which, in this context, likely means "lineage" or "clan." On this usage, see Hermann Wellenreuther and Carola Wessel, eds., *The Moravian Mission Diaries of David Zeisberger, 1772–1781,* trans. Julie Tomberlin Weber (University Park: Pennsylvania State University Press, 2005), 18n42; and Shekomeko Diary, December 16, 1742, 1/111/1 RMM.

60. The following is drawn largely from Atwood, *Community of the Cross,* 161–70.

61. Moravian choirs were not singing groups but rather peer groups who worshipped and often lived and worked together. Choirs were organized according to sex and life-stage, so for example, there was a Single Sisters, Married People, Widows, and Older Boys choir, among others. For a discussion of the development of the choir system, see Atwood, *Community of the Cross,* 173–78; Gillian Lindt Gollin, *Moravians in Two Worlds: A Study of Changing Communities* (New York: Columbia University Press, 1967), 67–89; and Beverly Prior Smaby, *The Transformation of Moravian Bethlehem from Mission to Family Economy* (Philadelphia: University of Pennsylvania Press, 1988), 10–11.

62. Atwood, *Community of the Cross,* 161, 184.

63. *Description of the New Netherlands,* 88–89.

64. *Historical Memoirs,* 11–12. Büttner was likely describing a similar ceremonial feast among the Delaware when he reported that the Indians from near Nazareth, Pennsylvania, had "gone to an Indian town for a feast to sacrifice a deer to the devil so that he would not harm them." Büttner Diary, November 21, 1741, 26/211/5/1 RMM.

65. *Description of the New Netherlands,* 88–89.

66. *Historical Memoirs,* 23–24.

67. *Zeisberger's History,* 136–37.

68. For information on Delaware and Mohican hunting practices, see *History, Manners, and Customs,* 12; and *History of the Mission,* pt. I, ch. 3. For a compelling analysis of modern Cree hunting practices, see Robert Brightman, *Grateful Prey: Rock Cree Human-Animal Relationships* (Berkeley: University of California Press, 1993), chs. 3 and 4.

69. For example, Jonathan hosted an anniversary lovefeast, Shekomeko Diary; October 9, 1743, 1/111/1 RMM. Nathanael hosted a lovefeast to thank the Savior for the birth of his son; Shekomeko Diary, April 4, 1745, 1/111/1 RMM. Gideon and his son, Joshua, celebrated the anniversary of their baptisms with a lovefeast; Pachgatgoch Diary, February 13, 1759, 4/115/8 RMM. A different Joshua celebrated the twenty-fifth anniversary of his baptism with a lovefeast; Friedenshütten Diary, September 16, 1767, 7/131/4 RMM.

70. Diary of Joseph [Augustus] and Mary Spangenberg [Eng.], February 28, 1745, 30/223/6/1 RMM.

71. Shekomeko Diary, November 28, 1745, 1/111/1 RMM.

72. Bragdon, *Native People of Southern New England,* 175.

73. Pachgatgoch Diary, December 10, 1752, 3/114/7 RMM.

74. Abraham's son, Jonathan, regularly returned to the community for the Christmas celebration, as did Nathanael.

75. Shekomeko Diary, December 22, 1743, 1/111/1 RMM.

76. Gnadenhütten Diary, January 1, 1748, 4/116/3/1 RMM.

77. Little can be known directly about Mohican naming practices, but practices among neighboring Northeastern Indian peoples are suggestive. On Delaware naming practices, see *Zeisberger's History,* 80, 145; and *History, Manners, and Customs,* 141–44. On Shawnee customs in the twentieth century, see C. F. and E. W. Vogelin, "Shawnee Name Groups," *American Anthropologist* 47 (1935): 617–35. On Iroquois "requickening" ceremonies, see Richter, *Ordeal of the Longhouse,* 32–33, 39–40, 43. See also Richard White, " 'Although I Am Dead, I Am Not Entirely Dead. I Have Left a Second of Myself': Constructing Self and Persons on the Middle Ground of Early America," in *Through a Glass Darkly: Reflections on Personal Identity in Early America,* ed. Ronald Hoffman, Mechal Sobel, and Fredrika J. Teute (Chapel Hill: University of North Carolina Press, 1997), 404–18.

78. Atwood, *Community of the Cross,* 167–70.

79. *Historical Memoirs,* 37.

80. *Description of the New Netherlands,* 86.

81. *History, Manners, and Customs,* 268–76.

82. The location of God's Acre in Shekomeko is shown in Johannes Hagen's sketch of Shekomeko, reproduced in chapter 8 below, in figure 6. It is marked as #14.

83. Büttner to Anton Seiffert, December 7, 1742, 1/111/7/7 RMM. See also Shekomeko Diary, December 6, 1742, 1/111/1 RMM.

84. Rauch Diary, April 4, 1744, 2/112/1/3 RMM; and Shekomeko Diary, March 23, 1744, 1/111/1 RMM.

85. Moravians described death as "going home to the Savior." Gnadenhütten Diary, April 24, 1748, 4/116/3/1 RMM.

86. Constance Crosby, "From Myth to History, or Why King Philip's Ghost Walks Abroad," in *The Recovery of Memory: Historical Archeology in the Eastern United States,* eds. Mark P. Leone and Parker B. Potter Jr. (Washington, D.C.: Smithsonian Institution Press, 1988), 191.

87. *Description of New Netherlands,* 104.

88. Gnadenhütten Diary, April 24, 1748, 4/116/3/1 RMM.

89. The evidence is scant, but we can still safely surmise that Tschoop in fact held the role of tribal speaker or orator. Among the baptized, Johannes seems to have had the greatest facility with European languages. He is noted as speaking in Dutch, German, English, and Mohican. Further, he seems always to have accompanied Abraham on his travels because he was the better speaker. Shekomeko Diary, April 29, 1745, 1/111/1 RMM. Another hint that he held the role of speaker comes from Pyrlaeus's history of the mission. Christoph Pyrlaeus, Historical Account of the Indian Mission Work, 1739–1751, 29/221/21 RMM.

90. On the role of tribal speaker, see *Zeisberger's History,* 143.

91. "We sent our Bro. John to Potatick, to tell the Indians there (who are in Part Naturally related to him) something of our Savior & His Wounds." Büttner's Diary [Eng.], February 22, 1743, 1/111/1/3b RMM.

92. "Mack's Journey to New England" [Eng.], February 27, 1743, 1/111/3/4 RMM.

93. "Mack's Journey to New England" [Eng.], February 27, 1743, 1/111/3/4 RMM. Abraham was described as "possessed of gifts to testify of our Savior with energy and power" and by Büttner as "worthy solid manly Brother who by his walking preaches" and who "has likewise received Gifts to bear testimony of the Lamb such as touches the heart." *History of the Mission,*

pt. II, p. 35; Gottlob Büttner to Anton Seiffert [Eng.], October 1742, 26/211/5/5 RMM; and Shekomeko Diary, October 4–7, 1742, 1/111/1 RMM.

94. Letter from Tschoop to "My dear Brethren and Sisters" [Eng.], 34/319/1/14 RMM. The original German is at 34/319/1/13 RMM.

95. Gottlob Büttner to Anton Seiffert, October 1742, 26/211/5/5 RMM.

96. "Mack's Journey to New England" [Eng.], March 10, 1743, 1/111/3/4 RMM.

97. "Mack's Journey to New England" [Eng.], March 4, 1743, 1/111/3/4 RMM.

98. Mack's Diary [Eng.], February 3, 1743, 1/111/3/3 RMM.

99. Gilbert Tennent accused Zinzendorf of universalism, which he denied. See Tennent, *Some Account of the Principles of the Moravians* (London: S. Mason, 1743); and Atwood, *Community of the Cross,* 82.

100. "Martin Mack's Journey to New England," March 6, 1743, 1/111/3/4 RMM. On another occasion, after a "Labourers' Conference," Mack preached on the words, "Come unto me all ye that are weary and heavey laden." Mack diary, January 19, 1744, 2/112/19/1 RMM.

101. Shekomeko Diary, January 9, 1746, 1/111/1 RMM.

102. Quoted in Gottlob Büttner's diary [Eng.], September 23, 1744, 2/112/19/5 RMM. The original German can be found at Shekomeko Diary, September 23, 1744, 1/111/1 RMM. Similar themes about the Savior's love for all regularly appeared in the greetings Shekome-koans sent to each other. One from Nicodemus to the Bethlehem congregation reads, "This I know that our Saviour loves the Souls in an astonishing degree. And tho' they were ever so wicked, yet has he great love for them." Nicodemus, Elder of the Indian Congregation at Gnadenhütten, January 1747, 34/319/3/2 RMM.

103. *History of the Mission,* pt. II, pp. 77–78.

104. Gnadenhütten Diary, January 13, 1751, 5/117/2/1 RMM.

105. Gnadenhütten Diary, January 1, 1748, 4/116/3/1 RMM.

106. Shekomeko Diary, December 15, 1745, 1/111/1 RMM; and Gnadenhütten Diary, August 1754, 5/118/2 RMM.

107. As Jon Sensbach has demonstrated, however, this fraternalism did not go so far as to attempt to obliterate worldly distinctions. Sensbach, *A Separate Canaan: The Making of an Afro-Moravian World in North Carolina, 1763–1840* (Chapel Hill: University of North Carolina Press, 1998).

108. On the differences (and similarities) between Indian and colonial British methods of diplomacy, see Nancy Shoemaker, *A Strange Likeness: Becoming Red and White in Eighteenth-Century North America* (New York: Oxford University Press, 2004), 35–60.

109. Bragdon, *Native People of Southern New England,* 157–59; and Hendrick Aupaumut, quoted in Electa F. Jones, *Stockbridge, Past and Present: Or, Records of an Old Mission Station* (Springfield, MA: Samuel Bowles and Company, 1854), 20.

110. Martin Mack diary, February 4, 1744, 2/112/1/1 RMM.

111. Maintaining peace was in fact the original purpose of the Covenant Chain that set the terms of relationship among the Iroquois, colonists, Delawares, and Mohicans. See Francis Jennings, *The Ambiguous Iroquois Empire: The Covenant Chain Confederation of Indian Tribes with English Colonies* (New York: W. W. Norton and Company, 1984); and Daniel K. Richter and James H. Merrell, eds., *Beyond the Covenant Chain: The Iroquois and Their Neighbors in Indian North America, 1600–1800* (Syracuse, NY: Syracuse University Press, 1987).

112. Gnadenhütten Diary, January 15, 1751, 5/117/2/1 RMM.

113. The council was part of an effort by the Shawnee and Nanticoke, as directed by the Iroquois, to populate the Susquehanna Valley with tributary tribes in order to reinforce Iroquois hegemony. See C. A. Weslager, *The Delaware Indians, A History* (New Brunswick, NJ: Rutgers University Press, 1972), 196–220.

114. "Litt. O. 14th Supplement to the Report on the Indians' Visit to Bethlehem in March 1753," 35/323/1/3 RMM. Jane T. Merritt discusses these councils but interprets their tenor quite differently. Merritt, "Metaphor, Meaning, and Misunderstanding: Language and Power

on the Pennsylvania Frontier," in *Contact Points: American Frontiers from the Mohawk Valley to the Mississippi, 1750–1830*, ed. Andrew R. L. Cayton and Fredrika J. Teute (Chapel Hill: University of North Carolina Press, 1999), 60–87.

115. "Report of a Treaty Held at Gnadenhütten on July 17th," 1752, 35/323/1 RMM.

116. Merritt, *At the Crossroads*, 184–88; and *History of the Mission*, pt. II, p. 158–71.

117. Jon Butler's famous essay challenged the idea of the Great Awakening, arguing that the chronologically and geographically disparate revivals cannot be understood as constituting a single phenomenon. Butler, "Enthusiasm Described and Decried: The Great Awakening as Interpretive Fiction," *Journal of American History* 69 (1982): 305–25.

CHAPTER 7. THE VILLAGE MATRIARCH AND THE YOUNG MOTHER

1. One of the goals outlined by Zinzendorf and Rauch was to baptize twelve Indians, presumably to serve as Mohican disciples. "Zinzendorf's Journey to the Mohican Town of Shecomeco," in *Memorials of the Moravian Church*, 54–57. Shekomeko Diary, August 11, September 4, December 12, 1742, 1/111/1 RMM. The dates in Zinzendorf's account and the Shekomeko are slightly off. The mission diary records the baptisms as occurring on August 11, while Zinzendorf's journal records his arrival in Shekomeko on August 17.

2. The account presented here is largely drawn from my article, "Women and Christian Practice in a Mahican Village," *Religion and American Culture* 13 (Winter 2003): 27–67. In representing dates in this article, I neglected to account for the difference between the Gregorian and Julian calendars. Brainerd's August 12 visit to Pachgatgoch would have corresponded to August 23 in the Moravian records. Shekomeko Diary, August 11, 1742, 1/111/1 RMM; "Zinzendorf's Journey to the Mohican Town of Shecomeco," in *Memorials of the Moravian Church*, 54–57.

3. *Works*, vol. 7, p. 176.

4. Ted J. Brasser, *Riding on the Frontier's Crest: Mahican Indian Culture and Cultural Change* (Ottawa: National Museums of Canada, 1974), 67; and Büttner Diary, February 15 and February 21, 1743, 1/111/2/1 RMM.

5. Kathleen J. Bragdon. *Native People of Southern New England, 1500–1650* (Norman: University of Oklahoma Press, 1996), 158–60.

6. If David Zeisberger's account of Delaware practices holds true for Mohican society as well, Sarah was likely born no later than 1705. According to Zeisberger, Delaware men generally married between eighteen and twenty and women at fourteen or fifteen. *Zeisberger's History*, 82–83. Sarah and Abraham had several sons of marriageable age when the Moravians arrived in Shekomeko. Information on Abraham and Sarah's children is drawn from Fliegel *Index*.

7. Büttner Diary [Eng.], December 11, 1743, 1/111/2/7 RMM. The German can be found in Shekomeko Diary, December 11, 1743, 1/111 RMM.

8. Conference minutes from 1744 show Sarah particularly active in domestic disputes. Worker's Conference Minutes, June 10, 17, December 16, 23, 1744 2/112/5/3 RMM. A sampling of the Gnadenhütten diary for 1752 suggests Sarah's continued community work. She served as a conference member, as a disciple [*Jüngerin*], she paid calls on other villagers, offered advice to parents, and attended to the sick. Gnadenhütten Diary, January 12, 17, February 7, 12, March 11, June 4, July 26, August 15, September 14, 29, 1752, 5/117/3 RMM.

9. The community had been in flux as the Moravians came under increasing suspicion due to the renewal of colonial hostilities and as Shekomeko residents felt ever greater pressure from an increasing population of New Yorkers. The Moravians secured land from the Delaware about thirty miles from Bethlehem, and most Shekomekoans eventually relocated to the Pennsylvania site. The dislocation and cramped quarters facilitated a devastating epidemic that claimed the lives of many Shekomekoans. Pachgatgoch Diary, April 22, 1747, 4/116/1 RMM.

10. Actually, he sought to stay in Wechquadnach, another Mohican village in New York near Shekomeko, where some of the villagers moved following the dissolution of Shekomeko.

11. Pachgatgoch Diary, May 6–8, 1747, 4/116/1 RMM.

12. Both sons would soon return: a 1749 list of farmland assigned in Gnadenhütten includes Abraham and his three sons David, Joachim and Jonathan. September 2, 1749, 6/119/1/4 RMM. Lists of communicants from the same year include Abraham and Sarah, David and Sarah, Jonathan and Anna, but not Joachim. December 17, 1749, 6/119/2/1 RMM. A similar list from 1752 includes all three couples. January 15, 1752, 6/119/2/3 RMM.

13. Pachgatgoch Diary, May 29, 1747, 4/116/1 RMM.

14. Abraham knew his wife did not want to accompany him, and he requested that the Brethren let her stay with them. Sarah insisted on following her husband. Gnadenhütten Diary, March 13, April 24, 1754, 5/118/1 RMM; and Meniolagomekah Diary, June 13, 1763, 6/124/2 RMM.

15. Gnadenhütten Diary, January 9, 15, 16, 1754, 5118/1 RMM.

16. Gnadenhütten Diary, April 24, 1754 5/118/1 RMM; and Sarah to Sister Spangenberg, August 31, 1754 34/319/4/9 RMM.

17. Meniolagomekah Diary, June 13–20, 1763, 6/124/4 RMM.

18. Philadelphia Diary, June 10, 1764, 7/127/2 RMM.

19. On the Schaghticoke tribe, see Paulette Crone-Morange and Lucianne Lavin, "The Schaghticoke Tribe and English Law: A Study of Community Survival," *Connecticut History* 43 (Fall 2004): 132–62.

20. Much of the information on Rachel's life is in the form of conference minutes and letters from Rachel to Maria Spangenberg, to whom she often turned for comfort and support. Rachel dictated these letters and her husband transcribed them.

21. Later baptized Boas, Annimhard was accused of beating his wife, Ruth, who was presumably his first wife, as suggested by the fact that Ruth had a daughter of marriageable age in 1750. Conference Minutes, September 23 and 30, 1744, 2/112/5/3 RMM; and Gnadenhütten Diary, December 5, 1750, 5/117/1 RMM.

22. She was baptized the same day as the chief of the village, Gideon Mawehu, two of his children, and two other men from Pachgatgoch. Shekomeko Diary, February 13, 1743, 1/111 RMM. Her father, Lucas, was baptized March 27, 1743. Her mother, Priscilla, was baptized August 2, 1743. Her sister, also named Priscilla, was baptized August 7, 1743. Her brother, Lucas was baptized March 14, 1749.

23. The other three candidates were Tachtamoa (daughter of Johannes, later baptized Debora); a thirty-two-year-old unbaptized widow; and eighteen-year-old Maria (daughter of Gideon, the chief of Pachgatgoch, and also object of affection of the chief of Stockbridge, probably Umpachenee). Büttner's diary, February 21, 1743, 1/111/2/1 RMM.

24. White Workers' Conference, August 19, 1743, 1/111/6/3 RMM; Shekomeko Diary, August 13, 24, 28, and September 10, 1743, 1/111/1 RMM; and Conference Minutes, September 19, and October 16, 1743, 1/111/6 RMM. Apparently, Rachel was not alone in having difficulty liking Post. He had a tendentious personality and seldom won admirers. The only full-length biography of Post is Thomas Christopher Chase, "Christian Frederick Post, 1715–1785: Missionary and Diplomat to the Indians of America," Ph.D. dissertation, Pennsylvania State University, 1982.

25. "Mittlerzeit wolte der Heyland sie solten ihre vereinigung haben, welches sie ihm aber eineige mahl nicht erlaubte." Büttner to Anton Seiffert, December 9, 1743, 1/111/8/7 RMM. The lot was not to be used by individuals but only by Elders acting in the interest of the *Gemeine*, or congregation. Beverly Prior Smaby, *The Transformation of Moravian Bethlehem from Mission to Family Economy* (Philadelphia: University of Pennsylvania Press, 1988), 24.

26. Büttner to Anton Seiffert, December 9, 1743, 1/111/8/7 RMM; and Conference Minutes, December 22, 1743, 1/111/6 RMM. The boy was born September 24, 1744. Rachel often confided in Johannes. Her child is likely named after Zinzendorf and Johannes. Many couples named their children after their own family members. That Rachel did not suggests that there may well have been tensions between her and her family.

27. That Rachel addressed Maria as "Liebe Mutter" rather than the more common "Schwester," as Sarah and others called her, suggests the uncommon bond between the women as well as Rachel's desire for a spiritual mother. Maria Spangenberg's given name was Eva-Maria, but she was known as Maria and her husband, Augustus, as Joseph. Referring to Spangenberg as "Mother" might also suggest that Rachel viewed Spangenberg as the embodiment of Mary, mother of Jesus, or as the Holy Spirit, commonly called "Mother" by Moravians. Native understanding of selfhood was quite different from prevailing European notions, stressing the relational basis of identity over inborn essence. For example, when an individual was named after an important person, the individual shared in the personhood of their namesake. Rachel may well have seen Maria Spangenberg as the present embodiment of the *Heiland*'s mother. She would have been encouraged in this belief by the European Moravians who clearly put great store in the power of names, so clearly evident in the baptisms of Abraham and Sarah, Isaac and Rebecca, and Jacob and Rachel. See Richard White, " 'Although I Am Dead, I Am Not Entirely Dead. I Have Left a Second of Myself': Constructing Self and Persons on the Middle Ground of Early America," in *Through a Glass Darkly: Reflections on Personal Identity in Early America*, ed. Ronald Hoffman, Mechal Sobel, and Fredrika J. Teute (Chapel Hill: University of North Carolina Press, 1997), 404–18; and Daniel K. Richter, *The Ordeal of the Longhouse: The Peoples of the Iroquois League in the Era of European Colonization* (Chapel Hill: University of North Carolina Press, 1992).

28. Rachel to Maria Spangenberg, 34/319/2/1 RMM. The original German letter can be found at 219/1/7 RMM. Neither letter is dated, but this letter presumably refers to her first pregnancy.

29. Moravians believed sex to be a sacrament, and newly married couples were often enjoined to consummate their marriage while others waited outside the small room [*Kabinet*] and prayed. The original German reads as follows: "O liebe muter. Ich wahr sehr arm in Bethlehem und weill wir zu sammen waren im Kabinet und Bruder Joseph bätte fühlt ich große Gnade der Heiland begoß mein Hertz recht mit Blut daß er hielt mich alle zeit wohl und vergnügt im Herzen ob ich gleich noch so elend bin." Rachel to Maria Spangenberg, October 1745, 34/319/1/10, RMM. On Moravian attitudes toward sexuality and marriage, see Craig Atwood, "Sleeping in the Arms of Christ: Sanctifying Sexuality in the Eighteenth-Century Moravian Church," *Journal of the History of Sexuality* 8 (1997): 25–51; and Peter Vogt, " 'Ehereligion': The Moravian Theory and Practice of Marriage as Point of Contention in the Conflict between Ephrata and Bethlehem," *Communal Societies* 21 (2001): 37–48.

30. Undated letter from Rachel, 28/219/1/7 RMM.

31. Rachel Post to Brethren and Sisters in Berbies, 1745, 34/319/3/5 RMM. Another letter further suggests reconciliation with her husband. In a letter to her fellow villagers, Rachel assured them that she loved her husband and her child (one-year-old Maria) was well. Rachel to Gnadenhütten, A. [April? August?] 1746, 28/219/1/7 RMM.

32. Büttner to Seiffert [Eng.], June 27, 1744, 2/112/19/4 RMM.

33. "Mack's Journey from Shekomeko to Bethlehem and Arrest at Esopus" [Eng.], March 1–5, 1745, 2/112/10/1 RMM.

34. Rachel dictated the letter in broken English to her husband who transcribed it using German phonetics. "En dis mey moder dus laf mie so mus en gret del mor den mey ohn moder." Rachel to Maria Spangenberg, September 9, 1746, 3/113/1/5 RMM.

35. "Mey hart was won dey were heffe ey did not noh wat did key so heffe mey hart ey was alwes kreyin Ples aur söfger hi schut scho mie wat it was eff mey men was sick mey hart did sey noh it is som oder tinks en den did Josua kom hohm tensing en schringin o mey hart did krey were mutz et was as iff was kot won off mey finger aff en ey did krey were mutz dat aur söfger mut help him egin ey kut not schlip hohlneit beloved moder ey tuckt iur letter aut de heus off aur söfger it was ius so es wen de söfger giwid mey hens en ey was so gled dat ey did krey." Rachel to Maria Spangenberg, September 9, 1746, 3/113/1/5 RMM. For references to Joshua, see Post's Pachgatgoch diary, July 22, 1746, September 1 and 9, 1746, 3/113/1/5 RMM.

36. A similar but more fragmentary bit of evidence suggests that other women experienced a similar power in giving birth and nursing their children. The Gnadenhütten diary reports, "Die Aeimel erzehlte bei der Gelegenheit wie ihrs in ihren Herzen wäre wenn sie Kinder vor den Hld trüge und wenn sie gebähre und säugete." June 7, 1747, 4/116/6 RMM. Rachel's letter reads, "Mey scheyld gros well en strang but it hes eh gret kaff ey wist auer söffger did meg him well egen. ey ken help him noting de söffger muß du alting. . . . wen ey giff mey scheyld suck en ey tenck an die blot en wouns off auer söffger ey fühl mey hat sam teims were wet en so ey tenck mey scheyld saks de blot off auer söffger en ey fähl de engels luck efter mey en mey scheyld. . . . ey em puhr but ey krey en pre vor dem dat de söffger wut giff dem eh fühling off his blot en wouns in der harts. beluvet moder ie mus tenck an mie dat hie giefs mutz gres. . . . wie er iur pur schilderen Rahel und Maria Post." Rachel to Maria Spangenberg, September 9, 1746 3/113/1/5 RMM.

37. Pachgatgoch Diary, December 26, 1747, 4/116/2 RMM.

Chapter 8. Mohican Women and the Community of the Blood

1. There is considerable literature on native women in the context of colonialism. Among the most important works are Mona Etienne and Eleanor Leacock, eds., *Women and Colonization* (New York: Praeger, 1980); Carol Devens, "Separate Confrontations: Gender as a Factor in Indian Adaptation in European Colonization in New France," *American Quarterly* 38, no. 3 (1986): 461–80; Kathryn E. Holland Braund, "Guardians of Tradition and Handmaidens to Change: Women's Roles in Creek Economic and Social Life during the Eighteenth Century," *American Indian Quarterly* 14 (Summer 1990): 239–58; Karen Anderson, *Chain Her by One Foot: The Subjection of Native Women in Seventeenth-Century New France* (New York: Routledge, 1991); Carol Devens, *Countering Colonization: Native American Women and Great Lakes Missions, 1630–1900* (Berkeley: University of California Press, 1992); Nancy Shoemaker, ed., *Negotiators of Change: Historical Perspectives on Native American Women* (New York: Routledge, 1995); Laura F. Klein and Lillian A. Ackerman, eds., *Women and Power in Native North America* (Norman: University of Oklahoma Press, 1995); and Theda Perdue, *Cherokee Women: Gender and Culture Change, 1700–1835* (Lincoln: University of Nebraska Press, 1998), and Perdue, ed., *Sifters: Native American Women's Lives* (New York: Oxford University Press, 2001). An entire issue of *Ethnohistory* was devoted to "Native American Women's Responses to Christianity," *Ethnohistory* 43 (Autumn 1996); see especially the introduction to the issue by Sergei Kan and Michael Harkin, 563–71.

2. Ted Brasser, *Riding on the Frontier's Crest: Mohican Indian Culture and Cultural Change* (Ottawa: National Museums of Canada, 1974), 28–29. Kathleen Bragdon discusses the marriage practices of southern New England native peoples. Bragdon, *Native People of Southern New England, 1500–1650* (Norman: University of Oklahoma Press, 1996), especially chs. 3 and 7.

3. Bragdon, *Native People of Southern New England,* especially ch. 1.

4. Historian Shirley Dunn has compiled data from dozen of deeds relating to Mohican lands through much of the seventeenth and eighteenth centuries. See especially Dunn, *The Mohicans and Their Land, 1609–1730* (Fleischmanns, NY: Purple Mountain Press, 1994), appendix A, "Recorded Land Transactions of the Mohicans"; and Dunn, *The Mohican World, 1680–1750* (Fleischmanns, NY: Purple Mountain Press, 2000), appendix A, "Recorded Land Transactions." Robert Steven Grumet discusses women's signatures on deeds among Coastal Algonquians in "Sunksquaws, Shamans, and Tradeswomen: Middle Atlantic Coastal Algonkian Women during the 17th and 18th Centuries," in *Women and Colonization: Anthropological Perspectives,* ed. Mona Etienne and Eleanor Leacock (New York: Praeger, 1980), 43–62; see also Henry Andrew Wright, *Indian Deeds of Hampden County* (Springfield, MA: 1905), 120–30.

5. Shekomeko Diary, May 6, 1745, 1/111/1 RMM; and Joachim Sensemann to Gottlob Büttner [Eng.], February 16, 1744, 30/223/3/2 RMM.

6. Bragdon, *Native People of Southern New England,* 181, 242. See also Wilbur R. Jacobs, "Wampum: The Protocol of Indian Diplomacy," *WMQ* 6 (October 1949): 596–604; Mary W.

Herman, "Wampum as a Money in Northeastern North America," *Ethnohistory* 3 (1956): 21–33; and George S. Snyderman, "The Functions of Wampum," *Proceedings of the American Philosophical Society* 98 (December 1954): 469–94.

7. Electa F. Jones, *Stockbridge, Past and Present; Or Records of an Old Mission Station* (Springfield, MA: Samuel Bowles and Company, 1854), 21. A string of wampum generally confirmed a single statement, while a belt of wampum was meant as confirmation of the whole message. Moravian missionary David Zeisberger noted that twenty to thirty belts of wampum were generally required to ratify an alliance or peace between two peoples. *Zeisberger's History,* 31–32, 94–95; and *History of the Mission,* pt. I, pp. 157–58.

8. Bathsheba may have seen contributions to the missionaries in much the same light: on one occasion she presented Martin Mack with a bear roast, and on another, sponsored a lovefeast for the missionaries. Gnadenhütten, April 6, 1748, 4/116/3 RMM; and Gnadenhütten Diary, September 28, 1748, 4/116/4 RMM. The Moravian diarist described the belt for the 1750 council as "sehr schön" (very beautiful); it measured 12 rows wide by 230 in length, using a total of 2,760 beads. The first was for a delegation to Shamokin in 1747, the second for a council with the Iroquois at Onondaga in 1750. Gnadenhütten Diary, April 15, 1747, 4/116/1 RMM; and Gnadenhütten Diary, February 8, April 9, 1750, 4/116/7 RMM.

9. Ruth owed "3 pieces of eight" to "Barnstats" and six guilders to George Jacobs. Copy of Ruth's testament at end of Hagen's diary [Eng.], 1745, 2/112/8/2 RMM.

10. Aupaumut, in Jones, *Stockbridge, Past and Present,* 21. Alison Duncan Hirsch has found the custom widespread in Pennsylvania in the eighteenth century; see Hirsch, "Indian, *Métis,* and Euro-American Women on Multiple Frontiers," in *Friends and Enemies in Penn's Woods: Indians, Colonists, and the Racial Construction of Pennsylvania,* ed. William A. Pencak and Daniel K. Richter (University Park: Pennsylvania State University Press, 2004), 71–72.

11. Rebecca was married to Isaac, one of the first to be baptized and who, according to the missionaries, had been known "as a great sorcerer"; he was related to the Mohican sachem, Corlaer. He died in the smallpox epidemic in Bethlehem in the summer of 1746. Indian Workers Conference, December 23, 1744, 2/112/5/3 RMM; and *Memorials of the Moravian Church,* 145.

12. Sensemann attributed the shortage instead to a failure to plant sufficient crops the previous spring. Joachim Sensemann to Gottlob Büttner [Eng.], February 16, 1744, 30/223/3/2 RMM.

13. Her husband, Boaz, may have still been living at the time; he appears in the records in March 1745, and Ruth died in April. Copy of Ruth's testament at end of Hagen's diary [Eng.], 1745, 2/112/8/2 RMM.

14. Shekomeko Diary, April 26, 1745, 1/111/1 RMM.

15. Indian Workers' Conference, May 20, 27, 1744, 2/112/5/3 RMM.

16. Fliegel *Index,* 113–16.

17. Brasser, *Riding on the Frontier's Crest,* 29. The significance of these changes will be discussed in greater detail below.

18. Tschoop to Zinzendorf, December 19, 1741, 34/319/1/2 RMM.

19. Pachgatgoch Diary, July 10, 14, 19, 1751, 3/114/4 RMM; Pachgatgoch Diary, March 12, 1752, 3/114/5 RMM; Pachgatgoch Diary, April 9, 1752, 3/114/5 RMM; Pachgatgoch Diary, April 26, May 16, 1752, 3/114/6 RMM; and Pachgatgoch Diary, December 6, 1753, January 8, 1754, 3/114/8 RMM.

20. Büttner Diary, January 30, 1743, 1/111/2/1 RMM.

21. Indian Workers Conference, June 17, 1744, 2/112/5/3 RMM.

22. Sarah, Tamar, and Rachel all expressed similar sentiments in the same batch of letters. Undated letters, 34/319/1/12 RMM. See also Bethlehem Christian Indians to Shekomeko and Pachgatgoch [Eng.], June 2, 1746, 34/319/2/8 RMM; and Rachel to Joseph Spangenberg, February 4, 1746, 34/319/2/1 RMM.

23. Indian Workers Conference, June 20, 1744, 2/112/5/3 RMM.

24. Extract from the Bethlehem Congregation Journal, June 4/15, 1749, 26/211/19/1 RMM.

25. Bethlehem Christians to Shekomeko and Pachgatgoch, June 2, 1746, 34/319/2/7 RMM.

26. Büttner refused to baptize her again. Büttner's Diary, July 10, 1743, 1/111/2/4 RMM.

27. "Probe einem Gesang-Bücher vor die Seeligen Herzel aus den Braunen Nationen der Mahikander Delawares und etliche Versgen in der Sprache der 6 Nationen. 1746," Archiv der Brüder Unität in Herrnhut. A copy can be found in 35/331 RMM.

28. Undated letters of Christian Indians at Pachgatgoch, 34/319/3/9 RMM.

29. Letter from Rachel, 28/219/1/7 RMM.

30. Indian Workers Conference, December 16, 1744, 2/112/5/3 RMM.

31. Men's experience of communion and the intersection with the rituals of mourning wars is discussed in chapter 6.

32. In their accounts of warfare and torture, neither Heckewelder nor Zeisberger call particular attention to the central role of women, suggesting either the authors' cultural bias or the waning of women's power—or perhaps both. Perdue suggests that women were often vulnerable to raiding warriors as they worked in the fields. If they were not immediately killed, they were more likely to be adopted than tortured. On the other side of the battle lines, women had once "avenged the deaths of their relatives personally through torture, but by the late eighteenth century torture had waned." Perdue, *Cherokee Women,* ch. 4, quotation p. 90.

33. *The Jesuit Relations* contain many examples of baptized Indians being taken captive and singing Christian songs while stoically bearing the tortures of their captors. In these instances, Christianity seems to have functioned as a means of enabling the captives to die with honor. A dying Huron who had earlier in his life endured torture among the Iroquois assured his wife: "Put a few questions to those who have seen me in the country of the Iroquois—in the midst of the torments, and on the point of being burned over a slow fire—and thou shalt know from them whether I have ever shown the least weakness in the face of all the cruelties that were exercised on my body." If he didn't fear death then, the man told his wife, when he had not experienced the sacraments, then "why should I fear to die now, when I see myself so powerfully sustained, and when God has given me a firm hope of soon seeing again, as Saints in Heaven, my children who died a short time ago?" Rueben Gold Thwaites, *The Jesuit Relations and Allied Documents: Travels and Explorations of the Jesuit Missionaries in New France, 1610–1791* (Cleveland: Burrows Bros. Co., 1896–1901), vol. 53, p. 105.

34. Women also likely placed a high value on stoicism, though the occasions for demonstrating stoicism and gaining power thereby would have been private (childbirth) rather than public (warfare and torture). Some scholars have suggested that the nearly universal European assumption of the day, that Indian women gave birth with far less pain than European women, is largely a function of a cultural imperative of stoicism. James Axtell, ed., *The Indian Peoples of Eastern America: A Documentary History of the Sexes* (New York: Oxford University Press, 1981), 3. Roger Williams noted of the Narragansett that "most of them count it a shame for a Woman in Travell to make complaint, and many of them are scarcely heard to groane." Quoted in Bragdon, *Native People of Southern New England,* 175. On the spiritual powers gained through suffering, Perdue writes, "although women could not avoid the physical and spiritual dangers brought on by menstruation, pregnancy and childbirth, they could gain a spiritual power through these trials." Perdue, *Cherokee Women,* 32–36.

35. David S. Jones, "Virgin Soils Revisited," *WMQ* 60 (2003): 703–42. Two notable epidemics hit the mission community in its first decades. During the summer of 1746, nineteen members of the Indian-Moravian community died in Bethlehem. *Memorials of the Moravian Church,* 143–48; *History of the Mission,* pt. II, pp. 93–97. And nearly half of the 121 Moravian Indians asylumed at the Philadelphia Barracks died in the course of the year from December 1763 to December 1764. "Departures and Burials on the Common Burying Ground of Indians departed in the Barracks at Philadelphia," Box-Philadelphia I, Register 1742–1822, p. 208, MAB.

36. Already in the mid–seventeenth century, Mohicans reported that "before the arrival of the Christians, and before the small pox broke out amongst them, they were ten times as numerous as they now are, and that their population had been melted down by this disease,

whereof nine-tenths of them have died." And in 1735, Ebenezer Poohpoonuc of Stockbridge reported that in his own lifetime he had seen a similar decrease: "Since my remembrance, there were Ten Indians, where there is now One." *Description of the New Netherlands,* 28, 64, 95; *Gospel Ministers,* iv; and Brasser, *Riding the Frontier's Crest,* 23, 29, 30.

37. *Description of the New Netherlands,* 106.

38. Calvin Martin has made this argument in "The European Impact on the Culture of a Northeastern Algonquian Tribe: An Ecological Interpretation," *WMQ* (1974): 17–21. A more recent study makes a similar case with respect to the Indians of the Massachusetts "Praying Town" at Natick. Harold W. Van Lonkhuyzen, "A Reappraisal of the Praying Indians: Acculturation, Conversion, and Identity at Natick, Massachusetts, 1643–1732," *NEQ* 63 (1990): 396–428. Alfred A. Cave has challenged the idea that shamans of southern New England practiced *maleficium,* suggesting that this interpretation is the result of the bias of the Puritan sources that saw shamanic healing practices as diabolic. See Cave, "Indian Shamans and English Witches in Seventeenth-Century New England," *Essex Institute Historical Collections* 128, no. 4 (1992): 239–54. Kathleen Bragdon's excellent study of Southern New England peoples in the sixteenth and seventeenth centuries suggests that shamans could use their power for good or ill. Bragdon, *Native People of Southern New England,* 203 passim. Van der Donck reported of the Mohicans that they "possess great fear of the devil, who they believe causes diseases, and does them much injury." *Description of the New Netherlands,* 102. Konkapot and Umpachenee of the nascent Stockbridge mission believed that they had been targeted by sorcerers in retaliation for their acceptance of the mission program. *Historical Memoirs,* 21–24. The Moravian records also contain numerous references to "poisonings" by spiritual means. For one such example, see "Bishop Cammerhoff's Journey to Shamokin, Pa 1748," 26/211/6/2 RMM, which tells of a Mohican woman married to an Oneida. When their child died, the couple believed it had been killed by Delaware sorcerers.

39. Interestingly, Moravian missionary David Zeisberger confessed that he came to believe in the powers and skills of native "sorcerers," as he called them. *Zeisberger's History,* 125–26.

40. Fliegel *Index,* entries for Priscilla, Lucas, Rachel, Esther, and Sarah.

41. Conference minutes, March 10, 1745, 2/112/15/1 RMM.

42. Büttner's Diary [Eng.], September 17, 1743, 1/111/2/7 RMM; and Shekomeko Diary, September 17, 1743, 1/111/1 RMM.

43. Bethlehem Christian Indians to Shekomeko and Pachgatgoch, June 2, 1746, 34/319/2/8 RMM.

44. "A short account wch Br. Rauch gave at the Lovefeast before the Lord supper 23 Aug 1746, of the happy departure of Br. Jonas, the Indian, in Gnadenhütten," 34/319/5/3 RMM.

45. Van der Donck observed that in cases of mortal illness, Mohicans were "faithful to sustain and take care of each other." *Description of the New Netherlands,* 82.

46. Büttner's Journal [Eng.], December 28, 1744, 2/112/19/6 RMM; and Shekomeko Diary, December 28, 1744, 1/111/1 RMM.

47. Most of the recorded instances of seeking treatment from Indian practitioners are from the Pachgatgoch records. The missionaries stationed there in the 1750s often sought treatment from Gideon for a variety of ailments. Pachgatgoch Diary, July 28, November 3, 1750, March 30, 31, August 14, 1751, 3/114/2–4 RMM. For references to use of the sweat lodge, see Shekomeko Diary, July 11, 1745, 1/111/1 RMM; Pachgatgoch Diary, August 20, October 11, November 1, 25, 29, 1750, 3/114/2 RMM; Pachgatgoch Diary, February 18, March 18, 19, 21 and May 13, 1751, 3/114/3 RMM.

48. "A short account wch Br. Rauch gave at the Lovefeast before the Lord supper 23 Aug 1746, of the happy departure of Br. Jonas, the Indian, in Gnadenhütten," 34/319/5/3 RMM.

49. *Description of the New Netherlands,* 104.

50. *History of the Mission,* pt. II, p. 102; and "Bishop Cammerhoff's Journey to Shamokin, Pa 1748," 26/211/6/2 RMM.

51. Undated letter from Gideon [Eng.], 34/319/3/9 RMM.

52. Letters from Pachgatgoch to Bethlehem, 1756, 34/319/4/12 RMM.

53. Shekomeko Diary, January 18, 1744, 1/111/1 RMM.

54. Büttner to Seiffert, Shekomeko, December 7, 1742, 1/111/7/7 RMM; and Shekomeko Diary, November 30, 1742, 1/111/1 RMM.

55. "Ltr from Br. Jonathan translated out of Low dutch by Br. Mack" [Eng.], undated, 34/319/2/19 RMM.

56. Presbyterian missionary David Brainerd observed the same phenomenon during his work at the Forks of the Delaware. There, a man identified as a "conjurer" came to hear Brainered preach. The missionary asked the man why he came if his heart was dead and the man answered "I love to hear you speak about Christ for all. . . . I would have others come to Christ if I must go to Hell myself." Brainerd commented that this separation from loved ones in the afterworld "seem'd to be a very dreadful Part of the Hell he thought himself doom'd to." David Brainerd, *Mirabilia Dei Inter Indicos* (Philadelphia: William Bradford, n.d.), 159.

57. Büttner Diary [Eng.], September 27, 1744, 2/112/19/5 RMM. See also Shekomeko Diary, September 23, 1744, 1/111/1 RMM. A very sick Delaware woman sent a request through her sons that a Moravian Brother be sent to baptize her before she died, perhaps in the hopes of securing a continued connection with her two baptized sons. Gnadenhütten Diary, July 22, 1750, 5/117/1 RMM.

58. Jannike is Jannetje Mack, who died in 1747. Gnadenhütten Diary, February 3, 1750, 4/116/7 RMM.

59. Copy of Ruth's testament at end of Johannes Hagen's diary [Eng.], 1745, 2/112/8/2 RMM; and Johannes Hagen to Maria Spangenberg [Eng.], Shekomeko, April 12, 1745, 26/211/17/2 RMM.

60. Beata to Maria Spangenberg [Eng.], January 1747, 34/319/3/1 RMM. Gideon's wife Martha expressed similar thoughts when their daughter went to live at Bethlehem. Gideon and Martha to Spangenberg and others in Bethlehem [Eng.], July 9, 1754, 34/319/4/8 RMM.

61. Her request was granted. Gnadenhütten Diary, February 15, March 1, 1748, 4/116/3 RMM.

62. Joshua in Gnadenhütten to Spangenbergs, January 4, 1747, 34/319/3/3 RMM.

63. Gnadenhütten Diary, August 23, 1747, 4/116/2 RMM.

64. David and Sarah made a similar request. Gnadenhütten Diary, February 10, 13, 23, May 13, 14, 1748, 4/116/3 RMM.

65. Gnadenhütten Diary, March 2, 1748, 4/116/3 RMM. Beata died later that year. Gnadenhütten Diary, August 18, 1748, 4116/4 RMM.

66. Joshua to the Spangenbergs [Eng.], January 1747, 34/319/3/3 RMM. See also Gnadenhütten Diary, January 3, 23, 1747, 4/116/1 RMM.

67. Apparently, the missionaries consented to Philip and Lydia's request, and just over a month later, in February 1747, the mission diary recorded that the couple was happy to have their children at Bethlehem. Philippus and Lydia [Eng.], Gnadenhütten Diary, January 1747, 34/319/3/4 RMM. Another account of the same event can be found in the Gnadenhütten Diary, January 5, 13, February 22, 1747, 4/116/1 RMM.

68. On Indian child-rearing practices, see James Axtell, *The Invasion Within: The Contest of Cultures in Colonial North America* (New York: Oxford University Press, 1985), 58, 209; and *Zeisberger's History,* 16–17, 80–81.

69. For Moravian views on children, see Craig D. Atwood, *Community of the Cross: Moravian Piety in Colonial Bethlehem* (University Park: Pennsylvania State University Press, 2004), 178–83. On the Moravian understanding of children's piety and their application at mission sites, see Amy C. Schutt, " 'What Will Become of Our Young People?': Goals for Indian Children at Moravian Missions," *History of Education Quarterly* 38 (Autumn 1998): 268–86. On New England childrearing styles, see Philip Greven, *The Protestant Temperament: Patterns of Child-Rearing, Religious Experience, and the Self in Early America* (New York: Knopf, 1977); and John Demos, *A Little Commonwealth: Family Life in Plymouth Colony* (New York: Oxford University Press, 1970).

70. While the Moravians may have been less strict than their New England neighbors when it came to parenting philosophies, they did expect mission residents to accept the disciplining of children who attended the mission school. The records, however, neither suggest just what sort of punishment might have been meted out nor record any actual instances of children being punished by the Moravians. White and Native Workers Conference, November 21, 1742, 1/111/6/2 RMM.

71. For a discussion of Indian marriages in seventeenth- and eighteenth-century eastern New England, see Ann Marie Plane, *Colonial Intimacies: Indian Marriage in Early New England* (Ithaca, NY: Cornell University Press, 2000).

72. The longhouses were constructed of hickory saplings supports covered with the bark of chestnut trees. *Description of the New Netherlands*, 79–80; Brasser, *Riding the Frontier's Crest*, 29; and "Plan of Shekomeko by Johannes Hagen," 2/112/17/1 RMM. Umpachenee's longhouse at Skatekook clearly served this function. Stockbridge schoolteacher Timothy Woodbridge witnessed a divining ceremony held at Umpachenee's longhouse, which Woodbridge estimated was nearly sixty feet in length. *Historical Memoirs*, 23–24.

73. I have yet to find any discussion of the process by which delegates were chosen to serve on the committee, but it is apparent that it was the Christian members in good standing who served most regularly. At times, these were people who were likely prominent members of the community even before the arrival of the Moravians. But it is also clear that the Moravians helped to disrupt traditional patterns of authority. Many native communities experienced a new factionalism between Christians and non-Christians. See, for example, Daniel K. Richter, "Iroquois Versus Iroquois: Jesuit Missions and Christianity in Village Politics, 1642–1686," *Ethnohistory* 32, no. 1 (1985): 1–16.

74. Rebecca, Isaac's wife, seems to have maintained a business in selling rum. Women were often the suppliers of alcohol within an Indian community, as Peter Mancall has found in his study of Indians and alcohol in early America. Mancall, *Deadly Medicine*, 60. See also Hirsch, "Indian, *Métis*, and Euro-American Women," 80–81; Shekomeko Diary, March 20, 1745, 1/111/1 RMM.

75. Büttner's diary, January 30, 1743, 1/111/2/1 RMM.

76. White Workers Conference, August 13, 1743, 1/111/6/3 RMM.

77. On the regulation of marriage at Bethlehem, see Peter Vogt, " 'Ehereligion': The Moravian Theory and Practice of Marriage as Point of Contention in the Conflict between Ephrata and Bethlehem," *Communal Societies* 21 (September 2001): 37–48.

78. Pachgatgoch Diary, June 8, 1751, 3/114/3 RMM. Benjamin, Anna, Bartholomeus, and Esther were siblings. Anna married Jonathan, Abraham, and Sarah's son, in 1744, discussed below.

79. On the death of Umpachenee's wife, Hannah, see *Historical Memoirs*, 83. On Gideon and Umpachenee (Aaron) as cousins, see Pachgatgoch Diary, August 8, 1751, 3/114/4 RMM.

80. Umpachenee was excommunicated by Sergeant in 1741. Indian and White Workers Conference, August 11, 12, 1743, 1/111/6/3 RMM. On Umpachenee's impending excommunication, see Sergeant Diary, March 30, 1740, Stiles Papers.

81. Indian and White Workers, October 16, 1743, 1/111/6/2 RMM.

82. Maria ultimately married Samuel in December 1743 and died the following September. Indian and White Workers, December 4, 1743, 1/111/6/2 RMM; and Shekomeko Diary, December 26, 1743, September 27, 1744, 1/111/1 RMM.

83. Gideon and Martha remained in Pachgatgoch, where there was a Moravian mission presence at least until the 1760s. Gideon died in 1760. Christina eventually married Benjamin in 1767 and was killed in 1782 in the Gnadenhütten, Ohio, massacre. Fliegel *Index*, 87; and Pachgatgoch Diary, January 25, 1760, 4/115/9 RMM. The last mention of Martha is November 1762, at which time she was reported to be moving to her winter house. Fliegel *Index*, 278.

84. Büttner Diary, February 21, 1743, 1/111/2/1 RMM. Interestingly, the copy of this part of Büttner's diary made by Seiffert does not contain this last discussion. See 1/111/2/2 RMM.

85. White Workers Conference, August 13, White Workers' Conference, August 13, 1743, 1/111/6/3 RMM.

86. Anna (and thus her siblings, Benjamin, Esther, and Bartholomeus) was related to both the chief sachem at Stockbridge and Gideon of Pachgatgoch. On her relationship to

the Stockbridge sachem, see Martin Mack Diary, February 18, 1744, 2/112/1/1 RMM. Anna's parents were Petrus (Peter) and Thamar; Thamar was apparently Gideon's sister-in-law. Shekomeko Diary, November 28–30, 1743, 1/111/1 RMM. Gideon's wife Martha was identified as the foster mother of Anna. Pachgatgoch Diary, January 12, 1755, 4/115/3 RMM.

87. The German term *Freunden* is used here to mean the extended family or lineages, rather than "friends." See Hermann Wellenreuther and Carola Wessel, eds., *The Moravian Mission Diaries of David Zeisberger, 1772–1781,* trans. Julie Tomberlin Weber (University Park: Pennsylvania State University Press, 2005), "Introduction," 18. Shekomeko Diary, December 26, 1743, 1/111/1 RMM.

88. Shekomeko Diary, January 3, 1744, 1/111/1 RMM. For the conference minutes about the timing and place of the wedding, see Indian and White Workers Conference, December 26, 28, 1743, 1/111/6/2 RMM.

89. *Description of the New Netherlands,* 83.

90. *Description of the New Netherlands,* 83; Bragdon, *Native People of Southern New England,* 177–78; and Plane, *Colonial Intimacies,* 24–26.

91. Indian Workers Conference, December 16, 1744, 2/112/5/3 RMM.

92. Indian Workers Conference, February 5, 1744, 2/112/5/1 RMM, and March 31, 1745, 2/112/5/3 RMM.

93. "Maria hat gesagt, sie hette erst solche böse gedancken gehabt, sie möchte ihren Mann mahl fragen wies ihm gefallen würde wen sie sein Kind den Hals abschnitte wen er nicht besser vors Essen sorgen wolte." Indian Workers Conference, March 17, 1745, 2/112/15/1.

94. Indian Workers Conference, March 24, 1745, 2/112/15/1 RMM. For references to Joseph's troubles with alcohol, see Shekomeko Diary, March 28, 1743, 1/111/1 RMM.

95. For a discussion of violence in Indian marriages in eastern Massachusetts, see Plane, *Colonial Intimacies,* 150–51.

96. Those couples that appear at least once include Boaz and Ruth, Jonas and Bathsheba, Joseph and Maria, Zacheus and Magdalena, all from Shekomeko, and Petrus and Thamar of Wechquadnach. On Jonas and Bathsheba, Zachaeus and Magdalena, see Indian and White Workers Conference, March 17, 24, 1745, 2/112/15/1 RMM. On Petrus and Tamar, see Indian and White Workers Conference, September 5, 19, 1743, 1/111/6/2 RMM; and Indian Workers Conference, January 1, and March 31 1745, 2/112/5/1, 3 RMM.

97. Indian Workers Conference, January 4, 22, 1744, 2/112/5/1 RMM. Indian Workers Conference, September 30, 1744, 2/112/5/3 RMM.

98. Gnadenhütten Diary, February 10, 1748, 4/116/3 RMM.

99. Jonas's wife did eventually return and was baptized, taking the name Bathsheba. Büttner's Diary, January 30, 1743, 1/111/2/1 RMM. See also Workers Conference, January 30, 1743, 1/111/6/2 RMM; and Shekomeko Diary, August 7, 1743, 1/111/1 RMM.

100. Ironically, just five months after Petrus's death in July 1746, Petrus's widow, newly baptized as Christiana, married John Jacob Bull, also known as Shebosch, a Palatine convert to the Moravians. The couple remained active in mission work well into the 1780s. Fliegel *Index,* 84, 327; and *Memorials of the Moravian Church,* 145.

101. Indian Workers Conference, May 27, 1744, 2/112/5/3 RMM.

102. Indian Workers Conference, January 22, 1744, 2/112/5/3 RMM.

103. For a discussion of the choir system, see especially Atwood, *Community of the Cross,* 173–78; Gillian Lindt Gollin, *Moravians in Two Worlds: A Study of Changing Communities* (New York: Columbia University Press, 1967), 67–89; and Beverly Prior Smaby, *The Transformation of Moravian Bethlehem from Mission to Family Economy* (Philadelphia: University of Pennsylvania Press, 1988), 236. Both Gollin and Smaby see the choir system primarily as a substitute for the authority of the nuclear family and as a means of social control, a view challenged by Atwood, who emphasizes the roots of the system in Zinzendorf's theology.

104. Johann Christoph Pyrlaeus, who served as teacher at Shekomeko while preparing for a mission to the Iroquois, was the first to marry. He married Susanna Benezet on June 29, 1742. Gottlob Büttner and Johann Martin Mack were both married on September 3, 1743, to

Margaretha Bechtel and Johanna Rauh, respectively. Johannes Hagen was married several days later to Margaretha Dismann on September 7, 1742. Christian Heinrich Rauch was married December 12, 1742, to Anna Elisabetha Robins. Joseph Shaw was married to Maria Jones on March 27, 1743. And finally, of course, Christian Friedrich Post married Rachel on August 24, 1743. Clarence E. Beckel, ed., *Marriage Records of The Bethlehem Moravian Congregation with Supplementary Biographical Material, 1742–1892* (Bethlehem, PA: Bethlehem Public Library, 1936).

105. Her given name was Johanna, but she was most often referred to as Jannetje and sometimes as Anna or Jannike.

106. Mack's Journal [Eng.], January 29–31, 1743, 1/111/3/3 RMM.

107. Mack's Journal [Eng.], February, 4, 6, 8, 1743, 1/111/3/3 RMM.

108. "Martin Mack's Journal of Journey to Shamoko" [Eng.], October 22, 1745, 28/217/12b/1 RMM.

109. Letters from the Indians in Bethlehem, 1757, 34/319/4/13 RMM.

110. House Conference, November 30, 1742, 1/111/6/2 RMM.

111. White and Native Workers, November 27, 1742, 1/111/6/2 RMM.

112. Shekomeko Diary, November 13, 1743, 1/111/1 RMM.

113. Shekomeko Diary, October 13, 1743, 1/111/1 RMM.

114. Gnadenhütten Diary, June 21, 1747, 4/116/1 RMM.

115. Shekomeko Diary, February 17, 1744, 1/111/1 RMM.

116. Mack's Diary from Shekomeko, March 12, 1743, 2/112/1/2 RMM; and Shekomeko Diary, March 1, 1743, 1/111/1 RMM. Mack's diary uses the new calendar.

117. "A Short Account of Brother Martin Mack's Journey to Checomeco," November 22, 1745, 28/217/12/b/2 RMM. Women also expressed their affection for Moravian men, as when Johannes's wife Martha lamented that Büttner had been taken into custody for questioning. She recounted for Johannes that when she was in the woods, she had thought about Büttner, and "her heart wept and cried and she thought 'what are they doing with my Brother? What has he done that they harass him so and don't let him be at home when he is so sick.'" Johannes tried to console his wife by saying that Jesus' disciples were also persecuted. Shekomeko Diary, October 18, 1744, 1/111/1 RMM.

118. Indian and White Workers Conference, March 31, 1745, 2/112/15/1 RMM.

119. Indian and White Workers Conference, April 11, 1745, 2/112/15/1 RMM.

120. Indian Workers Conference, June 30, 1744, 2/112/5/3 RMM.

121. Conference Minutes, June 4, 1745, 2/112/8 RMM.

122. For example, Heckewelder commented, "Although the Indians have no code of laws for their government, their chiefs find little or no difficulty in governing them." And further: "It may justly be a subject of wonder, how a nation without a written code of laws or system of jurisprudence, without any form or constitution of government, and without even a single elective or hereditary magistrate, can subsist together in peace and harmony, and in the exercise of the moral virtues." He went on to attribute the smooth operation of society to "the pains which the Indians take to instill at an early age honest and virtuous principles upon the minds of their children, and to the method which they pursue in educating them." In this task, parents were assisted by all members of the community, who employed public praise and scorn to shape behavior. Such education would have been largely the province of women. *History, Manners, and Customs,* 107, 113–14.

CHAPTER 9. THE DYING CHIEF AND THE ACCIDENTAL MISSIONARY

1. This task is complicated by the different calendars in use by the British and German worlds during this period.

2. In April 1750, Jephta, who had been baptized by the Moravians and whose son lived at Stockbridge, arrived in Pachgatgoch bearing a request for a Moravian brother, which the Moravians resolved to fulfill. Pachgatgoch Diary, April 20, 1750, 3/114/2 RMM.

3. As we shall see, it is unclear precisely what Umpachenee's status was: he may have been the new chief sachem (governor) announced in February 1744, or he may have continued as "captain," meaning the local chief. The Moravian records sometimes call him governor and sometimes captain. Shekomeko Diary, May 22, 1745, 1/111/1 RMM.

4. Although the passage refers only to the "Governor from Westenhuc," it is clearly a reference to Umpachenee because the passage also refers to the governor having been upset with the missionaries for objecting to his marriage to Gideon's daughter Maria the previous year. Pachgatgoch Diary, December 11, 1744, 2/112/6/1 RMM.

5. Umpeatkow's wife is identified by the Moravians as the sister of Nathanael, a Shekomeko resident. Pachgatgoch Diary, May 26, 1751, 3/114/3 RMM.

6. Pachgatgoch Diary, May 26, 27, 1751, 3/114/3 RMM.

7. For more on Nicodemus, see chapter 5.

8. Fliegel *Index*, 257. See also Fliegel's alphabetical catalog, 34/3191/3 RMM.

9. Elizabeth was closely related to a prominent Shawnee chief and a Mohawk captain. Fliegel *Index*, 107.

10. He had long been a defender of the Moravian missionaries and an important political leader, serving as the representative of his community within the Mohican confederacy. Gottlob Büttner's Diary [Eng.], August 19, 1744, 2/112/19/5 RMM.

11. Anna was baptized by Martin Mack in Shekomeko, July 31, 1743, Bartholomew by Christian Rauch, March 26, 1744, and Benjamin by Mack in Gnadenhütten, November 4, 1749.

12. The new governor at Stockbridge traveled to Wechqudnach when he heard the news of the impending marriage. No other reason was given other than that Anna was a *Freund* of his. As we have seen, the Moravians were likely using "*Freund*" to signify lineage rather than friendship. Shekomeko Diary, February 5, 1744, 1/111/1 RMM; and Martin Mack Diary, February 16, 1744, 2/112/1 RMM.

13. Pachgatgoch Diary, May 26, 1751, 3/114/3 RMM.

14. Pachgatgoch Diary, May 27, 1751, 3/114/3 RMM.

15. Pachgatgoch Diary, May 27, 1751, 3/114/3 RMM.

16. Gnadenhütten Diary, June 16, 1747, 5/117/2 RMM.

17. Apparently the lines of communication were not perfect. Büninger received word in mid-July that Umpachenee had died. Pachgatgoch Diary, July 12, 1751, 3/114/4 RMM.

18. For the rest of this chapter, Old Style dates will be used in the text for clarity. The Moravian records follow the Gregorian calendar, and the dates given there are New Style.

19. Abraham Büninger to David Nitschmann, August 3, 1751, 4/115/15/3 RMM; and Pachgatgoch Diary, August 8, 10, 11, 1751, 3/114/4 RMM.

20. Pachgatgoch Diary, August 12 [NS], 1751, 3/114/4 RMM.

21. Jonathan Edwards, "Fast before Installment, St. Ind. and Mohawks," Acts 16:9, August 1751, 14/1093, JEC. This verse was printed on the Massachusetts Bay colonial seal in 1629.

22. Amos reported in Pachgatgoch that "the old king who had been sick for so long died last Saturday." Pachgatgoch Diary, August 24, 1751 [NS], 3/114/4 RMM. The 21st, not the 22nd, was a Saturday, and August 21 New Style corresponds to August 10 Old Style. Samuel Hopkins's history of Stockbridge records Umpachenee's death as August 10. *Historical Memoirs*, 159.

23. Jonathan Edwards, 1 Cor. 4:18, August 1751 to the Stockbridge Indians and Mohawks, JEC.

24. In attendance were Brigadier General Joseph Dwight, Colonel Joseph Pynchon, Captain Timothy Dwight, Captain Martin Kellogg, and Captain Benjamin Ashley, their military titles signifying their loyal service in the recent King George's War. Martin Kellogg and his sister, Rebecca, now married to Benjamin Ashley, were taken captive at Deerfield in 1704.

25. JE to Hubbard, August 31, 1751, *Works*, vol. 16, pp. 394–405.

26. Solomon Stoddard, *Whether God is not Angry with the Country for Doing So Little towards the Conversion of the Indians?* (Boston, 1723), 10.

27. On Hendrick's life and career, see Erik Hinderaker, "The 'Four Indian Kings' and the Imaginative Construction of the British Empire," *WMQ* 53 (July 1996): 487–526; and Timothy J.

Shannon, *Indians and Colonists at the Crossroads of Empire: The Albany Congress of 1754* (Ithaca, NY: Cornell University Press, 2000), 30–36.

28. JE to Hubbard, August 31, 1751, *Works,* vol. 16, pp. 394–405.

29. The Mohawks' frustration was exacerbated by William Johnson's resignation from his post as New York's Indian agent. Shannon, *Indians and Colonists,* 30–51.

30. Another account of this meeting can be found in a report dated October 8, 1751, Mass. Archives, vol. 32, pp. 204–12.

31. JE to the Mohawks at the Treaty, August 16, 1751, *The Sermons of Jonathan Edwards, A Reader,* ed. Wilson H. Kimnach, Kenneth P. Minkema, and Douglas A. Sweeney (New Haven: Yale University Press, 1999), 105–10.

32. JE to Hubbard, August 31, 1751, *Works,* vol. 16, pp. 394–405.

33. JE to Hubbard, August 31, 1751, *Works,* vol. 16, pp. 394–405.

34. Shannon, *Indians and Colonists,* 1–16, 48–51.

35. The sermon quotations are from Psalms 1:3, August 1751, JEC.

36. Patrick Frazier, *The Mohicans of Stockbridge* (Lincoln: University of Nebraska Press, 1992), 183–88.

CHAPTER 10. INDIAN AND WHITE BODIES POLITIC AT STOCKBRIDGE

1. Several recent works explore British identity in the eighteenth century. See especially Linda Colley's seminal *Britons: Forging the Nation 1707–1837* (New Haven: Yale University Press, 1992). On various aspects of British-American identity, see Brendan McConville, *The King's Three Faces: The Rise and Fall of Royal America, 1688–1776* (Chapel Hill: University of North Carolina Press, 2006); Nancy Shoemaker, *A Strange Likeness: Becoming Red and White in Eighteenth-Century North America* (New York: Oxford University Press, 2004); Thomas S. Kidd, *The Protestant Interest: New England after Puritanism* (New Haven: Yale University Press, 2004); and John Wood Sweet, *Bodies Politic: Negotiating Race in the American North, 1730–1830* (Baltimore: Johns Hopkins University Press, 2003).

2. Harry S. Stout challenged Perry Miller's assertion that Edwards broke with his Puritan forebears on the issue of the national covenant. Stout's analysis of Edwards's Thanksgiving and Fast Day sermons led him to conclude that Edwards's theology was of a piece with the New England Puritan tradition in maintaining the idea of a national covenant. Mark A. Noll views the communion controversy as the beginning of Edwards's abandonment of the national covenant. Miller, *The New England Mind: The Seventeenth Century* (Cambridge: Harvard University Press, 1954), 463–91; Stout, "The Puritans and Edwards," in *Jonathan Edwards and the American Experience,* ed. Nathan O. Hatch and Harry S. Stout (New York: Oxford University Press, 1988), 142–59; and Noll, *America's God from Jonathan Edwards to Abraham Lincoln* (New York: Oxford University Press, 2002), 44–48.

3. David J. Silverman has explored this same phenomenon in the context of the Indians of Martha's Vineyard. Silverman, *Faith and Boundaries: Colonists, Christianity, and Community among the Wampanoag Indians of Martha's Vineyard, 1600–1871* (Cambridge: Cambridge University Press, 2005).

4. Shirley W. Dunn, *The Mohican World, 1680–1750* (Fleischmanns, NY: Purple Mountain Press, 2000), 36, 65–97.

5. A 1741 message sent to the Shawnee, whom the Mohicans considered their younger brothers, referred to Sergeant as their "elder brother." *Historical Memoirs,* 89.

6. During this time, residents of Wechquadnach (near Sharon, Connecticut) expressed interest, even paying several visits, but did not relocate to Stockbridge. *Historical Memoirs,* 74, 75; and Sergeant Diary, June 26, July 1, 1739, Stiles Papers. Most of the Wechquadnach Indians moved to Gnadenhütten in 1753. See especially Gnadenhütten Diary, May 24, 1753, 5/117/4 RMM.

7. Stephen Williams to the Commissioners, July 11, 1735, Box 2, NEC.

8. *Historical Memoirs,* 37.

9. For example, in May 1736, Sergeant reported that fifteen families were considering moving to Stockbridge, drawn by the promise of land to "improve" and the appeal they found in "the notion of husbandry." Sergeant to Benjamin Colman, May 20, 1736. John Davis Papers, 1730–1739, MHS. According to Sergeant, in 1736, a visitor from the Susquehanna "experienc'd something more than ordinary, whereby he had been changed from a very vicious, drunken Fellow, to a sober Man." *Historical Memoirs,* 36; and Sergeant Diary, January 6, 1740, Stiles Papers.

10. Sergeant Diary, March 30, 1740, Stiles Papers.

11. Sergeant visited Kaunaumeek in September 1736 with several Stockbridge Indian leaders. There he preached in Mohican to a gathering of about thirty. The Housatonic chiefs, according to Sergeant, "took pains to persuade them to embrace the Christian Religion and endeavour'd to answer those Objections they suppos'd might arise in their Minds against it." *Historical Memoirs,* 61. Wautaunukumeett was likely the same as Wauntaugameet, listed as one of four chiefs (including Umpachenee and Konkapot) who represented the Housatonic Mohicans at the 1735 Deerfield conference. *At a Conference,* 11.

12. David Brainerd took up the task of serving as missionary at Kaunaumeek in April 1743, but by the following year, he had been reassigned to serve among the Delaware. With his departure and a new war looming, most of the Kaunaumeek Indians moved to Stockbridge in April 1744. Patrick Frazier, *The Mohicans of Stockbridge* (Lincoln: University of Nebraska Press, 1992), 58–59, 70; *Historical Memoirs,* 61–62; John Sergeant to New England Commissioners, January 20, 1738, and May 9, 1738, NEC; and Sergeant Diary, June 10, 1739, Stiles Papers.

13. Hendrick Aupaumut, quoted in Electa F. Jones, *Stockbridge, Past and Present; Or Records of an Old Mission Station* (Springfield, MA: Samuel Bowles and Company, 1854), 16–17. John Sergeant and Moravian missionary and historian John Heckewelder recounted similar stories of the Mohicans' rescue of the Shawnee. Sergeant's version, the earlier of the two accounts, places the refugee villages along the Susquehanna, whereas Heckewelder suggests they settled somewhere in New England. Sergeant to Stephen Williams, May 14, 1739, Housatonic, Ayer Collection MS 800. According to Heckewelder, some of the refugee Shawnee settled with the Delaware in Pennsylvania and others were settled closer to the Mohicans in what became New England. Heckewelder, *Notes, Amendments and Additions to Heckewelder's History of the Indians,* 970.1 H35m, American Philosophical Society, Philadelphia; and Eric Hinkderaker, *Elusive Empires: Constructing Colonialism in the Ohio Valley, 1673–1800* (Cambridge: Cambridge University Press, 1997), 18–32.

14. Various land transactions involving land in and around Stockbridge confirm close Shawnee ties. See Dunn, *Mohican World,* 139–40 and appendix B, which includes a number of Shawnee individuals with ties in Stockbridge.

15. Sergeant Diary, June 10, 1739, Stiles Papers.

16. Aunauwauneekheek reported that the Shawnee had indeed "made an agreement among themselves to trade no more in Rum and that they have actually broken some caggs." Sergeant to Williams, May 14, 1739, Ayer Collection.

17. Sergeant to Williams, May 14, 1739, and John Sergeant to Stephen Williams, May 21, 1741, Gratz Collection, Box 23, American Colonial Clergy, Historical Society of Pennsylvania [HSP].

18. John Sergeant to Drummond, June 23, 1741, Gratz Collection, Box 23, HSP; and *Historical Memoirs,* 89.

19. Sergeant experienced firsthand Shawnee hostility toward Christianity, remarking that many in his audience had walked out when he attempted to preach. He suspected their aversion was "deriv'd ... from the French, and confirmed by their own Observation of the Behaviour of that vile Sort of Men the Traders, that go among them." *Historical Memoirs,* 89.

20. Evan Haefeli and Kevin Sweeney attribute St. Francis Indian participation in the 1704 raid on Deerfield to the fact that some of the St. Francis Indians were descended from Connecticut River Indians. Haefeli and Sweeney, "Revisiting the Redeemed Captive: New Perspectives on the 1704 Attack on Deerfield," *WMQ* 52 (January 1995): 9–16.

21. The most recent attacks had come in the 1720s, during Dummer's War; Abenakis raided towns on the Massachusetts frontier in retaliation for English intrusions into Abenaki lands. As Colin Calloway has shown, the Abenaki fought for reasons distinct from the interests of their French allies. Calloway, *Western Abenakis of Vermont, 1600–1800* (Norman: University of Oklahoma Press, 1987), 113–31.

22. The message was sent from "three of your Brethren...viz. from the High-lands, Mauhekun, and Skahttukook." By specifying "any of our people," the Stockbridges and the others were likely referring to those Mohicans and Schaghticoke who had joined the St. Francis in the seventeenth century when they were seeking relief from English intrusions on their lands. Sergeant Diary, January 20, 1740, Stiles Papers; see also *Historical Memoirs*, 77–78. Gordon Day, "Western Abenaki," identifies Wtanshekauntukko as St. Francis, or Odanak, Indians. Odanak was a refugee community first established by Sokokis of the upper Connecticut River area, later joined by other southern New England Indians from farther south in the valley. "Abenaki," *HNAI*, vol. 15, pp. 148–49, 159.

23. The final belt was delivered to a party of Norridgewocks hunting near Albany, accompanied by a more strongly worded address. The Stockbridges insisted (albeit without success) that Abenakis remain neutral: "Brother at Naunauchoowuk. Tho' you had begun a war with the English, you would regard us if we should desire you to desist—you will without doubt, not intermeddle, if we insist on advice to this purpose." The message met with a noncommittal deferral: the hunting party seemed to approve, "but said, they must first consult their Elder men, who were at home, before they came to any final determination." Sergeant Diary, January 20, 1740, Stiles Papers.

24. Since 1719, the Anglican Society for the Propagation of the Gospel had a missionary based at Fort Hunter working among the Mohawk populations of Canajoharie and Tionderoga. On the Anglican mission to the Mohawks, see William B. Hart, "For the Good of Our Souls: Mohawk Authority, Accommodation, and Resistance to Protestant Evangelism, 1700–1780," Ph.D. dissertation, Brown University, 1998.

25. James Merrell discusses the history of the ceremony, which likely had its origins in Iroquoia in the seventeenth century. Merrell, *Into the American Woods: Negotiators on the Pennsylvania Frontier* (New York: W. W. Norton & Co., 1999), 20–23.

26. This document is in Sergeant's hand and is housed not with Stockbridge records but at the Moravian Archives. "Speech of our Tribe of Indians to the Mohawks with their Answer," June 5, 1744, 35/323/8/1 RMM. The Shekomeko diary notes that six Highland Indians were passing through on their way to Stockbridge and then to the Mohawks to renew their alliance. Shekomeko Diary, May 21, 1744, 1/111/1 RMM.

27. The note at the top from Sergeant indicates that the speeches were exchanged the previous week. "Speech of our Tribe," June 5, 1744, 35/323/8/1 RMM.

28. On the fate of Stockbridge during King George's War, see Frazier, *Mohicans of Stockbridge,* 69–81.

29. Runners from Stockbridge arrived at Shekomeko in February 1744 to announce the appointment of their new governor (the Moravian term that seems to correspond to the English usage of "chief") and renew their friendship. Martin Mack Diary, February 4, 5, 1744, 2/112/1/1 RMM.

30. *Historical Memoirs*, 129.

31. In his one published sermon, Sergeant aligns himself with the anti-revivalist cause, arguing that the truth lies in the "middle way" between contending parties. He offered up his thoughts "to the Judgment of the Candid and Impartial." Sergeant, *The Causes and Danger of Delusions in the Affairs of Religion Consider'd and Caution'd against, with Particular Reference to the Temper of the Present Times* (Boston, 1743), 1. A letter from Sergeant to an unknown recipient defending his interpretation of Romans 7:1–7 also reveals his liberal leanings. John Sergeant, March 20, 1745, Henry Hopkins Collection, Family Papers MC23, Williams College Archives.

32. John Sergeant to Stephen Williams, February 22, 1741 [1742], Autograph Letters of Ephraim Williams, Williams College Archives, Williamstown, Massachusetts.

33. For a full account of the land transactions at Stockbridge, see Lion G. Miles, "Red Man Dispossessed: The Williams Family and the Alienation of Indian Land in Stockbridge, Massachusetts, 1736–1818," *NEQ* 67, no. 1 (March 1994): 46–76.

34. Umpachenee and other Stockbridge residents were likely quite well versed in varieties of Christianity. Kaunaumeek resident Waunaubauquus arrived in Stockbridge in 1738 and was baptized in February 1740. He had been baptized in his youth by a "popish priest," but Sergeant agreed to baptize him again because had lived "altogether in heathenism." Umpachenee surprised Sergeant when he asked the missionary his opinion of priestly celibacy and their "severe Methods of doing Penance." Sergeant responded by telling Umpachenee that such practices were the "vain Inventions of Men" and that the obligation of the Christian was to "mortify our Lusts and Passions, and to regulate our Lives by the revealed Will of God, and not to go beyond that." Sergeant Diary, January 26, 1736, quoted in *Historical Memoirs*, 43; and Sergeant Diary, February 17, 1740, Stiles Papers.

35. Sergeant Diary, October 21, 1739, February 5, 1740, Stiles Papers.

36. Umpachenee objected that fasts were simply "of human institution," offering as evidence the fact "there was no such thing in the neighbouring Government among the Dutch People." Perhaps Sergeant was correct in believing the example of the Dutch to be "a mighty thing with him," but perhaps Umpachenee was making a finer point than that and reminding Sergeant of Jesus' message in the Sermon on the Mount that his followers should anoint their heads "that your fasting may not be seen by men but by your Father who is in secret" (Matthew 6:16–18). Sergeant Diary, March 27, 1740.

37. Sergeant Diary, March 27, 30, 1740, Stiles Papers.

38. Büttner refrained from commenting on Sergeant's preaching in the official mission diary, but in a letter to a colleague, one can detect a bit of jealousy in his observation that Sergeant's main concern was not religion but displaying his language skills. Büttner went on to suggest that the Indians valued good Moravian preaching in English or Dutch over Sergeant's Congregationalist preaching in Mohican, noting that as soon as Sergeant left, the "foreign Indians" (the Stockbridges) asked the Moravians to preach again. Büttner obliged, preaching first in English and then in Dutch, with his words translated by Johannes. Shekomeko Diary, October 6, 7, 1742, 1/111/1/1 RMM; and Büttner to Anton Seiffert, October 16, 1742, 1/111/7/5 RMM.

39. Büttner Diary, April 16, 1743, 1/111/2/4 RMM; and Br. Rauch's Journey in 1743 [Eng.], 29/221/4/1 RMM.

40. Büttner's Diary [Eng.], August 26, 1744, 2/112/19/5 RMM. The original German can be found at Shekomeko Diary, August 26, 1744, 1/111/1 RMM. See also Indian Workers Conference, September 2, 1744, 2/112/5/3 RMM.

41. Although Umpachenee is not mentioned by name in this document, the governor is referred to as the one who was upset with the Moravians for interfering with his marriage to Gideon's daughter, Maria. In the discussion of that affair, the Stockbridge leader is referred to as the "captain of Westenhuc" and also as Aron, making it clear that they are referring to Umpachenee. Büttner to Spangenberg, December 11, 1744, 2/112/6/11 RMM; Shekomeko Diary, December 6, 9, 10, 1744, 1/111/1 RMM; and Brother Büttner's Journal [Eng.], December 3, 1744, 2/112/19/6 RMM.

42. Umpeatkow's name appeared among the sellers on deeds dated 1737 and 1740. Dunn, *Mohican World*, 360.

43. Pachgatgoch Diary, May 26, 1751, 3/114/3 RMM.

44. Büttner Diary, April 20, 1743, 1/111/2/4 RMM.

45. Gottlob Büttner Diary, April 19, 1743, 1/111/2/4 RMM; and Shekomeko Diary, April 19, 20, 1743, 1/111/1 RMM. Paul was reported in Shekomeko in October 1743 and October 1744 and headed to Bethlehem in May 1745. See Shekomeko Diary, October 12, 1743, 1/111/1 RMM; Indian Workers' Conference, October 21, 1744, 2/112/5/3 RMM; and Bischoff's Diary, May 27, 1745, 3/113/1/1 RMM.

46. According to Shirley Dunn, van Guilder had been raised in Rhinebeck, New York. During the mission era, van Guilder lived on a farm west of Sheffield. Dunn, *Mohican World,* 169–70; Büttner Diary [Eng.], April 21, 1743, 1/111/2/7 RMM; and Shekomeko Diary, April 21, 1743, 1/111/1 RMM.

47. Büttner's Diary [Eng.], December 5, 1743, 1/111/2/7 RMM; Büttner Diary, December 6, 1743, 2/211/5/1 RMM; and Shekomeko Diary, December 6, 1743, 1/111/1 RMM.

48. These included the wives of Abraham and Sarah's sons, Jonathan and David, and Daniel's sister Judith, who had been baptized by Sergeant. Later, in 1753, there was a substantial exodus from Stockbridge to Gnadenhütten, Pennsylvania, where many of the Shekomeko residents had relocated, likely an indication of the growing frustration in Stockbridge over the alienation of Indian lands. See, for example, Gnadenhütten Diary, May 24, 1753, 5/117/4 RMM.

49. *Historical Memoirs,* 128.

50. These tracts in part repeat the concerns raised in Europe about the Moravians. Tennent published two major pieces against the Moravians. The first was a compilation of three sermons preached in April 1742 at New York and published as *The Necessity of Holding Fast the Truth* (Boston, 1742). The second is a point-by-point refutation of Zinzendorf's ideas. The preface to this work was signed by Benjamin Colman, Thomas Prince, John Webb, William Cooper, Thomas Foxcroft, and Joshua Gee. Gilbert Tennent, *Some Account of the Principles of the Moravians, Chiefly collected from several Conversations with Count Zinzendorf; and from some Sermons preached by him at Berlin and published in London* (London, 1743). Samuel Finley, *Satan Strip'd of his angelick Robe: Being the substance of several sermons preached at Philadelphia, January 1742–3 from II Thessalonians 2:11,12, shewing the strength, nature and symptoms of Delusion, with an application to the Moravians* (Philadelphia, 1743).

51. Finley, *Satan Strip'd,* 40.

52. Tennent, *Some Account,* 45.

53. The Moravians provided Tennent with just the outlet he needed—he could recant some of the excesses of the revivals, particularly those that threatened ministerial authority, without having to acknowledge his own error. Tennent, *Some Account,* iv, vi, ix, 12, 18–19, 43.

54. Finley, *Satan Strip'd,* 19, 28, 29.

55. Jonathan Edwards to John Erskine, July 5, 1750, *Works,* vol. 16, p. 348.

56. Several of Edwards's treatises were devoted to defining the marks of true conversion, including *The Distinguishing Marks of a Work of the Spirit of God* (1741), *Some Thoughts concerning the Present Revival of Religion in New England* (1743), and *Treatise Concerning Religious Affections* (1746).

57. Christian Rauch, undated recollections of a journey into Mohawk country [Eng.], 29/221/4/1 RMM.

58. In May 1743, in response to the growing outcry against the Moravians, the Connecticut General Assembly passed an act that accused the Moravians of estranging the Indians from the government and inciting revolt. Charles J. Hoadly, ed., *The Public Records of the Colony of Connecticut From October 1735, to October 1743, Inclusive* (Hartford: Press of the Case, Lockwood & Brainerd Co., 1874), vol. 8, pp. 521–52. The colonial officials did not find the Moravians as offensive as the settlers did, finding them guilty of violating the recently passed act but not the greater charge of treachery, as some would have liked. All were fined £100 and released, with the exception of Pyrlaeus, who was not fined at all because he had only been passing through and was not employed as a missionary in the province.

59. "John Christopher Pyrlaeus's account of his arrest and trial" [Eng.], June 1743, 1/111/9/1 RMM.

60. Büttner also became suspected of papist leanings. English translation of a report of Gottlob Büttner's trial at New York in a letter to Peter Böhler, August 13, 1744, 2/112/3/5 RMM; and Büttner Diary, October 17, 1744, 112/19/5 RMM.

61. "An Account of What happened in the Indian Affairs at Schekomeko & Pachgatgoch viz the Arrest, Imprisonment & Examination of Br. Pyrlaeus, Martin Mack & Joseph Shaw at Milford in New England" [Eng.], June 7, 1743, 1/111/4/2 RMM.

62. As the council continued to debate, Pyrlaeus presented his ordination papers and glee-fully looked on as "they chewed a long while [at these] as they were all in Latin, of which not one of them understood anything." With his university education, Pyrlaeus was the exception among the Moravian missionaries, most of whom were craftsmen. Their lack of formal educa-tion would become an issue during their trials in New York, as we shall see. Pyrlaeus, "Account of his Arrest" [Eng.], June 1743, 1/111/9/1 RMM.

63. Gottlob Büttner to Anton Seiffert [Eng.], June 5, 1744 (May 25 according to the Julian calendar used by the English), 2/112/2/3 RMM.

64. Gottlob Büttner to Anton Seiffert [Eng.], June 27, 1744, 2/112/19/4 RMM.

65. Büttner Diary [Eng.], June 23, 1744, 2/112/2/3 RMM.

66. A thorough account of these events is contained in *History of the Mission*, pt. II, pp. 55–68.

67. Büttner to Seiffert [Eng.], June 27, 1744, 2/112/19/4 RMM. Even some nearby Indians were apparently afraid of the Shekomeko Indians. Missionary Shaw attributed the fear of the New York Highland Indians to the white people who "had told them that we came from the Pope and when they believed what we said to them they would all go to the Hell which has made them so as they are afraid to come to Shecomecko." Joseph Shaw to Peter Böhler [Eng.], April 11, 1744, 30/223/4/2 RMM.

68. Governor Clinton, July 5, 1744, 2/112/7/4 and 2/112/7/5 RMM.

69. Punctuation added for clarity. Büttner to Böhler [Eng.], August 13, 1744, 2/112/3/5; and Shaw to Seiffert and Böhler [Eng.], August 11, 1744, 2/112/4/2 RMM.

70. "An Act for securing of his Majesties government of New York," September 21, 1744, 2/112/7/9 RMM.

71. "Translation of Mack's Journey from Sheck. to Bethlehem and arrest at Esopus," March 3, 1745, 2/112/10/1 RMM.

72. Mark Valeri finds a similar shift in Edwards's thought on the nature of forgiveness, shifting from a Puritan ideal of forgiveness as a social act to an evangelical view emphasiz-ing forgiveness in a more generalized sense. Mark Valeri, "Forgiveness: From the Puritans to Jonathan Edwards," in *Practicing Protestants: Histories of Christian Life in America, 1630–1965*, ed. Laurie F. Maffly-Kipp, Leigh E. Schmidt, and Mark Valeri (Baltimore: Johns Hopkins University Press, 2006), 35–48.

73. George M. Marsden, *Jonathan Edwards: A Life* (New Haven: Yale University Press, 2003) 5–6, 36–37.

74. JE to Timothy Edwards, January 27, 1752, *Works*, vol. 16, p. 420.

75. See especially Edwards's farewell sermon to his Northampton congregation. Jonathan Ed-wards, *A Farewel Sermon Preached at the First Precinct in Northampton* (Boston: S. Kneeland, 1751).

76. The most extensive treatments of the controversy are Patricia Tracy, *Jonathan Edwards, Pastor: Religion and Society in Eighteenth-Century Northampton* (New York: Hill and Wang, 1979), ch. 8; Kevin Sweeney, "River Gods and Related Minor Deities: The Williams Family and the Connecticut River Valley, 1637–1790," Ph.D. dissertation, Yale University, 1986, ch. 5; and David Hall's introduction, *Works*, vol. 12.

77. For Edwards's own account of the relationship of Stockbridge affairs with the Williams family's involvement in the communion controversy, see especially his letter to William Hogg. *Works*, vol. 16, pp. 549–52.

78. "Minutes," December 4, 11, 1749, New England Company Records, 1685–1784 (here-after NEC Records), New England Historic Genealogical Society, Boston, Massachusetts; and December 6, 1749, Mass. Archives, vol. 32, pp. 30–32. For a more extended discussion, see Marsden, *Jonathan Edwards*, 379–80; and Edmund S. Morgan, *The Gentle Puritan: A Life of Ezra Stiles, 1727–1795* (New Haven: Yale University Press, 1962), 82–89.

79. The most famous line from this letter laments the shame that a "head so full of divin-ity should be so empty of politics." Ephraim Williams Jr. to Jonathan Ashley, May 2, 1751, in *Colonel Ephraim Williams: A Documentary Life*, ed. Wyllis Wright (Pittsfield, MA: Berkshire County Historical Society, 1970), 61.

80. *Works,* vol. 16, pp. 355–56; and Winslow, *Jonathan Edwards, 1703–1758* (1940; repr. New York: Collier Books, 1961), 243.

81. The terms proved acceptable to Edwards, and he was awarded a salary of £70 sterling (comparable to the £700 Old Tenor that he received in Northampton) from the New England Company, £6.13s4d. from the English congregants and 100 loads of firewood from the Indian and white congregations together. "Minutes," April 1, June 6, 1751, NEC. The arrangement apparently did not represent a drop in salary. See JE to Joseph Bellamy, June 28, 1751, *Works,* vol. 16, p. 374; McLaurin to Hogg, November 8, 1751, Firestone Library, Princeton; and Sarah Cabot Sedgwick and Christine Sedgwick Marquand, *Stockbridge, 1739–1939: A Chronicle* (Great Barrington, MA: Berkshire Courier, 1939), 60.

82. According to Edwards, Kellogg was "a man of pretty good understanding for one that was being an illiterate man, and a man in years," yet he could not be "persuaded to set up a school or turn out of his own disorderly way." J. E to Jasper Mauduit, March 10, 1752, *Works,* vol. 16, p. 453; JE to Secretary Andrew Oliver, February 18, 1752, *Works,* vol. 16, pp. 425–28; *Historical Memoirs,* iii, 143–44; and Sergeant, *A Letter from the Revd Mr. Sergeant of Stockbridge, to Dr. Colman of Boston* (Boston: Rogers and Fowle, 1743), 3.

83. On the departure of the Mohawks from Stockbridge, see JE to Andrew Oliver, April 12, 1753, *Works,* vol. 16, pp. 581–82.

84. Edwards believed the Williamses considered him to be an obstacle to their plans and "a great nuisance here." JE to Andrew Oliver, February 18, 1752, *Works,* vol. 16, p. 428.

85. *Works,* vol. 16, pp. 423–425, 428, 550–51. The Indians' contempt for Williams predated Edwards's arrival. Sergeant recorded in his journal that Stockbridge chief Umpachenee complained to him that, "Capt Williams and I were the occasions of his Apostacy." John Sergeant, diary entries dated October 21 and November 29, 1739, Stiles Papers.

86. *Works,* vol. 16, p. 590. Letters from Abigail Williams to her brother show increasing concern at their father's erratic behavior. Abigail Williams Sergeant Dwight to Brother, Stockbridge, November 1, 1752, Dwight Collection, p. 23, Williams College Archives.

87. JE to Andrew Oliver, February 18, 1752, *Works,* vol. 16, p. 427; JE to the Commissioners, February 19, 1752, *Works,* vol. 16, p. 431; JE to Thomas Prince, May 10, 1754, *Works,* vol. 16, p. 632; and JE to Isaac Hollis, July 17, 1752, *Works,* vol. 16, p. 499.

88. JE to Thomas Hubbard, March 30, 1752, *Works,* vol. 16, pp. 465–66; JE to Andrew Oliver, May 1752, *Works,* vol. 16, p. 472; and JE to Andrew Oliver, October 1752, *Works,* vol. 16, p. 534.

89. Timothy Woodbridge, who still maintained a separate day school for the Stockbridge Mohicans, could not have seen the plans for the boarding school as anything other than a slight. Williams accused Woodbridge of undermining the boarding school, and Woodbridge was called to Boston to answer to the Indian commissioners. He was accompanied by several Stockbridge Indians, who spoke in his defense. "Minutes," August 13, 1750, October 2, 1750, NEC.

90. Marsden, *Jonathan Edwards,* 405.

91. For a discussion of the relationship between Dwight and Edwards, see Marsden, *Jonathan Edwards,* 395–96. See also JE to Andrew Oliver, February 18, 1752, *Works,* vol. 16, pp. 425, 426; JE to Thomas Prince, May 10, 1754, *Works,* vol. 16, pp. 630–31; and JE to Isaac Hollis, July 17, 1752, *Works,* vol. 16, p. 497. In a fury one day, Dwight accosted Hawley (an Edwards appointee) at the schoolhouse and "continued him under his chastisement for three hours" in the presence of the Mohawk children in an effort to force his resignation. The result was to further confirm Mohawk uneasiness and eventually drive away Hawley, who left on a mission to the Oneida village of Onohquaga in the summer of 1753. JE to Thomas Hubbard, March 30, 1752, *Works,* 16, pp. 465–66; JE to Andrew Oliver, May 1752, *Works,* vol. 16, p. 472; and JE to Andrew Oliver, October 1752, *Works,* vol. 16, p. 534.

92. Boston Commissioners to Jaspar Mauduit, May 27, 1754, NEC; and JE to Sec. Josiah Willard, March 8, 1754, *Works,* vol. 16, pp. 626–27.

93. December 13, 1752, Mass. Archives, vol. 32, pp. 299–304. Woodbridge, together with eleven other English inhabitants of Stockbridge and forty-one Indians, submitted a memorial

of their grievances about the management of the school under Dwight and Kellogg and defending Edwards expressing themselves at "an intire loss" as to "when and by what means these gentlemen made the discovery of Capt. Kelloggs great knowledge of the value of the country of the western tribes of Indians, his extraordinary talents and prudence in the management of Indian Affairs, his zeal for the crown and the good of this province." Mass. Archives, vol. 32, pp. 365–72. Edwards, Dwight, and Ephraim Williams also sought to win the influential merchant and commander William Pepperell to their cause. JE to Pepperell, January 30, 1753, *Works,* vol. 16, pp. 552–63; and Ephraim Williams to Sir William Pepperell, August 29, 1753, New Misc. Mss. box 2, folder 17, Williams College Archives.

94. JE to Isaac Hollis, July 17, 1752, *Works,* vol. 16, p. 497.

95. Edwards's letter to Thomas Prince was largely an attempt to dispel the accusations leveled by Joseph Dwight that the Mohawks had left *because* control had been placed in the hands of Edwards. JE to Thomas Prince, *Works,* vol. 16, p. 637.

96. Something of this can be seen in Edwards's notes of a meeting at his house with the Mohawks when they announced their intention to leave. The notes read: "on Mr. Edwards asking what it was that discouraged 'em and made 'em go away whether it was any thing that they had observed in Him that had discouraged them replied no they found no fault with any thing in Him but it was instead those People that lately had the management of affairs at the Boarding School that had discouraged them." Notes at the end of sermon dated December 1753, Luke 1:77–79, JEC.

97. "Speech of our Tribe of Indians to the Mohawks with their Answer," June 5, 1744, 35/323/8/1 RMM.

98. Minutes, August 3, 1746, Box B, NEC Records, NEGHS; and JE to Isaac Hollis, July 17, 1752, *Works,* vol. 16, p. 496.

99. Quoted in *Historical Memoirs,* 120.

100. JE to William Hogg, July 13, 1751, *Works,* vol. 16, p. 392.

101. JE to Hubbard, August 31, 1751, *Works,* vol. 16, pp. 394–405.

102. JE to Joseph Paice, February 24, 1752, *Works,* vol. 16, pp. 436, 440.

103. At the time, Hawley was stationed as chaplain at Crown Point. JE to Gideon Hawley, October 9, 1757, *Works,* vol. 16, p. 690. For the decline of providential thinking, see Michael Winship, *Seers of God: Puritan Providentialism in the Restoration and Early Enlightenment* (Baltimore: Johns Hopkins University Press, 1996).

104. Not all of the Iroquois present at the negotiations were satisfied with the provisions promised by the colonial officials. When told there was no promise of clothing for those not attending the school, "several of them are gone away in disgust." JE to Hubbard, August 31, 1751, *Works,* vol. 16, p. 398; see also JE to Joseph Paice, February 24, 1752, *Works,* vol. 16, pp. 434–47.

105. *Works,* vol. 3, p. 151.

106. "Private meeting on occasion of Mssrs W——ge's Hawley going into the Country of the Six Nations," Acts 14:26–27, May 1753, JEC.

107. "Private meeting," JEC.

108. *Works,* vol. 16, pp. 407–14.

109. Edwards outlined his educational plans in a long letter to supporter William Pepperell in November 1751. *Works,* vol. 16, pp. 406–14, quotations 411, 413.

110. *Works,* vol. 16, p. 431.

111. *Works,* vol. 16, p. 409.

112. Noll, *America's God,* 44–48.

113. In writing to the commissioners for Indian affairs in Boston, Edwards reported, "I preach constantly to 'em once every Sabbath and go once a week to instruct their children." JE to Commissioners for Indian Affairs, February 18, 1751. Of roughly 1,200 surviving manuscript sermons, approximately 190 of these were composed for the Stockbridges. Counting these and repreached Northampton sermons, Edwards preached approximately 233 sermons to the Stockbridge Indians. All numbers are drawn from an analysis of the finding aid to the Jonathan

Edwards Collection Gen MSS 151, by Elizabeth A. Bolton, Beinecke Rare Book and Manuscript Library, New Haven, Connecticut, 1995. Numbers should be taken as approximate, as some sermon manuscripts Edwards marked with "St. Ind" are not identified in the index as Indian sermons. An updated sermon index is being prepared by the Jonathan Edwards Center at Yale.

114. Although the English and Indian members of the town technically belonged to the same congregation, the sermon manuscripts suggest that Edwards preached separately to the two groups, which is confirmed by a journal entry by Gideon Hawley. Hawley, July 14, 1754, The Papers of Gideon Hawley, American Congregational Library, Boston, Massachusetts; and JE to Major Ephraim Williams, Jr. et al., September 18, 1753. *Works,* vol. 16, p. 604.

115. Gideon Hawley, "A Letter from Rev. Gideon Hawley of Marshpee, containing an account of his services among the Indians of Massachusetts and New York, and a narrative of his journey to Onohoghgwage," MHS, *Collections,* ser. 1, vol. 4 (1794): 51.

116. I discuss Edwards's Stockbridge sermons at greater length in "Living upon Hope: Mahicans and Missionaries, 1730–1760," Ph.D. dissertation, Yale University, 1998, 160–83; and "'Friends to Your Souls': Jonathan Edwards' Indian Pastorate and the Doctrine of Original Sin," *Church History* 72 (December 2003): 736–65.

117. Of the 165 sermons marked as preached to the English congregation at Stockbridge, only 29 were original compositions. See also *Works,* vol. 16, pp. 504–9.

118. Indeed, New Testament texts outnumber Old Testament texts by a ratio of five to three, as compared to a nearly equal balance in those preached to his English congregations.

119. Wilson H. Kimnach's, "Introduction," in *Works,* vol. 10, pp. 213–27.

120. Proverbs 8:31, March 1752, JEC.

121. "To the Mohawks at the Treaty," August 16, 1751, in *The Sermons of Jonathan Edwards, A Reader,* ed. Wilson H. Kimnach, Kenneth P. Minkema, and Douglas A. Sweeney (New Haven: Yale University Press, 1999), 105–10.

122. Luke 24:47, October 1751, JEC.

123. Revelation 3:20, February 1751, JEC.

124. N.d. fragment from baptismal sermon on back of letter dated December 28, 1756, JEC.

125. Edwards, "To the Mohawks," in *The Sermons of Jonathan Edwards,* 105–10.

126. For an important new interpretation of this sermon, see Douglas L. Winiarski, "Jonathan Edwards, Enthusiast? Radical Revivalism and the Great Awakening in the Connecticut Valley," *Church History* 74 (December 2005): 683–739.

127. Revelation 3:20, February 1751, JEC. See also John 1:12, February 1751, JEC.

128. Luke 9:23, August 1753, JEC.

129. Patrick Frazier details the trials of the Stockbridge Indians during the French and Indian War. Frazier, *Mohicans of Stockbridge,* 105–23.

130. Revelation 22:5, August 1756, JEC. For Edwards's view of the state of the world at this time, see his letter to Gideon Hawley. *Works,* vol. 16, p. 690.

131. Romans 12:12, June 1755, JEC.

132. Genesis 1:27, August 1751, JEC.

133. Lecture to the Indian Children, February 1751, ANTS, reel 5. Edwards's *Defense of Original Sin* rested on his premise that all humans have a shared constituitive identity with Adam, so just as a leaf shares the identity of the tree with the root, so too do humans partake of Adam's identity.

134. Jonathan Edwards, 2 Corinthians 4:18, August 1751 to the Stockbridge Indians and Mohawks, JEC.

135. The manuscript provides no further hint as to the occasion or date of the lecture. Edwards, "Lecture on the Problem of Drink," JEC.

136. Matt 10:14–15, March 1755, JEC.

137. Ezekiel 33:7–9, November 1754, JEC; and Job 31:14, April 1756, JEC.

138. Commissioners to Jaspar Mauduit, January 2, 1755, NEC Records.

139. I have only identified about twenty original sermons to the English. More commonly, he resorted to his vast file of sermons from Northampton.

140. Psalms 119:18, October 1751, JEC.

141. Edwards, "To the Mohawks," in *The Sermons of Jonathan Edwards*, 105–10.

142. Proverbs 3:16, 1751, JEC.

143. 1 Corinthians 11:27, January 1751, JEC.

144. Matthew 13:3–4, 1740, repreached May 1756, JEC.

145. N.d. fragment from baptismal sermon. The script, the paper, and the format of the sermon mark it as belonging to the Stockbridge era.

146. Emphasis in the original. *Works*, vol. 3, p. 424.

147. Wauwaumpequunaut arrived at Stockbridge as a seventeen-year-old in 1740, requesting to be taught to read. John Sergeant diary, January 6, 1740, Stiles Papers; and *Works*, vol. 16, pp. 451–52, 476–77.

148. Diary and Memorandum Book, JEC. Pages 69 and 70 of this account book list at least one additional Indian marriage, between Jacob Cheeksunkun and Lydia, a Mohawk woman. These leaves are missing from the original but have been located in a copy of J. E. Woodbridge, *The Memorial Volume of the Edwards Family Meeting at Stockbridge, Mass.* (Boston, 1871) at the Huntington Library, San Marino, California. These pages also contain reference to paying "Hannis" for his interpreting service. This is likely Johannis Metoxon, a prominent leader at Stockbridge and a relative of Corlaer, the Mohican sachem also known as Metoxen. My thanks to Douglas Winiarski, who discovered these pages and provided me with his transcription. On Metoxon, see Shirley W. Dunn, *The Mohicans and their Land, 1609–1730* (Fleischmanns, NY: Purple Mountain Press, 1994), 356.

149. 1 Corinthians 10:17, JEC. Edwards preached at least eight other sacramental sermons during his tenure at Stockbridge.

150. Profession of faith, n.d., 21/1245, JEC.

151. Aupaumut was referring to *A Treatise concerning Religious Affections*, published in 1743, and *Freedom of the Will*, published in 1754. "Hendrick A." to "Hon'ble Timothy Edwards, Esq. Stockbridge or Wunnuqhqtoqhoke," Stockbridge Library, Stockbridge, Massachusetts. The letter has a date of 1775 added by a later hand. Lion Miles suggests a more likely date of the 1790s. Lion Miles, personal communication.

152. John Sergeant Jr. diary, May 18, 1795, Harvard Grants for Work among the Indians, Journals of John Sergeant 1790–1909, Harvard University Archives, Cambridge, Massachusetts.

153. John Sallaint's work on the African-American Congregational minister Lemuel Haynes persuasively documents the influence of Edwards's work via his New Divinity disciples on African-American Christians, who, like Aupaumut, grounded their calls for racial equality in Christian theology. Saillant, *Black Puritan, Black Republican: The Life and Thought of Lemuel Haynes, 1753–1833* (New York: Oxford University Press, 2003); Mark Valeri, "The New Divinity and the American Revolution," *WMQ* 46 (October 1989): 741–69; John Saillant, "Slavery and Divine Providence in New England Calvinism: The New Divinity and a Black Protest, 1775–1805," *NEQ* 68 (December 1995): 584–608; and Kenneth P. Minkema, "Jonathan Edwards on Slavery and the Slave Trade," *WMQ* 54 (October 1997): 823–43.

CHAPTER 11. IRONY AND IDENTITY

1. Patrick Frazier's history of the Stockbridge Indians continues through the Revolution. Frazier, *The Mohicans of Stockbridge* (Lincoln: University of Nebraska Press, 1992).

2. Lion Miles, "Red Man Dispossessed: The Williams Family and the Alienation of Indian Land in Stockbridge, Massachusetts, 1736–1818," *NEQ* 67, no. 1 (March 1994): 62–72, 75; and Alan Taylor, "Captain Hendrick Aupaumut: The Dilemmas of an Intercultural Broker," *Ethnohistory* 43, no. 3 (Summer 1996): 436.

3. James W. Oberly has chronicled the Stockbridges' political fate in the nineteenth and twentieth centuries. Oberly, *A Nation of Statesmen: The Political Culture of the Stockbridge-Munsee Tribe of Indians, 1815–1972* (Norman: University of Oklahoma Press, 2005).

4. On the formation of new tribal identities, see James H. Merrell, *The Indians' New World: Catawbas and Their Neighbors From European Contact through the Era of Removal* (Chapel Hill: University of North Carolina Press, 1989); on Christianity as the basis for expression of native identity, see David J. Silverman, *Faith and Boundaries: Colonists, Christianity, and Community among the Wampanoag Indians of Martha's Vineyard, 1600–1871* (Cambridge: Cambridge University Press, 2005).

5. My understanding of the Moravian community at Bethlehem has been shaped by Katherine Carté Engel's work, including *Pilgrims and Profits: Moravians in the Mid-Atlantic Marketplace* (Philadelphia: University of Pennsylvania Press, forthcoming). Older accounts include Gillian Lindt Gollin, *Moravians in Two Worlds: A Study of Changing Communities* (New York: Columbia University Press, 1967); and Beverly Prior Smaby, *The Transformation of Moravian Bethlehem from Mission to Family Economy* (Philadelphia: University of Pennsylvania Press, 1988).

6. Aupaumut's letter to Sergeant from Goshen is dated January 10, 1803, and is included at the end of Sergeant's diary covering July 1, 1802, to January 1, 1803, Harvard Grants for Work among the Indians. Journals of John Sergeant 1790–1909, Harvard University Archives, Cambridge, Massachusetts.

7. Mortimer noted in the mission diary that nine Stockbridge Mohicans had arrived, including "Hendrick Aupaumut, one of the principal chiefs of the nation, his brother Solomon Aupaumut, Andrew, chief warrior, John Quinney Junior, town clerk and one of the Schoolmasters there, and John Metoxen, who resided some years since for a considerable time in Bethlehem." Goshen Diary, January 7, 1803, 171/12 RMM.

CHAPTER 12. THE COOPER AND THE SACHEM

1. Shekomeko Diary, September 4, 1742, December 12, 1742, 1/111/1 RMM.

2. Abraham's grandmother, Manhat, had appointed Cornelius's father, Tatamshatt, to serve as guardian to Abraham and his brother's land until they came of age. Memorandum, September 1743, 3/113/5/2 RMM.

3. Pachgatgoch Diary, March 9, 1760, 4/115/9 RMM; and Shirley W. Dunn, *The Mohican World, 1680–1750* (Fleischmanns, NY: Purple Mountain Press, 2000), 282.

4. Bathsheba, Joshua senior's second wife, assisted in preparing wampum belts for important councils, suggesting her husband's role as runner, as defined by Aupaumut. Joshua's extensive travels with the missionaries were thus in effect a continuation of his prior office. On the role of runner, see Aupaumut, as quoted in Electa Field Jones, *Stockbridge, Past and Present; Or Records of an Old Mission Station* (Springfield, MA: Samuel Bowles and Company, 1854), 21. On Bathsheba's contributions, see Gnadenhütten Diary, April 15, 1747, 4/116/1 RMM; and Gnadenhütten Diary, February 8 and April 9, 1750, 4/116/7 RMM.

5. Shekomeko Diary, September 4, 1742, 1/111/1 RMM. Hymns attributed to Joshua can be found in 35/331/3 RMM.

6. Jane T. Merritt, *At the Crossroads: Indians and Empires on a Mid-Atlantic Frontier* (Chapel Hill: University of North Carolina Press, 2003), 169–97.

7. Gnadenhütten Diary, January 23, 1747, 4/116/1 RMM; and Gnadenhütten Diary, January 18, 1755, 5/118/4 RMM.

8. Martin Mack, November 19, 1755, 5/118/6/27 RMM. On the Gnadenhütten raid, see *History of the Mission*, pt. II, pp. 164–68.

9. Nain Diary, February 25, 1758, 7/125/1 RMM; Memorial, 1759, 125/2 RMM; *History of the Mission*, pt. II, p. 191; and Nain Diary, October 12, 1762, 7/125/3 RMM.

10. Gregory Evans Dowd provides an insightful analysis of Pontiac's Rebellion. Dowd, *War Under Heaven: Pontiac, the Indian Nations, and the British Empire* (Baltimore: Johns Hopkins University Press, 2002).

11. Philadelphia Diary, April 13, May 22, 1764, 7/127/2 RMM.

12. Philadelphia Diary, June 24, 1764, 7/127/2 RMM.

13. Philadelphia Diary, November 13, December 20, 1764, 7/127/2 RMM. Amy C. Schutt maintains that there were mounting ethnic tensions in the Friedenshütten mission between the older population of baptized Mohicans and the growing community of Munsee and Unami Delaware. Schutt calculates that in 1767 the population of Friedenshütten was roughly 19 percent Mohican, 22 percent Munsee, 33 percent other Delaware, and the rest from various different tribes. Schutt, "Tribal Identity in the Moravian Mission on the Susquehanna," *Pennsylvania History* 66 (1999): 378–98.

14. Friedenshütten Diary, February 4, April 14, 1770, 7/131/6 RMM.

15. Eric Hinderaker, *Elusive Empires: Constructing Colonialism in the Ohio Valley, 1673–1800* (Cambridge: Cambridge University Press, 1997), 168–70; and Michael McConnell, *A Country Between: The Upper Ohio Valley and Its Peoples, 1724–1774* (Lincoln: University of Nebraska Press, 1992), 248–53.

16. Gnadenhütten Diary, August 18, 1773, 9/144/1 RMM; and Gnadenhütten Diary, September 9, 10, 1773, January 23, 1774, 9/144/2 RMM.

17. Gnadenhütten Diary, August 1, 1775, 3/114/5 RMM. The move to Gnadenhütten on the Muskingum is detailed in *History of the Mission*, pt. III, pp. 62–85. See also Hermann Wellenreuther and Carola Wessel, eds., *The Moravian Mission Diaries of David Zeisberger, 1772–1781*, trans. Julia Tomberlin Weber (University Park: Pennsylvania State University Press, 2005), 49–51.

18. Gregory Evans Dowd, *A Spirited Resistance: The North American Indian Struggle for Unity, 1745–1815*, 65–89.

19. The suspicions of the British and the anti-American Indians were not altogether unfounded: missionaries Zeisberger, Heckewelder, and some of the mission Indians did offer assistance, mostly in the form of intelligence to American officials. Dowd, *Spirited Resistance*, 84–85.

20. Zeisberger's Diary, October 25, 1781, 10/151/1 RMM; *History of the Mission*, pt. III, pp. 148–69; and Richard White, *Middle Ground: Indian, Empires, and Republics in the Great Lakes Region, 1650–1815* (Cambridge: Cambridge University Press, 1991), 389–91.

21. *History of the Mission*, pt. III, pp. 170–86; and John Heckewelder, *A Narrative of the Mission of the United Brethren among the Delaware and Mohegan Indians, from its Commencement, in the Year 1740, to the Close of the Year 1808* (Philadelphia: McCarty and Davis, 1820), 310–28.

22. Traditionally Miami land, Woapicamikunk had since 1796 been home to a community of about forty Delaware families, including Buckongahelas. Within a few miles were other Delaware and Shawnee villages, including the residences of the Delaware-Munsee chiefs Tetepachsit and Hackinkpomska. In 1797, Tecumseh settled nearby. John Sugden, *Tecumseh: A Life* (New York: Henry Holt and Co., 1997), 99. Just a couple years earlier, Tetepachsit, according to Moravian missionary David Zeisberger, had expressed interest in "hearing the gospel," and his community extended an invitation to the Christian Delawares living at the Moravian community of Goshen in Ohio to resettle on the White River, an invitation that did not explicitly include the missionaries. Moravian leaders considered the situation and in August 1800 determined to send missionaries. Abraham Luckenbach and Johann Kluge arrived in March 1801 together with thirteen Christian Delaware. The mission was eventually closed in September 1806, citing the pressure from territorial governor William Henry Harrison and the influence of the Shawnee Prophet. For the founding of the Moravian mission, see Lawrence Gipson's introduction to *White River Mission*, 11–18.

23. *White River Mission*, 54–55, 113, 155–57; and Goshen Diary, March 4, 1802, 19/171/9 RMM.

24. *White River Mission*, 621.

25. *White River Mission*, 231.

26. *White River Mission*, 176.

27. On the history of "falling" in the revivalist traditions among the Methodists, Presbyterians, and Baptists, see Ann Taves, *Fits, Trances, and Visions: Experiencing Religion and Explaining Experience from Wesley to James* (Princeton: Princeton University Press, 1999), 104–9.

28. For a detailed description of Tenskwatawa's message, see R. David Edmunds, *The Shawnee Prophet* (Lincoln: University of Nebraska Press, 1983), 28–41; and Dowd, *Spirited Resistance*, 123–47.

Hendrick Aupaumut recorded another version of the Prophet's vision, brought by emissaries of the Prophet to the Delaware settlement on the White River. Aupaumut to John Sergeant, January 3, 1807 [1808], box 1, folder 6, Dean Family Papers, Indiana Historical Society, Indianapolis.

29. *White River Mission*, 407–8.

30. Caritas eventually confessed to being in possession of a medicine bundle. Her confession did not save her life: she was burned alive. A Delaware chief Tedapachsit was the next to be brought forward. Tedapachsit had been an important chief who had been disgraced for his participation in the cession of land at the Treaty of Greenville in 1795. Dowd, *Spirited Resistance*, 137; and White, *Middle Ground*, 496–99.

31. *White River Mission*, 397, 401, 413.

32. *White River Mission*, 417–18, 561.

33. *White River Mission*, 432.

34. Patrick Frazier, *The Mohicans of Stockbridge* (Lincoln: University of Nebraska Press, 1992), especially chs. 6, 10, 16, and 17.

35. Aupaumut's history was published as "Extract from an Indian History" MHS *Collections*, 1st ser., vol. 9 (1804): 99–102.

36. Jones, *Stockbridge Past and Present*, 14–20. Hilary Wyss has provided a thoughtful analysis of Aupaumut's history. Wyss, *Writing Indians: Literacy, Christianity, and Native Community in Early America* (Amherst: University of Massachusetts Press, 2000), 105–22.

37. I have written more extensively about Aupaumut's career in Wheeler, "Hendrick Aupaumut: Christian-Mahican Prophet," *Journal of the Early Republic* 25, no. 2 (Summer 2005): 187–220. See also Alan Taylor, "Captain Hendrick Aupaumut: The Dilemmas of An Intercultural Broker," *Ethnohistory* 43 (1996): 431–57; R. David Edmunds provides a more detailed description of the status of the Indian residents of the Old Northwest at the turn of the century. Edmunds, *Shawnee Prophet*, ch. 1.

38. That Mohican values remained strong despite the changing means of subsistence is suggested by the fact that following the feast, the remaining provisions were distributed to the aged and the poor. John Sergeant Diary, December 3, 1793, Harvard Grants for Work among the Indians, Journals of John Sergeant 1790–1909, Harvard University Archives, Cambridge, Massachusetts (hereafter Harvard Grants).

39. The following year, when some young Stockbridge men had advertised in the newspaper to lease their lands to white neighbors, Aupaumut became furious, preferring that the tribe worked the land themselves and fearing that such leases opened the door to abuse and, by providing an alternate source of income, kept the Stockbridges from learning the necessary farming and husbandry skills. He further informed Sergeant "that a number of us have good resolution to persevere in our labours in cultivating our lands. God has given us, in such a manner as to get a good living according to the custom of white people, by this we hope many or all our nation will be [inclined] to follow our example." John Sergeant Diary, September 9, 1794, Harvard Grants.

40. Aupaumut delivered the speech, and a written copy was given to the Delawares, signed by Aupaumut, John Quinney, and Solomon Aupaumut "in behalf of the rest." Goshen Diary, January 11, 1803, 19/171/12 RMM.

41. Goshen Diary, January 11, 1803, 19/171/12 RMM.

42. Goshen Diary, January 7, 1803, 19/171/12 RMM.

43. "Extract from the Indian Journal, being the 6th Speech that was delivered to the Delaware Nation residing at Waupekummekut, or White River, on the 15th day of April, 1803," printed in *Massachusetts Missionary Magazine* (April 1804): 467–71. On Joshua as interpreter, see *White River Mission*, 222–23.

44. Aupaumut to Sergeant, November 2, 1807, Ft. Wayne, transcribed in John Sergeant diary, December 30, 1807, Society for the Propagation of the Gospel among the Indians (hereafter SPGAI), box 4, folder 14, Phillips Library, Salem Massachusetts.

45. Aupaumut extract in Sergeant letter, March 25, May 30, 1808 SPGAI vol. 4, p. 14, Phillips Library.

46. John Sergeant Diary, August 11, 1805, Harvard Grants.

CHAPTER 13. EPILOGUE

1. John Sergeant, diary entry dated April 8, 1819, Society in Scotland for Propagating Christian Knowledge, Records, 1794–1892, Dartmouth Archives, Hanover, New Hampshire (hereafter DA). I write about this occasion at greater length in Wheeler, "Hendrick Aupaumut: Christian-Mohican Prophet," *Journal of the Early Republic* 25, vol. 2 (Summer 2005): 187–220.

2. Sergeant Diary, January 23, 1819, DA. On the Miami grant to the Stockbridges, see Sergeant diary, July 1, 1819, DA. An 1808 letter from Aupaumut to Massachusetts senator (and former Indian commissioner and secretary of state) Timothy Pickering noted that he had confirmation from President Jefferson specifying "our right to a certain tract of land of that have been granted by the Miamis to the Delaware-Muhheaconnuk and Monsies." Aupaumut to Pickering, December 29, 1808, vol. 43, p. 234, Timothy Pickering Papers, MHS. For the sale of the White River land, see Treaty with the Delaware, October 3, 1818, in *Indian Affairs: Laws and Treaties,* compiled and edited by Charles J. Kappler (Washington, D.C.: Government Printing Office, 1904), vol. II, pp. 170–71.

3. This letter is signed Aupaumut, listed as sachem, and five counselors. John Sergeant diary, April 8, 1819, DA. Lion Miles translates Unnannaumpauh as "Indians" but suggests it can also mean "people." Miles renders the last line as "In heaven will receive truth." Lion Miles, personal communication, August 19, 2004.

4. For a political history of the Stockbridges from Aupaumut's time through the 1970s, see James W. Oberly, *A Nation of Statesmen: The Political Culture of the Stockbridge-Munsee Mohicans, 1815–1972* (Norman: University of Oklahoma Press, 2005).

5. On foreign missions in the nineteenth century, the classic work is William R. Hutchison, *Errand to the World: American Protestant Thought and World Missions* (Chicago: University of Chicago Press, 1987).

6. *Tschoop and Shabasch, Christian Indians, of North America, A Narrative of Facts* (Dublin: M. Goodwin, 1824); and *History of the Mission,* pt. II, p. 14.

7. *Tschoop: The Converted Indian Chief* (Philadelphia: American Sunday School Union, 1842). Tschoop was in fact a corruption of Job, perhaps a reference to the calamities the Mohican had faced. He had been left lame by a fire. See Edmund de Schweinitz, *The Life and Times of David Zeisberger* (Philadelphia: J. B. Lippincott, 1871), 98n1.

8. Classic works on the Indian policy include Francis Paul Prucha, *American Indian Policy in the Formative Years: The Indian Trade and Intercourse Acts, 1790–1834* (Cambridge: Harvard University Press, 1962) and *The Great Father: The United States Government and the American Indians* (Lincoln: University of Nebraska Press, 1984); and Ronald N. Satz, *American Indian Policy in the Jacksonian Era* (Lincoln: University of Nebraska Press, 1975). Michael Rogin studied the era through the lens of psychoanalytic theory in *Fathers and Children: Andrew Jackson and the Subjugation of the American Indian* (New York: Alfred A. Knopf, 1975).

9. On Cooper's use of Moravian sources, see Edwin L. Stockton Jr., "The Influence of the Moravians upon the Leather-Stocking Tales," Ph.D. dissertation, Florida State University, 1964, published in *Transactions of the Moravian Historical Society,* vol. 20, pt. 1; and Will J. Alpern, "Indians, Sources, Critics," in *James Fenimore Cooper: His Country and His Art* (No. 5), ed. George A. Test (Oneonta: SUNY Oneonta, 1985), 25–33.

10. *Tschoop: The Converted Indian Chief,* 35–36.

11. See for example, Phebe Earle Gibbons, *"Pennsylvania Dutch," and Other Essays* (Philadelphia: J. B. Lippincott & Co., 1882), 184. Gibbons' essay was first published in the *Atlantic Monthly* in October 1869. See also Joel Cook, *America, Picturesque and Descriptive* (Philadelphia: H. T. Coates & Co., 1900), 229–30, which describes Tschoop's grave and cites him as the model for Uncas's father in Cooper's tales. Another guidebook claims Tschoop as model for Uncas. Anna Margaretha Archambault, *A Guide Book of Art, Architecture, and Historic Interests in Pennsylvania* (Philadelphia: John C. Winston, Co., 1924), 21.

Index